OCR Philosophy of Religion for AS and A2

Third edition

OCR Philosophy of Religion for AS and A2 is a textbook endorsed by OCR for students of Advanced Subsidiary or Advanced Level courses. Structured closely around the OCR GCE Religious Studies specification this updated third edition covers all the essential topics studied within philosophy of religion in an accessible and student-friendly way. Each chapter includes:

- OCR specification checklist, to clearly illustrate which topics from the specification are covered in each chapter
- explanations of key terminology
- review questions, thought points and activities to test understanding
- overviews of key scholars and theories
- chapter summaries and annotated further reading.

With a section dedicated to preparing for assessment this book provides students with the skills they need to succeed. The book comes complete with diagrams and tables, lively illustrations, a comprehensive glossary and full bibliography.

The companion website hosts a wealth of further resources to enhance the learning experience with additional resources including PowerPoint slides, flashcards, further reading, weblinks and handouts. It can be found at www.routledge.com/cw/mayled.

Jon Mayled is a chief examiner. He is author and editor of many popular books for the GCSE and GCE specifications.

Jill Oliphant was formerly Head of Religious Studies at Angley School in Kent. She is also an experienced examiner.

Matthew Taylor is Director of the International Baccalaureate at Brentwood School. He was previously Head of Philosophy and Religious Studies at Colchester County High School for Girls and Head of Religious Studies and Philosophy at St Gregory the Great Roman Catholic V.A. School in Oxford.

This textbook is endorsed by OCR for use with the Philosophy of Religion units of specification H172 OCR Advanced Subsidiary GCE in Religious Studies and specification H572 OCR Advanced GCE in Religious Studies.

OCR Philosophy of Religion for AS and A2

Third edition

JON MAYLED

JILL OLIPHANT

MATTHEW TAYLOR

Routledge
Taylor & Francis Group

LONDON AND NEW YORK

First edition published 2007
Second edition published 2009

This third edition published 2015
by Routledge
2 Park Square, Milton Park, Abingdon, Oxon OX14 4RN

and by Routledge
711 Third Avenue, New York, NY 10017

Routledge is an imprint of the Taylor & Francis Group, an informa business

British Library Cataloguing in Publication Data
A catalogue record for this book is available from the British Library

Library of Congress Cataloging in Publication Data
Taylor, Matthew, 1973-
    [Philosophy of religion for AS and A2]
    OCR philosophy of religion for AS and A2 / Matthew Taylor, Jill Oliphant, Jon Mayled.—Third edition.
        pages cm
    Includes bibliographical references and index.
    1. Religion—Philosophy.   I. Oliphant, Jill, 1949-   II. Mayled, Jon.
    III. Title.   IV. Title: Philosophy of religoin for AS and A2.
    BL51.T397 2015
    210.76—dc23   2014045616

ISBN: 978-0-415-52869-6 (pbk)
ISBN: 978-1-315-74887-0 (ebk)

Typeset in Charter ITC
by Keystroke, Station Road, Codsall, Wolverhampton

This book is dedicated to Belén, Beatriz and Francisco.

Contents

PART V THE NATURE OF RELIGIOUS BELIEF   241

Acknowledgements

TEXTS

The following publishers and individuals have kindly given copyright permission for extracts from their publications to be reproduced. Every effort has been made to trace copyright-holders of sourced material for permission to reproduce. Any omissions brought to our attention will be remedied in future editions.

Professor Richard Dawkins, for permission to quote short extracts from his books: *The Blind Watchmaker* (Penguin, 1986), *River Out of Eden: A Darwinian View of Life* (HarperCollins, 1995), *Unweaving the Rainbow: Science, Delusion and the Appetite for Wonder* (Penguin, 1998), and *The Selfish Gene* (Oxford University Press 1976, 1989).

The scripture quotations contained herein are from The New Revised Standard Version of the Bible, Anglicized Edition, copyright © 1989, 1995 by the Division of Christian Education of the National Council of the Churches of Christ in the United States of America, and are used by permission. All rights reserved.

Continuum International Publishing Group administers the copyright for *Catechism of the Catholic Church*, London, Geoffrey Chapman, 1994.

IMAGES

We are indebted to the people and archives below for permission to reproduce photographs or original illustrative material. Every effort has been made to trace copyright-holders. Any omissions brought to our attention will be remedied in future editions.

Bridgeman Art Library

Plato   4
Aristotle   31

The School of Athens	32
René Descartes	91
Thomas Aquinas	100
David Hume	129
Sigmund Freud	156
St Augustine	174
Maimonides	401
The Ancient of Days (William Blake)	420
Émile Durkheim	452
Max Weber	456
Carl Gustav Jung	464

Getty

A child	110
Damage caused by Hurricane Katrina	173
Stephen Hawking	203
Small child	204
Richard Dawkins	216
G.E.M. Anscombe	438

Istock

A cat called Erkenbrand	6
A modern car	28
The statue	31
Rosa Gallica	85
A domino rally	102
A bus	104
A lottery ticket	212
Lourdes	349
The crucifix	454

AKG Images

Anselm of Canterbury	82
Boethius	423

The Society of Jesus (British Province)

National Portrait Gallery, London

Professor Richard Dawkins

How to Use this Book

This book has been written for OCR students but it will be of use to all AS and A2 level Religious Studies students, as well as students taking the Philosophy of Religion section of AS/A2 Philosophy and Scottish National Examinations at Higher Level.

The book is designed for students to use in class and at home. Every chapter provides an overview of the major themes and issues of Philosophy of Religion on the OCR specification for Religious Studies. The following six features are designed to help you make the most effective use of the book:

1   **What you will learn about in this chapter**
    This highlights the key issue or issues you should think about while studying each chapter.

2   **OCR checklist**
    The box in each chapter about the OCR specification tells you which topics from the AS/A2 Religious Studies course are covered.

3   **Essential terminology box**
    At the beginning of every chapter there is a box listing the key terminology for that chapter. You should be able to use this terminology accurately in examinations.

4   **Examination questions practice**
    At the end of every chapter there is a section about answering examination questions on the topic, with an exam-style question. Please note: OCR does not endorse the exam-style questions as being examples of exam questions that may be set by OCR.

5   **Review questions**
    The review questions in every chapter are designed to test your understanding of topics discussed in the chapter. Make use of this section as a way to assess your learning about and from the issues raised in the chapter.

6 **Further reading**

The reading suggested at the end of each chapter suggests ways of exploring topics in greater depth.

Answering Examination Questions

To be successful in Advanced Level Religious Studies you must learn examination techniques. Some advice to guide you is given below, but there is no substitute for practising writing answers to examination questions. There are example questions at the end of the chapters in this book, and your teacher will give you plenty of other questions with which to practise.

Some important aspects to answering examination questions are explained below.

Your work will be assessed on how well you meet the following two Assessment Objectives (AO):

AO1 Demonstrate Knowledge and Understanding

- select and demonstrate clearly relevant knowledge and understanding through the use of evidence, examples and correct language and terminology appropriate to the course of study. In addition, for synoptic assessment, A Level candidates should demonstrate knowledge and understanding of the connections between different elements of their course of study.

AO2 Analysis, Evaluation and Application

- critically evaluate and justify a point of view through the use of evidence and reasoned argument. In addition, for synoptic assessment, A Level candidates should relate elements of their course of study to their broader context and to aspects of human experience.

All AS questions are in two parts (a) and (b). Part (a) assesses AO1 and Part (b) assesses AO2. These are weighted at 70 per cent for AO1 and 30 per cent for AO2.

All A2 questions are in one part. This combines both AO1 and AO2. The AOs are weighted at 70 per cent for AO1 and 30 per cent for AO2.

All questions are marked according to the OCR Levels of Response. See: http://www.ocr.org.uk/qualifications/as-a-level-gce-religious-studies-h172-h572/.

> ## Practise writing answers
>
> It is very important that you practise answering questions for Religious Studies examinations by handwriting answers. In an examination you have very little time to write answers and you have to write, not type. This takes practice; try to avoid typing answers when you practise doing examination questions at home.

SUBJECT KNOWLEDGE

At both AS and A2 level the majority of marks are given for your demonstration of a good understanding of the topic the question is examining. It is important not only that you learn the work you have studied, but also that you are able to select the knowledge that is relevant to an answer. For example, if the question is (AS level): *Explain how Augustine and Irenaeus use the concept of human free will in their theodicies,* your answer should be focused on human free will and these theodicies, not writing everything you know about the theodicies of Augustine and Irenaeus or free will.

When preparing for examination questions, it is a good idea to think about not only what a question is asking, but also what material you have studied that is relevant to the question.

> ## Selecting the correct information
>
> Think about how you would answer the two questions below. Make a list of the topics and information you need to include in any answer. Be specific. For example, do not just say 'the ontological argument' for question 1.
>
> 1   *Explain Anselm's version of the ontological argument.*
> 2   *Explain the weaknesses of the ontological argument.*

TIMING

It is very important that you learn how to complete questions in the time available. In an examination the time available is very limited. It is a good idea to practise timing yourself writing answers to examination-style questions. You will get a low mark if a question is incomplete, as this limits the maximum level your answer can reach.

Always try to spend equal amounts of time on each whole question you answer, as each question is worth the same number of marks. However, at AS level there are two parts within a question. In this case you may be expected to spend slightly longer completing the section of each question for which the higher mark is awarded.

UNDERSTANDING THE QUESTIONS

It is very important that you think carefully about what a question is asking you. The table below focuses on some of the common instruction words used in OCR questions and what they mean.

Instruction word	Explanation
Explain as in: **Explain** Anselm's ontological argument.	When a question uses the word **Explain**, it is telling you to demonstrate your knowledge of the topic in the question, and your ability to select and show understanding of relevant information and to use technical terms accurately.
	Thus, in the example question, you would need to demonstrate what you know about Anselm's ontological argument, such as its different forms and the terminology philosophers use to talk about this argument, such as *a priori*.
Discuss as in: 'Arguments from religious experience are never convincing.' **Discuss**.	The word **Discuss** in a question is telling you that you should examine the strengths and weaknesses of arguments for and against the statement in the question. You need to consider whether arguments in favour of and against the statement are successful. To do this, you will need to demonstrate an accurate understanding of one or more philosophers' views and the strengths and weaknesses of these views.
Assess as in: **Assess** Hume's reasons for rejecting miracles.	**Assess** is normally used as an **A2 level** instruction word. By **Assess** the examiner means that you should first **explain** the issue you are being asked to assess and second you should present arguments for and against the issue you have been asked to assess. Part of your assessment should present reasons analysing the strengths and weaknesses of arguments supporting or disagreeing with the issue. You should finish your answer with a conclusion which presents the result of your assessment.
	In the case of the example question you would need to explain clearly and precisely Hume's reasons for rejecting accounts of miracles. Second, you should present philosophers' and theologians' arguments for and against Hume's reasoning. You should analyse the strengths and weaknesses of the philosophers' and theologians' arguments concerning Hume's reasons.
	Remember that at A2 the two AOs are combined and that you need to demonstrate both in your answer.
	At AS **Assess** is sometimes used for part (b) questions and should be addressed in the same way although, obviously, more briefly.

To what extent as in:
To what extent can God be held responsible for moral evil?

The phrase *to what extent* is used in questions where you have to decide the level or extent of something. In order to do this, you need to explain the view suggested in the question and why some philosophers and theologians might hold this view. Then, you will need to assess the strengths and weaknesses of reasons for holding these views and compare the strengths of the different reasons for holding this view with each other. The extent will be limited or defined by the strongest view you have considered.

In the example question you will need to explain the strengths and weaknesses of reasons philosophers and theologians give when discussing God's responsibility for moral evil. The extent of God's responsibility will be decided by comparing the different reasons and arguments you present and deciding which one is the strongest.

Remember that at A2 the two AOs are combined and that you need to demonstrate both in your answer.

How fair as in:
How fair is the claim that moral language is meaningful, even if religious language is not?

How fair is another instruction phrase which occasionally might appear in the Philosophy of Religion A2 paper, such as 'How fair is the view that religious ethics are absolute?' To complete a task beginning with *how fair* you need to explain reasons why philosophers and theologians support this view and then, even if religious ethics are absolute, *assess* the strengths and weaknesses of these reasons. The *fairness* of the view in the question is decided by comparing the strengths of reasons for and against the view in the question and deciding which reasoning is strongest. The view in the question is only fair if you can demonstrate that the reasoning of the philosophers and theologians in agreement with the view in the question is stronger than that of those who disagree.

In the case of the example question, you would need to explain the reasons why philosophers and theologians might believe moral language is meaningful, even if religious language is not, and consider the strengths and weaknesses of these reasons when compared to the views of people who disagree with this view. The fairness of the view in the question is decided by considering whether arguments that moral language is meaningful even if religious language is not are stronger than views that disagree.

Remember that at A2 the two AOs are combined and that you need to demonstrate both in your answer.

Timeline

Scientists, Ethicists and Thinkers

This timeline gives the names and dates of people whose great ideas are discussed within the book. This list is not a comprehensive list of every important or significant philosopher of Western civilisation.

Socrates (c.470 BCE–399 BCE)
Plato (c.427 BCE–c.347 BCE)
Aristotle (384 BCE–322 BCE)
Epicurus (341 BCE–270 BCE)
Jesus of Nazareth (c.3 BCE–30)
Dionysius the Areopagite (1st century CE)
Saul of Tarsus/Paul (9–67)
Irenaeus (130–200)
Plotinus (205–270)
Augustine (354–430)
Boethius (480–524)
Pseudo-Dionysius (5th–6th century)
Muhammad ﷺ (571–632)
Avicenna (980–1037)
Averroës (a.k.a. Ibn Rushd) (11th century)
Anselm (1033–1109)
Gaunilo of Marmoutiers (11th century)
Maimonides (1135–1204)
Thomas Aquinas (1225–1274)
John Duns Scotus (c.1266–1308)
John Calvin (1509–1564)
Théodore de Bèze (1519–1605)
Luis de Molina (1535–1600)
Thomas Hobbes (1588–1679)
Pierre Gassendi (1592–1655)
René Descartes (1596–1650)
John Locke (1632–1704)
Isaac Newton (1642–1727)
Gottfried Wilhelm Leibniz (1646–1716)
David Hume (1711–1776)
Immanuel Kant (1724–1804)
William Paley (1743–1805)
Jeremy Bentham (1748–1842)

Thomas Malthus (1766–1834)
Friedrich Schleiermacher (1768–1834)
Georg Wilhelm Hegel (1770–1831)
John Stuart Mill (1806–1873)
Charles Darwin (1809–1882)
Karl Marx (1818–1883)
William James (1842–1910)
Friedrich Nietzsche (1844–1900)
Sigmund Freud (1856–1939)
Émile Durkheim (1858–1917)
Max Weber (1864–1920)
Bertrand Russell (1872–1970)
George Moore (1873–1958)
Carl Jung (1875–1961)
Albert Schweitzer (1875–1965)
Albert Einstein (1879–1955)
Bronislaw Manilowski (1884–1942)
Rudolf Bultmann (1884–1976)
Paul Tillich (1886–1965)
Karl Barth (1886–1968)
Ludwig Wittgenstein (1889–1951)
Karl Popper (1902–1994)
John Wisdom (1904–1993)
Jean-Paul Sartre (1905–1980)
Frederick Copleston (1907–1994)
A.J. Ayer (1910–1989)
Norman Malcolm (1911–1990)
G.E.M. (Elizabeth) Anscombe (1913–2001)
Ian Ramsey (1915–1972)
John Leslie Mackie (1917–1981)
Basil Mitchell (1917–2011)
Richard Hare (1919–2002)
John Hick (1922–2012)
Maurice Wiles (1923–2005)
Anthony Flew (1923–2010)
R.F. Holland (1923–2013)
Arthur Peacocke (1924–2006)
John Polkinghorne (1930–)
Russell Stannard (1931–)
Anthony Kenny (1931–)
Alvin Plantinga (1932–)
Nicholas Wolterstorff (1932–)
Richard Swinburne (1934–)
Keith Ward (1938–)
Richard Dawkins (1941–)
Stephen Jay Gould (1941–2002)
Stephen Hawking (1942–)
Simon Conway Morris (1951–)
Brian Davies (1951–)
Charles L. Griswold (1951–)
Michael Behe (1952–)
Alistair McGrath (1953–)

THE GOD OF PHILOSOPHY

PART I

THE ISSUE

What do you mean by the word 'God'? What do philosophers mean by God?

How are the two related?

Whatever your answer to these questions, it will probably be different from that of other people. Equally, your answer would probably be different from what a 5-year-old child would say, and perhaps different from what a philosophy professor would say.

For over 3,000 years philosophers have been thinking about what they mean when they talk about 'God'. Two Ancient Greek philosophers, Aristotle and Plato, have in their different ways both influenced the development of western Philosophy of Religion, particularly within Christianity.

However, many of the ideas of Plato and Aristotle are very different from Judaeo-Christian beliefs about God. The following two chapters introduce some of their thinking that has influenced the development of western Philosophy of Religion. They also examine possible links between religious beliefs and these aspects of Ancient Greek philosophy.

1 Plato and Philosophy of Religion

THE ISSUES

1   Plato: one of the most important philosophers in the history of the Western world.
2   Is there a World of Forms beyond the physical world?

WHAT YOU WILL LEARN ABOUT IN THIS CHAPTER

In this chapter you will be introduced to some of the ideas of Plato. In particular you will focus on his theory of Forms as well as examining some of the criticisms of his ideas.

STARTER

Look at the pictures opposite and then consider the questions below:

Questions

1   What animals are shown in the pictures?
2   Are all the animals of the same species? If not, what characteristics do they have which show that they belong to a particular species?

Thought Point

Five-minute challenge

Draw sketches of some of the following animals:

- Tiger
- Monkey
- Horse
- Toad
- Cow

When all the sketches are completed, put them together and ask people to identify which species the animal comes from. Do not be embarrassed about the quality of your sketches. Let people work out what they are. Do not tell them.

Plato the man (427–347 BCE)

Plato is one of the most famous philosophers in history. His writings influenced the development of philosophy throughout the western world and a large number of his books survive. Plato was taught by the first great western philosopher, Socrates. Most of the books he wrote have Socrates as their leading character. His early books are about Socrates' philosophy but the later ones present arguments from Plato's own thinking.

Plato wrote about many issues ranging from the existence of the soul and the nature of beauty, to who should run a government. Plato founded his own school of philosophy, like a university, called the Academia, from which we get the word 'Academy' in English. He died in 347 BCE, aged 81.

Thought Point

The harder challenge

What is meant by 'beauty'?

THE OCR CHECKLIST

Candidates are expected to have a basic knowledge of the thinking of Plato; they will not be expected to have first-hand knowledge of the texts. They should be able to highlight the strengths and weaknesses in the thinking of Plato in the areas specified below.

Plato: the Analogy of the Cave, *The Republic VII. 514A–521B*

Candidates should be able to demonstrate knowledge and understanding of what might be represented in the Analogy of the Cave by the following:

- the prisoners, the shadows, the cave itself, the outside world, the sun, the journey out of the cave and the return to the prisoners.

Candidates should be able to discuss critically the validity of the points being made in this analogy.

Plato: the concept of the Forms; the Form of the Good

Candidates should understand what Plato meant by 'Forms' and be able to demonstrate knowledge and understanding of:

- the relation between concepts and phenomena;
- the concept of 'Ideals';
- the relation between the Form of the Good and the other Forms.

Candidates should be able to discuss critically the validity of the above points.

From OCR A Level Religious Studies Specification H172.

PLATO'S THEORY OF FORMS

The starter exercises drew your attention to the difference between ideas and ideas expressed in reality. For example, you can recognise a cat because you know what a cat is, i.e. you have an idea of what a cat is. For Plato this distinction is crucial. First, the knowledge of what a cat is precedes your actually seeing a cat. Second, Plato suggests that the world we live in is a world of *appearances* but the *real world* is a world of ideas that he calls *Forms*.

In order to really understand what Plato means by the Forms we need to look at Book V of *The Republic*, 478a–b where Socrates tries to persuade Glaucon that any beautiful object can also seem ugly. He says that beauty may be limited in some way, for example a rose bush may seem absolutely perfect but when you look closely you see that there is black spot on the leaves, or the shape of the rose may be beautiful but the colour is not as beautiful as another rose. Socrates says that you can say the same of terms such as large and small, heavy and light – for example a cat is small when compared to a lion but it could be large when compared to other cats. So we cannot in fact say that anything in the world is unqualifiedly beautiful, large, small, light, heavy, just, etc. Plato then assumes that there must be something which is unqualifiedly beautiful, large, small, etc. These are the Forms – the Form of Beauty is always completely beautiful. There is only one Form of Beauty for many beautiful things; they are like a kind of reflection of Beauty.

The world we live in is a world of appearances, but it is not the most important or real world. In the material world things that exist like trees and plants will all die. What makes a tree a tree, however, or a cat a cat, is the way in which it corresponds to the Form of tree or cat.

By *Form* Plato meant the idea of what a thing is. There are many types of cat but they all conform to or match to some degree the idea of what a cat is. Plato argues that the true Form of cat must exist somewhere; it exists in the World of Forms. A Form is unchanging because it is a concept; it is not like physical objects that imitate or copy the Form – they die. The Form is everlasting. The Forms thus exist in a different reality.

Plato was not really interested in the Forms of objects like beds or, indeed, animals like cats. What concerned Plato were concepts such as beauty, truth, justice and the Good. Plato observed that concepts like beauty may be applied to many different objects. A flower and a person can both in some way reveal what beauty is. However, they are clearly not the whole story or definition of what beauty is because other things such as landscapes, actions and paintings can be beautiful. This led Plato to suggest that underlying all these images and examples of beauty is the real Form of beauty, to which these things correspond to a greater or lesser extent.

Form

By 'Form' Plato meant the idea of something. For example, if you say 'Look! There's a cat,' you have some idea of what a cat is and you can recognise lots of different types of cat. All the different types of cat embody the Form of a cat: some set of characteristics that resemble the idea of what a cat is. The Form of anything is not physical but the eternal idea of what a thing is.

A cat called
Erkenbrand

Thought Point

The harder challenge

If you attempted the harder challenge about beauty and found it difficult, this may interest you. Scientific research has shown that part of human beings' definition of beauty relates to symmetry. Subconsciously our minds assess the symmetry of anything we see. What scientists have shown is that people who are perceived to be beautiful, such as fashion models, have bodies that are more symmetrical than other people.

Forms, for Plato, are unchanging, timeless and eternal. This is why the real World of Forms is more important to Plato than the changing world of appearances. In the world there are only shadows and images of the Forms. Objects in the world imitate a form; for example, a beautiful person is only a shadow or image of the Form of beauty. In this sense the Forms go beyond human comprehension. Plato also talks of things in the world of appearance participating in the World of Forms – meaning, for example, that the Form of beauty is somehow present in a beautiful person.

When we are born we have a dim recollection of what Forms are, because Plato argues that we have an immortal soul that observed the Forms before being incarnated in a body. However, in the body the memories of the soul are only dim. Plato's evidence for this claim was the fact that people can have a basic understanding of something like truth, justice or beauty without being taught it. Instinctively we can know something is beautiful even if we do not know about the Form of beauty. This leads Plato to claim that humans have an immortal soul. The philosopher is someone who tries to escape the world of appearances and with their mind see the Forms that lie behind appearances. Because the true philosopher has knowledge of the Forms, Plato argues that they are the most suitable people to rule society.

Archetype

An initial model or idea from which later ideas and models of the same thing are all derived.

Thought Point

Justice and injustice

All the beliefs listed below are unjust according to many people, yet they are examples of practices that have occurred or are occurring in different parts of the world today.

continued opposite

1   Is this behaviour just or unjust?
2   Is there a single concept of justice that all these actions break? (In addition, can you identify a culture where this behaviour is seen to be just?)

(a) Discriminating against people on the grounds of race;
(b) Keeping women at home and not educating them;
(c) Discriminating against homosexual people;
(d) Stoning to death rebellious sons who refuse to obey their parents;
(e) Sterilising people who are mildly mentally disabled.

Education, according to Plato, is a matter of remembering and recalling the World of Forms, knowledge of which is in the soul but hidden by the incarnation of the soul in the body. For Plato people do not learn new things; instead learning is a process of understanding the reality of how things are. For example, if you learn that lying is wrong, for Plato this is a not a matter of being taught this. Instead, when you acknowledge lying is wrong, you are remembering the Form of truth that your soul knew before incarnation.

The most important Form is the *Form of the Good*. In the world of appearances we can label things as good, but this does not tell us all that goodness is. Plato argues that goodness is the most important Form. It is not clearly explained what this Form is – it is not pleasure as there can be bad pleasures nor is it knowledge as the only knowledge is knowledge of the Good. To explain it three analogies are used: the Sun, the Divided Line and the Cave.

Form of the Good
The highest of all the Forms. Plato said it was also the source of the other Forms.

THE ANALOGY OF THE SUN

Plato asks us to think about sight – in order to see we need an object to be seen, the eyes and light. It is the sun that provides the light. This applies also to the mind – just as in the visible world there are objects that can be seen by the eyes through the medium of light provided by the sun, so in the intelligible world things can be seen by the mind's or soul's eye through the medium of knowledge and truth provided by the Form of the Good.

Thus in his analogy of the Sun, Plato says that the Form of the Good makes things knowable and that the Form of the Good is the source of the other Forms. For Plato the Form of the Good enables us to understand and assess things. Plato's analogy to sight illustrates the importance of the Form of the Good.

Plato points out that sight requires both light and the eye to see clearly. Light symbolises the Form of the Good. The implication is that without the knowledge of the Form of the Good one does not see clearly, the same as trying to see in the dark. For Plato it is only in the light of the Form of the Good that anything can be known and that this has an ethical dimension – the world can only be understood from an ethical approach: through knowing the Form of the Good. Plato's approach can perhaps best be understood as teleological: the idea that everything aims towards a certain goal – the Form of the Good. The Form of the Good enables the philosopher who understands it to recognise good people, good actions and so to become a better person.

Thought Point

What is the Good?

How would you explain to a child what the word 'good' means? Justify your answer.

1   Would you say: good is a matter of what I approve of?
2   Would you say: good is what pleases me?
3   Would you say: good is what the government decides?
4   Would you say: good is what my community decides?
5   Would you say: good is what my religion says?
6   Would you say: good is what God says?
7   Something else?

THE ANALOGY OF THE DIVIDED LINE

This analogy is a continuation of that of the Sun, and is intended to be read as a reference to the Analogy of the Cave.

A   B   C   D   E

In Plato's *Republic*, Socrates uses the literary device of a divided line to teach basic philosophical ideas about the four different types of 'object' (of the intelligible world and the visible world) and the corresponding ways we come to knowledge about what exists, or come to mere opinions about what exists.

AB is opinions, beliefs, etc.; BC is scientific knowledge (knowledge of the physical world); CD is mathematical knowledge (geometry, trigonometry, etc.); DE is philosophical knowledge (knowledge of the Forms and especially the Form of the Good).

Philosophical knowledge is the most important knowledge for Plato and this is shown by the length of DE. BC and CD are equal, suggesting the interdependence between mathematics and the physical world. AB would represent the view or reality of the prisoners in the cave analogy.

THE ANALOGY OF THE CAVE

The Analogy of the Cave is one of the most famous passages in Plato's *Republic*. It is one of three similes that Plato uses to illustrate his theory of Forms. The Cave is often said to be allegorical, meaning that different elements of the story are symbolic of the situation in which people find themselves. Plato used the story to illustrate his theory of Forms, although philosophers debate how to interpret it.

Imagine people chained up in a cave, far underground. The people are all facing the wall and are chained up in such a way that they can only look ahead of them at the wall of the cave. The only light in the cave comes from a fire. There is a wall behind the prisoners and there is a fire located behind the wall. Behind the wall other people are walking up and down carrying statues on their heads. What the chained prisoners see is the shadows cast by the statues on the wall in front of them. The prisoners believe that the shadows are real because that is all they see. If they hear the people behind the wall speaking they assume that the echoes come from the shadows.

Suppose that one or more of the prisoners is freed. At first when he is turned round, he will be confused and not understand what he sees. Gradually the released prisoner becomes accustomed to the firelight and is able to see the statues. He is in a confused state, as he believes reality is the shadows.

Then if the released prisoner is dragged up a steep long ramp at the back of the cave into the sunlight, he will be blinded by the light and will try to flee back into the cave. However, gradually, if he is prevented from going back underground, he will be able to see the world around him. Finally, he will look up and realise the role of the sun, supporting life and the seasons of the year. Once in this situation he will not wish to go back underground.

However, out of duty the prisoner goes back underground again to teach the other prisoners about reality. When he goes back underground from the light of the sun to the darkness, he once again cannot see clearly and at first

Analogy
The act of comparing one thing with another that shares similar characteristics, to help a person learn about the first thing. For example, if you say a person is 'as cunning as a fox', you are explaining something about how cunning and crafty the person is.

The Cave
A famous analogy written by Plato which he uses to explain some parts of his theory of Forms.

The Analogy of the Cave

The text of the Analogy of the Cave is in Plato's *Republic* at 514a–521b. The 'Further reading' section suggests some books that are good guides to Plato's text.

Plato's other analogies

Plato's Cave is one of a set of three analogies that he used to explain some of the features of his theory of the Forms. The other two analogies, the Similes of the Line and the Sun can be found in Plato's *Republic* at 506e–511e.

sees nothing at all. When the other prisoners hear his story and observe that he sees little they are convinced it is better not to go above ground, even wishing to put to death anyone who tries to free another prisoner.

Thought Point

Philosopher

Before reading the commentary on the cave discuss what your image of a philosopher is.

Key features of the Analogy of the Cave

The tied prisoners are in an illusory world. What they think is reality, the shadows, is not reality at all. Plato says that their situation is no different from ours – in Plato's thinking people do not see the Forms clearly, only the illusory physical world. In addition, the people in the cave are prisoners; they need to be set free. In this sense the physical world imprisons a person by stopping them seeing the Forms.

The statues that people carry are also images of the Forms. These images are themselves only imitations or copies of the true reality of the Forms. The people who carry the statues on their heads are often thought to be people who share the same views as those chained up in the cave. The people who carry the statues shape the prisoners' views, because all the prisoners see is the shadows of the statues. However, these statues are themselves only images of the Forms and show that the people carrying the statues have no more idea of the Forms than do the people chained up in the cave. In the *Republic* Plato criticised philosophers and politicians who lead the people but do not actually know the truth (the Forms). The people carrying the statues are like these politicians and philosophers.

The prisoner is eventually set free, but this is described as being forced on the reluctant prisoner. Plato believed that people needed to be taught how to understand the Forms so that they could see clearly. However, the actual act of teaching people could be distressing and force people to change their views. This is why the prisoner is described as being dragged up into the sunlight. In addition, Robin Waterfield (ed., Plato, *Republic*) suggests that the prisoners being attracted to the shadows from the fire-light rather than the real world above represent the way in which culture, tradition and upbringing limit people's ability to see the world in any way other than how they were brought up.

Above ground the prisoner gradually starts to see. This is an analogy to the philosopher gradually learning to distinguish Forms from the images and copies of them in the world. Eventually the released prisoner comes to contemplate the sun. The sun represents the Form of the Good. This analogy also illustrates the sun as source of the other Forms. In the Analogy of the Cave the sun sustains all the living things in the world above ground.

The released prisoner wants to stay above ground to contemplate the Forms, but out of duty he feels that he must go below ground again to educate the other prisoners. This represents Plato's idea that those who can see the Forms (i.e. what is true) should be the leaders of society, not the politicians who want to rule out of a desire for power and fame. For Plato, knowledge of the Forms is an essential quality of any ruler, so that a ruler governs wisely for society's good, not to further her or his self-interests.

When the released prisoner goes below ground, he at first cannot see clearly. This illustrates the difficulties of seeing the Forms within the world. The other prisoners laugh at the released prisoner's talk of life above ground and Plato remarks that they would kill him if they could. Quite possibly Plato could have had two things in mind here: first, the general view of philosophers in Ancient Greek society was that they were rather odd. (An Ancient Greek playwright, Aristophanes, wrote a play called *Clouds* in which one of the characters is Socrates, who is described as wearing a cloud costume. During the play Socrates wanders on and off stage saying things that do not make much sense.) Second, the statement that the other prisoners would kill the released prisoner if they could is perhaps referring to the death of Socrates – an event which always haunted Plato.

THE DEATH OF SOCRATES

Socrates was one of the first Western philosophers. Although he wrote nothing himself, many of his ideas were recorded by Plato, his student. Socrates died after drinking hemlock, a poison. He had been condemned to death by a court in Athens for impiety and corrupting the youth of Athens by teaching them philosophy. The duty of a citizen was to end their own life if condemned to death; Socrates put obeying the law above himself and drank the poison.

Plato records the days leading up to Socrates' death in *Crito* and *Phaedo*. These books contain ideas from Plato as well as from Socrates.

Throughout his life Plato defended Socrates' memory and was distrustful of all politicians because of what had happened to Socrates.

The Analogy of the Cave raises issues about who is the most suitable person to rule society and about the state in which most people exist – one of ignorance of the Forms – and also the fact that people do not want to be released from this state.

There is no one way to interpret the Cave. Plato used it as an illustration of the theory of Forms, but it does not explain everything about the theory of Forms. How do you interpret the Cave?

The Cave Analogy – In Summary

1 The prisoners are chained up underground by their legs and necks so they cannot turn their heads

People who do not understand the true eternal knowledge of the Forms are trapped in the physical world imprisoned by desires, temptations, superficial sights and possessions.

2 There is a wall behind the prisoners behind which there is a fire

The setup of the Cave is that shadows are cast onto the wall in front of the prisoners and voices can be heard.

3 People walk up and down between wall and fire with images of animals, statues and pots on their heads; some of them are talking

All the things being carried create shadows on the wall in front of the prisoners. The prisoners can hear the voices and see the shadows of the objects balanced on people's heads. The objects are copies of things in the world above, so the shadows are copies of copies.

4 One prisoner is released and turns around to see the wall and the fire

The released prisoner realises that the shadow world is not actually the *Real* world.

5 The prisoner is dragged up to the surface

Being shown a different way of seeing the world is frightening, overpowering and something to try to avoid.

6 At first the released prisoner is overwhelmed by the glare of the light above ground

Over time you adjust to the different way of seeing things in the same way as an adult way of seeing the world is very different from a child's. Young children often find adults' activities bewildering or frightening.

7 The released prisoner first sees shadows, then reflections in the water, then the moon and stars and finally plants, trees and the sun by day

Gradually an understanding of the true, real nature of the world is gained. The world above the surface represents the Forms; the Sun is the highest Form and represents the Form of the Good. The Sun gives light and governs the seasons symbolising the Form of the Good as the Source of the other Forms of knowledge.

8 Remembering the prisoners still in the Cave the released prisoner pities them

The released prisoner pities the prisoners who still don't see what the true reality is, somewhat like more educated people pitying ignorant people.

continued opposite

which can be discovered through using the mind (i.e. it is *a priori*). According to Plato, once we understand the Good people will not disagree about moral issues or differences across cultures about what is right or wrong.

Others hold a relativist point of view and argue that there is no such thing as an absolute good. They say that ideas of right and wrong develop in the world of time and space through human relationships and situations (i.e. they are *a posteriori*). Society's values and morality change over time and also differ in different parts of the world, and so the Form of the Good is not valid.

Of what are there real Forms?

Are there really Forms of everything, such as bus tickets, types of deodorant, televisions and so on? Plato is not really interested in the question of Forms of material objects; he is interested in the Forms of concepts such as good, truth and justice. He rarely discusses the Forms of material objects. According to Bertrand Russell, Plato's ideas of the Forms when taken to their extreme fall into 'a bottomless pit of nonsense'. Plato himself seemed to struggle with the implications of his theory: sometimes he says there is a Form for everything but at other times he seems unsure. While he does mention the Form of a bed in the *Republic*, it is not even clear if this is a serious remark. Griswold has suggested this was a joke.

It is possible to think of Forms of good things or even things that we can imagine, such as a perfect circle, but it is more difficult to imagine the ideal Form of disease or disability, or even death. Augustine argued that evil does not really exist but is simply a privation of good, just as blindness is a privation of sight. However, even if this idea of Augustine's is accepted there is still some confusion as to what exactly the World of Forms applies to. Even if we could know the true ideas of beauty, truth and justice from the World of Forms, how could they affect our everyday lives? The Forms are so far removed from our experience that it would be impossible to put knowledge of the Form of the Good into practice.

The link between Forms and the physical world

Plato never clearly explains the relationship between Forms and the world of appearances (e.g. what is the link between the Form of justice and instances of justice in the world?). This is unclear.

Also, Plato presents a very depressing picture of the world of appearances in which we live, depicting it as a gloomy cave. Plato ignores any beauty in the physical world and sees it as inherently 'evil' as it is subject to change.

---

cannot be challenged. *A priori* arguments are common in philosophy, critical thinking and mathematics.

A famous example of an *a priori* argument is:

> *Premise 1*: Socrates is a man.
> *Premise 2*: Men are mortal.
> *Conclusion*: Socrates is mortal.

However, there are three ways in which an *a priori* argument can be criticised:

(i) The validity (truthfulness/accuracy) of the starting principles can be challenged.
(ii) The coherence of the argument (whether its steps are logical) can be challenged.
(iii) The appropriateness of the assumptions the argument makes can be challenged.

This at first sight seems plausible as the task of the philosopher is to seek out true reality by training himself not to see the 'shadows' of the physical world.

However, Karl Popper thought that Plato's World of Forms was simply a way of coping with the uncertainty of life. For Popper it makes sense to find truth in a changing reality.

Aristotle also suggested that something does not have to be eternal to be pure. Something white does not become more white if it is eternal – eternity and whiteness are different qualities. Thus for something to be real it does not depend on remaining unchanged as Plato thought.

The World of Forms

The existence of any other world apart from the world of appearances cannot be proved.

Plato's dualist view about the nature of reality has been criticised by others who believe that abstract ideas (e.g. 'cat', 'beauty', 'justice') are actually only names that have been invented to help people describe their experiences of the physical world. This is a materialist view because it says that the ordinary, material world is the true reality and that ideas develop only because of our experience of physical things. From this point of view, the idea of 'cat' exists because human beings have had experience of cats and needed an idea or word to describe them. 'Cat' is not some eternal idea waiting to be discovered independently with the intellect – we only come up with the idea because we have first experienced the physical object. This way of achieving knowledge is known as *a posteriori* – knowledge that comes through sense experience. Aristotle argued that the ideas or Forms are developed from our continued experience of physical things – they do not exist eternally or independently. They exist only in language – not in some independent World of Forms.

In Plato's defence . . .

Modern genetics could be used to support Plato's argument that what is really real are ideas or Forms. People and animals are members of a particular species because they share a common genetic code. The genetic code comes first, and the individual is able to grow and become a member of a certain species only as a result of the genetic code.

Additionally, rationalist philosophers such as Descartes could be used in support of Plato. Descartes agreed that we have concepts that exist in the mind first and are then used to help us construct reality. However, Descartes believed that these ideas existed in the mind and not somewhere else such as the World of Forms.

Kant was also a rationalist and thought there were two realities: the world of sense experiences which he called the phenomenal world which depends on the mind; and the world of things themselves, the reality or noumenal world. He thought that our ideas of the world come from how we ourselves perceive or interpret it, whereas the noumenal world can never be known.

If Kant's ideas are right then he would back up Plato's ideas of the World of Forms, since for Kant we can never really know the world around us as it really is because we interpret it through our sense experiences.

A scientist such as Dawkins would completely disagree with this, as he would say the empirical world has evidence to back up its existence. However, the advances in quantum physics show that we can no longer be absolutely certain that our experiences of the physical world are accurate so maybe there is a noumenal world that exists without anything experiencing it.

The third man argument

Plato's famous student Aristotle put forward a well-known criticism of the theory of Forms: suppose that a man is a copy of the Form of the man. What is the origin of the Form of the man? Well, the Form of the man is a copy of a previous Form of a man. How many men is that? Three – hence the title. In effect, Aristotle was saying that a copy of a Form could turn out to be an infinite series that never stopped; this would render the Theory of Forms meaningless as a way of explaining the ultimate origin of concepts such as the Good, truth and justice. Plato tried to answer this criticism in his later work *Parmenides*. It is also necessary to take account of the journey made by the soul to explain Aristotle's *a priori* notion of knowledge.

PLATO'S DEMIURGE

Plato's Demiurge and the OCR specification

Plato's Demiurge is not part of the CCR specification. However, it can provide a useful point of comparison with the Judaeo-Christian concept of God

Plato's later philosophical book the *Timaeus* discusses the origins of the universe, including the role of the Demiurge, the creator-like being who makes the universe. The *Timaeus* was written after the *Republic* and consequently the concept of the Forms is also important in Plato's account of the origins of the world (universe). In the later part of the *Timaeus* the Forms are discussed in detail and Plato develops his earlier work on the Forms in the *Republic*.

Plato starts by considering whether the world has always existed or whether it had a beginning; he distinguishes between a thing that 'always is' and a thing that is 'becoming', i.e. changing from not existing to existing. He concludes that things that always exist are known by intelligence, but things that are 'becoming' are known by opinion. This links back to the *Republic*. The Forms are known by intelligence and reason, whereas the visible changeable world is known only by opinion.

This leads Plato to suggest that the visible world known by opinion is caused to exist. Nothing observable in the visible world always exists. Given that the world is visible, changes and exists, Plato concludes that there is a Creator who made it exist. This Creator is a craftsman who is the Demiurge who made the universe as a visible, changeable copy of a model, i.e. the true unchanging Form of the world.

The name Demiurge means 'public worker', reflecting the fact that the world is a physical, visible copy of the true Forms. The Demiurge makes the universe as a copy of the original model of the world (Form of the world).

The Demiurge is a Craftsman – a shaper and maker of the world like an artist making a model out of clay. The Demiurge/Craftsman is not the inventor of the universe. Instead the Demiurge makes a copy of the true model of the universe which it is implied is a Form or collection of Forms; he imposes order but he does not create the pre-existing matter. The universe is supremely beautiful because the Craftsman made it as copy or image of the model of the universe (the Form of the world). The goodness of the world is visible because the world is spherical and the sphere without edges is the perfect and beautiful shape; the globe is endless and has no edges.

Since the World is visible Plato also describes it as 'tangible' (touchable/ feelable) and this leads him to suggest it consists of the solids 'Fire', 'Earth', 'Water' and 'Air'.

The World itself is described as an animal by Plato because it is a copy of a Form. Time is also a creation of the Demiurge; the universe is as near a copy of the Model Form of the universe as it can be but the universe being a copy is temporal; time passes. This is observed in the celestial motion of the planets (called 'wandering stars' by Ancient Greeks). Plato describes the world as a moving copy of the eternal Form of the World (universe).

The World also has a soul because it is a living animal. This is important in Plato's later Cosmology in which he describes the Demiurge making the gods and instructing the gods to make human beings. Human beings consist of soul and body in Plato's thought and the soul of human beings comes from what is left of the world's soul after creation.

PLATO'S DEMIURGE AND THE CREATION OF THE WORLD IN PLATO'S OWN WORDS (*TIMAEUS*)

1   What is that which always is and has no becoming?
2   That which is known by intelligence and reason [i.e. The Forms].

   (a) A question: was the world always in existence and without beginning? Or created, and had it a beginning?
   (b) Created, I reply, being visible and tangible and having a body.
   (c) Now everything that becomes or is created must of necessity be created by some cause, for without a cause nothing can be created.
   (d) The work of the creator – he looks to the unchangeable and fashions the form and nature of his work after an unchangeable pattern,
   (e) Now that which is created must, as we affirm, of necessity be created by a cause.

3   But the father and maker of all this universe is past finding out; and even if we found him, to tell of him to all men would be impossible.
4   There is still a question to be asked about him: Which of the patterns had the Craftsman in view when he made the world?

   (a) If the world be indeed fair and the artificer good, it is manifest that he must have looked to that which is eternal [The Forms];
   (b) Everyone will see that he must have looked to the eternal; for the world is the fairest of creations
   (c) And having been created in this way, the world has been framed in the likeness of that which is known by reason and mind [i.e. the Forms] . . . and must therefore of necessity be a copy of something.

5   Let me tell you then why the creator made this world of generation.
6   He was good, and the good can never have any jealousy of anything. And being free from jealousy, he desired that all things should be as like himself as they could be.
7   He desired that all things should be good and nothing bad, so far as this was attainable and out of disorder he brought order, considering that this was in every way better than the other.

ANALYSIS OF PLATO'S DEMIURGE AS THE CREATOR OF THE WORLD

The argument presented by Plato is uncontroversial as far as the claim that what exists is caused to exist. However, Plato does not consider the possibility that the cause of the universe could be random or not caused by an intelligent being.

The concept of the Demiurge is similar to the Christian idea of God as a craftsman who makes the universe. However, God in the Judaeo-Christian tradition is different from the Demiurge in many respects.

First, God is the Creator who acts intentionally; God is not simply making a visible copy of the Form of the World. The Craftsman/ Demiurge is in this sense a lesser being than God. The Christian belief that God creates *ex nihilo* contrasts markedly with Plato's Demiurge working like an Artist to make the World which is a visible copy of the real World Form. Unlike the God of monotheism the Demiurge is a lesser being who does not create from nothing, is lower than the Forms and has a limited role as a Craftsman.

In contrast, God in the Judeao-Christian tradition is omnipotent and omniscient, and nothing is greater than God. Furthermore, in Christianity, Creation is the intentional act of God and reveals God's Providence (goodness) to people. The Demiurge's world is only the copy of the eternal Form of the World.

Thought Point

Compare the Judaeo-Christian account of Creation with Plato's account. Which account is more persuasive in your opinion? Why?

Plato Summary

The Forms	1	Two worlds: Appearances (this world) and Reality (the Forms)
	2	Characteristics of Forms: Transcendent, Unchanging, Perfect, Archetypes for things that physically exist, Immortal

continued opposite

The Form of the Good	1	Highest Form
	2	Source and origin of the Other Forms
	3	Knowledge of the Form of the Good is intrinsic other knowledge, i.e. Knowledge is not morally/ethically neutral
Criticisms of the Forms	1	No convincing reasons to suppose the Forms exist
	2	Forms could just be ideas in the mind
	3	Unclear link between Forms and the physical world of appearances
	4	No proof that the World of Forms exists
	5	Aristotle's third man argument
The Cave	1	Tied up prisoners – people trapped in the physical world of appearances
	2	The fire and shadows – imitations and copies of the Forms
	3	The world above ground – the World of Forms
	4	The sun – the Form of the Good: by which other forms are known
	5	Cave Simile – illustrates the theory of the Forms
The Demiurge	1	Demiurge literally 'Public worker'
	2	Artist or Artisan or Craftsman who makes the visible, tangible world
	3	The World is the copy of its eternal Form
	4	The World is less than the eternal Forms
Analysis of the Demiurge	1	No reason to suppose that the cause of the World/universe is the Demiurge; the cause could be random or unintelligent
	2	Judaeo-Christian concept of God is different because: God creates *ex nihilo*, creation is an example of God's Providence, and nothing is higher/greater than God

SUMMARY

1   Forms

Two worlds

Appearances (this world)
Reality (the Forms)

Characteristics of the Forms

Transcendent
Unchanging

Archetype for things that physically exist
Immortal

Form of the Good

Highest Form
Source of the other Forms

Criticisms

Forms could just be ideas in the mind
Unclear link between Forms and the world of appearances
No proof that the World of Forms exists
The third man argument

2 Cave analogy

Key elements

Tied up prisoners – people trapped in the world of appearances
The fire and shadows – imitations and copies of the Forms
The world above ground – the World of Forms
The sun – the form of the Good

REVIEW QUESTIONS

Look back over the chapter and check that you can answer the following questions:

1 Explain in less than a side of A4 what is meant by Plato's theory of Forms.
2 Do you agree with Plato that Forms exist? Justify your answer with reasons.
3 Explain the link between Plato's Forms and the Cave analogy.
4 Explain the Analogy of the Cave.
5 Is there any reason to believe that anything exists except what we can observe?

continued opposite

Terminology

Do you know your terminology?

1   Try to explain the following ideas without looking at your books and notes:

    (a)   Form
    (b)   Form of the Good
    (c)   The Analogy of the Cave.

Examination Questions Practice

EXAM MISTAKES TO AVOID

When writing answers to questions about Plato, make sure you avoid the mistake of only describing what Plato says. In most examination questions on Plato you will be asked to explain some aspect of his thinking. In particular, make sure you do not just tell the story of the Cave if the question requires you to explain its meaning.

Remember: (a) assesses AO1 and (b) AO2. To help you improve your answers look at the AS Levels of Response. See: http://www.ocr.org.uk/qualifications/as-a-level-gce-religious-studies-h172-h572/

SAMPLE AS EXAM-STYLE QUESTIONS

1 (a) **Explain Plato's analogy of the cave.**
      (25 marks)

Explain how the analogy was used by Plato to explain his theory of Forms. Key elements to include in your answer would be:

- The sun – represents the Form of the Good, which is the source and origin of the other Forms. This links in with Plato's earlier analogy of the sun.

- The real world – the world of ideas; more important than the physical world for Plato.

- Shadows on the wall – the illusions of the physical world. Only shadows and images of the Forms are seen in the physical world.

- The prisoners – represent people trapped in the physical world and unable to see the reality of the World of Forms. The prisoner who is dragged out of the cave takes time to adjust to the sunlight. This represents the person who gradually adjusts to seeing the world differently when they recognise the reality that Forms exist.

(b) 'Plato does not value experience enough.' Discuss. (10 marks)

- You could argue that Plato's emphasis on the Forms limits knowledge to the few who see the Forms clearly. However, in daily life most people gain knowledge from experience of the physical world around them. You could argue that experience and study of the physical world, not knowledge of the Forms, has led to discoveries such as electricity or penicillin.

- One common argument is to suggest that there is no way to demonstrate the existence of the Forms or their non-existence. Philosophers might say that the Forms are unverifiable (uncheckable) and therefore philosophically meaningless, whereas the physical world is visible and available for us to study through science.

- On the other hand, you could argue that Plato's suggestion of the existence of the Forms has developed from studying the physical world and realising that there is more to reality than just what can be seen and observed.

- Plato's theory of the Forms might suggest that a moral life is possible only if you understand the Forms yourself or follow the instructions of those who understand them. Clearly, people can be moral even if they do not believe in or see the Forms.

2   (a) **Explain what Plato meant by the Form of the Good.**

    (b) **'Plato's "Forms" are no more than an invention.' Discuss.**

3   (a) **Explain criticisms that have been made of Plato's Theory of Forms.**

    (b) **'Criticisms of Plato's Theory of Forms are valid.' Discuss.**

FURTHER READING

The Beginner's Guide to Ideas by W. Raeper and Linda Smith (1991) is an introduction to philosophy for A Level students and well worth reading.

There are a number of histories of philosophy available and you will discover a lot more about Plato from them. They are often available in public reference libraries.

There are many versions of Plato's *Republic* available. Two very readable editions that both contain helpful footnotes and commentaries are those translated by Desmond Lee (2003) and Robin Waterfield (1994).

The moving story of Socrates' death can be found in Plato's book *Crito*. Many modern versions of it have been published, often under titles such as *The Last Days of Socrates* (1972).

2 Aristotle and Philosophy of Religion

Essential terminology

The body
The Four Causes
The prime mover

THE ISSUES

1   How do we explain the existence of things?
2   What did Aristotle mean by the prime mover?

Key scholars

Plato (c.427 BCE–c.347 BCE)
Aristotle (384 BCE–322 BCE)

WHAT YOU WILL LEARN ABOUT IN THIS CHAPTER

In this chapter you will examine Aristotle's idea about cause and purpose in the world and its link to God.

STARTER

Look at the picture overleaf. Explain how this object came into existence, identifying as many factors that contribute to its existence as you can.

'ALL MEN DESIRE TO KNOW'

These words open Aristotle's book *Metaphysics* and they sum up Aristotle's fascination with learning about and understanding the world. Part of Aristotle's philosophy investigated the nature of things and how we explain why things exist.

In the starter exercise you identified as many causes of the existence of the car as you could come up with. Quite possibly you identified not only the metal and parts the car is made from, but also the fact that people and machines made it, that the car had a design and the arrangement of the parts was for some purpose. Quite clearly a pile of parts from a car is not the same as having a real car.

Aristotle's interest was in explaining 'why' things exist as they do. However, Aristotle rejected the idea that things which exist in some way

participate in or imitate an ideal Form of that object as Plato suggested. Instead, Aristotle is interested in why a particular piece of matter exists in the way it does. So, a car is made of matter, but all the bits of matter in it have a particular arrangement and structure as part of the car. They have a particular 'form', but this form is not a copy of an ideal Platonic 'Form' of a car.

This interest led Aristotle to suggest that there are four different types of cause or explanation of why any object exists. In modern philosophy these four types of explanation are usually called the 'Four Causes'.

THE OCR CHECKLIST

Aristotle: ideas about cause and purpose in relation to God
Metaphysics Book 12

Candidates should be able to demonstrate knowledge and understanding of:

* Aristotle's understanding of material, efficient, formal and final cause;
* Aristotle's concept of the prime mover.

Candidates should be able to discuss critically the validity of the above points.

From OCR A Level Religious Studies specification H172.

ARISTOTLE'S FOUR CAUSES

The Material Cause

The Material Cause answers the question: what is it made of?

The Material Cause refers to the matter or substance that something is made from (e.g. a book is made from paper). The matter that the book is made from is paper. The material cause also explains the properties of something: paper can be written on, it can be torn, it can be burnt etc. Aristotle also divided the material cause into prime matter and proximate matter. Proximate matter is matter that has some properties such as paper, wood, stone etc. Prime matter has no properties. Aristotle actually thought that prime matter did not exist but was theoretically necessary.

However, knowing what something is made of does not give us the whole answer. We know that a book is made of paper, and perhaps glue, ink etc. but knowing this does not help us understand exactly what a book is.

The Formal Cause

The Formal Cause answers the question: what are its characteristics?

The Formal Cause refers to what gives the matter its 'form' or 'structure'. A book is not just any old piece of paper, but it is pieces of paper arranged in a particular way. So the difference between a collection of pieces of paper and a book is that a book has properties and functions that come from the particular arrangement of the pages and the words/pictures printed on them.

The Efficient Cause

The Efficient Cause answers the question: how does it happen?

The Efficient Cause refers to the cause of an object or thing existing. In other words, the answer to 'why' the thing exists. A book exists because someone wrote it and printed it. The author of the book is the cause of the book existing rather than it just being a pile of paper.

The Final Cause

The Final Cause answers the question: what is it for?

The Final Cause is concerned with the reason why something is the way it is, and is the most important part of Aristotle's thinking. This cause is concerned with the function of any thing or object. If you take the example

Metaphysics

Metaphysics means 'after physics'. This is nothing to do with what you more commonly mean by 'physics' – what this is actually referring to is Aristotle's book *Physics*; 'after physics' is just a reference to the fact that this book was classified as following on from his book *Physics* by later philosophers.

The Four Causes

1 *The Material Cause* – what a thing is made of.
2 *The Efficient Cause* – the agent or cause of the thing coming to exist as it is. The existence of a painting or work of art is brought about by the artist who makes it. The artist is the efficient cause.
3 *The Formal Cause* – what makes the thing recognisable: its structure, shape and activity.
4 *The Final Cause* – The ultimate reason why the thing exists.

Teleological

An argument relating to the study of ultimate causes in nature or a study of actions relating them to the ends.

of a book, you could ask why it is printed and laid out in the way it is, and of course an answer would be to say that it is laid out in this way so as to be readable. This Final Cause is teleological – it is concerned with the function of a particular object or the reason an action is done (Aristotle, *Metaphysics*). Aristotle is not saying that there is a purpose or sign of design in nature; he is saying that when you consider any object or thing it has some function which is the ultimate reason why the thing is as it is.

According to Aristotle the purpose or telos is an intrinsic part of the object itself and the most important. For Aristotle every single object and even the universe itself has a purpose. Something is good if it achieves its end purpose, and its telos defines it as good. According to Aristotle if we could discover the telos of an organism, we could also discover what needs to be done to reach that purpose.

Aristotle gave a large number of examples to explain these ideas. One such example was that of a marble statue. You could ask what caused the statue, and you might expect the following answers:

Material Cause:	It is made of marble.
Formal Cause:	It has the shape of a statue.
Efficient Cause:	A mason made it.
Final Cause:	Its function is to be a beautiful statue that honours, remembers or recalls someone/thing.

Thought Point

Aristotle's Four Causes

How would you explain each item on the list in terms of Aristotle's Four Causes?

1   A house
2   A car
3   The sun
4   A flower
5   A human being

ARISTOTLE

Aristotle was a remarkable person. He tutored students on most traditional subjects that are taught at universities today. He was fascinated with understanding the physical world around him and the universe. His biology books were not superseded by anything better until 2000 years later. Aristotle also wrote about other areas of study, including drama, rhetoric (public speaking), meteorology, sport and physics.

Plato and Aristotle

Aristotle was taught by Plato and always admired Plato and his philosophical work. Many of the areas of study that so interested Aristotle were first worked on by Plato. However, Aristotle often approached topics of study in different ways from Plato, which leads to some of Aristotle's philosophy being very different from Plato's.

Plato and Aristotle are often thought to represent two different approaches to philosophy: Plato emphasising the world of ideas and reason as the source of knowledge, Aristotle emphasising the physical world and experience as the basis of knowledge. However, Aristotle's writings always recognised the value of what he had learned from Plato and many of his books refer continually to the ideas of Plato. Anthony Kenny has stated that:

> Aristotle always acknowledged a great debt to Plato, whom on his death he described as the best and happiest of mortals 'whom it is not right for evil men even to praise'. (Anthony Kenny, *A Brief History of Western Philosophy*)

However, Aristotle's philosophy is different from Plato's in a number of important ways:

Aristotle emphasises the value of studying the physical world. Aristotle's approach is empirical and he is not as concerned as Plato with the World of Forms.

- Aristotle rejected Plato's theory of Forms; some of the reasons included the fact that the relationship between Forms and the objects in the physical world was not explained.
- Aristotle rejects a dualist view of the world and Plato's understanding of the soul.

The School of Athens by Raphael

The picture overleaf shows Plato pointing upwards towards heaven and the world of ideas and carrying his book *Timaeus*, while Aristotle carries his book *Ethics* and points towards the Earth and the physical world. Why?

Formal Cause

Make sure you do not confuse Aristotle's Formal Cause and forms with those of Plato.

The statue

Aristotle the man (384–322 BCE)

Aristotle was born in Macedonia. At the age of 17 he moved to Athens where he joined Plato's Academy. In 347 BCE he moved to Turkey due to the growing political tensions between Macedonia and

continued overleaf

Athens. He spent his time there investigating science and particularly biology. In 341 BCE he moved with his family back to Macedonia to become tutor to King Philip II of Macedonia's son Alexander (who would later become Alexander the Great). After Alexander became king, Aristotle returned to Athens and founded a school called the Lyceum. He remained in Athens teaching until 323 when Alexander the Great died. After Alexander's death it became difficult for Aristotle to stay in Athens as he was Macedonian. Worried that he might die like Socrates, Aristotle and his family moved to Chalcis, where he died a year later.

The School of Athens by Raphael

Aristotle and Plato: detail from the School of Athens in the Stanza della Segnatura, 1510–1511 (fresco) (detail of 472) by Raphael (Raffaello Sanzio of Urbino) (1483–1520) Vatican Museums and Galleries, Vatican City, Italy/The Bridgeman Art Library
Nationality/copyright status: Italian/out of copyright

Evaluating Aristotle's Theory of Causality

Aristotle criticises Plato's belief in the World of Forms as there is no evidence for their existence, but by the same count there is no evidence that only the material world is the source of true knowledge. As we saw in the chapter on Plato, rationalists such as Descartes and Kant thought that there were other sources of true knowledge apart from sense experience which could always be mistaken (see pp. 18–19).

Many scientists and philosophers would also part company with Aristotle over his belief that everything has a telos, final cause or purpose. Some would say that things exist simply by chance or as Bertrand Russell said the universe simply is – it is 'brute fact' and it makes no sense to ask what caused it or to think that it has a purpose. Existentialist philosophers such Albert Camus and Jean-Paul Sartre also thought it was pointless to think that the universe had any purpose.

If things happen by chance or luck they do not fit into Aristotle's categories. It is also difficult to find a material or formal cause for emotions, and even their efficient and final causes raise problems: is there a final cause for despair?

Kant and Hume would also argue that the idea of cause cannot be easily located in the material world.

However, today scientists do work in a similar way to Aristotle as theories about the universe are based on prior experience and observation of the universe.

Aristotle used the Greek word *aition*, in the sense meaning *an explanation that accounts for something*. Aristotle's theory shows that there can be several explanations for the existence of something, all of which increase our understanding of it. For example, we know the material cause of a human being and all the chemical components involved, but we can also accept other explanations for the existence of humans such as life being a gift from God. Aristotle shows that both scientific and religious explanations can work together – the Big Bang can be seen as the efficient cause of the universe and at the same time God can be seen as the final cause.

Aristotle's ideas have been developed by many other philosophers. As well as being influential in the development of modern science, his ideas have been adopted by Christian thinkers like Thomas Aquinas.

THE PRIME MOVER

Aristotle observed that everything that exists was in a permanent state of 'movement' or 'motion'. By 'motion' Aristotle did not mean moving around or taking a walk. The Latin word *motus* from which motion comes refers to change. He noticed that everything in the universe is in a state of change. One example could be the ever-varying weather. You could also think about the fact that human beings are in a process of change. Every day your body changes, you grow and age, you lose hair and skin cells.

Aristotle observed four things:

1   The physical world was constantly in a state of motion and change.
2   The planets seemed to be moving eternally.
3   Change or motion is always caused by something.
4   Objects in the physical world were in a state of actuality and potentiality.

From these four points Aristotle concludes that something exists that causes the motion and change without being moved and that is eternal.

Aristotle reached this conclusion by observing that if something can change, it exists in one 'actual' state and has the 'potential' to become another state. A cow in a field is potentially a piece of roast beef. An actual child is potentially an adult. Aristotle used this distinction between potentiality and actuality in his philosophy. He realised that if things come into existence they must be caused to exist by something else. Second, he argued that if something is capable of change that means it is potentially something else. This led him to ask: what is the cause of motion and change in the universe? Aristotle is not asking what started the chain of events off like a domino rally. Instead he is considering what the continual cause of change is. The motion of the planets is significant at this point. Aristotle understood the motion of the planets to be eternal, but clearly if they are in motion eternally there must be an eternal cause of motion – a prime or first mover.

The prime mover

The unchanging cause of all that exists.

Thought Point

Potentiality and actuality

How does Aristotle's distinction between potentiality and actuality apply to the following?

1   An acorn
2   An embryo
3   The Prime Minister
4   A computer
5   A pig.

NB: Aristotle did not suggest that the prime mover starts everything off like lighting a firework. For Aristotle the prime mover is the originating cause of all motion eternally that sustains the pattern of change from actuality to potentiality in the physical world.

What are the characteristics of the prime mover?

According to Aristotle the prime mover exists by necessity – meaning that the prime mover could not fail to exist. The prime mover is not capable of change and so Aristotle says that it is pure actuality by nature, and so its nature is good. The reason for this is that lack of goodness means that people can do better, meaning they can change. Something that is pure actuality clearly is not lacking some quality it should have; it is just what it should be – i.e. it is good.

For Aristotle, the prime mover is the Final Cause, meaning that the prime mover is the ultimate explanation of why things exist (think of Aristotle's Four Causes). Aristotle also suggests that the Final Cause leads to movement like the action of being loved. This is a somewhat strange idea, but one way to understand it might be to think of love not just as being about your actions but also about attraction. The prime mover is the ultimate reason and final goal of movement. Another way to understand this could be to think of a magnet that attracts iron objects towards it. Aristotle says that all action is ultimately aimed at the prime mover and this is like attraction because the prime mover is the cause of all motion (that which moves without being moved).

In his book *Metaphysics* Aristotle also associates the prime mover with God and concludes that God is 'a living being, eternal, most good, so that life and duration continuous and eternal belong to God; for this is God' (Aristotle, *Metaphysics*). Therefore, for Aristotle, God is the prime mover. The characteristic of this prime mover is that it is without parts and indivisible. In philosophy the term for being without parts is 'divine simplicity'. God is pure actuality having no potentiality. God is also described as being 'complete reality'.

Aristotle considered how it is possible to explain divine thought if God is pure actuality. For instance, he rejected the idea that God was like a person who is constantly asleep. Aristotle suggested that God's activity was thinking and thought, but thinking about what? His conclusion is that: 'Therefore it must be of itself that the divine thought thinks (since it is the most excellent of things)' (Aristotle, *Metaphysics*). This phrase may be interpreted in many ways, but Aristotle rejected any idea of God thinking about the universe and what happens in it, as this would mean that God changes, because God's knowledge would change. Hence, Aristotle's answer is that God reflects only on being God as a perfection.

Finally, Aristotle considers how God relates to the universe. He suggests two ways (Aristotle, *Metaphysics*):

1   As a leader
2   In the order of the universe.

Aristotle argues that the first is more important than the second as the universe depends for its existence on the prime mover, but he also points out that all things in the universe are ordered to some 'Final Cause' and ultimately to the prime mover. This exemplifies the importance he places on the last of his Four Causes.

It is important to note that the prime mover – God in Aristotle's thinking – is a necessary being but one who does not in any way interact with or act in the world. The God of Aristotle is an eternal, transcendent and impersonal being.

Evaluating Aristotle's prime mover

The relationship between the prime mover and the universe which the mover causes to move is unclear. According to Aristotle the prime mover started the chain of cause and effect in the universe without himself being moved. However, some Greeks believed that matter is eternal and therefore the prime mover would not be an efficient cause.

For many philosophers this would seem to be a contradiction and an impossibility. How can something that is unmoved itself initiate movement in other things? While Aristotle does link the prime mover with God, Aristotle's prime mover is transcendent and cannot interact in the universe in the way that religious believers often talk about God's activity in the world. Nor can any sense be made of religious believers' claims to have experiences of God, or to believe that God hears and answers prayer.

The causal relationship between the prime mover thinking and the universe is unclear. Aristotle said that the prime mover was pure thought, but how can something that is pure thought move the physical universe? Surely also this immaterial view of God contradicts his materialist and empirical view of the universe as explained in his theory of the Four Causes?

However, the prime mover does share characteristics with the Christian view of God in that he is eternal and omnipotent. It could be argued that there must be a first cause for the universe, and his ideas again influenced Christian philosophers such as Thomas Aquinas and his Cosmological argument.

SUMMARY

1　Aristotle

Aristotle's Four Causes

The Material Cause – the matter or substance from which something is made

The Formal Cause – what gives the matter its form or structure
The Efficient Cause – the cause of an object or thing existing
The Final Cause – the reason why something is the way it is

2   Plato and Aristotle

Aristotle's philosophy is different from Plato's

It emphasises the value of studying the physical world
It effectively rejects Plato's theory of Forms
It rejects dualism and adapts Plato's understanding of the soul

3   The prime mover

The source that causes the motion and change of the universe without
   being moved and that is eternal
The prime mover exists of necessity
The prime mover is the Final Cause
The prime mover is linked with God and in Metaphysics *Aristotle also*
   calls this being 'God'

The prime mover is related to the universe

As a leader
In the ordering of the universe

Problems

The relationship between the prime mover and the universe is unclear
Aristotle's prime mover is transcendent and cannot interact in the universe
   in the way that religious believers often talk about God's activity in the
   world
The causal relationship between the prime mover thinking and the universe
   is unclear
Is there a final cause or purpose to the universe?

4   Aristotle and Christianity

Aquinas developed early forms of cosmological arguments
The philosophy of Aristotle is used to explain Roman Catholic beliefs about
   the presence of Jesus in the bread and wine used in the Eucharistic
   service, the Mass
The prime mover idea influenced medieval thinking about the nature of
   God

REVIEW QUESTIONS

1   What is the difference between Plato's and Aristotle's use of the word 'Form'?
2   Is the prime mover anything like the God of the Judaeo-Christian tradition?
3   Whose definition of the soul do you have more sympathy with, Aristotle's or Plato's? Give reasons to support your answer.

Terminology

Do you know your terminology?

1   Try to explain the following ideas without looking at your books and notes:

    (a)   Aristotle's Four Causes
    (b)   Necessary being
    (c)   The prime mover.

Examination Questions Practice

EXAM MISTAKES TO AVOID

Make sure that you do not confuse the philosophy of Plato and Aristotle. Students often lose marks in this way, which is a great pity. In addition, in examination questions try to show that you understand Aristotle's ideas rather than just describing them.

Remember: (a) assesses AO1 and (b) AO2. To help you improve your answers look at the AS Levels of Response. See: http://www.ocr.org.uk/qualifications/as-a-level-gce-religious-studies-h172-h572/

THE GOD OF FAITH   PART II

WHAT COMES INTO YOUR HEAD?

1   What thoughts immediately come into your head if:

   (a) Some unknown person walks up to you in the street and says 'I believe in God'?
   (b) A person stands in the street talking about their belief in God and giving out leaflets to anyone who wants them?
   (c) Your friend says that belief in God has become really important to them?
   (d) Some unknown person knocks at your door to talk to you about belief in God?

2   What would you think each of these persons means by 'God'?

The understanding of God in religious faiths such as Judaism, Christianity and Islam is in some ways very different from that in Greek philosophy.

The chapters on Plato and Aristotle presented ideas which suggest that God is a distant, separate, transcendent being; God is neither part of the universe nor clearly understandable or observable from within the physical universe.

The next two chapters explore two of the most important beliefs about God within the Judaeo-Christian tradition: God as Creator and God's goodness. In these chapters you will explore what these concepts mean to religious believers, as well as some of the issues and challenges raised in response to these ideas.

Essential terminology

Creatio ex nihilo
Creator
Deism
Genesis 1–3
Omnibenevolence
Omnipotence
Omnipresence
Omniscience
Theism

3 God the Creator

THE ISSUE

What do people from the Judaeo-Christian tradition mean by 'God'?

WHAT YOU WILL LEARN ABOUT IN THIS CHAPTER

In this chapter you will examine what followers of the Judaeo-Christian tradition believe about the nature of God. In particular, you will be thinking about what it means to say that God is the Creator. You will also examine some of the imagery used to talk about God in the Bible and some of the philosophical terms used to describe God.

STARTER

Imagine a person who came to study English in Britain from a country which forbade religious belief. This person knows nothing about what is meant in most cultures by the words 'God' and 'religion'. How would you explain to someone like this:

1 What people mean by the word 'God';
2 What people mean by the word 'religion'.

THE OCR CHECKLIST

Judaeo-Christian influences on philosophy of religion

Candidates should be familiar with biblical texts to exemplify the topics below. There are no prescribed texts.

The concept of God as Creator

Candidates should be able to demonstrate knowledge and understanding of:

- the way the Bible presents God as involved with his creation;
- the imagery of God as a craftsman;
- the concepts of omnipotence, omniscience and omnipresence;
- the concept of 'creatio ex nihilo'.

Candidates should be able to:

- compare this view with Aristotle's prime mover;
- discuss whether, if God created the universe, God is therefore responsible for everything that happens in it.

Candidates should be able to discuss these areas in a critical manner.

From OCR A Level Religious Studies specification H172.

INTRODUCTION

How do we explain what is meant by God? The starter activity at the beginning of this chapter was designed to highlight this issue.

Philosophy of religion uses the word 'attributes' to refer to the characteristics of an object or person. When talking about God, 'attributes' refer to the qualities and characteristics commonly associated with God, such as being the Creator, omnipotent (all-powerful), omniscient (all-knowing), good, just and so forth.

There is a great contrast between the way Greek philosophy talks about the nature of God or a prime mover, and the way the Bible refers to God as

Creator. This chapter will examine the biblical teaching concerning the nature of God as *Creator*.

GOD THE CREATOR

In the Bible God is described as the Creator. This is accepted without question rather than being a matter of debate. The nature of God as Creator is most clearly seen in a few passages from Genesis, Job, Psalms and Isaiah.

Thought Point

What is a creator?

1   How would you define what a creator is? Think of your own definition or pick one of the following options. Make sure you can explain your choice:

A creator is

> (i) . . . someone who makes things
> (ii) . . . someone who invents new things
> (iii) . . . someone who designs things
> (iv) . . . someone who produces great artistic works.

Within the Judaeo-Christian tradition there are a number of key things that are meant when God is described as Creator:

1   God causes the universe to exist.
2   God is responsible for the universe coming into existence and existing at every moment.
3   God is responsible for everything which exists within the universe. These ideas all derive from the Bible.

GOD AS CREATOR

The Judaeo-Christian tradition belief is that God is the Creator and this is taken for granted. For example, an early summary of Christian belief called the Apostles' Creed opens with the words 'I believe in God, the Father almighty, creator of heaven and Earth.'

Creator
A title applied to God. In the Judaeo-Christian tradition it refers to God creating the world as recorded in the Bible, for example in Genesis 1–3, Psalm 8 and Job 38.

Deism
Belief in a God who starts the world off or creates it and then leaves it to run by itself. This view makes God completely separate from, and not involved with, his creation. Also, simply the principle of the universe, but not the one humans have a relationship with.

Theism
Refers to belief in a God who creates the world and continues to sustain it and be involved with it. This is the traditional view of God held by the Jewish, Christian and Islamic traditions.

Genesis 1–3
The Book of Genesis is the first book of the Christian Bible and Jewish Torah. Chapters 1–2 contain two different accounts of the creation of the world by God, and the Fall is in Chapter 3.

Thought Point

Read the text

The OCR specification says that you should be able to use biblical texts to discuss the concept of God the Creator.

Make sure you at least read Genesis 1–3 carefully.

It is also a very good idea to read other relevant biblical texts such as Psalm 8 and Job 38–39.

Although you do not need to learn any of the Bible passages off by heart, the biblical ideas about God the Creator come from these texts and you will understand the ideas better if you have read the Bible passages.

'In the beginning when God created the heavens and the earth' (Genesis 1: 1)

The belief in God as Creator centres on the idea of God creating the Earth. In the story, God's spirit, or more literally breath/wind, moves over the Earth and shapes it. God commands that there is light, darkness, stars, sun, moon, fish in the sea, birds in the heaven, animals on land and people. It is important to note that it is God who brings everything into being in this story.

In Genesis 2 the second creation story also refers to God creating people – Adam and Eve. God is referred to as walking in the garden in the cool of the day. The image of God walking in the garden is a very human one but this is not to say that God is like a human being. God the Creator is elsewhere in the Bible pictured as being above creation, responsible for everything in it and the universe itself continuing to exist.

Isaiah 40 describes God watching over creation and the people in the creation are compared to grasshoppers in the sight of God. What matters in the Judaeo-Christian tradition is that God is in control of his creation and is responsible for the creation existing every second of every day.

Thomas Aquinas pointed out that whether the world had a beginning is not the major issue. What really matters is that God causes everything that exists to exist.

The craftsman

God the Creator is compared to a craftsman and this is clearly seen in Job 38, where God is described as the designer who laid the very foundations of the Earth, decided its dimensions and supported the pillars on which the

Earth stands. God is also pictured as being in control of the sun and the moon whereas we know today that the sun and the moon follow regular patterns of activity that are explainable in scientific terms.

In Genesis 2 God making Adam from the dust is likened to a potter shaping the clay. This is a human-like image of God. An image which likens some aspect of God's nature to that of a human being is called *anthropomorphic* (meaning human-like).

God is in control

God as Creator is clearly viewed as being in control in the Bible. For example, in Isaiah 40: 22–23 God is described as sitting above the Earth and having the power to reduce princes to nothing. The same idea of God being in control is shown through the Genesis creation stories when God throws Adam and Eve out of the Garden of Eden.

Creation out of nothing

A key part of Christian belief in God the Creator is that God created the world out of nothing. This belief derives from both Genesis and Job: Genesis because it records God creating the world and people from darkness, and Job because God is pictured as laying the foundations of the Earth. This idea of God creating the universe out of nothing is usually referred to as *Creatio ex nihilo*.

However, it is also worth noting that while Christian tradition believes God created out of nothing, there are some hints in the earliest writings of the Bible that God was originally pictured as a craftsman shaping pre-existent unformed matter. In Genesis 1: 2 God's spirit hovers over the formless void and the chaos of the waters and controls it. The biblical scholar John Day has pointed out that this is the same idea as that found in Psalm 104: 26. John Day suggested that God's 'control of the waters is simply a job of work' ('Creation Narratives'). This very early idea was replaced in Christian belief with the idea that God creates out of nothing. To many people today the idea of *Creatio ex nihilo* is appealing because it fits in with the idea of the universe and time all beginning at the Big Bang.

Human beings' place in creation

One important thought that pervades the Jewish Scriptures is about the place of human beings at the top of a hierarchy of all life. In Psalm 8 God is said to have made human beings:

Anthropomorphic

An image which likens some aspect of God's nature to that of a human being is called anthropomorphic. For example, in the Bible God is described as having a 'strong right arm' and being a 'king'.

Creatio ex nihilo

This phrase is Latin for *'creation out of nothing'*. It is often used by Christians to communicate the idea that God created the universe out of nothing. God creating the world as described in the Genesis creation stories is often described as being an act of creation *'out of nothing'*.

. . . little lower than God, [*than the divine beings* or *angels*] and crowned them with glory and honour.

  You have given them dominion over the works of your hands; you have put all things under their feet. (Psalm 8: 5–6)

This passage echoes the statement in Genesis 1: 26 that human beings are made in the image of God.

  Human beings are described as being made in the image of God. What this means is unclear, but some ideas are:

1   Human beings are superior to and placed above the rest of the living creatures of the world by God. There is a hierarchy of creatures and human beings are at the top.
2   God gives human beings a privileged place in the world.
3   Imago Dei suggests that humans share some of God's attributes.

The Genesis 2 creation story is concerned specifically with the place of human beings in creation. Adam and Eve in the Garden of Eden are tempted by the snake and are thrown out of the garden and punished. The interpretation of this story of Adam and Eve's disobedience to God (Genesis 3) is discussed in Chapter 11 of this book on the problem of evil but what concerns us here is the fact that God is in charge of the Garden. God is pictured as providing a paradise for human beings as long as they follow his laws about not eating the fruit from the tree of life and the tree of knowledge of good and evil. Part of the belief in God as Creator is that he provides for human beings and puts them in charge of creation.

  Christians today often interpret the comment about human beings 'made in the image of God' as referring to humans' rationality, their ability to think and reason. What Christians do not believe is that the idea of God being a potter or walking in the Garden of Eden in the afternoon means that God is in any way like a human being.

Paradise

The word 'paradise' originates from ancient Persia. In ancient Persian 'paradise' means 'garden'.

The serpent

The serpent in the Garden of Eden is linked with Satan in Christian beliefs, but it is worth noting that this link was only made a long time after the Genesis story was written. Belief in Satan only originated after 537 BCE.

Thought Point

How observant are you?

Look at Genesis 1: 26 and Psalm 8: 5. There is something odd about the language, particularly in Genesis 1: 26. Can you work out what it is? You will find the answer at the end of this chapter, in the box before the 'Further reading' section.

The beauty of creation

The final point to note is that the Bible pictures God as the Creator of an ordered, beautiful and harmonious world. This is seen clearly in the peaceful Garden of Eden before the Fall of Adam and Eve. For Christians the beauty of creation reveals the Creator. The Roman Catholic Church, for example, has stated that:

> The order and harmony of the created world results from the diversity of beings and from the relationships which exist among them. Man discovers them progressively as the laws of nature. They call forth the admiration of scholars. The beauty of creation reflects the infinite beauty of the Creator and ought to inspire the respect and submission of man's intellect and will. (*The Catechism of the Catholic Church* §341)

According to Genesis 2–3, disharmony within creation is caused by human beings disobeying God and going against God's wishes. (See Chapter 9 on the problem of evil for further information.)

Thought Point

Visit a park

Go for a walk in a park or in the countryside. Take time to stand and stare and look at the scenery. Why do you think looking at the natural world makes religious people believe in God the Creator?

GENESIS AND MYTH

In biblical interpretation a myth is a story which communicates a set of values or beliefs through imagery. What matters in a myth is the message, not the literal truth of the imagery.

This is not the same as saying that creation stories are not literally true – it is saying that *what matters is the message of the creation stories*. Of course, for many Christians and Jews throughout history the Genesis creation story has been interpreted as literally true.

Myths usually communicate a key set of values that form part of the identity of a society. In most religious traditions there are very early creation stories which are myths; they communicate the religious person's belief in God the Creator. The Genesis creation stories are examples of myths. They communicate the beliefs of the Jewish people about God being Creator of the world (Genesis 1) and human beings as the most important part of creation (Genesis 1).

A different example from the United Kingdom is the stories surrounding King Arthur. Most of these stories are mythological; they communicate values about loyalty, promise-keeping and national identity. Very few of the stories of Arthur have any historical basis and all the parts loved by television and film, such as Lancelot, Guinevere and the Holy Grail, are much later additions.

Is the seven-day creation story literally true?

There are a number of reasons to suggest that the Genesis story is a myth rather than literal truth:

1   Scientific research strongly suggests that the world is 4.5 billion years old and that many species of animals, such as dinosaurs, lived and walked the Earth long before humans or the writing of the Bible.
2   The creation story in Genesis 1 appears to have adopted ideas from the culture in which it emerged. In particular, it may have been influenced by Psalm 104, which many scholars believe is a much earlier piece of writing that refers to the events of creation in the same order as the seven-day creation story.
3   The Genesis seven-day creation story may have developed ideas from Canaanite creation myths associated with the ancient city of Ugarit (in modern-day Syria). In particular, God moving over the water is an idea found in earlier Canaanite texts.

The use of the word *spirit* or *breath* to describe God moving over the Earth to control its making and development is significant. God moving on the wind is a mythological image showing his power over the Earth. The first two verses of Genesis refer to God moving over the waters, which is an idea found in earlier Canaanite creation stories in which God the Creator battles the chaotic god of the oceans.

Creationists

Christians who interpret the Genesis stories in a literal way are called *Creationists*. They reject Darwin's theory of evolution and believe that God directly created human beings in some way. If you would like to know more about ways in which the Genesis story has been interpreted, have a look at some of the books listed in the 'Further reading' section.

Thought Point

Biblical creation stories

It is important to note that biblical scholarship strongly suggests that the creation narratives in the Bible are influenced by earlier Canaanite stories, and not by stories from Babylon as is often claimed. On the other hand, the story of Noah and the flood is related to the much earlier Babylonian *Epic of Gilgamesh*.

Mythology is explored in greater depth in Chapter 16 on religious language for A2 religious studies.

DATES DO NOT MATTER

It is important to be clear about the fact that when the Bible refers to God the Creator it is not concerned with the date when the Earth began, whether it was 6,000 years ago or 4.5 billion years ago. As Aquinas pointed out, the belief in God as Creator is concerned with God causing the universe to exist and continuing to cause it to exist. While people are very interested in the question of when the Earth began, properly speaking this is not what calling God the Creator is concerned with.

THE OMNI QUALITIES OF GOD

Within the Bible God is given many titles, such as almighty or warrior, which tell the reader something about the nature of God. These titles are not to be interpreted exactly literally. For example, when God is said to have a *mighty hand* or to be like a *potter* (Genesis 2: 7) Jews and Christians do not necessarily mean that God has arms like a human being. Instead, the image of God being a *potter* is telling the reader something about God's nature as a *designer* or *craftsman*. This use of language is said to be analogical.

Omnibenevolence
Used as a title for God to say that God is 'good'. Means that God 'always wills goodness or good things towards people', or 'all-loving'.

What is meant by 'analogy' in philosophy of religion?

Making an analogy is the act of comparing one thing with another thing that has similar characteristics in order to help explain the first thing. The *Oxford Advanced Learners' Dictionary* gives a good example, saying that a teacher could compare a human heart with a pump to help explain how the heart works. In the Bible analogies are often used to say something about the nature of God. For example, Psalm 8 says: 'I look up at your heavens, made by your fingers' (Psalm 8: 3). The image of God having fingers is used to tell us about God creating the world and shaping it, but it is not necessarily the biblical writer's aim to say that God actually has fingers.

It is important to remember that God is elsewhere described as a *Warrior, King* or even a 'Mother hen' (Luke 13: 34). All these images tell us something about the character or nature of God, not the literal physical appearance of God. Clearly, if God is the Creator of the universe, God is a being who is unique and unlike any other being in the universe.

(The use of analogy to talk about God is discussed in greater depth in Chapter 15 on religious language.)

Analogy
Refers to comparing two or more related items, using the less complex item to communicate or highlight something about the more complex one. For example, the human brain is like a computer. Thomas Aquinas divided analogy into two types:

1 *Proportion* – telling us the extent to which a thing corresponds to what it should be
2 *Attribution* – telling us about the qualities of a particular thing.

Omnipotent

Means infinite or unlimited power. It is a philosophical word often used to describe God.

Qualities of God

Three qualities of God are clearly linked with the image of God as Creator revealed in the Bible. The three qualities are:

1   Omnipotence
2   Omniscience
3   Omnipresence.

OMNIPOTENT

'Omnipotent' infinite or unlimited power. Within philosophy of religion the possible meaning of omnipotence is much discussed but what is clear within the Bible is that omnipotence is a quality of God the Creator and it tells people about the limitless nature of God's power. This is depicted with God creating the world and controlling the chaos in the waters (Genesis 1: 1–2). God also lays the foundations of the Earth and governs day and night:

> Have you commanded the morning since your days began, and caused the dawn to know its place. (Job 38: 12)

Within the Bible the greatness of God's power compared with that of human beings is continually emphasised:

> Have you an arm like God,
> and can you thunder with a voice like his? (Job 40: 9)

The title 'omnipotence' is also telling the reader of the Bible that God's power is present through his creation. This is seen very clearly in that God is not only pictured as the Earth's Creator, but also as controlling day and night, the weather and even holding back the sun:

> the LORD threw down huge stones from heaven on them as far as Azekah, and they died. . . . And the sun stood still, and the moon stopped, until the nation took vengeance on their enemies. (Joshua 10: 11b, 13)

It is important to note that the logical possibility of God throwing hailstones or making the sun stand still is not the main issue. (How this particular story is to be interpreted is discussed in Chapter 5 on God's activity in the world.) For the Judaeo-Christian tradition God's power works throughout creation and this is the meaning of omnipotence. The world is imbued with God's power and this is accepted by the biblical reader without question.

In the Bible God's omnipotence is also an indication of his supremacy and greatness compared to people:

See, God is exalted in his power;
who is a teacher like him? (Job 36: 22)

Later philosophers of religion defined this idea of omnipotence as God being able to do anything that is logically possible. Aquinas writes that God is 'active power' and 'that his power has no limits' (Aquinas, *Summa Theologiae*, 1a, 25, a.1) which develops the notion of omnipotence in the Bible. (For more information about omnipotence look at the 'Further reading' section of this chapter.)

> **Imbued**
>
> '*Imbued* ' refers to being filled with something. In the Judaeo-Christian tradition creation is filled with God's power and presence.

Thought Point

Omnipotence problems

Some classic problems in philosophy of religion concerning omnipotence are put forward by Brian Davies, C. Wade Savage and others:

1   Can God climb a tree?
2   Can God make a rock too heavy to lift?
3   Can God make square circles?

What do you think the answers are? More importantly, what point do you think the questions are getting at?

> **Logical problems with omniscience**
>
> There are many philosophical problems with God's omniscience, such as how we can truly have free will if God appears to know what we will do before we do it. This and other philosophical problems are addressed in Chapter 16 on the nature of God.

OMNISCIENCE

Omniscience means 'infinite knowledge'. From the Bible God is shown to be all-knowing. God the Creator is aware of his creation and knows exactly what happens within the creation. There are numerous examples in the Bible of God being aware of what happens, such as when Eve eats the fruit of the tree of knowledge of good and evil, or when David commits adultery with Bathsheba (2 Samuel 11–12).

Second, in the Bible, God's omniscience is about the limitless nature of God's knowledge. God has knowledge of the creation of the Earth and how every part of the Earth functions. In Job 38–39 God's words to Job emphasise the full extent of God's knowledge, far beyond that of human beings:

> **Omniscient**
>
> Means infinite knowledge. Most philosophers today use the word as a quality for God to indicate that God knows everything it is logically possible to know.

> Can you bind the chains of the Pleiades,
>   or loose the cords of Orion?
> Can you lead forth the Mazzaroth in their season,
>   or can you guide the Bear with its children?
> Do you know the ordinances of the heavens?
>   Can you establish their rule on the earth? (Job 38: 31–33)

In this particular passage God's knowledge includes that of the stars and understanding the celestial laws – what we today would call the laws of physics governing the movement of the planets.

Later philosophy reflects on what it means to be all-knowing, considering questions such as: can God know the future if it has not already happened?

However, within the Bible, omniscience is about emphasising the limitless nature of God's knowledge of both the act of creation and all that happens within creation.

Thought Point

A bit of astronomy

What Job says about the Pleiades and Orion may sound a little strange. Actually it is referring to constellations of stars in the sky. In ancient Israel it was believed that the motion of the stars affected the weather.

If you want to get an idea of why the stars were thought to be 'chained' or tied with 'cords', stand in a garden which is not near street lights on a clear night and observe one patch of the sky for about an hour. What do you notice happens?

Want to know more?

If you would like to know more about philosophers' discussions of omniscience look at the 'Further reading' section at the end of this chapter.

Thought Point

Brain teaser

Can God know the future if it has not already happened?
If God knows the future do we really have a choice about decisions we make?
What do you think?

OMNIPRESENCE

Omnipresence is a quality of God which refers to God being present throughout creation.

Omnipresence is linked to the idea of omnipotence in the Bible. Within the Judaeo-Christian tradition, God the Creator is seen as sustaining all his creation and being present throughout all creation through all time. The idea of omnipresence expresses the idea of God being responsible for everything that exists and continues to exist.

Second, God being omnipresent relates to God being omniscient. Within the Bible, God is shown as being omnipresent and aware of what happens as well as being the Creator who is separate (transcendent). For example, in Genesis 3 God is depicted in a human-like way as walking in the Garden in the cool of the evening and aware of Adam and Eve's sin. In Job 38, God's presence is everywhere from the stars, weather and animals to the gates of death. Job emphasises the extent of creation being beyond human comprehension, but God is present within all creation.

The extent of God's presence is continually repeated in the creation stories. God is present in creation when he moves over the Earth (Genesis 1), present in the Garden of Eden (Genesis 3), present at the foundations of the Earth and in the heavens (Job 38).

Omnipresent
All-present. It is used in philosophy as a quality for God to refer to God being present throughout every part of creation.

THE UNIQUENESS OF GOD

1   The Judaeo-Christian belief in a Creator is a belief in a unique being completely different from anything which exists and lives in the universe.
2   Within the Bible God's uniqueness is highlighted by the qualities which he is described as having, such as being omnipotent and omniscient.

What the Bible is not interested in

The Bible is not concerned with difficulties explaining concepts like omnipotence and omniscience. For example, many people who experience evil events question whether God is omnipotent and good, if God does not stop evil events happening. These questions *are* important and they are considered in later chapters of this book, but they are not what concerned the biblical authors writing about God the Creator. The Bible reveals God as:

THE CREATOR

Who is:

UNIQUE
Supreme above all creation
All-knowing (omniscient)
All-powerful (omnipotent)
All-good (omnibenevolent)
Ever-present (omnipresent)

This picture is of a God who is often described using human (anthropomorphic) imagery and who is involved and active in creation (immanent). The picture of God revealed in the Bible is very different from that of Greek philosophy. The relationship between the God of the Bible and the God of philosophy is explored in the summary 'The gods of faith and philosophy compared' on p. 78.

GOD'S RESPONSIBILITY FOR WHAT HAPPENS WITHIN THE UNIVERSE

The issue

The problem for many people with saying that God is the Creator is that people usually associate a creator with the object that has been created. For example, if you design a car and sell it to the public, you will be held responsible if it turns out that the car's design has a fault that causes it to explode when the car drives at over 60 miles per hour. Similarly, pacifists have criticised the designers of nuclear weapons as 'immoral'.

So, when it comes to the world, if earthquakes happen in it, is God responsible for them? If God's responsibility is like yours for the faulty car, God could, and possibly should, be held accountable for the problems that earthquakes cause.

An alternative

An alternative view would be to say that if we look at all the problems in the natural world like volcanoes, earthquakes and hurricanes, it is clear that, if God is the *craftsman* who made the world, he did a pretty poor job. This is effectively a challenge to the claim that God is omnipotent. The implication is that:

1   The world could be better than it is if God is omnipotent
2   Therefore, God cannot be omnipotent.

Because of the Judaeo-Christian belief that God is omnipotent, it could be argued that if the world could be somewhat different then surely an all-powerful God could have made an earthquake-free world.

However, although God the Creator is often thought of as being like a craftsman, theologians like to make three important points here:

1   God is not like a car designer and should not be compared to a human designer of any sort.
2   God omnipotently made a world that is full of change and follows natural laws. Earthquakes and their consequences are the result of the world working in a regular way. This makes the world understandable to human beings; it is a world in which they can learn things. Are people really saying they do not want a world in which change and development take place? Human life would not have evolved in a world in which there was no change and development. If there was no change and development there might be no deaths, but equally no births.
3   There are many possible explanations for why a good God might create earthquakes in his universe. One explanation that appears harsh but is factually true would be to say that earthquakes are a problem only if you live in an earthquake zone. This would be equivalent to saying you can hardly blame the designer of a car if someone steps in front of the car while it is moving and is injured as a result. (These ideas are explored in greater depth in Chapter 9 on the problem of evil.)

Thought Point

Think about the following problem

Imagine that a mother starts a campaign against hand-guns. Her son was killed in a gangland shooting. As part of her work, she campaigns against the manufacturer and seller of the gun used to shoot her son.

continued overleaf

The mother considers a range of arguments she could use:

1   You are to blame for my son's death as you made the gun that killed him.
2   It is your fault my son died. You sold the gun that killed him.
3   Gun shops like yours should be banned. Selling guns just helps criminals to kill people.
4   Making a gun is just as bad as using it to kill someone.
5   Why make a gun if you think killing is wrong?
6   Selling guns helps people to be violent. That is wrong.

Which of these arguments are strong and which are weak? Why?

For more information about this idea and the *Free Will Defence* look at Chapter 9 on the problem of evil.

A different approach

In most cases, when the Judaeo-Christian tradition calls God 'Creator' it does not envisage God as being like a craftsman who makes guns or cars. Instead, what Christians, Jews, Muslims and many other religious believers are saying is that God is responsible for the fact that there is any universe at all. God's omnipotence is about saying that God is responsible for everything that comes into existence. How things behave within the universe is either according to the natural laws of science or, if the thing in question can think, it is a personal decision as to how it behaves. Rain falls downwards because of gravity, while on the other hand you decide what time to get up in the morning. The philosopher Brian Davies has put it like this:

> At the end of his *Tractatus Logico-Philosophicus* Ludwig Wittgenstein wrote: 'Not how the world is, is the mystical, but that it is.' For Wittgenstein, **how the world is**, is a scientific matter with scientific answers (even if we do not have all the answers yet). He insists however that even when the scientific answers are in, we are still left with the **thatness** of the world, the **fact** that it is. And it is with this fact that we surely need to grapple if we are reasonably to arrive at the notion of creation apart from the testimony of scripture. ('Creationism and All That')

Most religious believers would argue that people cause much of the evil and many of the problems in the world, whether it be murders and rapes, or climate change caused by global warming. This idea is called the *Free Will Defence* and it emphasises the fact that God is the Creator but God also created a world with human beings who have free will. How human beings use their free will is their decision. If God omnipotently intervenes and always stops people using their free will if they are doing something bad, then people do not have real free will, as they are prevented from choosing some things.

However, it is worth noting that while some scientists agree with these ideas, others strongly disagree. Those who disagree might put forward the following arguments:

1   That the world and universe exist is a fact, but saying that God is responsible for what happens in the universe is a mistake.
2   As many theologians have pointed out, science explains how the world and universe work. Classic examples are the theory of evolution and Newton's Law of Gravity.
3   In addition, science can increasingly explain why the universe is that particular way.
4   God is not responsible for what happens in the world because there is no need to believe in God to explain what happens in the world.

The scientist Richard Dawkins commented:

> The desire to see purpose everywhere is a natural one in an animal that lives surrounded by machines, works of art, tools and other designed artefacts, an animal, moreover, whose waking thoughts are dominated by its own personal goals. A car, a tin-opener, a screwdriver and a pitchfork all legitimately warrant the 'What is it for?' question. Our pagan forebears would have asked the same question about thunder, eclipses, rocks and streams. Today we pride ourselves on having shaken off such primitive animism. . . . But the old temptation comes back with a vengeance when tragedy strikes – indeed, the very word 'strikes' is an animistic echo: 'Why, oh why, did the cancer/earthquake/hurricane have to strike my child?' And the same temptation is often positively relished when the topic is the origin of all things or the fundamental laws of physics. . . . Behind the question there is always an unspoken but never justified implication that since science is unable to answer 'Why' questions, there must be some other discipline that is qualified to answer them. This implication is, of course, quite illogical. (*River Out of Eden*)

God being responsible for everything in the world obviously only creates a dilemma if you believe in God, but this is important for many people in the world. Belief in God is a very real issue.

Science can in no way explain why the universe exists. It can speculate, but there is no physical or even logical way to get outside of the universe to investigate why it is that it exists. What Dawkins and like-minded scientists object to is people believing in a Creator God as an explanation for why there is a universe.

Believing in or rejecting God as the Creator responsible for everything that happens in the universe is a faith choice for all people.

Thought Point

God's responsibility for what happens in the universe

1   The existence of evil, whether caused by humans or natural disaster or illnesses, raises questions about the world we live in.

2   If God is the Creator, God chose to create the world this way and, if so, this raises the question: is God responsible for everything that happens in the world?

   (a) **Yes:** this raises questions about God's omnipotence (why did he not make the word differently?) and his omniscience (did God knowingly choose to make a world like this?) and his goodness (should God say sorry for making a world with so much evil in it?).

   (b) **No:** this raises questions about God's nature (is God really omnipotent, omniscient?) and about whether God exists (God is not responsible for what happens in the universe as he does not exist).

3   Answers:

   (a) Many religious believers emphasise the link between free will and responsibility.

   (b) Atheists say God is not responsible as God does not exist.

SUMMARY

1   **God the Creator**

   The Creator

   Anthropomorphic imagery

   Craftsman – a potter (Genesis)
   Designer – lays the foundations of the Earth (Isaiah)

Creatio ex nihilo
Humans' place in creation

Authority over the Earth

Harmony and beauty of creation

Ruined by people's evil actions (Genesis 3)

Omni titles in the Bible

Omnipotence

God's power is limitless
God's power is present throughout and supreme above creation

Omniscience

God has limitless knowledge of creation

Omnipresence

God is present throughout all creation

God's responsibility for creation

The problem of evil challenges the omni titles applied to God

REVIEW QUESTIONS

Look back over the chapter and check that you can answer the following questions:

1   Explain, with reference to biblical imagery, what is meant by 'God the Creator'.
2   What can be learnt about the Judaeo-Christian belief in God as Creator from Genesis 1–3, Job 38, Psalm 8 and Isaiah 40? Summarise your conclusions in a table or bullet-pointed list.
3   What does it mean to describe God as a 'craftsman'? Why can this term also leave God open to criticism?
4   If God is the architect of the world, what feedback would you give the architect about the project? Write a report to give your views, supported by reasons.
5   The scientist Stephen Hawking once remarked that:

continued overleaf

It would be completely consistent with all we know to say that there was a being who is responsible for the laws of physics. (*A Brief History of Time*)

Does this comment relate to belief in God as Creator? If so, why does it relate to God being Creator? If not, why not?

Terminology

Do you know your terminology?

1   Try to explain the following ideas without looking at your books and notes:

(a) Deism as opposed to theism
(b) All the 'omni' qualities of God in the Judaeo-Christian tradition
(c) *Creatio ex nihilo*
(d) The story of Adam and Eve
(e) The seven-day creation story.

Examination Questions Practice

This is a good topic on which to complete examination questions. The OCR specification identifies particular topics that you should be able to explain and critically discuss. If you understand and can discuss the issues raised in this chapter, you should do well.

Remember: (a) assesses AO1 and (b) AO2. To help you improve your answers look at the AS Levels of Response. See: http://www.ocr.org.uk/qualifications/as-a-level-gce-religious-studies-h172-h572/

EXAM MISTAKES TO AVOID

If you are asked to describe beliefs about God being the Creator, do not spend your time describing the seven days of creation or the story of Adam and Eve in great detail. If you are asked about God being the Creator, the examiner wants you to explain the nature and meaning of this title the 'Creator' when it is applied to God.

SAMPLE AS EXAM-STYLE QUESTIONS

1 (a) **Explain how the Bible presents God as Creator.** (25 marks)

To answer this question you need to discuss what is learnt about the nature of God from the Bible, particularly the passages that concern God being the Creator, such as Genesis 1–3 and Job 38.

You need to explain what is learnt about God from these passages; you could discuss the following beliefs which are based on the Bible texts:

- God creating out of nothing (*Creatio ex nihilo*) (link to Genesis 1 and 2, Job 38 or Isaiah 40).
- God's omniscience (link to Genesis 2: 4 to 3: 1).
- God's omnipotence (link to Genesis 1–3, Job 38 or Isaiah 40).
- God as an omnipresent craftsman (link to Job 38 or Isaiah 40).
- God being the ruler of the world.
- God being the Creator involves God continuing to sustain the world in existence.

(b) **'God is responsible for everything that happens in the universe.' Discuss.** (10 marks)

This question asks you to discuss the extent to which God is responsible for what happens in the world. There are a number of approaches that you could take to answer this question. A selection of ideas are given below:

- Discuss the meaning of omnipotence and point out what this means God is responsible for. Reach a judgement about whether God is responsible for everything that happens in the world
- Consider the meaning of omniscience and examine whether God is responsible for everything that happens in the world if God:
  - knows what is happening
  - has the power to control what is happening.
- Does the presence of evil in the world mean that God is not in control, or, if God is in control, why is there evil in the world? Is God not good?

Later in the course you will study the problem of evil. Some aspects of the problem of evil are relevant to this question and you could discuss them in your answer, although this is not necessary at this stage.

2 (a) **Explain what is meant in the Bible by describing God as creator.**

(b) **'The creation stories in the Bible are fiction.' Discuss.**

3 (a) **How do the writers of the Bible explain the creation of the world?**

(b) **'God created humanity for a purpose.' Discuss.**

Thought Point

The answer

Have a look at some different translations of Genesis 1: 26 and Psalm 8: 5 and you will find that the word 'gods' not 'a god' appears. This is actually

continued overleaf

a clue pointing to the very early origins of the story because in early cultures (1,000 or more years before Jesus) God was one but there was also a heavenly court or council of lesser gods. This is thought by biblical scholars to be the explanation of the curious phrase in Genesis 1: 26 'Let us make. . .'. It is worth noting that some later Christians interpreted this curious phrase as a reference to the Christian Trinity of God the Father, Son and Holy Spirit.

FURTHER READING

As in many areas of Religious Studies, there is a huge number of books available that deal with these topics. The most important distinction is between books that are Bible commentaries – these examine how to interpret the text, usually line by line – and books that explain people's ideas about the meaning and significance of 'God being Creator'. The books suggested below cover both of these areas:

Bible commentaries

There are many commentaries available. Perhaps the easiest ones to access are the all-in-one whole Bible commentaries (e.g. Raymond E. Brown, Joseph A. Fitzmyer and Roland E. Murphy, *The New Jerome Biblical Commentary* (1989)). Public libraries usually have copies of these commentaries in their reference sections.

If you would like to read a book about biblical theology, you could have a look at works by Adrian Graffy and also John Drane.

God and science

If you are interested in questions about how belief in God relates to modern science, look at *Belief in God in an Age of Science* (2003) by John Polkinghorne. This is a challenging and interesting read with a good introduction to the wider issues about God and science which relate to this topic.

Philosophy and the omni titles

If you would like to investigate issues raised by omnipotence and omniscience, a good starting point is to look at the relevant chapters in Peter Vardy's book *The Puzzle of God* (1995) and also Brian Davies' book *An Introduction to the Philosophy of Religion* (2003). A good, thought-provoking book is Michael Clark's *Paradoxes from A to Z* (third edition, 2012).

4 The Goodness of God

Essential terminology

Decalogue
God as judge
God as lawgiver
Perfection

THE ISSUES

1   In the Bible is God morally good/perfect?
2   Does God command good things? Or are things good because God commands them?

The Euthyphro dilemma

It is well worth reading the dilemma in Plato's own words. Have a look at a modern translation of the dilemma.

WHAT YOU WILL LEARN ABOUT IN THIS CHAPTER

In this chapter you will examine what makes actions morally good. The crucial issue is often presented as a question:

> Are things good because God commands them, or
> Are things good and that is why God commands them?

Key scholars

Plato (c. 427 BCE–c. 347 BCE)

Second, you will examine the Judaeo-Christian belief of God's goodness. You will consider whether or not God is the source of moral values.

STARTER

If you say 'murder is wrong', one question to ask is: why is it wrong? Come up with as many explanations as you can of why murder is wrong.

Thought Point

Adultery

God says that adultery is wrong. In fact, in the Bible God says that any form of sexual activity apart from that between married couples is wrong.

Would you say that adultery is wrong? Explain your answer.

If you said that 'adultery is wrong', is the main reason adultery is wrong because:

1   God judges it wrong?
2   I personally just feel it is wrong?
3   It is wrong for some other reason?

WHAT MAKES AN ACTION GOOD?

In philosophy of religion there is a classical problem called the Euthyphro dilemma which comes from the writings of Plato. The key point of the dilemma is a question that Socrates raises about how goodness is defined: Is an action 'good' because:

1   God commands it, or
2   What is good, God commands?

The choice to be made is double-edged. If you choose (1) God's commands make things good, it would mean that if God commanded that 'rape is not wrong', then there would be nothing morally wrong with rape. God could even command trivial things such as all men should have beards and this would be morally right because God had commanded it. It is possible to find some examples in the Old Testament where the commands of God seem to be morally questionable, such as when God commanded Moses to kill all of the male Midianites and then:

> Now therefore, kill every male among the little ones, and kill every woman who has known a man by sleeping with him. But all the young girls who have not known a man by sleeping with him, keep alive for yourselves. (Numbers 31: 17–18)

The virgins were presumably raped, but how could the soldiers know which women were virgins? Similarly, consider the command of God that Abraham should sacrifice his son Isaac Genesis 22: 2. Some philosophers do not agree with this view as it could mean that God is a divine dictator because whatever God commands is the law, and any act, however horrific it might seem, is good if it is commanded by God.

This is also questioned by Kierkegaard who suggests that we must, like Abraham, have faith in God, even if we have no way of explaining that or if it may seem to demand what to us seem unethical actions . . . the will of God comes above ethics. However, many religious believers could not accept this and both Augustine and Aquinas believe that God cannot will evil as he is perfectly good. This leaves us with option (2), the preferred choice of Plato, that good is independent of God's will.

Option (2) suggests that God only commands what is good. The problem with this is that goodness does not originate from God. Instead goodness is some sort of independent standard and God is the enforcer of this standard. This view is not supported in the Christian tradition, which emphasises the goodness of God's commands, and the fact that goodness originates from God. Additionally, if the moral law lies outside God we have no need of God

Kierkegaard – the man

Søren Aabye Kierkegaard (1813–1855) was a Danish poet, philosopher, religious author, and social critic who is widely considered the first existentialist philosopher. He was born into a wealthy family in Copenhagen.

From 1830, Kierkegaard attended the School of Civic Virtue, Østre Borgerdyd Gymnasium in Copenhagen, where he studied Latin and history among other subjects. He then went on to study theology at the University of Copenhagen.

Kierkegaard's writings were written in Danish and were therefore initially only known in Scandinavia. However, by the turn of the twentieth century, they had been translated into major European languages including French and German. By the mid-twentieth century, his thought was exerting a substantial influence on philosophy, theology, and indeed Western culture as a whole.

The goodness of God

This God – his way is
perfect;
the promise of the LORD
proves true;
he is a shield for all who
take refuge in him.
(2 Samuel 22: 31)

Revelation

Revelation refers to an act
in which God is made
known to people either
directly (e.g. in a vision) or
indirectly (e.g. through
admiring God's creation).
See Chapter 12 on
revelation and holy
scripture for more
information.

The goodness of
creation

God saw everything that
he had made, and indeed,
it was very good. (Genesis
1: 31a)

The near sacrifice
of Isaac

You can read the whole
story in Genesis 22: 1–19.

to be moral. Indeed why should we worship a God who is bound by the same moral laws as we are?

In the Bible God is pictured as being perfectly good and his commands are the moral law. For example, the Ten Commandments express God's will and state what is good according to God. On this view, things are good because God commands them – God sets the standard of what is good and bad.

Both options given by the Euthyphro dilemma cause a problem for believers – the first makes genocide morally good and the second places morality outside of God. The only way out of this dilemma is to place the source of morality and goodness not in God's commands but somewhere entirely different. A possible solution is that offered by both Aristotle and Aquinas: that creation, life, the universe and everything in it has a purpose or telos and something is good when it fulfils this purpose or telos. An alternative solution is that God's love is a source of morality rather than his commands, but this depends on people being able to recognise love in the first place and to know how to put this into practice in different ethical situations.

THE GOODNESS OF GOD IN THE BIBLE

Two key ideas emerge about God's goodness in the Bible: first, that God is good and, second, that God's actions are good.

The Jewish Scriptures and the New Testament paint a clear picture of God being 'good'. Many passages state that God is good and perfect. God's goodness is revealed directly to people through God's activity in the world. God is the Creator, and God's creation is repeatedly stated to be good and to reveal God to the world. By saying that creation reveals God, Christians mean that something is learned about the nature of God through creation.

God's action in the world is specifically seen as good in the Bible. The creation myths in Genesis show that God's goodness is visible: in the creation of and sustaining the world.

Furthermore, God's goodness is seen through his actions for the benefit of people, such as healing miracles or support for God's followers in battle at Jericho. The picture that emerges is of God acting within the world, and God's activity is plainly seen to be good.

The goodness of God's actions is not a matter of human judgement, and this is nowhere more obvious than in the story of Abraham's obedience to sacrifice Isaac at the command of God. The story concerns duty and faithfulness to God, but the fact that God is clearly stated to challenge Abraham to do something which most people believe to be immoral (sacrificing a child) raises important questions about the nature of God's goodness.

The story of the near sacrifice of Isaac presents an image of God as the lord and master of all, whose will is beyond human comprehension. This story, probably more clearly than any other in the Bible, indicates that God's commands are what make an action good. The duty of people is to respond to and obey those commands – in this story Abraham's faith in God is put to the test and what matters is Abraham's response to God's commands. One important aspect of the story is that faith in God involves surrendering your will and wishes to God.

The story of the near sacrifice of Isaac ends with God intervening to prevent the sacrifice, but the fact remains that, for many Christians today, the story presents a strange and uncomfortable image of God.

Thought Point

What would you sacrifice?

Which of the following things would you be prepared to sacrifice to help or save someone:

1   If the person was your friend or partner?
2   If the person was your enemy?

    (a) Your clothes;
    (b) Your food;
    (c) Your car;
    (d) Your house;
    (e) Your savings;
    (f)   Your life.

The Ten Commandments

God's revelation of the Ten Commandments in Exodus 20 is a good example of God setting the standards of what is morally right and wrong. The status of the Commandments as revelations from God is shown by the fact that God is revealed through what is called a Theophany – a manifestation or appearance of God or a god to human beings.

God commands what is good, and in some parts of the Bible it states that God wrote the Commandments on tablets of stone, rather than Moses hearing them and writing them down (Genesis 31:18; 32:19; 34:1; 27–8). The giving of the Decalogue illustrates the fact that God's goodness is also a matter of moral action – meaning that God intervenes in the world in good ways.

> **The Ten Commandments**
>
> One text suitable for studying for this topic is Exodus 20. When reading the set text it is worth starting at Exodus 19: 16 which sets the scene for the revelation of the Ten Commandments.

Decalogue

Another term for the Ten Commandments revealed to Moses on Mount Sinai.

God as lawgiver

An image of God commonly used in the Bible, for example when God reveals the Ten Commandments to the Israelites on Mount Sinai.

God as judge

A common image of God throughout the Jewish Scriptures and the New Testament. In the parable of the Last Judgement (Matthew 25: 31–46), God is pictured as a king judging people, separating the good from the bad. The good go to heaven, the bad to hell.

> **On keeping the Ten Commandments**
>
> Now this is the commandment – the statutes and the ordinances – that the LORD your God charged me to teach you to observe in the land that you are about to cross into and occupy, so that you and your children and your children's children may fear the LORD your God all the days of your life, and keep all his decrees and his commandments that I am commanding you, so that your days may be long. (Deuteronomy 6: 1–2)

continued opposite

Within the Commandments God is described as 'impassioned' (this is often translated in bibles as 'jealous', but what it actually means is that God is passionately committed to Israel). The Ten Commandments are a gift to the people of Israel to enable them to lead a good life.

Within the Jewish Scriptures God is also passionate about punishing sinners who do not follow his laws – consistency in action is part of God's goodness. In the later parts of the scriptures the prophets are called by God to announce his message to the people and to condemn injustice. For example, the prophet Amos condemns market traders for conning people in the market.

Child sacrifice

Child sacrifices did occur in the ancient world in parts of the Middle East around the time of Abraham. What is significant about the story of Abraham is that God does not let Abraham carry out the sacrifice. Ancient Israel was unusual in many ways for its time – one such way is the fact that child sacrifices were banned.

The Ten Commandments are part of God's covenant with Israel. By covenant, the Jewish people mean the relationship between them and God. The relationship is a two-way one – God sets out moral standards of behaviour and duties for the Israelites, but the Israelites are also God's chosen people whom God protects. In the ancient world a covenant is a sacred agreement between two groups which cannot be broken. Both parties (groups) of the agreement have duties and responsibilities towards each other. God's goodness in the Bible is revealed through his covenant with the people of Israel and the fact that God is seen to keep the covenant even when the people break it.

However, the imagery used to describe God's activity in the Bible is clearly anthropomorphic and even within the Bible there is an awareness that God is not really like a fighter, a warrior, a king or a mother hen (these and many other images are used in the Bible). What the images attempt to communicate is the awareness by religious people of the goodness of God and God's activity within the world. God is seen to intervene in the world.

In the New Testament, the Gospels and Epistles show the Christian belief in the goodness of God, which is most obviously revealed in Jesus Christ. For Christians, Jesus is God made flesh (incarnate), and Jesus' life, death and resurrection reveal God's love for people. Jesus is crucified as an innocent sacrifice for the sins of human beings. A sacrifice in the ancient world was something innocent that was offered to God to take away sin. Jesus' death is an example of God's goodness in the Christian tradition, as God, through Jesus, saves people from their sin and wrongdoing.

Thought Point

Think again

Look back at the exercise *What would you sacrifice?* (p. 69). How would Christians relate Jesus' death to this exercise?

Jesus' mission preached repentance and the forgiveness of sins (Mark 1: 12–14) – it called people to turn away from sin and return to God. Healing people was a sign of the forgiveness of sins by God, as illness in the ancient world was often connected with wrongdoing. God's goodness is revealed through the fact that God offers forgiveness to people.

PLATO'S FORM OF THE GOOD AND GOD IN THE BIBLE

Both Plato's Form of the Good and God are sources of goodness. First, God is clearly pictured as being 'good' and the source of goodness and the Form of the Good self-evidently is 'good'.

Second, Plato states that the Forms are not material, physical things and, in similar manner, God is transcendent – utterly separate from the world. While God is described in the Bible as acting in human-like ways, there is also an awareness that God is different from human beings and thus God's goodness is not always understandable in human ways.

However, there is a difference between God and the Form of the Good. The Form of the Good is the source of the other Forms; the Form of the Good does not act in the physical world. Whereas God is not just a source of goodness who decides what is right and wrong, God also acts in morally good ways in the world. Examples of such activity are the creation and miracles.

WHAT DOES 'GOD IS "GOOD"' MEAN?

The biblical answer is that by saying God is good we are making a statement about God's nature and actions – that they are good. Hence, God is described as perfect and good in the Bible, and God's actions (e.g. creation) are good.

However, within Christian tradition there is a second way in which the goodness of God is explained. Augustine pointed out that evil could be defined as not living up to how you should be. In other words, evil was

> **On exploitation of the poor**
>
> Hear this, you that trample on the needy,
>   and bring to ruin the poor of the land,
>   . . . and practice deceit with false balances,
>   . . . The LORD has sworn by the pride of Jacob:
>   Surely I will never forget any of their deeds.
> (Amos 8: 4, 5b, 7)
>
> Do not rob the poor because they are poor,
>   or crush the afflicted at the gate;
> for the LORD pleads their cause
>   and despoils of life those who despoil them.
> (Proverbs 22: 22–3)

Anthropomorphism

Anthropomorphism refers to using human imagery to describe God. For example, if you say 'God is a King', you mean God is kingly in some sense, not that God is a human king.

Biblical authors on: God is not human

God is not a human being, that he should lie, or a mortal, that he should change his mind. (Numbers 23: 19a)

. . . for I am God and no mortal. (Hosea 11: 9b)

The goodness and justice of God's actions

In this way God makes his justice known; first, for the past, when sins went unpunished because he held his hand, then, for the present age, by showing positively that he is just, and that he justifies everyone who believes in Jesus. (Romans 3: 25–6)

The sign in the Temple

Read the story of the cleansing of the Temple and the cursing of the fig tree in the New Testament, Mark chapter 11. Then investigate the priests of Jesus' time.

described as a lack of something. When it came to moral evil, Augustine suggested that an action is evil if it is lacking in goodness. According to Augustine's view, if you say that a human being is evil, or their actions are evil, you are saying that the way they behave does not match expectations of how a human being should behave (e.g. if you torture people you are not living up to the standards expected of human beings).

Perfection means that something cannot be any better than it is – it lacks nothing. 'God is perfectly good' is a statement that God is the standard of what is good and the standard cannot be different. Hence, option (2) in the Euthyphro dilemma is incorrect because it suggests that God commands something because it is good.

RIGHTEOUS INDIGNATION

Another aspect of God's goodness within the Old and New Testament is righteous indignation. Righteous indignation refers to justified anger about an action or event that is morally wrong.

The Old Testament refers on many occasions to God's righteous indignation or anger with people who stray from God's law. This can be seen in stories ranging from the destruction of Sodom and Gomorrah to the death of Beersheba's first child by King David as a punishment for David planning the death of Beersheba's husband Uriah the Hittite. In the Old Testament the righteous indignation of God culminates in the destruction of Jerusalem in c. 586 BCE and the deportation of many people into exile in Babylon. The theme which runs through the Old Testament passages is that God's justice is offended by wrongdoing and the indignation that follows is righteous or justified. God is innocent of blame for this anger; instead the indignation is just punishment that is provoked and deserved. The righteous indignation of God can be against individuals, such as Onan (Genesis 38) or the whole people of Israel (e.g. the Prophet Amos), although aimed at its leaders.

In the New Testament the righteous indignation of God is not a common motif. However, one incident in Jesus' ministry that stands out is the cursing of the fig tree for having no fruit. Jesus curses the tree as he enters Jerusalem. In Jerusalem Jesus cleanses the Temple and then leaves Jerusalem again for the night. His disciples notice that the fig tree has died (Mark 11: 12–14). The fig tree story appears to represent the judgement of God. The story is described by commentators such as Fr Henry Wansbrough OSB, as a 'Markan sandwich'. The fig tree is cursed and Jesus enters the Temple and smashes it up, a sign representing the destruction of the old covenant and of the rule of the priests and teachers of the law. Jesus was not simply cleansing the Temple because the money changers in the Temple were doing precisely what the Old Testament Mosaic law permitted. Instead Jesus' actions symbolise the overthrow of the Temple and its leaders. The fig tree dying mirrors the symbolic sign about the fate of the Temple in Jesus' teaching.

In the letter to the Ephesians Paul advises the Ephesians that as Christians they are to turn their back on their old lives and warns people not to 'sin in their anger' (Ephesians 4: 26). One possible interpretation of this is that anger and sin do not always go together.

The crucial point in all these incidents of righteous indignation is that God's anger is justified and that it is not a moral failing of God to be angry. Rather, God's justice demands that God *should* be angry at the wrongdoing that has occurred.

WHAT PROBLEMS ARE RAISED BY GOD'S GOODNESS?

1　Over the centuries many Christians and non-Christians have questioned whether it is possible to believe in a good God given the amount of evil and suffering in the world. This issue is explored in Chapter 11.
2　Some people would question whether God does intervene in the world because they have not witnessed or experienced events such as miracles or visions. This issue is explored in greater depth in Chapter 5.
3　Many people in the modern world have questioned whether God is good by examining some of the incidents in the Bible, such as the destruction of the city of Ai (Joshua 8) and the sacrifice of Isaac (Genesis 22: 1–19).
4　Some philosophers have suggested that we cannot talk directly about what it means for God to be good. The reason for saying this is that God is not a physical being like human beings and so to describe God's actions as good is not the same as saying, for example, that an action of the prime minister is good, where you can assess the prime minister's action against some standard of behaviour, such as the Ten Commandments.
5　God's acting for the good in the world is a problem for philosophers of religion who argue that God is unchangeable. In Western Christianity from the fourth century onwards, theologians have argued that God is unchanging and perfectly good. This has led to problems reconciling the image of God acting in the world in response to people's needs with the belief that God is eternal and unchanging. This issue is explored in greater depth in Chapters 5 and 15.

Righteous indignation in the New Testament

Read each of the following passages and identify what happened and the source of God's righteous indignation.

1　Genesis 38: 1–11
2　2 Samuel 6: 1–7
3　Deuteronomy 1: 34–37
4　Exodus 3: 14, 24
5　Numbers 12: 1–9
6　1 Samuel 15
7　Joshua 7.

The characteristics of God

Ancient and modern theologians have traditionally believed that God is: good, perfect, all-powerful, all-knowing and eternal.

The goodness of God is considered in this chapter and many of the other characteristics of God are considered in other chapters of this book.

A traditional view of God's goodness

God is infinitely good and all his works are good. (*The Catechism of the Catholic Church* §385)

Thought Point

Two views on the sacrifice of Isaac story

This story is a masterpiece, presenting God as the Lord whose demands are absolute, whose will is inscrutable, and whose final word is grace. . . . Such a Western judgement [as Kant's below] reduces the climactic encounter between God and Abraham to an extrinsic moral debate. (R.J. Clifford, 'Genesis')

There are certain cases in which man can be convinced that it cannot be God whose voice he thinks he hears; when the voice commands him to do what is opposed to moral law, though the phenomenon seems to him ever so majestic and surpassing the whole of nature, he must count it a deception. (C. Westermann citing Kant in his book *Genesis 12–36*)

1 What do you think the two authors are saying?
2 Which author do you most agree with?

Perfection

A philosophical term used to indicate the goodness of God. To be perfect means that you lack nothing and could not be better in any way. God is said to be perfect, as God is totally good and could not be more 'good'.

Evil as a lack of goodness

More information about this topic is given in Chapter 9, 'The Problem of Evil'.

SUMMARY

1 God's goodness

What makes an action good?

God commands it
God commands what is good?

In the Bible

God is good
God's actions are good

The goodness of Creation

God's goodness is visible in the creation and sustaining of the world
God acts for the benefit of people (e.g. healing miracles or support for God's followers in battle)
The goodness of God's actions is not a matter of human judgement (e.g. the sacrifice of Isaac story)

The Ten Commandments

God's commands are what makes an action good
The duty of people is to respond to and obey those commandments
The Ten Commandments set the standards of what is morally right and
*   wrong*
Enable people to lead a good life
Part of God's covenant with Israel

Imagery of God

Anthropomorphic (e.g. a fighter, a warrior or a king)

Jesus and goodness

Christian belief in the goodness of God, most clearly revealed in Jesus
For Christians, Jesus is God made flesh (incarnate)
Jesus' life, death and resurrection reveal God's love for people
Jesus is crucified as an innocent sacrifice for the sins of human beings
Jesus' mission preached repentance and God's forgiveness of sins

God's goodness and Plato

Similarities
Plato's Form of the Good and God are sources of goodness
Plato states that the Forms are not material, physical things and God is
    transcendent

Differences
The Form of the Good does not act in the physical world
God also acts in morally good ways in the world (e.g. creation)

Criticisms of God's goodness

The amount of evil and suffering in the world
People may doubt that God acts in the world if they have not witnessed or
*   experienced an event such as a miracle*
Many people have questioned whether God is good by examining Bible
*   stories (e.g. the destruction of the city of Ai)*

REVIEW QUESTIONS

Look back over the chapter and check that you can answer the following questions:

1   Explain a biblical view of God's goodness.
2   Is the goodness of God in any way similar to Plato's Form of the Good?
3   Why might people reject belief in a good God?
4   How would you solve the Euthyphro dilemma?

Terminology

Do you know your terminology?

1   Try to explain the following ideas without looking at your books and notes:

    (a) Decalogue
    (b) God's goodness
    (c) Anthropomorphism.

Examination Questions Practice

You will be tested on the goodness of God as revealed in the Bible. Your answers will need to be linked to some biblical examples.

EXAM MISTAKES TO AVOID

As always with questions involving the Bible, do not just tell stories. Make sure that you explain the relevance of biblical examples to the question you are answering.

Remember: (a) assesses AO1 and (b) AO2. To help you improve your answers look at the AS Levels of Response. See: http://www.ocr.org.uk/qualifications/as-a-level-gce-religious-studies-h172-h572/

SAMPLE AS EXAM-STYLE QUESTIONS

1   (a) **Explain what is meant in the Bible by the phrase 'God is good'.** (25 marks)

Focus your answer on the ways in which God's goodness is revealed in the Bible, such as:

- The Ten Commandments, creation and miracles.
- God's goodness demands a response (e.g. law-breaking is punished, not only in earthly life but also through eternal punishment).
- Good behaviour is rewarded (e.g. in the Jewish Scriptures Abraham is promised land and descendants).
- God commands what is good because God is good.
- The goodness of God may not be understood by human beings (e.g. the sacrifice of Isaac).

(b) **'It is difficult to believe in a God who is perfectly good.' Discuss.** (10 marks)

To answer this question well you need to consider whether the picture of God as good presented in the Bible matches up with reality:

- Some of the qualities with which God is associated within the Jewish Scriptures do not necessarily match people's ideas about goodness. For instance, God is described as vengeful.
- Discuss why the existence of evil in the world could be a reason to doubt the goodness of God and creation.
- Explain why some biblical stories challenge people's ideas of goodness (e.g. the sacrifice of Isaac and the destruction of Ai).

2   (a) **Explain the Biblical idea of the 'goodness of God'.**

(b) **'A good God would not punish people.' Discuss.**

3   (a) **Explain how the Bible shows the goodness of God.**

(b) **'A good God would not make so many rules.' Discuss.**

FURTHER READING

If you would like to read more about God's goodness, a helpful starting point is Brian Davies' *An Introduction to the Philosophy of Religion* (2003). It is very readable and widely available.

Also try *Goodness, God, and Evil* by David E. Alexander (2014).

SUMMARY PARTS I AND II: THE GODS OF FAITH AND PHILOSOPHY COMPARED

This table is a brief summary of some of the points raised in Parts I and II. The table is designed to highlight contrasts between different views. It presents a generalised overview of the issues, but you should make sure you also know the different ideas, theories and beliefs in detail.

	FAITH	PHILOSOPHY
GOD	1 The view of many believers 2 Derives from tradition and Holy Books like the Bible	1 Understanding of God developed in philosophical argument 2 Emphasis on the logical and rational explanation of belief in God
GOD'S EXISTENCE	1 Known through faith, revelation and religious experience 2 Existence of God is beyond doubt	1 Demonstrated through rational argument (natural theology) 2 The cosmological, teleological arguments
CREATOR	1 Genesis (creation narratives), Psalms, Job and Isaiah 2 Immanent	1 God is the Final Cause (Aristotle), or the prime mover (Aquinas) 2 God's relationship to the world is non-interventionary
GOODNESS OF GOD	1 Revealed through God's actions, such as miracles, God's gifts to the world, such as the Ten Commandments, and people's experiences of God (e.g. Paul's) 2 God's actions are described as those of a person acting morally	1 God is the ultimate source of Good 2 God is perfect and immutable 3 God is incapable of lacking goodness 4 Links between Plato's Form of the Good and Christian ideas about God's goodness
LANGUAGE APPLIED TO GOD	1 Described using anthropomorphic and anthropopathic language 2 God is love, a warrior, the lord, king 3 God is immanent and personal	1 God is impersonal and transcendent 2 Language used to described God is not anthropomorphic or anthropopathic

THE EXISTENCE OF GOD

PART III

THE ISSUE

Does God exist? Discuss what other people think and why. Do their friends or families share this view?

This question has puzzled human beings for centuries, and it puzzles most people at some time in their lives.

The vast majority of people who have ever lived, not to mention the vast majority of people living today, believe in God. They will disagree about what this means, but they believe.

However, saying you believe in something is not the same as actually demonstrating your belief is correct. Suppose you were ill and needed an operation to save your life: you can say that you will not have the operation as you *believe the Martians will save you*. Doctors who do not share your belief in Martians would probably not be impressed. They would want evidence that Martians exist and that Martians save people in your situation.

The chapters on the cosmological, teleological, ontological and moral arguments introduce traditional ways in which religious people have tried to demonstrate that their belief in God is true. The chapter on the problem of evil explores some ways in which arguments for belief in God have been challenged or undermined.

5 The Ontological Argument

THE ISSUES

1 Is it true that once you have some idea of what sort of a being God is, you can think that it is impossible for God not to exist? Or, to put it another way: God has to exist, no doubt about it.
2 Is it part of the nature of God that God has to exist in reality, not just in people's minds?

WHAT YOU WILL LEARN ABOUT IN THIS CHAPTER

1 You will examine whether religious people are correct to say 'God has to exist in reality, there is no doubt about it.'
2 You will understand the ontological argument for God's existence.
3 You will have analysed some of the strengths and weaknesses of the ontological argument.

THE OCR CHECKLIST

The Ontological argument from Anselm and Descartes; challenges from Gaunilo and Kant.

Candidates should be able to demonstrate knowledge and understanding of:

- the Ontological argument from Anselm and Descartes;
- challenges to it from Gaunilo and Kant;

continued opposite

- Anselm's understanding of God – his understanding of the differences between contingent and necessary existence;
- Descartes' understanding of existence as a perfection which God cannot lack;
- Gaunilo's analogy of the island in *On Behalf of the Fool*.

Candidates should be able to discuss critically these views and their strengths and weaknesses.

From OCR A Level Religious Studies specification H172.

STARTER

Look at the following statements. How would you prove the truth of each of these statements?

1 Father Christmas has a red coat.
2 Unicorns are white.
3 Adolf Hitler's actions were evil.
4 God exists.
5 Murder is wrong.
6 Two plus two equals four.
7 The prime minister is mortal.

INTRODUCTION

This chapter examines an argument for God's existence, the ontological argument, which claims to demonstrate that the statement 'God exists' is analytically true – meaning that it would be simply nonsense or incoherent to doubt God's existence. Another way of putting this is that the ontological argument claims that once you have understood the meaning of the word 'God' you must recognise that God exists.

Anselm of Canterbury (1033–1109)

Anselm of Canterbury, Scholastic philosopher and saint

Anselm was born in Aosta (Piedmont), Italy. As a young man he became a monk at the famous monastery of Bec, in Normandy, France. Eventually he became abbot of the monastery and in 1093 he was chosen as Archbishop of Canterbury. During his life he wrote a large number of works examining both the nature of God and the relationship between the Church and the State in medieval Europe. Anselm's writings were influenced by the philosophy of Plato and he was an important early figure in the Scholastic movement.

Thought Point

Analytic and synthetic statements

Anselm wanted to show that the statement 'God exists' is logically true. Philosophers call this type of statement an analytic statement. What does that mean?

Consider the following statements:

1   A triangle has three internal angles which add up to 180 degrees.
2   Yetis walk the Himalayas.
3   Unicorns are white and have a horn on their head.

Which of these statements are:

A   True?
B   Need to be proven true with evidence?

Analytic statements

An analytic statement is a statement which it is impossible to think false. For example, a triangle having three internal angles adding up to 180 degrees is an analytic statement, because it is impossible to think of a triangle in any other way. Richard Swinburne gives the following example:

> An analytic or logically necessary proposition is one which it would be incoherent to suppose to be false; 'all squares have four sides' and 'red is a colour' are logically necessary, because it would be incoherent, make no sense to suppose that red could be anything except a colour, or that a square could have only three sides. (*The Existence of God*)

For example, once you have understood what is meant by 'a square' you understand that by a square you mean something with four sides and four internal right angles which add up to 360 degrees.

continued opposite

Synthetic statements

A synthetic statement is a statement in which the statement's truth or falsity depends on evidence which has to be collected. An example of a synthetic statement is statement (2) above. The truth or falsity of this statement depends on evidence one collects.

A **Deductive Argument** is a form of argument where the conclusion logically follows from the given premises. If the premises are true and strongly support the conclusion, then the conclusion of the argument must also be logically true. It essentially has three parts: (1) the major premise, (2) the minor premise, and (3) the conclusion. E.g.

All men are mortal.

Socrates is a man.

Therefore, Socrates is a mortal.

ANSELM'S ONTOLOGICAL ARGUMENT

Anselm's principle was 'faith seeking understanding' which for him meant 'an active love of God seeking a deeper knowledge of God'. Anselm's book *Proslogion* (Deane (trans.), *St Anselm: Basic Writings*) suggests one way in which the existence of God could be 'demonstrated' to people. Anselm begins by reflecting on a psalm from the Bible which says that 'Fools say in their hearts, "There is no God"' (Psalm 14: 1).

Anselm's reflections on this passage have become known as the ontological argument for God's existence. The name for Anselm's argument is derived from two Greek words – *ontos* (being) and *logos* (reason or word). As the name suggests, the ontological argument is concerned with the being or nature of God.

ANSELM'S FIRST ONTOLOGICAL ARGUMENT

Anselm puts forward two closely related ontological arguments. His first argument may be summarised as follows:

1   God is the greatest possible being which can be conceived (thought) of.
2   God may exist either in the mind alone (*in intellectu*) or in reality (*in re*) as well.
3   Something that exists in reality and in the mind is greater than something that exists as an idea in the mind alone.
4   Therefore, God must necessarily exist in reality and in the mind.

Anselm's argument is a reply to the fool who says there is no God and this gives Anselm his starting point. For the fool to say 'there is no God' the fool has to have an idea in her or his mind of what God is. Anselm suggests that the definition in mind is that God is the 'greatest possible being'. Hence Anselm says that God is the greatest possible being that can be 'conceived' – meaning 'thought of'.

Analytic

The concept of the subject is contained in the predicate, where the predicate is the part of the sentence which follows after the subject, e.g. triangles have three sides.

Synthetic

Refers to a proposition or statement the truth or falsity of which has to be verified through experience. Predicates of synthetic propositions are not intrinsic to the subject of the proposition (e.g. the car is green – this may or may not be true).

Predicate

A quality or property of a subject expressed in a sentence.

Anselm then points out that it is greater to exist in reality than in the mind alone. For example, people have an idea of what a unicorn is and can give a description of it. However, while we can happily talk about the idea of a unicorn and its nature or qualities (e.g. a white, horse-like creature with a horn) it does not make it exist. Unicorns may be brought to life using computer animations in films or in books such as the *Harry Potter* series, but they do not exist in reality. What matters for Anselm is that what exists in reality as well as in the mind is greater than something that is only an idea in the mind.

It is worth noting that, up until this point, Anselm's argument depends on the assumption that existence in reality and in the mind is greater than existence in the mind alone. In other words, an idea that exists in reality and in the mind has some extra quality that an idea in the mind alone lacks. What is that quality? Anselm's answer is of course: existence.

Thought Point

Watch the film the *Matrix* Part 1 (1999) and ask yourself whether it supports Anselm's claim that existence in reality is better than existence in the mind alone.

Existence is a predicate

The word 'predicate' is used in philosophy to indicate an intrinsic property or quality of something. For example, a predicate of a particular species of rose might be its form or its fragrance. In other words, predicates tell us something about the nature of a thing.

Anselm claims that it is part of God's nature that God exists. In philosophical terms: *a predicate of God is God's existence.*

Philosophers would say that the predicates of something are included in the subject you are talking about. The term 'widow' refers to a woman whose husband has died. The predicate of being a widow is that your husband has died. This is part of the nature of being a widow. Hence, you do not need to say: *Mrs Smith is a widow whose husband has died.*

Anselm's claim is that existence is a predicate of God (i.e. a property or quality of God's nature). Therefore, God, being the greatest possible being, has to exist, since an idea in the mind is not as great as an idea that exists in reality. The idea that exists in reality has the extra property of actual 'existence'. To be the greatest possible being, God must, necessarily, have his property of existence.

Rosa Gallica or the Gallic Rose

The conclusion that Anselm reaches is that because God is the greatest being that can be thought of, part of being a 'being' or 'thing' of any sort is that you exist. So God must exist. For Anselm, God's existence is thus analytic.

ANSELM'S SECOND VERSION OF THE ARGUMENT (*PROSLOGION* 3, 1078)

Anselm's second version of the ontological argument adds a further important point: that it is impossible for this being, God, not to exist. In other words, 'this being' has to exist. Furthermore, if you say 'God does not exist', you are, according to Anselm, contradicting yourself.

1   God is that being nothing greater than which can be thought of.
2   Something which cannot be thought not to exist is greater than anything which can be thought not to exist.
3   Therefore, it is impossible to think that this being cannot exist.
4   And this being is what we call 'God'.

Anselm thinks this because he believes that it is part of God's nature to exist. As Peter Van Inwagen states:

> The interesting thing about this [Anselm's] argument was that it claimed to show that the non-existence of God was impossible, owing to the fact that any assertion of non-existence of God must be self contradictory. (*Metaphysics*)

> **Anselm's second ontological argument**
>
> God cannot be conceived not to exist. – God is that, than which nothing greater can be conceived. – that which can be conceived not to exist is not God . . . and this being thou art, O Lord, Our God. (Deane (trans.), *St Anselm: Basic Writings*)

Necessary

The word used in philosophy to say that something has to be that way and cannot be any different (e.g. if a philosopher was discussing necessary existence he or she would be talking about something which has to exist and could not fail to exist).

Gaunilo's own words

On gossip!

The being is said to be in my understanding already, only because I understand what is said. . . . For, suppose that I should hear something said of a man absolutely unknown to me, of whose existence I was unaware. Through that special knowledge by which I know what man is, or what men are, I could conceive of him also, according to the reality itself. . . . And yet it would be possible if the person who told me of him deceived me, that the man himself, of whom I conceived, did not exist. (Deane (trans.), *St Anselm: Basic Writings*)

The island analogy

For example: it is said that somewhere in the ocean is an island . . . [and] that

continued opposite

Contingence and necessity

Anselm's second argument concludes that God has to exist and cannot fail to exist. In philosophical terms this is called necessary existence. Anything which has to exist and cannot fail to exist is said by philosophers to exist by *necessity*.

Most things that exist depend on something else for their existence. For example, your house only exists in reality because someone built it. You cannot say your house had to exist, because it was up to the builder to decide whether to build it. This type of existence is called 'contingent existence'.

'*Contingent existence*' refers to something which depends on referring to something else to fully explain why it exists.

Anselm argues that God must necessarily exist because if God existed only contingently, God would depend on something else for existence, and therefore would not be as great as a being that had to exist and could not fail to exist.

Thought Point

Why are human beings said to be 'contingent' by philosophers?

This being is what Christians mean by God

Anselm's final claim is that the greatest possible being is what Christians mean by God. This passage has led some commentators to suggest that Anselm was not so much proving God's existence as reflecting on the fact that God existed necessarily. This would fit in with Anselm's claim that you contradict yourself if you deny God's existence.

GAUNILO'S RESPONSE TO ANSELM'S ARGUMENT

Many criticisms have been made of Anselm's argument, but the most famous one is that put forward by a Benedictine monk called Gaunilo. His argument was entitled *On Behalf of the Fool* and it is a defence of the fool against Anselm's ideas.

GAUNILO'S ARGUMENT

Gaunilo argues that Anselm's conclusion, that God cannot fail to exist, is 'unintelligible' – it cannot show that God necessarily exists. Gaunilo suggests that the fool mentioned in Psalm 14 might reply to Anselm in the following way.

1 Gossip!

First, the fool could have in mind all sorts of things that do not exist in reality. Gaunilo gives the example of someone hearing about a person from gossip. However, he says that gossip is unreliable, and the person and event in question were made up to trick you.

2 Defining things into existence

Furthermore, Gaunilo argues that you cannot demonstrate the existence of something by just having an idea about it; you cannot define the idea into existence. Philosophers of the Middle Ages would say you cannot prove from what is said (*de dicto*) what exists in reality (*de re*).

3 Gaunilo's island

The most famous argument put forward by Gaunilo is that of a perfect island. He suggests that anyone can think of a most perfect paradise island: *beautiful palm trees swaying in the breeze, waves breaking on golden beaches*. Gaunilo argues that while the most perfect island can be conceived of, this does not mean that it exists.

Gaunilo's island analogy implies that it is absurd to say that just because you have an idea of something it must exist. Following Gaunilo's argument you can also have, for example, a clear idea of what a perfect aeroplane is; it does not mean that the aeroplane exists. This leads Gaunilo to claim either that the argument about the perfect island is a joke or that the man making the argument is a fool, or that the person believing the argument is a fool.

In the same way, Gaunilo concludes that Anselm cannot demonstrate or prove that the idea of God as the greatest possible being means that God exists in reality.

> this island has an inestimable wealth of all manner of riches and delicacies that is told of the island of the Blest . . . it is more excellent than all other countries. . . . Now if someone should tell me that there is such an island, I should easily understand his words, in which there is no difficulty. But suppose that he went on to say, as if by a logical inference: 'You can no longer doubt that this island which is more excellent than all lands exists somewhere, since you have no doubt it is in your understanding. And since it is more excellent not to be in the understanding alone, but to exist both in understanding and in reality, for this reason it must exist.' (Deane (trans.), *St Anselm: Basic Writings*)

> If a man should try to prove to me by such reasoning that this island truly exists, and that its existence should no longer be doubted, either I should believe that he was jesting, or I know not which I ought to regard as the greater fool: myself . . . or him, if he should suppose that he has established with any certainty the existence of the island. (Deane (trans.), *St Anselm: Basic Writings*)

Thought Point

A newspaper story reports that 'Elvis was seen in London yesterday'. How might Anselm have used his arguments in response to this?

Anselm's reply to Gaunilo

Anselm responded to Gaunilo using the claim that God's existence is necessary:

1   Anselm not only said that God is the greatest possible being but that God's existence is necessary. Gaunilo's argument is different, because the island, while being the greatest possible island, does not have to exist. In other words its existence is contingent.

2   In his *Liber Apologeticus Contra Gaunilonem* chapter 3 Anselm argues against Gaunilo that if you conceive of the greatest possible being you *conceive of a being which cannot be even conceived not to exist*. Guanilo's island is not a thing which can be conceived not to exist, so Anslem rejects Gaunilo's argument that the island's existence can be proved from the idea of it alone.

3   The philosopher Alvin Plantinga has suggested that Anselm could also reply to Gaunilo by suggesting that however great an island is, there could always be one better, as there is no 'intrinsic maximum' or limit to the qualities of wealth, treasures and beautiful scenery that Gaunilo's island can have.

Incoherent

A philosophical argument which fails because it is illogical.

> No matter how great an island is, no matter how many Nubian maidens and dancing girls adorn it, there could always be a greater one with twice as many for example. The qualities that make for greatness of an island . . . most of these qualities have no intrinsic maximum. . . . So the idea of a greatest possible island is an inconsistent or incoherent idea; it's not possible that there be such a thing. (Plantinga, *God, Freedom and Evil*)

On the other hand, God, according to Plantinga, is maximally great in Anselm's thought – nothing greater is possible. Therefore, the greatest possible being and the greatest possible island are not comparable.

Why Thomas Aquinas rejected Anselm's argument

Aquinas rejects claims that the existence of God is self-evident to human beings. For Aquinas, human beings are not in a position to understand God's nature; hence they cannot know that 'God exists' is an analytic statement.

> 'God exists,' of itself is self-evident, for the predicate is the same as the subject, because God is His own existence as will be hereafter shown . . . Now because we do not know the essence of God, the proposition is not self-evident to us; but needs to be demonstrated by things that are more known to us (*Summa Theologiae* 1a q2 a1)

For this reason Aquinas' cosmological or design arguments are synthetic arguments that look for evidence to prove God's existence.

SOME FINAL THOUGHTS ABOUT ANSELM'S ARGUMENT

Anselm's argument is not proof of God's existence like the Cosmological argument, because Anselm does not think that God's existence is a matter of debate. Instead Anselm is 'demonstrating' what is true, like a scientist repeating an experiment to prove to other people that his ideas are true.

DESCARTES' ONTOLOGICAL ARGUMENT

In Meditations 3 and 5 of his *Meditations on Philosophy* Descartes wrote about the existence of God. Meditation 5 particularly concerns us, as it presents a version of the ontological argument.

The background to Descartes' ontological argument

Prior to actually presenting the ontological argument for God's existence, Descartes, in his earlier meditations, reached the following conclusions. You should be aware of these as a background to his ontological argument:

1   In the third meditation Descartes claimed that God has placed in every person the idea of God. Descartes likened this idea to a trademark or stamp that identifies an object as belonging to a 'craftsman'. A modern equivalent might be a company logo.

Boethius and Anselm

Some philosophers have suggested that the development of Anselm's ontological argument had been influenced by the classical philosopher Boethius' book *The Consolation of Philosophy*.

In particular, Boethius suggested that:

> The universally accepted notion of men proves that God, the fountainhead of all things, is good. For nothing can be thought of better than God, and surely He, than whom there is nothing better, must without doubt be good. Now reason shows us that God is so good, that we are convinced that in Him lies also the perfect good. For if it is not so, He cannot be the fountain-head; for there must then be something more excellent, possessing that perfect good, which appears to be of older origin than God: for it has been proved that all perfections are of earlier origin than the imperfect specimens of the same: wherefore, unless we are to prolong the series to infinity, we must allow that the highest Deity must be full of the highest, the

continued overleaf

perfect good. (Boethius [1902]) *The Consolation of Philosophy*)

Boethius suggests that God is perfect and there is nothing better than God, which is similar to Anselm's ontological argument. However, Boethius' argument is not quite the same as Anselm's: Anselm's ontological argument focuses on the point that God is the greatest conceivable being. The extract from Boethius suggests that God is the most perfectly good being that exists, which is not quite the same as Anselm's argument that God is the greatest conceivable being (there is more about Boethius in Chapter 16 on the nature of God).

2   Some things cannot be doubted, such as the truths of mathematics. Descartes argues that God's existence is a truth somewhat similar to those of mathematics; it cannot be doubted once it has been clearly demonstrated.

3   Demonstrating God's existence is not about proving the idea of God true or that it is more than an intuition; it is about showing there is no reason to ever doubt that God exists.

What Descartes suggests in his ontological argument is that the existence of God cannot be doubted just as the truths of mathematics cannot be doubted, and his version of the ontological argument is meant to demonstrate this.

Triangles and Descartes' ontological argument

Descartes uses the triangle as an example. The nature of a triangle is that it has three sides and three interior angles adding up to 180 degrees. The nature of the triangle is called 'immutable' by Descartes – meaning 'incapable of change/being different'.

Second, triangles are what they are. So far as Descartes is concerned it makes no difference if I have an idea of what a triangle is or not. In fact even if no one knows what a triangle is, a triangle is still this shape with three sides.

The crucial point is that, like a triangle, God also has an 'immutable' nature. A triangle's nature (three sides and three interior angles equalling 180 degrees) tells us something about the essence of what a triangle is.

According to Descartes, part of God's nature is that God exists. This is immutable; it tells us something about God.

Part of God's essence is therefore existence. Descartes argues that God existing is as fundamental to the nature of God as the interior angles of a triangle adding up to 180 degrees are an essential part of what a triangle is. For Descartes, the essence of God is that God exists and existence is a predicate of God.

Descartes' argument

1   God is a supremely perfect being.
2   A property of perfection is existence.
3   Therefore, God exists.

Existence as perfection

Descartes argues that it is part of the essence or nature of God to exist and the reason for this is that existence is a perfection.

By perfection Descartes means that something is not lacking in any way. If you have the idea of a perfect car, it is only an idea; it is not the perfect car unless it exists in reality. Descartes gives the example of it being impossible to think of a mountain existing without also the concept of a valley that goes with it.

Existence, so far as Descartes is concerned, is a perfection of God in the same way as a mountain and a valley going together. You cannot talk about God unless God exists, because God is perfect, and part of perfection is existence.

Thought Point

Think of the characteristics of your dream car. Could your dream car be described as the 'perfect' car? What would Descartes say?

But why should we believe God exists?

Descartes gives two answers:

1 If you study the idea of God carefully enough it is clear that the perfection of existence is part of the way God is, necessarily.
2 To a possible claim that one can happily think of mountains and valleys but that does not mean they exist, Descartes just insists that existence is a perfection, and hence God being perfect must exist.

FURTHER OBJECTIONS TO THE ONTOLOGICAL ARGUMENT

KANT AND WHY EXISTENCE IS NOT A PREDICATE

Immanuel Kant, in response to Descartes, argues that existence is not a predicate. For example, one can have an idea of what a unicorn is. However, that does not mean it exists in reality, even though we can think about unicorns as living creatures.

Descartes the man (1596–1650)

René Descartes was born in La-Haye, France. He joined a Jesuit school in Anjou, and later on studied at the University of Poitiers. He joined the army of the Prince of Orange in 1618, but did not actually fight in any battles. From 1628 to 1649 he lived in Holland. In 1649 he became the tutor of Queen Christina of Sweden. He died of pneumonia in 1650.

Descartes wrote widely on philosophy, and he is significant because many philosophers see him as the founder of modern philosophy; he developed new approaches to philosophy which differed from the traditional philosophies of Europe that came from the great Greek philosophers of the ancient world. He wrote many books, but the most famous is his *Meditations on First Philosophy* (1641), which examines the nature of reality and God. It is this book which contains his version of the ontological argument.

Another way some philosophers put this point is to say that Kant is saying that existence is part of the concept of God (an analytic statement) but it does not prove that God exists in reality. For Kant, all philosophical statements or propositions about existence are *synthetic* – they need to be verified as true or false. God's existence, like any other thing's existence, is synthetic and needs to be verified.

Thought Point

How do you think Descartes would reply to Kant's claim that existence is not a predicate? (Clue: Think about Descartes' claim that existence is a perfection.)

Replies to Kant

Is Kant right to say that existence is not a predicate? For example, one can have an idea of what the Yeti is and list the particular properties of the Yeti such as size, hairy, human-like, living and so forth. However, if I have actual evidence that the Yeti exists, that adds something to the idea of a Yeti – it adds 'existence'.

Charles Hartshorne pointed out that:

> The conceptual description of a kind of thing may at most account for so much of its quality or value as is expressible in merely abstract terms. But the full quality is not thus expressible. (*Anselm's Discovery*)

Another way of putting what Hartshorne says could be to claim that there is a big difference, for example, between describing the symptoms of an illness such as a cold in theory, and the reality of having the illness in real life. For Hartshorne, the problem with Kant's argument is that there is a big difference between an idea of God and God existing in reality as well. Hence, Hartshorne rejects Kant's claim that existence is not a predicate.

Norman Malcolm ('Anselm's Ontological Argument') has suggested that necessary existence could be a predicate of God. Malcolm argues that the existence of God is either impossible or necessary. Following Anselm's second formulation of the ontological argument, Malcolm suggests that God cannot contingently exist; otherwise God is not the greatest possible being. Malcolm reasons that God's existence is impossible only if God's existence is both self-contradictory and illogical.

However, the problem with Malcolm's claim that God necessarily exists is that you cannot prove God exists by stating what is not the case. Even if God's existence is not impossible or contradictory, this only shows that God's existence is possible, not that God necessarily exists.

IS EXISTENCE REALLY A PERFECTION WHICH GOD CANNOT LACK?

Pierre Gassendi (et al.) wrote a reply to Descartes' idea that existence is a perfection which God cannot lack. He argued that something either exists or it does not. It is only relevant to discuss perfection of something if it exists. If something like a unicorn, Yeti or God does not exist, then these things are neither perfect nor imperfect; they just do not exist ('Descartes replies to critics').

A reply to Gassendi

Descartes responded to Pierre Gassendi's idea, stating that existence is necessarily part of the nature or essence of God, and *the relation between existence and essence is manifestly quite different in the case of God from what it is in the case of a triangle* ('Descartes replies to critics'). To put it another way, Descartes is saying that God is a different sort of thing from triangles and it is the essence of God to exist.

Thought Point

Descartes and Gassendi

Does Descartes' reply really solve Gassendi's criticism? What do you think?

SUMMARY

1 The ontological argument

Anselm of Canterbury

Starting point: Psalm 14: 1, 'Fools say in their hearts, "there is no god"'
Anselm's first ontological argument

Something which exists in reality and in the mind is greater than something which exists as an idea in the mind alone. Therefore, God must exist in reality and in the mind

Anselm claims that existence is a predicate of God

Anselm's second version of the argument
God's existence is necessary
The greatest possible being is what Christians mean by God
Some suggestions that Anselm was reflecting on, not proving, God existed necessarily

Gaunilo's response to Anselm's argument
Necessary existence is 'unintelligible'
You cannot define the idea into existence
Gaunilo's island
Gaunilo argues that while the most perfect island can be conceived of, that does not mean that it exists; the same reasoning applies to Anselm's ontological argument

Anselm's possible reply to Gaunilo
Gaunilo's argument is different, because the island, while being the greatest possible island, does not have to exist, its existence is contingent.
Plantinga argued that God is maximally great in Anselm's thought. Therefore, the greatest possible being and the greatest possible island are not comparable.

Thomas Aquinas

Rejected Anselm's argument as God's existence is not self-evident, and human beings are not in a position to understand God's nature

Descartes

Claimed that there is the idea of God in every person, like a trademark or stamp
Some things cannot be doubted, such as the truths of mathematics or God's existence
Demonstrating God's existence is about showing there is no reason to ever doubt that God exists
Triangles and Descartes' ontological argument
God and triangles have an 'immutable' nature/essence Part of God's essence is existence

God is the supremely perfect being
Descartes' example: the concept of mountains and valleys

Further objections to the ontological argument

Kant argues that existence is not a 'predicate'
Replies to Kant
Charles Hartshorne – there is a big difference between an idea of God and God existing in reality as well
Norman Malcolm suggested that necessary existence could be a predicate of God
Pierre Gassendi argued that it is only relevant to discuss the perfection of something if it exists

REVIEW QUESTIONS

Look back over the chapter and check that you can answer the following questions:

1   Briefly explain Gaunilo's criticism of the ontological argument.
2   What are the two most serious weaknesses of the ontological argument in your opinion? Justify your choice.
3   Summarise Anselm's and Descartes' version of the ontological argument.
4   What is the difference between an analytic and a synthetic statement? Explain with reference to an example.
5   Explain what Kant means when he says existence is not a predicate.
6   Descartes says that existence is a perfection of God. What does this mean?

Terminology

Do you know your terminology?

Look back at the key terminology list from the beginning of the chapter. Make sure you can explain every term and how the terms relate to the ontological argument. The ability to use terminology accurately will help you to gain a high mark in your examination.

Examination Questions Practice

In order to achieve a high mark when answering questions about the ontological argument, you must make sure you understand the different forms of the argument. It is all too easy to achieve a low mark if you confuse the different writers, ideas and terminology of this topic.

EXAM MISTAKES TO AVOID

Remember: (a) assesses AO1 and (b) AO2. To help you improve your answers look at the AS Levels of Response. See: http://www.ocr.org.uk/qualifications/as-a-level-gce-religious-studies-h172-h572/

SAMPLE AS EXAM-STYLE QUESTIONS

1   (a) **Explain Anselm's ontological argument.** (25 marks)

- First hint: stick to the question – write about Anselm. Do not include irrelevant material such as Descartes' version of the argument.
- Second, to gain a high mark you should be able to write about both versions of Anselm's ontological argument. Remember that the different arguments deal with slightly different ideas.
- Third, you could discuss the analytical nature of Anselm's ontological argument.
- Fourth, to achieve a high mark you need to show the examiner that you understand and can explain the following ideas of Anselm:

  – God is the greatest being that can be conceived.
  – The superiority of existence in reality over existence in the mind.
  – Existence as a predicate of God.
  – God's necessary existence.

(b) **'Logic cannot prove the existence of God.' Discuss.** (10 marks)

This question is asking you to consider whether the existence of God is an analytic claim that can be shown to be true by deductive argument. The word 'logic' in the question tells you this.

This is an evaluation question, so you will need to present and assess some differing views. For example, you could discuss and evaluate some of the following ideas:

- Assess whether the existence of God is an analytic statement. Use ideas from the ontological argument to support your argument. Think about some commentators' criticisms of the ontological argument, such as Kant's.
- Put forward an argument that defends the existence of God as an analytic proposition. For example, you could put forward and assess Descartes' response to criticism of his argument.

- Look at the chapters of the book on the cosmological or design argument. In your answer suggest some reasons why Aquinas would agree with this statement.

2 (a) **Explain the ontological argument from Anselm and Descartes.**

   (b) **'The ontological argument will never be of any use in trying to prove God's existence.' Discuss.**

3 (a) **Explain Descartes' ontological argument.**

   (b) **'The ontological argument will only convince those who already believe in God.' Discuss.**

FURTHER READING

'The Ontological Argument' (J. Frye, in *Dialogue* 20, April 2003) provides an excellent overview of the mistakes students often make when answering questions about the ontological argument. It is written for advanced level students and is well worth reading.

The Puzzle of God (P. Vardy, 1995) provides a very readable account of the ontological argument, particularly Anselm's argument and Gaunilo's response. It also provides an easy-to-read explanation of analytic and synthetic statements.

The Existence of God (R. Swinburne, 2004) provides a detailed and well-articulated examination of arguments in favour of God's existence. Richard Swinburne examines both arguments for God's existence and some of the responses these arguments have drawn.

The Miracle of Theism (J.L. Mackie, 1982) presents a stimulating account of the ontological argument and the main philosophical debates about its validity. Mackie attempts to answer the arguments for God's existence put forward by Richard Swinburne.

On Behalf of the Fool provides a clear analysis of Anselm's argument and includes some other analogies apart from those mentioned in this chapter. (A readily accessible extract from Gaunilo's writings may be found in *Philosophy of Religion: The Big Questions*, ed. E. Stump and Michael J. Murray (1999).)

6 The Cosmological Argument

Key scholars

Thomas Aquinas
(1225–1274)
David Hume (1711–1776)
Bertrand Russell
(1872–1970)
Frederick Copleston
(1907–1994)
G.E.M. (Elizabeth)
Anscombe (1913–2001)

THE ISSUES

Why does anything exist rather than nothing?
Does God cause everything to exist?

WHAT YOU WILL LEARN ABOUT IN THIS CHAPTER

Whether there are any arguments which show that God causes the universe
to exist.
Why David Hume and other philosophers reject arguments which claim to
show that God causes the universe.

STARTER

Look at the picture below. Explain why the Earth exists. Try to include as
many relevant reasons in your explanation as you can.

THE OCR CHECKLIST

The Cosmological argument from Aquinas and Copleston; challenges from Hume and Russell

Candidates should be able to demonstrate knowledge and understanding of:

*   the Cosmological argument from Aquinas and Copleston;
*   the arguments put forward by Copleston in the 1948 radio debate with Russell and Russell's counter arguments;
*   Hume's criticisms of the Cosmological argument.

Candidates should be able to discuss critically these views and their strengths and weaknesses.

From OCR A Level Religious Studies specification H172.

INTRODUCTION

The Cosmological argument is perhaps the most famous example of an attempt by philosophers to show the logic (rationality) of believing in God. The Cosmological argument claims that from examining the fact that the universe exists, it is possible to work out the cause of the universe's existence.

The Cosmological argument is appealing because it seems so obvious to say:

> *Everything that exists has a cause. The universe exists. So, the universe was caused.*

In this chapter we will examine whether this appealing argument is as logical as it sounds.

A very long history

The Cosmological argument is the modern title for a collection of arguments for God's existence that have been a matter of debate in various forms for over 2,000 years in philosophy. This chapter focuses on the arguments of Aquinas and Copleston and the critics of these two. There are plenty of other related ideas from Aristotle, Avicenna, the Kalam tradition and Richard Swinburne. See the 'Further reading' section if you wish to investigate these other cosmological arguments.

Aquinas the man (1225–1274)

Thomas Aquinas was born in 1225. As a young man he joined the Dominican Order. He was a brilliant academic and studied under Albert the Great.

continued opposite

Thought Point

Aristotle and Plato

The writings of Aristotle and Plato have greatly influenced philosophers such as Thomas Aquinas and their work on the Cosmological argument. It is worth reviewing the work you have completed on Plato and Aristotle while studying the Cosmological argument.

AQUINAS' COSMOLOGICAL ARGUMENT: THE FIVE WAYS

The final work of Thomas Aquinas was his *Summa Theologiae* which summed up his ideas about theology. The first part of it sets out to demonstrate the rationality of belief in the existence of God. Near the beginning of the work Aquinas put forward a collection of related ways of demonstrating the existence of God. Collectively, these demonstrations of God's existence are known as the Five Ways. The first three are often referred to by modern philosophers when they discuss the Cosmological argument.

WAYS 1 AND 2: THE ARGUMENTS FOR AN UNMOVED MOVER AND UNCAUSED CAUSER

Both of these first two ways are causal versions of the Cosmological argument. Thomas Aquinas' first two ways to demonstrate God's existence are similar and may be set out as follows:

Thomas Aquinas' first way

1   We can observe that things in the world are in a process of motion.
2   Everything that is in motion is in the process of changing from a potential state to an actual state.
3   The same thing cannot be at the same time potentially and actually the same thing.
4   For example, if something is actually hot, it cannot be potentially hot, but it can be potentially cold.

5   So, everything that is in a state of motion must be put into this state by another thing.

6   But the chain of movers 'cannot go on to infinity, because then there would be no first mover, and, consequently no other mover' (Aquinas, *Summa Theologiae*).

7   **Conclusion**: 'It is necessary to arrive at a first mover, put in motion by no other; and this everyone understands to be God' (Aquinas, *Summa Theologiae*).

Thomas Aquinas' second way

1   Nothing is an efficient cause of itself.

2   Efficient causes follow in order: a first cause causes a second, a second a third and so on.

3   It is not possible for efficient causes to go back infinitely, because if there is no efficient first cause, there will not be any following causes.

4   Conclusion: 'It is necessary to admit a first efficient cause to which everyone gives the name of God' (Aquinas, *Summa Theologiae*).

Through this argument Aquinas is showing that there cannot be an infinite regress of causers (movers) and there must be some explanation that is not part of the chain of causation and this explanation must be the source of all causation without itself having a cause. For Aristotle this would be the unmoved mover, whereas for Aquinas this is God.

POINTS TO NOTE ABOUT AQUINAS' FIRST AND SECOND WAYS

Motion, potentiality and actuality

The First Way sounds rather strange because of the odd use of the word 'motion'. What Aquinas means by 'motion' is the way or method by which some thing or object becomes something else. If you think of a hot cup of coffee, it is actually hot. However, the cup of coffee is also potentially cold. In Aquinas' way of thinking, you cannot be both potentially and actually the same thing at the same time. For example, it makes no sense to talk of the cup of coffee being potentially hot when it is actually hot.

Efficient cause may be understood as Aquinas' way of saying that the cause is necessary. If you want to make a hot cup of coffee, you necessarily have to heat the coffee. The efficient cause is that which gives heat to the coffee.

> He is renowned both in the Catholic Church and the history of philosophy for his writings. His most famous work was the *Summa Theologiae* which he began in 1256. He died before completing it. He was later made a Doctor of the Church in recognition of the quality of his theological and philosophical writings.

> **The Five Ways**
>
> Way 1 – argument for an unmoved mover
>
> Way 2 – argument for an uncaused causer
>
> Way 3 – argument from contingency
>
> Way 4 – argument from gradation
>
> Way 5 – argument from teleology

Look at the questions at the beginning of this chapter again. What the Cosmological argument concerns is why there is a universe at all. In Aquinas' case he suggests that there is a *'first efficient cause'* of everything, i.e. a cause of everything. This idea comes from Aristotle.

INFINITE REGRESSION

An infinite regression is a chain of events that goes backwards for ever. You can explain this with the example of a domino rally. If you ask what caused the final domino in the chain to fall, you would say the previous one caused it. If you asked what caused the domino before last to fall, you would say that it was the one before that, and so on. If you imagine this chain of dominoes to continue backwards an infinite number of times, you have an example of what is called *an infinite regression*.

If we analyse this chain of dominoes using Aquinas' terms *potentiality* and *actuality*, what we find is that every domino in the chain is potentially the cause of the next one falling.

Aquinas' claim is that, to explain why there is any chain of events at all, you need to have an actual cause that is *pure act* and not a potential cause, because if the cause of everything is only potential, then it needs to be acted on to achieve its potential, and so the chain of regression begins again. Aquinas' claim is that the chain is caused by a pure act not a potential act. Aquinas' conclusion is that the being that is pure act is God.

Beware of the domino example

Often Aquinas' argument is illustrated, as above, with the example of a domino rally and the claim is made that God starts the domino rally off. This is similar to watching a football fly through the air and saying the cause of it moving was someone kicking it. It does not matter whether that person is there any longer or not. The football kicker may have kicked the ball and run off while the ball is still moving.

Aquinas is not making this type of claim, as it would allow the possibility that God does not now exist, like the football kicker who wanders off.

What Aquinas really means

Many philosophers argue that the way to understand the idea of *first mover* or *first efficient cause* is that Aquinas is talking about an ontological

---

Extract from Thomas Aquinas' *Summa Theologiae*, 1a, 2, 3:

Way 1

[W]hatever is in motion must be put in motion by another. If that by which it is put in motion be itself in motion, then this also must needs be put in motion by another and that by another again. But this cannot go on to infinity because then there would be no first mover, and, consequently no other mover.

Way 2

In the world of sense we find there is an order of efficient causes. . . . Now to take away the cause is to take away the effect. Therefore, if there be no first cause among efficient causes, there will be no ultimate, nor any intermediate cause.

Infinite

Refers to something which has neither a beginning nor an end. Most commonly the idea of infinity is used in mathematics to describe series of numbers

first mover or *first efficient cause*. By this, philosophers mean that Aquinas is talking about the reason why anything exists at all. Aquinas is not just talking about who starts a chain of actions such as a domino rally.

Philosophers would say that Aquinas is concerned with why there is any motion or causation at all and why there continues to be motion and causation. The philosopher F.C. Copleston called this an 'ontologically ultimate cause'.

Copleston (*Aquinas*) explained this point by distinguishing between:

1   Winding up your watch at night, and
2   Writing on a piece of paper.

The second activity stops if you stop writing. Copleston's claim is that Aquinas' arguments are making a point more like the second than the first. The watch, once it is wound up, continues on its own. Copleston argues that this is not what Aquinas meant when discussing Ways 1 and 2. Instead, Aquinas is talking about a *first mover* or *first efficient cause* that is the reason for there being motion or causation at all. An example may help to illustrate this point:

> According to the Big Bang theory our universe began around 15 billion years ago. Scientists have inferred much about its origins and development. However, that does not explain why there is and continues to be a universe.

that have no beginning or end. For example, the series . . .
−3,−2,−1,0,1,2,3 . . . could continue without end.

F.C. Copleston (1907–1994)

By kind permission of The Society of Jesus (British Province)

Is Aquinas correct to say that you cannot have an infinite regression of causes?

Two points can be made here.

First, it is quite true that in mathematics one can think of a series of numbers without end, which might be like this: . . . −3,−2,−1,0,1,2,3 . . .

This series of numbers could of course continue both positively and negatively forever. If infinite regressions are possible in reality, then there could be an infinite series of causes and effects which had no beginning, though why there was such a series could be questioned. Equally, if God is proposed as the explanation for why there is anything rather than nothing, a person supporting infinite regressions could ask who caused God.

Second, many commentators have criticised Aquinas' argument that if every contingent thing at one time did not exist, nothing would come to exist. Philosophers criticise this point by saying that it is quite possible for

Contingent

Philosophers use the word contingent to mean that something is not immortal but depends on something else for its existence. For example, human beings are caused to exist by their parents. They do not just exist. So, philosophers would say human beings are contingent beings.

all contingent things at different points in time to not exist and later exist. However, this does not mean that at some time nothing existed.

WHY DAVID HUME REJECTS ARGUMENTS SUCH AS AQUINAS' FIRST AND SECOND WAYS

The philosopher David Hume questioned the idea that every event has a cause. Hume pointed out that human beings assume that every event has a cause, but we cannot prove this. The following example may help to illustrate this view.

Necessary

The word used in philosophy to say that something has to be that way and cannot be any different (e.g. if a philosopher was discussing necessary existence he or she would be talking about something which has to exist and could not fail to exist).

Thought Point

The bus

If you are waiting at a bus stop and you want the bus to stop, you put your hand out and the bus should come to a stop (providing the driver does not ignore you or fail to see you).

What causes the bus to stop?

If you had never before seen a bus or a person requesting a bus to stop, why would it be wrong to conclude that the person putting out their hand caused the bus to stop?

Cause and effect

The word cause is used in philosophy to refer to something which brings about an effect or result. For example, the cause of a football flying through the air could be the person who kicked it. The effect is the result of the action – in this case the ball moving. For more information about cause and effect see the section on Aristotle pp. 27ff.).

This example illustrates the fact that we may make assumptions about cause and effect which can be mistaken. Hume argued that we assume that there is a relationship between cause and effect, because our minds have developed a habit of seeing causes and automatically associating effects with them. Hume argues that if there is an explanation for every event in a series it is not necessary to ask what caused the whole series. According to Hume the fact that every event must have a cause is taken for granted as that is simply the way we see and understand things. Hume concludes that we expect future experiences to somehow conform to past experiences, and this repetition of instances reinforces our belief that A causes B. We see 'uniformity of nature' because that is the way our mind thinks: we organise events by establishing necessary connections between them. Past experiences make us believe that A and B must be connected but Hume stated that, as a matter of logic, one cannot always claim or assume that every effect has a cause. If this is true, it undermines Ways 1 and 2 of Aquinas' argument which assume that there is a relationship between cause and effect when he states in Way 2: 'In the world of sense we find that there is an order of efficient cause' (Aquinas, *Summa Theologiae*).

It is very important to understand what Hume is claiming: Hume is arguing that the proposition 'Whatever has a beginning of existence must have a cause' (Anscombe, '"Whatever Has a Beginning of Existence Must Have a Cause": Hume's Argument Exposed') is not certain. If Hume's point is correct, it would mean that the Cosmological argument's claim that the universe has a first cause cannot be proved.

The fallacy of composition and David Hume

David Hume also questioned whether it is necessary for the whole universe to have a cause just because everything that is within the universe could be explained by reference to a preceding cause. This is called the fallacy of composition.

For Hume there is no reason why God should be the first cause as the first cause could simply be the universe itself. This idea fits in with what we now know about the world as it evolved from primordial matter and so effectively actualises itself, and so it is completely possible that the universe came into being without a cause, or that it had always existed and so had no beginning.

One often quoted example is from Bertrand Russell, who pointed out that saying every man has a mother is not proof that the human race has a mother. Russell's closing comment was that:

> Obviously the human race hasn't a mother, that's a different logical sphere. (*Why I Am Not a Christian*)

If we apply the fallacy of composition to the Cosmological argument, it would mean that you cannot deduce that the universe has a cause just because you can identify the cause of contingent things within the universe.

Is David Hume correct?

David Hume is very sceptical of a special link between causes and effects. While it is quite true that we cannot *demonstrate* that every effect is *caused*, believing that effects are caused is a reasonable working approach to everyday life.

Elizabeth Anscombe ('"Whatever Has a Beginning of Existence Must Have a Cause": Hume's Argument Exposed') has responded to Hume's argument by pointing out that you could conclude that 'existence must have a cause' without believing or knowing that 'such particular effects must have such particular causes'. Anscombe gives the example of a magician pulling a rabbit out of a hat, pointing out that you can imagine a rabbit 'coming into being without a cause', but this tells us nothing about 'what is possible to suppose "without contradiction or absurdity" as holding in reality' (ibid.).

Furthermore, Anscombe suggests that even if you are able to imagine something coming into existence without a cause this does not tell you anything at all about what is possible in reality. You can imagine something, such as the rabbit in Anscombe's example, coming into existence without a cause. However, 'from my being able to do that, nothing whatever follows about what is possible to suppose "without contradiction or absurdity" as holding in reality' (ibid.).

REALITY AND SPECULATION

When considering the issue of causation and infinite regression it is very important to remember the difference between speculation and reality.

Reality refers to our experience of the universe and the way in which it works.

Speculation is an activity of the mind thinking about the various logical possibilities regarding any given point or issue. For example, scientists could speculate about the possibility of teleportation, but in reality this is currently impossible.

It is reasonable to ask whether discussion of the possibility of an infinite regression is a piece of logical speculation, or whether it seems to relate to reality. Points to consider here might include the idea that astronomers state that the universe did indeed have a beginning, though, of course, no scientist or for that matter any other person can do more than speculate about events outside of our universe.

Analysis of Aquinas' First and Second Ways

You could argue that a first cause, God, did exist once, but that does not mean that he still exists and is active in the world. Alternatively you could argue that, if causation implies keeping something going once it has begun, then God could be understood as a sustaining cause of the universe.

The arguments of the first and second ways seems to rely on a contradiction – first Aquinas says that everything must have a cause; then he says that something must exist that is the cause of itself. Alternatively, you could argue that if there wasn't an exception to this general rule then the universe would have no cause. Thus something must exist which had no cause. This is similar to Anselm's reply to Gaunilo, that God is a being who must exist. This argument can again be countered by saying that the universe requires no explanation – it just is. You could also argue that an infinite regress is possible, but Mackie agrees with Aquinas using the analogy of a train. He argues that there can be an infinite number of carriages, each of which may move the next one, but it only makes sense if there is a railway engine. Therefore, the most obvious objection to Aquinas' theory greatly damages it and brings into dispute the basis of the whole argument, for if an infinite regress is possible, then the need for a prime mover is questionable. Mackie's argument is of little use, as whilst he defended the argument for a prime mover, he questioned whether Aquinas' three ways could be related to his analogy.

Finally, the first and second ways only highlight the possibility of God as an explanation and the argument fails if we are not satisfied with the idea of God as a being who requires no further explanation.

WAY 3: THE ARGUMENT FROM CONTINGENCY

Thought Point

Check your ideas

Check the meaning of *necessity* as explained earlier in this chapter.

Aquinas' Third Way is called an argument from contingency or necessity, and it could be put as follows:

1   Things which exist in nature at one time did not exist and in the future will not exist. These things at any time may or may not exist (philosophers call this *contingent existence*).
2   If everything at one time did not exist, there would have been nothing in existence.
3   If point 2 were true, then there would be nothing in existence, because there would be nothing to bring anything into existence.
4   Interim conclusion: 'There must exist something the existence of which is necessary' (Aquinas, *Summa Theologiae*).

5   But every necessary thing either has its necessity caused by another or not.

6   An infinite regression of necessary things is impossible, as shown in Way 2.

7   Final conclusion: There exists 'some being having of itself its own necessity . . . causing in others their necessity. This all men speak of as God' (Aquinas, *Summa Theologiae*).

Thought Point

In Aquinas' Third Way God necessarily exists. You could say that God is a necessary being.

Which other argument for God's existence is this similar to? What are the similarities?

POINTS TO NOTE ABOUT AQUINAS' THIRD WAY

Contingent existence

Aquinas' key claim is that if everything exists contingently, it is possible to have a time when nothing exists. If you had a time when no contingent beings existed, none would come to exist, as there would be no contingent beings around to cause them. Hence, Aquinas concludes that there must be something the existence of which is necessary and which cannot fail to exist.

Links with Ways 1 and 2

Note that Aquinas links Way 3 with the rejection of infinite regression in Ways 1 and 2. In addition, Aquinas' concept of a necessary being fits in with Copleston's interpretation of the first two ways. Copleston suggested that the world is the sum total of all objects. None of these objects contain within themselves the reason for their own existence. Therefore, every object in the world depends on some other object for its existence. The world is the sum total of all these things. If everything within the world requires something else to exist, the cause of the entire universe must be external to the universe. This explanation must be a being which exists, but which contains within itself the cause of its existence. Its existence is 'self-explanatory'. Copleston refers to this as an *ontologically necessary being*.

CRITICISMS OF WAY 3

Immanuel Kant rejected Aquinas' Third Way for the same reason that he rejected the concept of necessary existence with respect to the ontological argument. However, this is not entirely fair as the Cosmological argument is fundamentally different from the ontological argument in that it is *a posteriori*. In other words, the cosmological argument starts from the fact that the universe exists and then explores why it exists, whereas the ontological argument starts from the idea that God exists.

The philosopher J.L. Mackie (Mackie, *The Miracle of Theism*) questioned Aquinas' argument in favour of a necessary being. He argued that Aquinas assumes that anything which does not have the predicate (or Mackie's word *essence*) of existence requires the existence of a necessary being, whom Aquinas calls God. However, Mackie questions why people should accept this assumption. He suggests that you could equally argue that there is 'a permanent stock of matter whose essence did not involve existence from anything else' (Mackie, *The Miracle of Theism*). In other words, Mackie is questioning the assumption that there is a necessary being. In addition, Mackie points out that while Aquinas' arguments appear convincing, he does not give any reason why God should be the necessary being.

What does Aquinas mean when he says that God is a necessary being?

One idea is that God is a logically necessary being, like Anselm's idea of God in the ontological argument. Aquinas believed that the existence of contingent beings would ultimately necessitate a being which must exist for all of the contingent beings to exist. This being, called a necessary being, is what we call God. However, the problem with this idea is that it would mean that the criticism of the idea of a logically necessary being from the ontological argument applies to Aquinas' argument.

Michael Palmer (*The Question of God*) has suggested that what might be meant is 'factual necessity', by which people mean that God exists independently of everything else. This is different from the idea of logical necessity and avoids this weakness.

WHAT DO WAYS 1 TO 3 SHOW?

For Aquinas, Ways 1 to 3 demonstrate that there is a first efficient cause and prime mover of the universe that is pure actuality not potentiality. This being's existence is necessary. Aquinas claims that this being is that which we call God. It is worth noting that at this point in the *Summa Theologiae* Aquinas has not demonstrated the existence of the Christian God. Aquinas spends much of the rest of Part 1a and 1a2ae of the *Summa Theologiae* exploring and demonstrating this relationship. It is very important to realise that the God of Aquinas is spoken of in a very different way from the personal attributes often attributed to God in the Christian tradition.

In an article about the Cosmological argument, one Christian philosopher reaches the following conclusion. What do you think he meant?

> What I have been saying may seem to make God both remote and irrelevant. He is not part of the universe and he makes no difference to it. (H. McCabe, 'A Modern Cosmological Argument')

Thought Point

Look at the picture. When this child is a bit older how would you explain to her why the stars in the sky exist? Would you want to give an ultimate explanation – one that a philosopher like Copleston would call a sufficient explanation?

CONCLUSION

Given the controversy and debates that surround the Cosmological argument it is certainly the case that it does not provide a demonstration of God's existence that is beyond doubt. That having been said, for many people the cosmological argument remains today an appealing and credible argument.

THE RUSSELL–COPLESTON DEBATE

INTRODUCTION

The BBC broadcast a debate entitled *The Existence of God – A Debate* in 1948. This debate was between two great philosophers of their day: Bertrand Russell and Frederick Copleston. The debate has become a world-famous example of two differing approaches to the Cosmological argument.

Copleston reworked Aquinas' argument and centred on contingency. This is a summary of his argument:

1   There are things in this world that are contingent – they might not have existed, e.g. we would not exist without our parents
2   Everything in the world is like this – everything depends on something else for its existence
3   Therefore there must be a cause of everything in the universe that exists outside of it
4   This cause must be a necessary being – one which contains the reason for its existence within itself
5   This necessary being is God

Russell refused to accept the idea of a necessary being as one that cannot be thought not to exist and concluded that the regress of causal events did not lead to the existence of everything in the universe:

> what I am saying is that the concept of cause is not applicable to the total

Just because each human has a mother does not mean the entire human race has a mother. He said that the universe is a mere, brute fact, and its existence does not demand an explanation.

> I should say that the universe is just there, and that's all.

Russell saw the argument for a cause of the universe as having little meaning or significance. He established it as a 'question that has no meaning' and thus proposed: 'Shall we pass on to some other issue?' Copleston's response to Russell's refusal to accept the importance of the issue was to claim:

> If one refused to sit at the chess board and make a move, one cannot, of course, be checkmated.

Thought Point

The chess problem

With a chess set, try to think of as many strategies to avoid losing as you can. Ask a friend for help if you are not a strong chess player. Then read the next section of the textbook about the Copleston–Russell debate and try to work out the link with the debate.

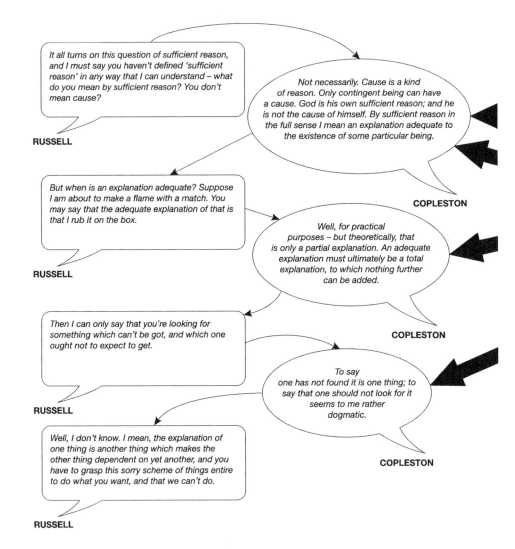

RUSSELL

It all turns on this question of sufficient reason, and I must say you haven't defined 'sufficient reason' in any way that I can understand – what do you mean by sufficient reason? You don't mean cause?

COPLESTON

Not necessarily. Cause is a kind of reason. Only contingent being can have a cause. God is his own sufficient reason; and he is not the cause of himself. By sufficient reason in the full sense I mean an explanation adequate to the existence of some particular being.

RUSSELL

But when is an explanation adequate? Suppose I am about to make a flame with a match. You may say that the adequate explanation of that is that I rub it on the box.

COPLESTON

Well, for practical purposes – but theoretically, that is only a partial explanation. An adequate explanation must ultimately be a total explanation, to which nothing further can be added.

RUSSELL

Then I can only say that you're looking for something which can't be got, and which one ought not to expect to get.

COPLESTON

To say one has not found it is one thing; to say that one should not look for it seems to me rather dogmatic.

RUSSELL

Well, I don't know. I mean, the explanation of one thing is another thing which makes the other thing dependent on yet another, and you have to grasp this sorry scheme of things entire to do what you want, and that we can't do.

The extracts of the text from the debate are taken from copies of the debate in C. Hamilton, *Understanding Philosophy for AS Level AQA* (2003); Palmer, *The Question of God* (2001); Vardy, *Puzzle of God* (1995); J. Hick (ed.), *The Existence of God* and Copleston, *Aquinas* (1991). The original text *The Existence of God – A Debate* (BBC: 1948), is also reprinted in Russell, *Why I Am Not a Christian* (2004).

Russell and Copleston agree that one of the key turning points in the debate is the principle of sufficient reason. When applied to the cosmological argument Copleston and Aquinas argue *that the universe can only be sufficiently explained by reference to God*. This claim is the point that Russell and Copleston argue about.

Note that Copleston is stating that God is different from contingent beings as he is '*his own sufficient cause*'. This makes God a different kind of being in a class of God's own.

Russell and Copleston dispute the adequacy of explanation that is required. Take the example of the Gulf War in 2003. How would you explain to someone why it started? You could blame George Bush and Tony Blair, but just saying they alone are responsible is not satisfactory, as you would want to understand something about the circumstances that led up to the war: for example, George Bush's '*war on terror*' or the atrocities which Saddam Hussein committed during his time in power. Where would you draw the line in the debate? How far back does your explanation have to go to be sufficient?

This section of the debate concludes with Russell and Copleston adopting two opposed positions. Russell argues that whether an explanation for the universe as a whole is possible or not, the explanation is beyond the reach of human beings. Second, Russell's argument through the whole debate suggests that it is unnecessary for human beings to have a sufficient explanation of the universe that goes beyond the contingent universe.

Copleston's point is slightly different. First, Copleston argues that a sufficient explanation of the universe that includes explaining why there is any unverse at all is important. Second, Copleston uses the word '*dogmatic*' to describe Russell's refusal to enter into the debate about the ultimate cause for the universe existing and continuing to exist. The use of the word 'dogmatic' is interesting as a dogma is a word used by Roman Catholics to describe a belief which is held beyond any doubt and debate. Copleston is accusing Russell of not being open minded.

The comments below about the Cosmological argument indicate how far apart Russell's and Copleston's views are.

It is a matter of personal judgement for you to decide whether Russell's or Copleston's arguments are stronger.

I should say that the universe is just there and that is all.

RUSSELL

If one does not wish to embark on the path which leads to the affirmation of transcendent being, however the latter may be described, one has to deny the reality of the problem and assert that things 'just are' and that the existential problem in question is just a pseudo-problem. And if one refuses to even sit down at the chess board and make a move, one cannot, of course, be checkmated.

COPLESTON

Sufficient reason

The principle of sufficient reason states that nothing is without reason. It is a powerful and controversial philosophical principle stipulating that everything must have a reason or a cause.

Copleston put forward a defence of the Cosmological argument which centred on a reformulation of some of the ideas found in the Third Way of Thomas Aquinas. Russell rejected Copleston's arguments and suggested that the universe was not explainable in the way Copleston wanted. At the heart of their debate is the issue of contingency and necessity, and what is a sufficient reason to explain why anything exists. Study the debate and comments on the following pages, and then try to complete the questions which follow it.

THE PRINCIPLE OF SUFFICIENT REASON

In order to understand the debate between Russell and Copleston you should be aware of what is meant by the *principle of sufficient reason*. The principle comes from the work of the philosopher G.W. Leibniz, who developed a new version of the Cosmological argument. At the heart of it was the idea that explaining the truth of a fact, or the existence of a thing, includes an explanation of why it is like that and not different. Leibniz defined the principle of sufficient reason as that:

> in virtue of which we hold that no fact could ever be true of or existent, nor statement correct, unless there were a sufficient reason why it was thus and not otherwise. (Leibniz, *Philosophical Texts*)

By this he meant that you should be able to give an explanation of why, for example, a car exists that includes how it came to exist. This idea of explaining how a thing came to exist he called the principle of *sufficient reason*.

A *sufficient reason* to explain the universe's existence would thus explain how and why the universe exists.

Thought Point

1 Who do you most agree with? Why?
2 What does Copleston mean by a *sufficient* reason?
3 Which person's argument is stronger in this extract?
4 Do you think it is, or will be, possible to ever prove your own point of view regarding the Cosmological argument in such a way as to end debate about it?

SUMMARY

Cosmological arguments

Aquinas' cosmological arguments

Ways 1 and 2: The arguments for an unmoved mover and uncaused causer
Concerned with why there is any motion or causation
Argues that there is a first mover which causes all that exists
God is the first efficient cause of the universe
Infinite regression is rejected
God is pure act
Copleston called this an 'ontologically ultimate cause'

Way 3: The argument from contingency
Aquinas argues that God necessarily exists
Criticisms of Way 3
Immanuel Kant rejected Aquinas' Third Way for the same reason that
    he rejected the concept of necessary existence with respect to the
    ontological argument
Mackie questioned the assumption that there is a necessary being and
    that God should be the necessary being

David Hume

Questioned the idea that every effect has the same cause
One cannot always claim or assume that every effect has a necessary cause
The fallacy of composition
Hume questioned whether it is necessary for the whole universe to
    have a cause just because everything that is within the universe
    could be explained by reference to a preceding cause
Bertrand Russell's example: the mother of the human race

The Russell–Copleston debate

Copleston
Presented a reformulation of some of the ideas found in the Third Way
    of Thomas Aquinas
Argued that the universe can only be sufficiently explained by reference
    to God
God is different from contingent beings as he is 'his own sufficient cause'
Argued that explaining why there is a universe is important

Russell
Rejected Copleston's arguments and suggested that the universe was
    not explainable in the way Copleston wanted

Russell argued that whether an explanation for the universe as a whole is possible or not, the explanation is beyond the reach of human beings

It is unnecessary for human beings to have a sufficient explanation of the universe that goes beyond the contingent universe

Russell stated: 'I should say that the universe is just there and that is all.'

REVIEW QUESTIONS

Look back over the chapter and check that you can answer the following questions:

1   Review the information in this chapter about infinite regression. Do you think that the idea of infinite regression is a serious weakness in Aquinas' argument or just philosophical speculation? Justify your answer with reasons.
2   Outline the main steps of Ways 1 to 3.
3   Do Hume's and Mackie's criticisms fatally wound the Cosmological argument?
4   The philosopher Anthony Kenny once used the title of his book *The God of the Philosophers* to refer to the way God is spoken of in arguments such as the Five Ways. What do you think he meant?
5   Is Aquinas' God of the Five Ways the same as the Christian God? Justify your answer with reasons.

Terminology

Do you know your terminology?

1   Try to explain the following ideas without looking at your books and notes:

(a) Necessity and contingency
(b) Infinite regression
(c) First efficient cause.

Examination Questions Practice

The Cosmological argument has been popular for thousands of years in different forms. Make sure that you understand it really well before the examination.

EXAM MISTAKES TO AVOID

Make sure that you use the terminology properly. In addition, when discussing Aquinas' Ways 1 and 2 try to avoid suggesting that God starts the domino chain off, as academic philosophers regard this as an incorrect way of understanding Aquinas.

It is a good idea to work out a quick and easy way of explaining Aquinas' key points before you go into the examination. Remember that in the examination you have to be able to discuss the philosophers' ideas and not just describe them.

The OCR specification states that you must be able to discuss Russell and Copleston's debate. Make sure you understand and can assess the different views that Russell and Copleston presented.

Remember: (a) assesses AO1 and (b) AO2. To help you improve your answers look at the AS Levels of Response. See: http://www.ocr.org.uk/qualifications/as-a-level-gce-religious-studies-h172-h572/

SAMPLE AS EXAM-STYLE QUESTIONS

1 (a) **Explain Hume's criticisms of cosmological arguments.** (25 marks)

Hume criticised the cosmological arguments in many ways. You should give a selection of points in your argument. Avoid the trap of spending all your time describing Hume's ideas and not leaving enough time for the other part of the question.

Points in your answer could include:

* Hume's discussion of infinite regression
* Hume's claim that you cannot move from a thing within the universe existing to the universe itself existing (the fallacy of composition)

* Why Hume argued that you cannot prove that any being is necessary
* Why Hume suggests that some things might be uncaused or have other causes than God
* Why Hume suggested that the universe may not have a cause even if things within it are caused.

(b) **'Hume's criticisms of the Cosmological argument do not succeed.' Discuss.** (10 marks)

There are a lot of ways to approach this question; it is up to you to pick the approach that you think you could use to best effect in an examination. I have suggested two approaches below. You could combine these approaches, focus on only one or, if you can, invent another approach.

- Approach 1: Discuss the criticisms of Hume's arguments, for example by the philosopher G.E. Anscombe
- Approach 2: Discuss some modern philosophers' use of Hume's arguments and whether the modern philosophers approach Hume's ideas positively or negatively. Bertrand Russell would be an example of a person who presents a view similar to that of Hume; Mackie also puts forward arguments that agree with some of Hume's points. Copleston and Anscombe are philosophers who would disagree with some of Hume's ideas.

2 (a) Explain Aquinas' Cosmological argument.

  (b) 'No convincing explanation for the existence of the universe has yet been found.' Discuss.

3 (a) Explain why Hume and Russell reject the Cosmological argument.

  (b) 'God is the most likely explanation for the existence of the universe.' Discuss.

FURTHER READING

The Cosmological argument remains really popular as a topic in modern philosophy. If you would like to extend your reading beyond what the OCR specification requires, you could look at some of the following books:

The philosopher Richard Swinburne has put forward what has become a well-known defence of cosmological arguments which avoids some of the weaknesses of Aquinas' arguments. If you would like to investigate his ideas it is worth looking at two of his books. *Is There a God?* (1996) is an introduction to his ideas about the philosophy of religion and is easier reading than his main work on this topic, entitled *The Existence of God* (2004). Both of these books are published by Oxford University Press.

If you would like to read something about the Big Bang and cosmology by a scientific writer, Paul Davies has written an excellent book called *The Mind of God* (1993).

A modern philosopher's rejection of the Cosmological argument in all its forms may be found in Chapter 5 of *The Miracle of Theism* (1982) by J.L. Mackie. Mackie examines the different forms of Cosmological argument and explains some of the weaknesses found in them.

7 The Teleological Argument

Essential terminology

Assumption
Cause
Effect
Inference
Natural laws
Natural selection
Telos

THE ISSUES

If we examine the world around us, is it obvious that someone designed it? If someone did design the world, was that someone 'God'?

WHAT YOU WILL LEARN ABOUT IN THIS CHAPTER

1   You will be introduced to two of the most famous teleological or design arguments written by Thomas Aquinas and William Paley.
2   You will examine:

(a) Why David Hume thought there could be other explanations for the way the universe is apart from design
(b) Why John Stuart Mill thought the state of the world could mean that its designer, if any, was cruel
(c) Why some biologists think that the apparently sophisticated design of living organisms can be explained by science without any need to believe in a creator.

Key scholars

Thomas Aquinas
(1225–1274)
David Hume (1711–1776)
William Paley (1743–1805)
Thomas Malthus
(1766–1834)
John Stuart Mill
(1806–1873)
Charles Darwin
(1809–1882)

STARTER

Look at the pictures overleaf and try to answer the following questions:

1   Which picture(s) show(s) things that have been designed? List the features of these things that show they have been designed.
2   What purpose, if any, do the things in the picture have?
3   Is there any evidence that the things in the picture were made or designed by someone/something?

Thought Point

Do something!

If you have access to a dartboard, throw some darts at it. If not, try taking penalties as in a football match.

If you miss, who or what is to blame? The darts? The football? Why do the darts/football move at all?

The Teleological argument from Aquinas and Paley; challenges from Hume, Mill and Darwin

Candidates should be able to demonstrate knowledge and understanding of:

* the teleological argument from Aquinas and Paley;
* the challenges to it from Hume, Mill and Darwinism.

Candidates should be able to discuss critically these views and their strengths and weaknesses.

From OCR A Level Religious Studies specification H172.

TELOS AND TELEOLOGICAL ARGUMENTS

'*Telos*' is the Greek word for the end or result of some course of action.

The phrase *teleological argument* is used to refer to arguments for God's existence which work by looking at things in the universe and trying to show that they have been designed for some reason or purpose (e.g. you could say the human ear is fit for hearing and that is its purpose). For some people the question that then arises is: has the ear been designed for this purpose? If so, by whom? If not, why is it so suited for hearing?

Teleological arguments explore whether there is a designer of things that appear to have been designed, and whether the designer is God.

The teleological argument, like the Cosmological argument, is an example of an *a posteriori* argument. In this case the argument starts from observing apparent design and order in the natural world and tries to demonstrate that there is a designer of it. This is the evidence from which the argument is developed, as we shall see below.

The teleological argument is backward-looking, meaning that it starts from the results and tries to work out what causes the result.

For example, if you found a mobile telephone and you had never seen one before, you could examine the mobile telephone and work out whether it had:

1   A purpose or function
2   Parts that fit together to achieve any function or purpose.

THE TYPES OF TELEOLOGICAL ARGUMENT

It is important to be clear that philosophers often divided teleological arguments into two types:

1   *Arguments based on purpose* (e.g. William Paley's ideas)
2   *Arguments based on regularity* (e.g. Thomas Aquinas' ideas).

Paley's and Aquinas' ideas and the meaning of these two types of argument are explained below.

TELEOLOGICAL ARGUMENTS BY THOMAS AQUINAS

As already shown in Chapter 6 on the Cosmological argument, Thomas Aquinas set out Five Ways (Aquinas, *Summa Theologiae*) in which he thought he could demonstrate that God exists. The last of these Five Ways is a form of design argument. A summary of it is set out below:

1   When you look at the natural world you can see that everything in it follows natural laws, even if the things are not conscious, thinking beings.
2   If things follow natural laws they tend to do well and have some goal or purpose.
3   However, if a thing cannot think for itself it does not have any goal or purpose unless it is directed by something that thinks:

> Take an arrow as an example. It can only be directed to its goal and used for its purpose by someone, such as an archer.

4   **Conclusion**: Everything in the natural world that does not think for itself heads towards its goal or purpose because it is directed by something which does think. That something we call 'God'.

Note what Aquinas wrote next:

> Similarly, even though human beings think for themselves and cause things to be aimed at some goal or result, the reason why human beings exist has to be explained, as human beings are not immortal and die.

Telos

The Greek word for 'end' or 'result' of a process or course of action.

Assumption

A belief or statement which is accepted without being supported by evidence or argument.

Inference

The philosophical word for a conclusion that is reached through a process of reasoning in an argument.

Aristotle and Aquinas

Aquinas read and used Aristotle's philosophy. It is a good idea to revise Aristotle while studying the teleological argument.

WHAT IS AQUINAS SAYING?

Aquinas' key claim is that everything in the natural world is directed to some goal and follows natural laws, whether intelligent or not. For example, if you drop anything, it falls, obeying the law of gravity.

Aquinas suggests that the reason for this is that natural laws direct things and these were set up by something which thinks (i.e. God).

Argument by regularity

It is very important to note that Aquinas' argument is in favour of what is called *regularity of succession*. This means that he bases his argument on the fact that things in nature follow certain laws that lead to certain results. For example, if you let go of a glass and it falls to the floor, the event that follows is that the glass smashes. Natural laws are often given by philosophers as examples of regularities of succession, by which they mean that events follow scientific laws that are predictable, regular and unvarying.

A good example is the aforementioned law of gravity.

Aquinas' own example is of an archer shooting an arrow. He implies that just as the arrow goes nowhere without an archer to shoot it, so everything in the natural world that does not think for itself needs to be directed to follow natural laws by something intelligent. He concludes that this intelligent thing is God. The argument could be set out as follows:

1 An arrow hits a target even though it does not have a mind of its own (*an effect*).
2 The archer (someone with a mind of their own) shot the arrow (*a cause*).
3 Things in the natural world follow natural laws even though they do not necessarily have a mind of their own (*an effect*).
4 Someone with a mind of their own caused the natural world to behave in this way. We call this someone God (*a cause*).

Of course the appropriateness of this analogy to the argument concerning natural laws can be questioned, because one could argue that an arrow being shot at a target is of a very different order and type from things following natural laws.

Natural laws

When discussing the teleological argument, this phrase refers to the physical laws of science such as gravity. It must not be confused with the ethical theory called natural (moral) law.

Effect

The result of a *cause*. For example, the *cause* of a football flying through the air would be the person who kicked it. The *effect* is the result of the action – in this case the ball moving. For more information about *cause* and *effect* see the section on Aristotle.

Weaknesses of analogies

For more information about weaknesses of analogies, see the section on David Hume (pp. 130ff.).

Cause

That which produces an effect; that which gives rise to any action, phenomenon, or condition. In philosophy this concept is often linked to the so-called Four Causes of Aristotle.

Thought Point

Can you recall the Four Causes of Aristotle and what they are? Try to explain them without looking at your notes, and then check your answers.

Aristotle and Aquinas

It is important to remember that Aquinas was a follower of Aristotle, and Aquinas' teleological argument is influenced by Aristotle's theory of the Four Causes. Aristotle linked the Final Cause to God. What Aquinas does is link Aristotle's idea of a *Final Cause* to the Christian God (which is quite different from Aristotle's idea of God). So, for Aquinas, the first and the final cause that things have a particular design, goal and purpose and follow natural laws is because of God.

The argument links in with Aristotle's thinking and the Cosmological argument. Aquinas is implying that while human beings do exist and think for themselves, ultimately the reason why they exist is because an uncaused cause made the natural laws that led to Human existence (i.e. God). This last part of the argument links in with Ways 1 and 2, which are forms of the Cosmological argument.

Cosmological arguments

For more information about the Cosmological argument see Chapter 6.

WEAKNESSES IN AQUINAS' ARGUMENT

It is very important to note the assumptions that Aquinas makes in his argument, as he does not provide evidence to support them:

1   Aquinas assumes that things in the natural world have some purpose and are aimed at some goal. He never provides examples to back this up. However, to be fair to Aquinas, he does explain this point in much greater depth in a separate book called *On the Truth* (Aquinas, *De Veritate*) in which he discusses God's providence.

Natural selection

For more information see pp. 136ff. below.

2   Is it correct to assume that everything follows a general law set down by a designer? Some people would say that the natural world is just the way it is and that does not mean it has a purpose given to it by a designer. The philosopher Anthony Flew suggests that Aquinas' claim that things in nature are directed to some purpose goes against the available evidence.

3   Richard Swinburne has pointed out that Aquinas' argument is not entirely satisfactory as it states that 'everything in the natural world that does not think for itself heads towards its goal or purpose because it is

directed by something which does think'. Swinburne claims that this is mistaken as it assumes what is at issue – whether God imposes regularity and laws on the universe (Swinburne, 'The Argument from Design').

Thought Point

A problem

If you found a rock, an orange and a mobile telephone on the ground, which one would you say was suited to a particular purpose or activity? Why would you make this choice?

If you had never seen any of these objects before, would there be any way of deciding whether the objects occurred 'just like that' or whether they were 'designed'?

WILLIAM PALEY'S TELEOLOGICAL ARGUMENT

William Paley's argument claims that you can clearly distinguish rocks from objects that are designed. He argued that the natural world was full of apparent examples of design. His most famous argument compares a stone and a watch. It comprises two parts:

Part 1

1   Paley suggested that if you went for a walk and found a stone, you could conclude that it had been there forever and not think any more about it. Whereas if you found a watch (an old-fashioned watch with cogs and springs) you could examine it and find that it had moving parts which demonstrate that:

    (a) The watch was for a *purpose*: telling the time
    (b) The parts *work together* or are *fit* for a purpose

Paley the man (1743–1805)

William Paley was Archdeacon of Carlisle. He was fascinated by discoveries being made about the natural world in his time, particularly the increase in knowledge of the complex organs and systems in the bodies of people and animals. He was famously impressed by the structure of the human eye: its sophistication, complexity, its fitness for seeing and so forth. This fascination with the natural world influenced his book *Natural Theology: or, Evidences of the Existence and Attributes of the Deity*, which was published in 1802.

(c) The parts are *ordered* and put together in a certain way to make the watch function

(d) If the parts are *arranged* in a different way the watch does not work, i.e. it does not fulfil its purpose.

This first part of the watch analogy is known as *design qua purpose*.

2   **Conclusion**: the watch had a maker who 'must have existed, at some time, and at some place or other, an artificer or artificers who formed it for the purpose which we find it actually to answer; who comprehended its construction and designed its use' (Paley, *Natural Theology*).

Paley also stated that it does not matter if the watch sometimes goes wrong or is not perfect. The point is that the watch's existence suggests it was designed for a purpose. This point is important when you study David Hume's writings about the teleological argument.

Part 2

Paley continues his watch analogy with his inductive argument:

1   Suppose the watch had another imaginary function: that of producing other watches.
2   If this were the case, your admiration for the watch and therefore the watchmaker would be increased.
3   Conclusion: Any person finding such a watch would conclude that the design of the watch implies 'the presence of intelligence and mind' (Paley, Natural Theology).

Paley also used evidence from astronomy and Newton's laws of motion and gravity to prove design in the universe. The universal laws governing the rotation of the planets could not, he said have come about by chance. This is *design qua regularity*.

What does the watch analogy show?

Paley argued that just as the watch being designed necessitates a designer to explain why it exists, so by analogy all of nature requires a much greater designer. Paley pointed out that the complexity of nature is far greater than any machine human beings can make. Thus the whole of nature requires a grand designer. That designer is God.

One famous example Paley gave to illustrate this is that of the complexity of the human eye.

It is most important that you understand the analogy that Paley's argument makes. It could be simply set out as follows:

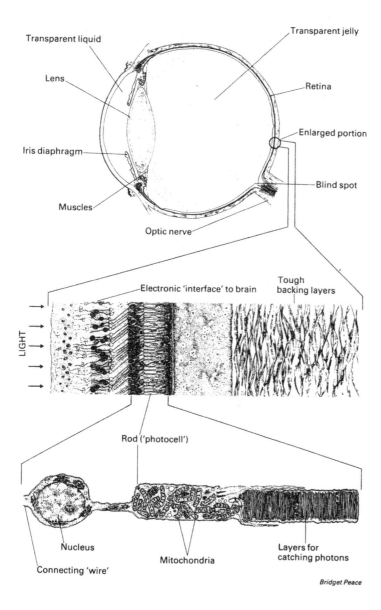

Bridget Peace

1 **Proportion** – telling us the extent to which a thing corresponds to what it should be
2 **Attribution** – telling us about the qualities of a particular thing.

'The Human Eye' by Bridget Pearce, from *The Blind Watchmaker* by Richard Dawkins

1 A watch is a machine designed for the purpose of telling the time (an effect).
2 The features of design in the watch suggest an intelligent designer (a cause).

3   The natural world and, in fact, all of the universe show features of design (an effect).
4   Conclusion: Therefore, the universe must have an intelligent designer (a cause).

Thought Point

Think about why Paley would liken the working of the natural world to that of a watch. Why is Paley's assumption considered to be weak by many philosophers?

Note the assumption that supports the analogy. Paley's watch is a machine – it is mechanistic. Paley's analogy assumes that the natural world is mechanistic in a similar manner to a watch.

One weakness of using analogy is that Paley's argument is only as strong as his analogy. For example, Paley is impressed with the human eye, but would it really be appropriate to compare the working of an eye to that of a camera?

Many writers have criticised the comparison Paley makes of nature with machines, arguing that the natural world is not mechanistic in the sense of a man-made machine.

Thought Point

Give a reason why the natural world is not like a machine.

If you do not believe that the elements in the analogy are comparable, you cannot argue that the causes of each effect are similar, so the analogy would not work.

How is Paley's argument different from that of Aquinas?

Paley's argument is different from that of Aquinas in one very important way. Paley focuses on the manner in which things like a watch fit together in a particular way for a purpose. Hence, this type of argument is sometimes called a *purpose argument*.

Paley was, as already noted, famously impressed with the human eye, the complexity of its parts and the way in which the parts fit together for the purpose of seeing. He is not commenting on one thing following another according to some law, as Aquinas argued.

CRITICISMS OF PALEY'S ARGUMENT

William Paley himself identified a number of potential weaknesses in his argument and attempted to respond to these weaknesses.

One important point he makes is that it is not enough to suggest that things happen because they follow some general law. He suggests that it is meaningless to talk about natural laws without presuming an agent responsible for these laws. Is this claim correct? The question is much debated.

However, it is in the writings of David Hume that the weaknesses of arguments such as Paley's have been most famously stated.

> ## *Thought Point*
>
> ### David Hume's books
>
> When was David Hume's *Dialogues Concerning Natural Religion* first published? Why does the date matter?
>
> The answer is important: William Paley published his book 23 years after David Hume's book was published. Curiously this was 27 years after Hume's death, as *Dialogues Concerning Natural Religion* was published posthumously. Do not make the mistake of claiming that David Hume criticised William Paley. It is much better to point out that Paley tried to respond to some of the criticisms of teleological arguments that were being made around that time. Some of Paley's responses are explained in the main text.

DAVID HUME'S CRITICISM OF TELEOLOGICAL ARGUMENTS

The year 1779 saw the first publication of David Hume's book *Dialogues Concerning Natural Religion*. In it he suggests a number of weaknesses found in teleological arguments which are based on analogy,

Hume the man (1711–1776)

David Hume was born in Edinburgh and went to university there. As a young man he became passionately interested in philosophy and started to develop the ideas for which he would become famous posthumously. During his life he worked as a clerk for a sugar merchant, and later carried out diplomatic work in Vienna and Turin. However, in later life, while working as a librarian in Edinburgh, he published his *History of England* (1754–1762) which became a bestseller. It was this book of history rather than his philosophy which made him famous in his own lifetime. His *Dialogues Concerning Natural Religion* was published in 1779.

such as Aquinas' and Paley's arguments. Some of these criticisms are outlined below.

Why David Hume rejected the use of analogy to prove the teleological argument

1   Hume argues that analogy is, in general, limited in strength to the points of similarity of the two or more things being compared. He suggests the example of concluding from a study of the human blood circulatory system that by analogy animals had the same system. However, he then states that it would be a weak and in fact mistaken analogy to compare human or animal circulatory systems with the way sap circulates in a plant. His argument is that the analogy is not very close.

It is important to note that this criticism applies directly to Paley's watch analogy. However, because Aquinas' argument focuses on things following natural laws, this criticism does not apply to his argument, though it may apply to Aquinas' archer example.

2   Hume gives a second analogy. He suggests that we can conclude that a house had a builder and an architect. He argues that we cannot deduce a builder or architect of the universe in the same way, as there is no similarity between the two. Equally, if the house is faulty, what does this suggest about the designer? If God does design the world, is God directly responsible for evil within it?

However, it is worth noting that Paley rejected this point because he considered the issue to be whether the universe exhibited signs of design; he was not concerned with questions relating to issues of quality concerning the design. Is Paley's response satisfactory? If God is directly responsible for the purpose of the designed thing, then any negative results from the design are God's responsibility. These issues are examined in greater depth in Chapter 9 concerning the problem of evil.

3   Hume concludes that there is nothing within the universe to which a universe can satisfactorily be compared. Therefore, any argument by analogy is weak from when it begins because it relies on experience. We do not have any other universe-like objects to which we can compare our universe to infer that it has an intelligent designer.

Hume is not here doubting belief in a God or deity, but is questioning whether the teleological argument can show that God or a deity exists. However, William Paley rejected this type of argument by claiming that lack of knowledge of how to make something only increases our sense of wonder at the individual who can make such a rare object (e.g. think of the skill required to make a mobile telephone). Most people do not know how to make them, but Paley might say that it does not stop us concluding something about the nature of the person who designed it.

The philosopher of religion Richard Swinburne disputes Hume's point. He suggests that if you have any explanation for why some event occurs, then it would be reasonable to say more about the cause of the event other than just *it causes the event*.

An example may help to illustrate this point. If a window gets broken because a football hits it, it would be quite reasonable to decide that something caused the football to go through the window, and that it has other characteristics than just causing footballs to go through windows. Furthermore, Swinburne adds that just because the universe is 'singular' – meaning: one of a kind, unlike anything else – this is not a reason to say that we cannot deduce anything about the regularity found within the universe. He gives the example of cosmologists investigating the origins and development of the universe and their investigation of the general laws of science which govern the whole universe.

Why David Hume argues that there are other possible explanations than God for apparent design in the universe

1   As well as the possibility that there is a grand designer of the universe, Hume argues that it is equally possible that 'matter may contain the spring of order originally within itself, as well as mind does' (Hume, 'Dialogues Concerning Natural Religion'). Hume then argues that unless there is perfect similarity between the object of comparison and what is being compared, you cannot draw a conclusion with any certainty.

Is this fair? Certainly many scientists in their work would investigate the properties of one substance by making comparisons with other substances that seem to be similar and then testing the comparisons. One example of this is the way in which similar properties of groups of elements in the periodic table can be inferred (worked out) from knowledge of the properties of one element in a group.

2   Any effects we observe within nature may be caused by a wide variety of causes. This insight has gained support in the modern world from the discovery of natural selection, not to mention DNA and its role in shaping the growth of all living organisms. Hume suggests that philosophers should be different from the 'precipitate march of the vulgar' (i.e. ordinary people). What he meant is that philosophers should clearly investigate the relationship between each effect and its cause(s) and not just follow opinions that are fashionable with the general public.

Natural selection
The phrase coined by Charles Darwin to explain his idea that: 'If variations useful to any organic being ever do occur, assuredly individuals thus characterised will have the best chance of being preserved in the struggle for life; and for the strong principle of inheritance, these will tend to produce offspring similarly characterised' (in M. Palmer, *The Question of God*).

However, although theists would not dispute this point, they could equally well suggest that their investigations of examples of order in the universe suggest that there is an intelligent designer.

3   Hume asks on what grounds we should compare our intelligent design of things with a possible cause of the universe as a whole, and he questions whether there is evidence that the world has a single designer. He suggests the analogy of a great ship. We may look at it and think 'Wow! What a great design', but actually the ship may be the result of years, even generations, of trial and error. Second, the ship may actually be the product of many hands, not just one great designer. This leads him to conclude that there is no evidence to suggest the 'unity of the deity' (Hume, 'Dialogues Concerning Natural Religion'). In addition, Hume argues that we could just as well say that the universe is one attempt among a limited number of others, so it was bound to happen like this.

However, some philosophers, such as Richard Swinburne, have disagreed with this because they claim that it is making the explanation more complex than it need be, in other words breaking the philosophical principle often known as *Ockham's Razor*. Hume claimed that this principle did not apply to the universe because it is a matter of debate whether one or more gods caused the universe. Richard Swinburne makes two important points in reply:

> When postulating entities postulate as few as possible. Also, suppose one murderer, unless the evidence forces you to suppose a second. If there were more than one deity responsible for the order of the Universe, we should expect to see the characteristics of different deities in different parts of the Universe, just as we see different kinds of workmanship in different houses of a city . . . it is enough to draw this absurd conclusion to see how ridiculous the Humean objection is. ('The Argument from Design')

Why Hume argues that random activity can lead to orderliness rather than disorder

1   Hume also considers the idea that matter may have first been arranged at random, by pure chance. He considers that if whatever force started the universe is to continue in motion, the tendency will be to move from disorder to order, so we could get an ordered world to live in out of disordered chaos in the past, i.e. the universe is the way it is and has life in it because of random changes tending to bring about order rather than disorder, not because anyone directed these changes in a particular

Ockham's Razor

A philosophical principle named after William Ockham, a fourteenth-century English philosopher and friar. The principle states: 'Do not multiply entities beyond necessity.' It is used in philosophy to suggest that when explaining anything you should do so in the most straightforward way possible, because usually the simplest explanation of any event or occurrence is the correct one. Often, Ockham's Razor is expressed as 'the simplest explanation is usually the best one'.

However, Paley's criticism does not quite address the issue Hume raises. Hume is claiming that random changes will tend to orderly situations rather than disorder, as disorder brings the process of change to an end, whereas order may continue the process of change. Hume's idea would later be seen more positively due to the work of Charles Darwin (see pp. 135ff. below).

way. (You may find some books refer to this as the Epicurean hypothesis, since the idea of random arrangement of matter can be traced back to the writing of the Greek philosopher Epicurus.)

However, Paley himself rejected this kind of argument as unsatisfactory, i.e. to attribute something so clearly ordered as a watch to luck:

> Nor . . . would any man in his senses think the watch, with its various machinery, accounted for, by being told that it was one out of possible combinations of material forms. (*Natural Theology*)

Thought Point

Look at the weather outside today. Can you explain all the different possible causes that make the weather as it is? Is it a matter of chance whether it is sunny, cloudy or rainy?

Swinburne has rejected this criticism because he claims that over time we have more and more evidence of events following each other in a regular way. He gives the example that while:

> in 1960 matter is behaving in a regular way, our claim [Hume's] becomes less and less plausible as we find that in 1961 and 1962 and so on it [the universe] continues to behave in a regular way. ('The Argument from Design')

This may, perhaps, defend Aquinas' argument but not Paley's, which focuses on examples of order being found in the world.

WHERE DO HUME'S IDEAS LEAVE THE TELEOLOGICAL ARGUMENT?

It is important to realise that David Hume criticises the teleological argument, but he does not suggest any alternative to the teleological argument that would explain the apparent order and design that can be seen in the world. As one scientist of today has put it:

> That great Scottish philosopher disposed of the Argument from Design a century before Darwin. But what Hume did was criticise the

logic of using apparent design in nature as positive evidence for the existence of a God. He did not offer any alternative explanation for apparent design, but left the question open. (Dawkins, *The Blind Watchmaker*)

MILL AND TELEOLOGICAL ARGUMENTS

John Stuart Mill is more famous for his work on liberty, ethics and utility theory. However, within his work on *Nature, the Utility of Religion, and Theism*, first published in 1874, Mill raised a most important question that has challenged religious belief from ancient times. He questioned the goodness of nature given the apparent cruelty to be found within nature. One example given by Richard Dawkins may serve to illustrate:

> A female digger wasp not only lays her egg in a caterpillar (or grasshopper or bee) so that her larva can feed on it but, according to Fabre and others, she carefully guides her sting into each ganglion of the prey's central nervous system, so as to paralyse it but not kill it. (*River Out of Eden*)

Mill and others have considered the state of nature to be a reason to reject notions of design. In particular, you should note that if the suffering of animals is included in a calculation of the amount of suffering in the world, the amount of goodness in nature is far outweighed by the amount of suffering.

Two points should be noted here:

1   Whether terms like 'cruel' can suitably be applied to nature, and what the state of the world might suggest about any designer, are valid questions and they are examined in greater depth in Chapter 9 concerning the problem of evil.
2   Paley's and Aquinas' question concerned whether the universe exhibits signs of design that point to a designer; they were not at that point concerned with questions raised by the nature of the design (though both addressed this topic separately). It is worth noting that Paley made this very point within his discussion of the watch analogy and that Aquinas' Five Ways in his opinion demonstrate 'that which we call God'. Aquinas spent much of his book *Summa Theologiae*, in which the Five Ways are presented, exploring the nature of God, including whether the existence of suffering in nature challenges belief in a designer.

DARWIN'S GREAT IDEA

Thought Point

Who was Charles Darwin? Why is he famous?

The voyage of the Beagle

During the voyage of HMS *Beagle*, Darwin studied a range of species found on the Galapagos Archipelago. He noticed that many species on the islands first seemed to be the same but, actually, when studied more closely, were slightly different. Perhaps his most famous example is that of finches. He noticed that, on the different islands, the species of finches were not the same but varied slightly. For example, the shape of the different species of finches' beaks corresponded to the type of food they ate. Some of them had beaks suitable for crushing seeds, others for biting insects. Darwin realised that very small changes from one generation to the next, over time, would build up into large changes. This idea was partly inspired by reading Sir Charles Lyell's *Principles of Geology* (1830–33) which proposed that the Earth's landscape had developed through a process of small changes over thousands of years and not as a result of catastrophes in the past, such as Noah's flood.

Darwin's second important insight came from reading the work of Thomas Malthus (1766–1834).

Thomas Malthus' idea

Malthus put forward the idea that food supplies increase arithmetically and population grows exponentially: 'The power of population is indefinitely greater than the power in the earth to produce subsistence for man' (*An Essay on the Principle of Population*). As a cleric, Malthus saw this situation as divinely imposed to teach virtuous behaviour. Malthus wrote:

> that the increase of population is necessarily limited by the means of subsistence; that population does invariably increase when the means of subsistence increase, and, that the superior power of population is repressed, and the actual population kept equal to the means of subsistence, by misery and vice

Darwin the man (1809–1882)

Charles Darwin came from an educated and wealthy background. Having commenced university life studying medicine, and later divinity, he became interested in botany – the study of plants. As a result, at the age of 22, he became the ship's naturalist on the now famous voyage of HMS *Beagle*. During the five-year mission of the ship he studied a huge range of plants and animals, and he began to think about the 'species problem'. By the phrase 'the species problem', Darwin meant the question concerning the origins, development and relationship of different species. By 1842 he had developed an outline of what would eventually become his famous theory of evolution by 'natural selection'. His most famous work, *On the Origin of Species*, was published in 1859 and became a bestseller. He went on to write other works developing and expanding on his idea. He died in 1882 and is buried in Westminster Abbey.

What this means is that if you start off with a small population, the population will grow with each child probably having more than one child themselves, so that over time the effect is that the population increases. Malthus was arguing that the Earth regulated its population growth. Of course, if modern medicine is available, disease will not kill as many members of a population as Malthus predicted, challenging his idea of the Earth regulating its growth.

From Malthus' work, Darwin realised that species die if they reproduce in excess of the food supply and this led him to develop the idea that 'life struggles to exist'. What Darwin went on to realise is that if two organisms are competing for food and one organism has evolved in a way that makes it better at getting food than the other, this species will thrive while the other one will die out. Darwin also realised, though he could not explain why it happened, that the offspring of parents, whether animal or human, inherit a mixture of characteristics from their parents. The word in biology for this is that there is variation. For example, children are similar to their parents, not the same as them. If one of these characteristics gave you an advantage over a person lacking it, Darwin argued that the advantageous characteristic would be more likely to be passed on to the next generation. Think about why.

Thought Point

The albino

Albinos are very rare. The word refers to a member of any species that has completely white skin, lacking any colour pigment whatsoever. Suppose you are an albino lion living in the grassland savannah of Africa. What disadvantage would you have compared with other lions that have orange-brown skin?

Natural selection

Darwin called his idea *natural selection*. By this he meant that if small variations in a living organism's characteristics occur from one generation to the next, an organism with an advantageous characteristic, such as running faster or better hunting skills, will be at an advantage over others and will be more likely to survive. For example, sickle-cell anaemia is a distressing and incurable genetic illness (you cannot catch it) caused by red blood vessels being misshapen. It is very common in some parts of the world. What is interesting is that, originally, it came from a part of the world where malaria is endemic, and sickle-cell anaemia gives the person suffering from it resistance to catching malaria. In other words, there was an advantage to having it in the area from where the illness originates.

Darwin himself wrote that:

> If variations useful to any organic being ever do occur, assuredly individuals thus characterised will have the best chance of being preserved in the struggle for life; and for the strong principle of inheritance, these will tend to produce offspring similarly characterised. This principle of preservation, or the survival of the fittest, I have called Natural Selection. (*On the Origin of Species*)

How does natural selection relate to the teleological argument?

Natural selection raises a very important challenge to the teleological argument because it provides a way to explain how Paley's examples of regularity and order in the world, like an eye, can exist without referring to a designer. Darwin showed very clearly why beneficial characteristics would be passed on more favourably to the next generation than non-beneficial ones. This would support Hume's suggestion that there may be other explanations of apparent design in the universe than a designer and fits in with Hume's argument above.

The reason why natural selection is such a challenge to the teleological argument is that the process of natural selection has been demonstrated to be true by numerous scientific studies of the natural world.

IS THE GOD OF THE TELEOLOGICAL ARGUMENT ANYTHING LIKE THE CHRISTIAN IDEA OF GOD?

It is very important to realise that the teleological argument is not proving the existence of the personal God of the Christian religion. It is not about showing that God the Creator is a caring figure, like a father, or any other biblical idea of God. The teleological argument is concerned with whether there is a designer of the universe. Christians would not dispute the belief that God designed or created the universe, but they would want to say more than this alone.

Is the teleological argument of value today?

What does the teleological argument prove? The answer really depends on who you ask. For some people, it draws attention to the observable order and regularity within the universe, which suggests a designer. For others, the order and regularity in the universe are remarkable but there are other explanations for it, such as natural selection.

1   The teleological argument continues to appeal to philosophers and the wider public, and its truth or falsity has never been demonstrated in such a manner as to end the philosophical debate about it.
2   There are a number of other design arguments by modern writers which avoid or answer the criticisms of Hume and they are worth investigating. Some sources of information are suggested in the 'Further reading' section.
3   Perhaps the truth of the matter is that the teleological argument is a reflection on the questions that arise in people's minds on seeing the wonder of the universe, whether they are atheist, theist or agnostic. The reason why questions concerning the teleological argument continue to interest us is that it is important to know the answer, one way or another.

Thought Point

A question: would you agree with this author? Why?

After sleeping through a hundred million centuries we have finally opened our eyes in a sumptuous planet, sparkling with colour, beautiful with life. Within decades we must close our eyes again. Isn't it a noble, enlightened way of spending our brief time in the sun, to work at understanding the universe and how we have come to wake up on it? . . . To put it the other way round, isn't it sad to go to your grave without ever wondering why you were born? Who, with such a thought, would not spring from his bed, eager to resume discovering the world and rejoicing to be part of it? (Dawkins, *Unweaving the Rainbow*)

SUMMARY

1   The teleological argument

Thomas Aquinas

Way 5 is a design argument
Aquinas argued that everything in the natural world is directed to some
    goal and follows natural laws set up by something which thinks
    (i.e. God)
Regularity of succession argument – Aquinas' archer example
Aquinas was influenced by Aristotle's theory of the Four Causes; he
    links Aristotle's Final Cause to God

Weaknesses in Aquinas' argument
Does everything follow a general law set down by a designer?
Anthony Flew suggests that Aquinas' claim that things in nature are
    directed to some purpose goes against the available evidence
Swinburne claims that Aquinas assumes what is at issue – whether God
    imposes regularity and laws on the universe

William Paley

Paley presents a purpose argument
Paley compares a rock and a watch, and notes that the watch
    demonstrates:

fitness for a purpose
parts work together/fit for a purpose
the parts are ordered

Part 2 of the argument

imaginary function of the watch: producing other watches
watch like this suggests the existence of something conscious and
    intelligent

Argues by analogy that nature requires a much greater designer than
    the watch
The complexity of nature is illustrated by the human eye

2   Challenges to design arguments

David Hume

Nothing to which a universe can be satisfactorily compared
Paley – lack of knowledge increases our sense of wonder

Swinburne – reasonable to say more about the cause of the event other than just it causes the event

Hume's analogy of the house builder and an architect; challenge about the design's quality (the problem of evil)

Paley – rejected this; he considered the issue to be whether the universe exhibited signs of design

There are other possible explanations than God for apparent design in the universe (e.g. DNA today)

Is there evidence that the world has a single designer? The analogy of a great ship

Random activity can lead to orderliness rather than disorder (supported by the discovery of natural selection)

J.S. Mill

Questioned the goodness of nature given the apparent cruelty to be found within nature (e.g. the behaviour of a digger wasp)

Natural selection

Darwin's discovery was influenced by:

Discoveries during the voyage of the *Beagle*

Sir Charles Lyell's *Principles of Geology*

Thomas Malthus' idea that food supplies increase arithmetically and populations grow exponentially

Natural selection can explain the emergence of complex living organisms without any need to refer to design, a designer or purpose

REVIEW QUESTIONS

Look back over the chapter and check that you can answer the following questions:

1   Richard Dawkins entitled a book *The Blind Watchmaker*. What point do you think he was making?
2   Outline Paley's analogy of the watch.
3   In what way is Aquinas' teleological argument different from Paley's?

4 Can you explain the difference between a teleological argument based on order and a teleological argument based on regularity?

5 Read the sections on Paley and Hume again. Which argument is stronger?

6 Charles Darwin once wrote: 'The old argument from design in Nature, as given by Paley, which formerly seemed to me so conclusive, fails, now that the law of natural selection has been discovered.' Explain why Darwin believed 'the old argument from design' now fails (*Charles Darwin and T.H. Huxley: Autobiographies*, ed. G. de Beer).

Terminology

Do you know your terminology?

1 Try to explain the following ideas without looking at your books and notes:

    (a) Variation

    (b) Paley's watch analogy

    (c) Natural selection

    (d) Why Hume would have rejected Paley's watch analogy.

Examination Questions Practice

Remember that Hume wrote before Paley and consequently never criticised Paley directly. It is also worth noting that Darwin certainly read Hume and Paley (we know this from his writings) but he did not come up with his idea of natural selection just to support Hume or weaken Paley's argument; Darwin's ideas are of much greater significance than Hume's or Paley's in terms of their impact on the world of today.

Remember: (a) assesses AO1 and (b) AO2. To help you improve your answers look at the AS Levels of Response. See: http://www.ocr.org.uk/qualifications/as-a-level-gce-religious-studies-h172-h572/

SAMPLE AS EXAM-STYLE QUESTIONS

1   (a) **Explain Paley's teleological argument.**
    (25 marks)

Stick to the question. Describe Paley's argument and do not even mention any other teleological arguments you have studied, but do not just tell the story of Paley walking across the heath. Explain its key points. For example, you could explain that:

- Paley's argument is an analogy.
- The watch shows signs of design, complexity and being fit for a purpose.
- The natural world is compared to the watch; the natural world is likened to a really complex machine.
- Paley compares the watch to examples of complexity in nature which he viewed as far superior (e.g. the human eye).
- Paley's analogy is concerned with the design suggesting a designer; it is not concerned with any other qualities of the designer.

    (b) **'Darwinism shows that Paley's argument is false.' Discuss.** (10 marks)

Do not discuss Hume in your answer. Stick to Darwin and Paley. Remember that you only have a little time in your examination to write your answer to evaluation questions.

- Discuss the significance of Darwin's theory of natural selection as a mechanism to explain why there is apparent order in nature without any need to refer to a designer or creator.

- Refer to the fact that Darwin, because of his life experiences, described himself as an agnostic.
- It is fair to point out that natural selection can be demonstrated by scientific research. Paley's analogy cannot be defended in this way.
- You could argue that while Paley's analogy is problematical, his point that the natural world seems to show signs of design is valid when you look at the sheer complexity of nature and the fact it exists.
- If you have studied creationist criticisms of the idea of evolution by natural selection it may be appropriate to use them here.

2   (a) **Explain criticisms of teleological arguments.**

    (b) **'Mill's objection to teleological arguments is stronger than those of Hume.' Discuss.**

3   (a) **Explain Hume's objections to teleological arguments.**

    (b) **'God is the most likely explanation for design in the universe.' Discuss.**

4   (a) **Explain Aquinas' teleological argument and Darwinist objections to it.**

    (b) **'Arguments from design must fail because they do not prove the existence of a God who is all-powerful.' Discuss.**

FURTHER READING

This chapter has explored what you need to know for the OCR AS Religious Studies examination. However, there are many other important developments and ideas in modern writings about the teleological argument. Some areas for investigation are suggested below:

The Question of God by Michael Palmer is an excellent source of information if you would like to examine the debate concerning Darwin, Hume and Paley in greater depth. Have a look at the chapter on the design argument (pp. 92–179). The book is a great introduction to detailed study of arguments for God's existence and it also contains extended extracts from the original authors' writings.

If you would like to read some short, well-written philosophical articles from today debating the teleological argument, it is well worth having a look at *Think* (summer 2003 and spring 2004). *Think* is the Royal Institute of Philosophy's journal which is designed to be readable by anyone interested in philosophy, not just university professors.

To investigate a modern biologist's view of natural selection and evolution you could read Richard Dawkins' book *The Blind Watchmaker*. This book is eloquently written and sets out in clear terms the theory of evolution as well as Dawkins' own reasons for rejecting teleological arguments and Paley in particular. A general introduction to Richard Dawkins' thinking may be gained by reading his book *River Out of Eden*: *A Darwinian View of Life*.

Essential terminology

Autonomy
Ego
Id
Postulate
Summum bonum
Super-ego

8 The Moral Argument

Key scholars

Immanuel Kant
(1724–1804)
Sigmund Freud
(1856–1939)

THE ISSUE

Does the fact that we have ideas about what is right and wrong mean that God exists?

WHAT YOU WILL LEARN ABOUT IN THIS CHAPTER

1   Why Immanuel Kant argued that moral reasoning had to lead you to the idea that God exists.
2   Why Sigmund Freud's ideas about the mind undermine Kant's moral argument.

STARTER

Consider the following problems and then answer the questions which follow:

1 You are sitting in a back office in the bank when, on the CCTV screen, you see a man burst in, order the customers to lie on the floor and demand money from the bank staff. Would you call the police? Would it make a difference if the man said he was robbing the bank to get cancer treatment for his dying child in the USA?

2 You are sitting on a bus. You notice that a purse has slid down the side of the seat. Opening it up you find £60 inside it and the pension book of an old lady with her address on it. Would you return the purse and its contents to the old lady?

3 You are sitting on a bus. You notice that a purse has slid down the side of the seat. Opening it up you find £60 inside it and the pension book of an old lady. You realise that the pension book belongs to your grandmother. Would you return the purse and its contents to your grandmother?

4 You are shopping in the supermarket. As you walk through the baby food section you notice a scruffy young woman pushing a pram containing two babies. As you watch you realise that she is putting tins of baby food into her handbag, not the basket. Would you tell the security guard?

Questions

1   What would you do in each case?
2   What reasons would you give to explain why, if at all, stealing is wrong in each case?
3   What are the consequences of your action or inaction in each case?
4   Is there one reason that makes taking things without permission wrong in all cases?

INTRODUCTION: CAN WE KNOW GOD EXISTS FROM OUR SENSE OF MORALITY?

This chapter will examine the philosophical idea that we can show the necessity of God existing from the fact that we have a sense of morality.

The phrase 'the moral argument' is used in philosophy of religion to cover a wide range of arguments that use the existence of morality as evidence for God's existence. For example, some people have argued that there is no point in being moral unless God exists, while other people have argued that the fact that there is such a thing as morality is because God made it – i.e. morality depends on God.

Immanuel Kant put forward the most famous of what are now called moral arguments for the existence of God and it is only his argument that you are required to know by OCR. The other moral arguments are very different from Kant's. When you research the moral argument for your AS examination, make sure that you focus your attention on Kant, as it is only his argument with which you have to be familiar.

KANT'S MORAL ARGUMENT

Immanuel Kant's writings contain the most famous example of the moral argument for God's existence. However, it is important to realise that Kant never put forward his argument for God's existence as a free-standing argument like the teleological argument. Instead, Kant's moral argument is part of his ethical theory. It is essential that you understand Kant's ethical theory in order properly to understand Kant's moral argument. According to Kant a moral action must be an autonomous action; it must be completely free.

Kant's moral theory is explained in the *Groundwork of the Metaphysics of Morals* (1785) (*Moral Law*) and tries to show the objectivity of moral judgement and the universal character of moral laws. It attempts to base morality on reason as opposed to feelings, inclinations, consequences or religion. Kant roots his view of morality in reason to the exclusion of everything else, and rejects especially Hume's idea that morality is rooted in desires or feelings. He does not reject desires and feelings, but says that they have nothing to do with morality. Only reason is universal, as feelings can change from person to person and they cannot be autonomous as they simply happen to a person – emotions are a spontaneous reaction to a situation, not a freely chosen response. In the same way any action that seems to be moral cannot be if it is something a person is ordered to do. For example, if a lifeguard rescues a drowning person because he is ordered to do it, this is not, according to Kant, a moral action as he was told to do it and it was not freely chosen. So just because God commands something that does not make it moral as only reason is the basis for morality. Only by exercising reason can a person do a completely free action, and then only if they are able to do it. For example, there is no obligation to jump in and rescue a drowning person if one cannot swim.

According to Kant we have a duty to be moral and to achieve the highest good (the *summum bonum*) which is a combination of virtue (doing one's duty) and happiness. Kant, however, was aware that many people lead morally good lives and yet misfortunes, unhappiness and suffering seem to be their lot in this life. Kant resolves this problem by saying that only if we postulate the existence of God can we be assured of achieving happiness, assured of achieving the *summum bonum*. Additionally if we cannot achieve the *summum bonum* in this life then we will achieve it in the next life, and only a benevolent and omnipotent God can guarantee that we achieve it. Kant does not think that he has proved God's existence, but that without God we cannot fulfil our duty to strive for a life of moral fulfilment and happiness. Only by postulating the existence of God and an afterlife do we have a practical reason to be moral.

Postulate

Kant uses the word postulate to mean 'assuming as true for the purposes of argument or set forward as a plausible hypothesis'.

This can be summarised as follows:

1   We all have an innate moral awareness – from this we have a duty to be virtuous.
2   An average level of virtue is not enough – we must aim for the highest standard possible.
3   True virtue should be rewarded with happiness.
4   There is an ideal state where human virtue and happiness are united which Kant called the *summum bonum*.
5   Kant's moral argument can be summarised as follows: moral statements are prescriptive – 'ought' implies 'can'.
6   Humans can achieve virtue in a lifetime but we cannot be certain that we are rewarded with happiness.
7   Therefore there must be a God who has power to ensure that virtue and happiness coincide.

Kant's moral argument does not postulate that God is necessary for morality but that God is required for morality to achieve its end, 'Therefore it is morally necessary to assume the existence of God.'

Kant's rejection of other forms of argument for God's existence

As seen in previous chapters, Kant rejects arguments that attempt to prove that God exists. Kant argued that because God's existence, or not, was a matter beyond human knowledge, attempts such as the cosmological or design arguments cannot succeed in demonstrating God's existence. However, he [Kant] goes on to argue that: 'It is morally necessary to assume the existence of God' ('Kant: The Existence of God as a Postulate of Pure Practical Reason', in M. Palmer, *The Question of God*).

WHAT DOES 'GOD AS A POSTULATE OF PURE REASON' MEAN?

By this phrase, Kant meant that through rational moral reasoning we end up having to put forward the idea that God exists as part of our explanation of morality. Kant uses the word *postulate* to mean something which is thought of and put forward (postulated) as a rational way of solving a problem.

So Kant is saying that in order to explain morality you have to include the belief that God exists. Kant would say that he was 'morally certain' God exists; but this is not the same as a traditional argument to prove that God exists.

Autonomy

Liberty to follow one's will; personal freedom. Used in philosophy to refer to a person who is able to exercise free will to make decisions. It literally means self-governing. If you are autonomous you are able to use reason to make your own free choices.

THE BACKGROUND TO KANT'S MORAL ARGUMENT

His ethics

The key ideas

The following ideas from Kant's ethical theory are very important. They are summarised below. You should make sure that you understand the ethical theory fully and how to apply it.

1 Kant emphasises the autonomy of morality

Autonomy

What Kant meant by this is that an action is only a matter of morality if this action is one that has been freely chosen. An action is a moral one if you choose to do it. For example, if you choose to rob a bank, that is your moral choice. If, on the other hand, you are a paranoid schizophrenic who hears voices telling you to rob the bank and you then do it, this is not a moral decision, as paranoid schizophrenics are incapable of distinguishing between voices and thoughts they hear in their mind and in reality. It is important to note that we, as human beings, experience ourselves as autonomous decision-makers in daily life.

Autonomy also leads Kant to reject the idea that God is a divine lawgiver who orders people to follow his rules out of fear of punishment.

2 If we are autonomous what is morally right behaviour?

Do your duty

Kant aimed to work out the principle of moral behaviour bearing in mind that we are autonomous human beings. Kant wanted to establish a universal basis for morality. He observed that all people impose moral duties on themselves and this leads him to question what is the good reason itself for moral action. Kant concludes that the only intrinsically good reason for moral action is the 'good will'.

Act according to the good will

By this Kant meant that you do an action because it is good to do, not because of any consequences such as: making you happy, making a profit, getting a result, and so on. Kant gave the example of a shopkeeper not overcharging his customers and explained that the only intrinsically good reason for not stealing from your customers is because it is wrong to do so.

Good moral actions are aimed at the highest good (the summum bonum)

Kant concludes that the act which is in accordance with the 'good will' is doing an action because it is the right thing to do and it achieves the *summum bonum* (the highest good). Kant called this idea the 'categorical imperative'. The word 'imperative' means a command or duty and the word 'categorical' means something that you 'have to do'. So, for Kant, your duty is something you should do – philosophically something you 'ought to do'. It is important to note that consequences do not matter. So, if it is your duty to tell the truth, you should tell the truth, whatever the consequences or cost of doing this.

3 What is meant by the summum bonum?

For Kant, the *summum bonum* or highest good is the achievement of moral goodness (virtue) and happiness together. What Kant meant by this is that the moral action is the one that is right to do – i.e. your duty – and also that because the action is virtuous it should lead to happiness and fulfilment.

4 How do you work out what is your duty?

Moral duties are the same universally

Kant stated that your duty is something which you work out through reason, and consequently it is something which applies universally. What this means is that an action that is truly the right thing to do does not depend on any factors such as whether doing the action will harm you or benefit you. The action is good to do because it is good to do. This leads Kant to suggest that through reason we can work out what is the right thing to do because the right thing to do has to be applicable universally – everywhere. Thus Kant suggested that a principle like 'break promises whenever it suits you' is not a duty because if everyone, universally, broke promises whenever they liked, the idea of promise-keeping would be meaningless.

5 What does Kant mean by God's law?

God's moral law is followed by acting according to reason alone

Kant rejects any idea that God makes laws we have to obey because that stops people being autonomous. Instead, he suggests that we act according to the moral law by following reason. What exactly Kant means by God's will is unclear.

Summum bonum

Summum bonum

Literally means the highest good. In Kant's moral thinking the *summum bonum* is the final goal or aim of all moral actions. For Kant the *summum bonum* is the act of both doing your moral duty and willing that doing your duty is rewarded with (or results in) a state of happiness and fulfilment.

KANT'S MORAL ARGUMENT

Kant's moral argument follows on from his conclusion that one's moral duty is known through reason. He argues that it would be illogical for the point of acting morally (the achievement of the *summum bonum*) to not be possible. Kant's argument could be summarised as follows:

In steps 1 and 2 the suggestion is that human beings can work out their moral duty by reason and they should aim to succeed in their moral duty – i.e. achieve the *summum bonum* of moral goodness (virtue) and happiness.

By the 'highest good' in step 2 Kant means two things. First, that you should do what is moral – i.e. your duty. Second, doing your duty should bring you fulfilment *because* it is the right thing to do.

Why do your duty if it will not lead to virtue and happiness?
Kant's answer is important. He argues that you ought to do your duty if it can be achieved, so duty can lead to moral goodness and happiness. Kant's argument is that doing your duty is either meaningful or it is not. He rejects the idea that concepts of duty and moral goodness are meaningless as this idea does not fit in with human experience. Kant points out quite clearly that we experience ourselves as being subject to moral values, duties and laws.

The important point in Kant's argument is at step 3. Kant accepts that the reality of the world will often mean that doing your duty and being morally virtuous in your behaviour do not always lead to happiness and fulfilment. For example, think of the phrase 'crime does not pay' – is this really true? In many situations around the world you can observe that crime does seem to pay; corruption makes you wealthy; honesty is viewed as a weakness to be exploited and loyalty is regarded as outdated. For Kant this is a real problem. Kant says do your duty because it's the right thing to do; happiness can result from doing the right thing, but it is never a motive for morally good actions. Kant is well aware that doing your duty sounds distinctly unappealing if ultimately it will not lead to the *summum bonum* – moral goodness (virtue) and happiness.

He then asks the crucial question: *How is doing your duty 'meaningful' if you cannot guarantee that the summum bonum will be achieved in this world?* His answer: you have to postulate (put forward) the idea of God's existence as a matter of reason. God's existence is the guarantee that ultimately moral virtue and goodness (the *summum bonum*) go together and are achievable.

1   Moral action is about doing one's duty.

2   The reason to do one's duty is to achieve the *summum bonum* (the highest good).

3   However, in the world people can do their duty and yet still not achieve happiness because of corruption and wickedness in the world. If the highest good is not achievable, what is the point of aiming to achieve it?

4   Therefore, the highest good must be achievable.

5   What could make the highest good achievable?

6   Answer: God.

7   Therefore, we should postulate the existence of God.

Kant's own words

[H]appiness is the condition of a rational being in the world, in whose whole existence everything goes according to wish and will.... Not being nature's causes, his will cannot by its own strength bring nature, as it touches on happiness, into complete harmony with his practical principles. Nevertheless, in the practical task of pure reason, i.e., in the necessary endeavour after the highest good, such a connection [i.e. a correspondence between virtue and happiness] is postulated as necessary: we should seek to further the highest good (which therefore must be at least possible). Therefore the existence is postulated of a cause of the whole of nature, itself distinct from nature, which contains the ground of the exact coincidence of happiness with morality.... Now it was our duty to promote the highest good; and it is not merely our privilege but a necessity connected with duty as a requisite to presuppose the possibility of this highest good. This presupposition is made only under the condition of the existence of God, and this condition inseparably connects this supposition with duty. Therefore, it is morally necessary to assume the existence of God. It is well to notice here that this moral necessity is subjective, i.e. a need, and not objective, i.e. duty itself.... A need of pure practical reason, on the other hand, is based on a duty to make something (the highest good) the object of my will so as to promote it with all my strength. In doing so, I must presuppose its possibility and also its conditions, which are God, freedom, and immortality. (Kant, 2007, Critique of Pure Reason)

WEAKNESSES IN KANT'S ARGUMENT

Thought Point

Crime does not pay – is this really true?

Consider whether this is true. Try to come up with reasons and examples to support your view.

THE *SUMMUM BONUM*

Kant argues that the *summum bonum* should be achievable, but is he right to make this claim?

Hollywood blockbuster films thrive on good overcoming evil, often against overwhelming odds. For example, think of the success of the *Lord of the Rings* films in which Frodo overthrows Sauron. While these stories may make appealing films, is reality like that? Do we have any reason to suppose that justice will in the end overcome evil and injustice? If God exists, we may have good reason to believe that good ultimately wins over evil. It is philosophically reasonable to hope this will happen, but it is rather difficult to argue that God exists based on what we hope or believe to be the case.

Kant argues that we should aim to achieve the highest good, but that does not necessarily mean this is possible, or that some powerful being like God exists to ensure that we have the possibility of achieving the highest good. As J.L. Mackie stated:

> [E]ven if, as Kant argues elsewhere, 'ought' implies 'can', the thesis that we ought to promote the highest good implies only that we can seek to promote it, and perhaps, since rational seeking could not be completely fruitless, that we can to some extent actually promote it. But this does not require that the full realisation of the highest good should be possible. (*The Miracle of Theism*)

If Mackie is correct, Kant cannot claim that if God exists as a 'postulate of pure reason' this is not a moral case for God's existence.

Furthermore, many philosophers have pointed out that even if we accept that a being of sufficient power is required to ensure that good ultimately is rewarded and evil is punished, it does not mean that the being is God. Brian Davies has argued that we can accept that the amount of power and knowledge required to enable people to achieve the *summum bonum* is not necessarily the same as omnipotence and omniscience. Davies explains this point using the example of an angel. The power and knowledge required to ensure that the *summum bonum* is achievable is just greater than that which we have, but it does not make the angel God or equivalent to God.

Does it matter if the *summum bonum* is unachievable?

Kant's argument suggests that the choice is between:

1   The *summum bonum* being achievable in reality and therefore moral behaviour is meaningful, and
2   The *summum bonum* being unachievable in reality and therefore moral behaviour is meaningless.

Behind these two choices is Kant's claim that we *ought* to achieve the *summum bonum* – meaning that the *summum bonum* can be achieved. Philosophers describe this as 'ought' involves 'can'.

As many philosophers have pointed out, this claim is false. Just because you ought to aim at achieving the highest good (the *summum bonum*) it does not mean that the highest good can be achieved, or even that it has to be achievable. Furthermore, the fact that a person makes an effort to achieve the *summum bonum* is good, and the goodness of the achievement is not undermined if the *summum bonum* is not achieved.

Every year students sit GCSE examinations. Teachers aim to ensure that their students pass. This is what teachers 'ought' to do. If the teachers have done their best for their students and the students have made all the progress it is possible for them to make, the fact that some students fail does not make the efforts of the teachers meaningless.

Does postulating the existence of God help people to be moral?

The answer to this question is clearly 'no' from a Kantian view-point. Kant would say that we are autonomous, rational decision-makers and we need no more than free, autonomous reason to act morally.

Second, even if one accepts Kant's claim that God is a postulate of pure practical reason, that does not help an individual solve a moral problem or dilemma. The choice for a Kantian or any other person is: what is the right course of action that leads to the *summum bonum*? Whether

God exists and guarantees that you ultimately achieve the *summum bonum* is not the issue.

Kant and happiness

Kant links the final achievement of the *summum bonum* with the achievement of happiness. There are two problems with this:

1   In his *Groundwork of the Metaphysics of Morals* Kant specifically says that the only appropriate attitude to the categorical imperative (the right thing to do) is to do it out of a sense of duty, not expecting it to lead to anything. Fulfilment is defined as doing one's duty.
2   While people may like their actions to lead to happiness this is not necessarily the motive for action. For example, a soldier going into battle may well be acting out of a sense of duty and be satisfied with doing his or her duty. This does not necessarily mean that the soldier's actions have to lead to happiness.

However, it is perhaps possible to make sense of this by reference to Kant's example of truth-telling.

Kant suggests the scenario of a man searching for someone whom he intends to kill. The intended victim is staying with you. If the potential murderer asks you where his victim is, should you say that the potential victim has been staying in your house?

Kant suggests that telling the truth overrides any concerns for the safety of the person whose life is at stake. It is possible to better understand this strange answer to the scenario above in the context that doing your duty ultimately leads to the achievement of the *summum bonum*.

Kant's argument only makes sense given his idea that moral actions are those carried out solely out of a sense of duty and not for any other motive. If you believe that consequences matter, as, for example, egoists or utilitarians do (i.e. that the death of the victim in the scenario is a result of your truth-telling to the murderer), then Kant's arguments fail because what matters is the result of an action, not just whether the *summum bonum* is achievable.

Kant and moral awareness

Kant's theory is also unclear because he stresses the autonomy of every person as a rational agent who can deduce the morally right course of action. Kant rejects the idea that morality derives from the will of God or that it is a divine command ('sanction' as he calls it). He does not accept the idea of God threatening punishments like hell on those who reject his law or providing rewards like heaven for people who are good. At the same time Kant states that God wills the moral law which we discover through reason, and this is why he links good moral behaviour with ultimately achieving the *summum bonum*.

Confusion

Kant's moral argument is not entirely clear, as he makes a range of points in his books which do not seem to fit very happily together. As we have seen in earlier chapters, Kant wrote in his *Critique of Pure Reason* that it was impossible to prove the existence of God by reason. Hence, Kant criticises and rejects the ontological, cosmological and teleological arguments. However, in his *Critique of Practical Reason* Kant argues that moral reasoning leads to an argument for God's existence. If we accept Kant's argument, what does saying God is a 'postulate of pure reason' actually tell us about whether God exists? Second, the argument that the *summum bonum* is achievable implies the idea of a divine reward for a good moral life. This undermines Kant's key claim that our decisions must be autonomous to be moral. A divine reward of happiness could be a motivating factor to act in a particular way, along the line of: *Be morally good to get the reward of happiness*.

Is Kant's moral argument teleological?

Kant specifically rejects the idea that moral behaviour is defined by any goal, purpose or result. It is for this reason that Kant emphasises the autonomy of reason and that morality is a matter of duty dictated by reason. Kant claims that his moral argument is a practical proof, as it starts from one's experience of moral decision-making. However, Kant still suggests an argument that appears rather like other arguments for God's existence, which he called 'theoretical arguments'. This is a problem for Kant, as Kant specifically rejects 'theoretical arguments' for the existence of God. Michael Palmer has suggested that Kant's moral argument on this point 'looks suspiciously like trying to keep your cake and eat it' (Palmer, *The Question of God*).

What do you think Palmer meant?

Thought Point

Compare the two arguments below

Argument 1

1 The *summum bonum* is the goal of moral action.
2 If the *summum bonum* is the goal of moral action it has to be achievable.
3 *Postulating* the existence of God makes the *summum bonum* achievable.

Argument 2

1 The universe exhibits signs of order and purpose.
2 If the universe exhibits these signs of order and purpose it has to have a designer.
3 *Postulating* the existence of God explains the fact that there is design.

Questions

1 In what ways are the arguments different?
2 In what ways are the weaknesses of these arguments different?
3 Are any of the weaknesses you have identified in these arguments similar or the same?
4 Look again at Michael Palmer's comment in the quotation above. How does studying these arguments relate to Palmer's comment?

FREUD'S CRITICISMS OF KANT

INTRODUCTION

Kant's moral argument only works within Kant's own moral framework with an objective moral law and a duty to achieve the *summum bonum*. If we do not need to achieve this state which seems to be out of our reach, we do not need God to enable us to do so. Freud does not give a direct criticism of the moral argument, but instead gives an alternative explanation for the idea of God and the source of our morality.

Sigmund Freud is famous as a psychologist and a founder figure of the theories of psychoanalysis. His ideas concerning the source of our moral values concern us here, because he claims that our moral values are in no way objective. According to Freud our sense of duty and moral awareness can be explained by socialisation. Kant said that our sense of duty was

Oedipus Rex

The story of Oedipus the King is well worth reading if you like Greek myths and legends. Translations and modern versions of the original story are readily available in bookshops.

Sigmund Freud was born
in Freiberg in 1856. He
trained as a doctor and
went on to specialise in
mental care, practising the
then new form of treatment
called 'psychoanalysis'.
He emigrated to the United
Kingdom in 1938 following
the Nazi invasion of
Austria. He wrote a large
number of works on both
psychology and religion, of
which the most important
is *The Interpretation of
Dreams*, in which he
develops his key ideas.
   Freud's theory of
psychoanalysis is
important, as it put forward

continued opposite

based on reason, but according to Freud our conscience was a product of the unconscious mind or super-ego. This is Freud's challenge: that our sense of moral obligation is not objective and simply comes from our own mind.

Freud distinguished between three components of the mind or human psyche:

1   Id – basic instincts and primitive desires e.g. hunger, lust etc.
2   Ego – perceptions of the external that makes us aware of the 'reality principle', one's most outward part and personality.
3   Super-ego – the unconscious mind which consists of:

   (a) the Ego-ideal which praises good actions
   (b) the conscience which makes you feel guilty for bad actions

Freud considers that the mind of a newborn child is 'id-ridden': full of instinctive drives and impulses which need immediate satisfaction. The ego seeks to please the id in ways that are in the long term beneficial. Freud saw the superego as reflecting the internalisation of cultural rules, mainly taught by parents. The super-ego works in opposition to the id and controls our senses of right, wrong and guilt.

Freud's claim, and its significance, are explored below, because if Freud is correct Kant's claim that God can be postulated from the existence of morality fails.

This idea was ground-breaking, but it was linked with Freud's idea of a so-called Oedipus Complex. The name is a reference to a character in Greek legend called Oedipus who ends up killing his father and replacing him as king and as husband to his own mother, though he does not at that point in the story know that he has killed his own father and married his own mother.

Freud proposed the theory that children develop a sexual attraction for the parent of the opposite sex. It is worth noting that Freud places great emphasis on this idea but it is both controversial and rejected by the majority of psychoanalysts today. In particular, modern psychology distinguishes different levels of maturity in moral development.

Freud is also important as one of the first people to see the relationship between sexuality and human behaviour, though his conclusions about the relationship are often rejected today. Human sexuality shapes human feelings, thoughts, culture and so forth. Freud realised that this is often at an unconscious level, since society shapes the way one thinks and behaves at the conscious level.

Thought Point

Where do our moral ideas come from?

Look at a common code of ethical values that many people claim are universal, such as the Ten Commandments or the European Convention on Human Rights.

1 Do you agree with these moral principles?
2 Do you believe that they are objective principles (i.e. not just limited to a particular society or group of people)? Justify your views.
3 Where do you believe your own moral values come from?
4 Which sources of moral values have most influenced you?

what were new and ground-breaking ideas about human psychology. He suggested that the mental life of a human being is dominated by the unconscious, not the conscious mind. The existence of our unconscious is revealed through dreams, trivial mistakes (e.g. slips of the tongue) and neuroses.

Models of moral development

If you wish to know more about some modern models of moral development you could investigate the work of Kohlberg or Spitzer.

Neuroses

Freud uses the word 'neuroses' to describe problem experiences in life, such as traumas or bereavements, that are not solved but instead are repressed by the mind. For example, some people find it very difficult to cope with a bereavement and may even deny that the person they cared for has really died. In this case the elements of the mind are not in harmony because while one part of the mind may deny the fact that the person has died, the person's mind is also in some other way aware of the truth that the person has died.

Freud argued that traumas which have been suppressed show themselves as 'obsessive neuroses' in adulthood, by which he meant compulsive, repetitive and irrational behaviour. An example of a minor obsessional neurosis is being obsessed by cleanliness in the house: not being able to rest if there is the tiniest speck of dust in the house or a room is left uncleaned for a day or even an hour.

FREUD'S VIEW OF RELIGION AND MORAL AWARENESS

1 Religion is an *obsessional neurosis*

Freud argued that religion is an obsessional neurosis (*The Future of an Illusion*). In particular, he stated that religion provides a way for people to satisfy their desires, such as that the world be ordered and that life be meaningful. The answers religion provides are appealing, for example the

Id

Freud's name for the part of the mind in which human instincts such as desire and appetite are based.

Super-ego

The name in Freud's model of the mind for the part of the ego with which humans reason and make decisions. Freud emphasised the way in which parental influence and values mould the super-ego and leave their mark on it.

Ego

Freud's name for the part of the mind which is shaped by 'external influences' such as traumas, bereavements, education and upbringing.

Neurosis

A neurosis is a medical term used of a person who suffers feelings of fear, worry and anxiety which can become obsessions that inhibit one's life. For example, some people have a neurotic obsession with cleanliness, others with checking that windows are shut or the oven hob is turned off.

FREUD'S MODEL OF THE MIND

The id
Freud gave the name 'id' to the part of the mind in which human instincts such as desire and appetite are based. These desires are often repressed by our conscious mind into the unconscious, but they can surface through dreams.

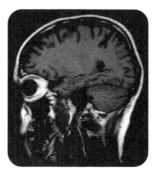

The superego
The super-ego is part of the id. The super-ego is in some ways similar to the conscience. For Freud it is a form of reasoning ability with which human beings make decisions. It is shaped by the influences that have affected people during their development. In particular, Freud emphasised how parental influence is reflected in the way children often share the value system of their parents.

The ego
The ego is the part of the systemising aspect of the mind which is shaped by what Freud called 'external influences' such as life experiences like traumas, bereavements, education and so forth. It also translates the appetitive drive of the id into conscious thought.

In later life Freud developed a model of the mind in three parts. A healthy mind he thought was one where these three elements, the id, ego and superego, are in harmony.

Freud particularly emphasised the role of parents in shaping the moral decision-making ability of their children as illustrated by the following quotation:

> The long period of childhood, during which the growing human being lives in dependence on his parents, leaves behind it as a precipitate the formation in his ego of a special agency in which this parental influence is prolonged. It has received the name of the superego. (S. Freud, *An Outline of Psychoanalysis*)

promise of reward for good behaviour after death. By using the phrase 'obsessional neurosis' Freud was indicating that religious people place faith in God because it answers their desires, such as that God exists and there is a life after death.

Freud's claim that religion is an obsessional neurosis would, if true, also refute Kant's moral argument, which claimed that God exists as a postulate of pure reason who ensures that the *summum bonum* is achievable. A Freudian response would be that the *summum bonum* being achievable is a very persuasive human desire, but this in no way makes it or God, as the postulate of pure reason, a reality. God for Freud is the result of guilt caused by a traumatic event in human history.

2 Moral values are the results of our experiences

It is important for the discussion of the moral argument to note that Freud's model of the mind argues that our moral values are the results of our experiences through upbringing and their interaction with the unconscious. As he remarked, parents preserve their influence on their children by the education and values they give them, and this includes the moral values that parents pass on to children.

If Freud is correct – and there is considerable evidence from modern psychology to support Freud's claim that experience and upbringing shape our moral ideas – Kant's claim that morality is objective and can be discovered through reason is vulnerable. Freud would argue that morality is the product of society and upbringing and not something objective to be discovered. If Kant's claim that morality is rational and objective is false, his argument for God's existence as a postulate of pure reason fails.

It is worth noting that the idea that there are objective moral values is a matter of debate in the writings of many modern moral philosophers as well.

CONCLUDING REMARKS ABOUT THE MORAL ARGUMENT

Kant's moral argument is only convincing if you are already a believer in God. It will not persuade you to believe in God for, as many philosophers including J.L. Mackie and Brian Davies have suggested, aiming at achieving the *summum bonum* or saying you ought to aim to achieve the *summum bonum* is one thing; it does not mean that the *summum bonum* has to be achievable. Second, psychoanalysis raises important questions about the origins of our moral values. While some people may believe that the moral argument contributes to a cumulative case that demonstrates the existence of God, it fails as a proof of God's existence.

Modern philosophy and objective moral values

One example of a defence of the claim that there are no objective moral values may be found in Chapter 1 of J.L. Mackie's *Ethics: Inventing Right and Wrong* (1990). It is also worth noting that there are a large number of moral philosophers who believe that there are objective moral values. An interesting perspective on the debate may be found in the work of Raimond Gaita, such as *Good and Evil: An Absolute Conception*.

Note well

Freud was not concerned directly with moral arguments for God's existence. Freud is important with regard to the moral argument because his ideas may also be used to criticise Kant's moral argument, but Freud developed his ideas as part of his theory of psychoanalysis.

Cumulative argument for God's existence

This phrase is used to refer to some modern approaches to proving God's existence which suggest that no one argument demonstrates God's existence, but the combined weight of lots of arguments could be evidence that God exists.

For more information about this idea have a look at the 'Further reading' section at the end of this chapter.

SUMMARY

1 The moral argument

Kant

Human beings
Rational, autonomous moral decision-makers

Kant and morality

Moral duty is something you should do
The summum bonum *is the achievement of moral goodness (virtue) and happiness together*
Through reason we can work out what is the right thing to do because the right thing to do has to be applicable universally – everywhere

The actual moral argument of Kant

Moral action is about doing one's duty
The reason to do one's duty is to achieve the summum bonum *(the highest good)*
The highest good must be achievable; otherwise moral goodness is pointless
What could make the highest good achievable?
Answer: God
Conclusion: we should postulate the existence of God

Weaknesses in Kant's argument

Is the summum bonum *achievable?*
Just because you ought to aim at achieving the summum bonum, *it does not mean that the highest good has to be achievable*
Is Kant's moral argument teleological?

2 Freud

Freud's model of the mind

The id
The super-ego
The ego

Explanation of religion and morality

The Oedipus Complex
Religion is an obsessional neurosis
Moral values are the results of our experiences

REVIEW QUESTIONS

Look back over the chapter and check that you can answer the following questions:

1   Outline in no more than 300 words Kant's moral argument.
2   Explain three weaknesses of the moral argument by Kant.
3   Do you agree with Freud about the source of human moral values? Explain your answer with reasons.
4   The philosopher Richard Swinburne wrote in his book *The Existence of God* that 'man's moral knowledge does not wear its source on its face'. What do you think Swinburne meant?

Terminology

Do you know your terminology?

1   Try to explain the following ideas without looking at your books and notes:

- God is a postulate of pure reason
- The *summum bonum*
- Ego, id and super-ego
- Neurosis.

Examination Questions Practice

The moral argument appears fairly regularly on examination papers. Make sure you really understand it well before the examination. In particular, study Kant's moral argument as opposed to the many other types of moral argument that philosophers and theologians have described.

EXAM MISTAKES TO AVOID

1   Make sure that you can use the terminology properly. Many students enter the examination confused about the meaning of postulate and

summum bonum in Kant's moral argument. Make sure that you are able to use these words accurately and explain their relationship to the moral argument in a clear way.

2 Kant's argument relates to his ethics, but if all you do is write about his ethics you will get a low mark in the Philosophy of Religion examination. Remember that the questions for this examination will focus on the moral argument of Kant.

3 The specification states that you must understand why Freud's ideas undermine Kant's argument. Make sure that you can explain the relationship between the two.

4 Finally, as stated at the beginning of this chapter, Kant's argument is very different from other moral arguments for God's existence. Do not take ideas from other moral arguments and say 'Kant says . . .'.

Remember: (a) assesses AO1 and (b) AO2. To help you improve your answers look at the AS Levels of Response. See: http://www.ocr.org.uk/qualifications/as-a-level-gce-religious-studies-h172-h572/

SAMPLE AS EXAM-STYLE QUESTIONS

1 (a) **Explain Freud's challenge to Kant's moral argument for the existence of God.** (25 marks)

This question is asking you to explain how Freud's ideas undermine Kant's moral argument. In order to complete this question well you will need to clearly state Kant's main ideas and explain how Freud's comments relate to them. Make sure the focus of your answer is on Freud's theory rather than just describing Kant.

Points in your answer could include:

- Why Freud's argument undermines Kant's claim that belief in God is known through reason
- Morality and belief in God are a product of parental influence, which undermines the claim that morality is rational
- Freud's 'super-ego', if true, suggests parental influence over children continues through the values that parents give their children. In one sense this suggests that human beings are not as autonomous as Kant claims
- Freud's notion that religion is an obsessional neurosis suggests that postulating the existence of God to guarantee a system of objective moral values is just part of the neurosis.

(b) **'Kant's understanding of morality leads convincingly to God's existence.' Discuss.** (10 marks)

This question is more straightforward than it sounds; it is asking you to assess whether or not Kant's moral argument is successful. The clue phrase that gives this away is 'leads convincingly. . . . Discuss'. You can use a range of approaches to answer this question. Some ideas are suggested below. You could discuss a selection of them or one of them in detail, if you felt you knew enough about it to gain 17 marks. The challenges that Freud's argument raises could be discussed. You could explain why his claim that religion is an obsessional neurosis is damaging to Kant's argument and, second, why Freud's ideas about moral development undermine Kant's claim that God's existence is a postulate of reason.

Assess a number of the criticisms of Kant's argument, such as:

- Why some philosophers say that the *summum bonum* does not have to be achievable
- Why philosophers claim the argument is inconsistent or confused
- Why other philosophers believe that God's role in the theory undermines the role of reason
- Why some scholars claim Kant attempts to 'have his cake and eat it'
- Morality is the product of society, education and upbringing.

Alternatively, you could put forward a defence of Kant's argument, pointing out that morality comes not just from people but also from God.

For example, you could refer to the fact that Kant stated that God guaranteed that the *summum bonum* is achievable and he also stated that human beings are aware of God's law when they act rationally – God's law is found through reason.

2 (a) Explain Kant's version of the moral argument for the existence of God.

   (b) How far have psychological explanations of religious belief disproved such moral arguments?

3 (a) Explain Kant's reasons for believing that human morality points to the existence of God.

   (b) Assess the idea that Freud's objections destroy Kant's moral argument for the existence of God.

4 (a) Explain Kant's moral argument including his concept of the *summum bonum*.

   (b) 'Human immorality proves that there is no God'. Discuss.

FURTHER READING

There is a wide range of reading available about the moral argument. A few books to investigate are suggested below.

Brian Davies' *An Introduction to the Philosophy of Religion* provides a readily available detailed examination of many of the topics found on the OCR examination paper, including the moral argument.

Richard Swinburne's book *The Existence of God* provides a detailed and excellent analysis of the moral argument's strengths and weaknesses.

Dialogue, the journal of religion and philosophy, contains a number of articles relating to Kant and the relationship of morality with religion. The articles by Dennis Brown on the moral argument (Issue 18, April 2002) and by Robert Kirkwood on morality and religion (Issue 9, November 1997) are particularly relevant to this topic.

If you would like to explore some ideas from psychology about moral development it would be well worth investigating the work of people such as Spitzer and Kohlberg. (See e.g. William Damon's 'The Moral Development of Children' in *Scientific American* (August 1999), 281(2)).

CHALLENGES TO THE BELIEF IN GOD

PART IV

THE ISSUE

Why might people say that God does not exist?

Discuss what other people think and why. Do their friends or families share this view?

This question is the opposite to the one being considered in Part II.

Although many people do believe in God there have always been others who feel that there are good arguments against God's existence. Many people also feel that the discoveries of science and other disciplines have suggested that there is no such thing as God.

The chapters in Part II introduced traditional ways in which religious people have tried to demonstrate that their belief in God is true.

The chapters here on the problem of evil and religion and science explore some ways in which arguments for belief in God have been challenged or undermined.

9 The Problem of Evil

THE ISSUE

The existence of evil is a problem for all people. Evil leads to people suffering great pain, being treated unjustly or dying tragically. However, the question is:

Does the existence of evil disprove the existence of God?

WHAT YOU WILL LEARN ABOUT IN THIS CHAPTER

1   Why the existence of evil is a challenge to belief in God.
2   Different ways in which Christians have tried to answer the problem of evil.
3   The strengths and weaknesses of traditional Christian attempts to solve the problem of evil.

STARTER

For many people, acts of wickedness and evil in the world and the suffering caused by natural disasters are the strongest arguments against belief in God. Working with other people, try to determine how a religious believer such as a Jew, Christian or Muslim might view the problem of evil.

1   Write up your answer as a set of questions.
2   Can you think of any answers or solutions to the questions you have thought of?

Some clues:

1 Think about what the traditional qualities of God are.
2 Study the pictures on this page. Use the pictures to help you work out what the problem of evil is.

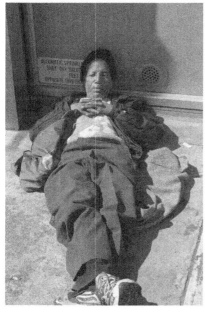

THE OCR CHECKLIST ✓

In this chapter you will cover the following aspects of the OCR specification:

Candidates should be able to demonstrate knowledge and understanding of:

• the problem of evil: the classic theodicies of Augustine and Irenaeus;

Theodicy
A philosophical attempt to solve the problem of evil.

continued overleaf

> • the nature of the problem of evil and the possible differences between natural and moral evil;
> • the origins of evil and the role of human free will.
>
> Candidates should be able to discuss critically these approaches and their strengths and weaknesses.
>
> From OCR A Level Religious Studies specification H172.

A DEFINITION OF THE PROBLEM OF EVIL

Perhaps the most famous definition of the problem of evil is the one put forward by the Greek philosopher Epicurus over 2,000 years ago:

> Is God willing to prevent evil, but not able to? Then he is not omnipotent.
> Is God able to prevent evil, but not willing to? Then he is malevolent (evil).
> Is God able to prevent evil and willing to? Then why is there evil?

The same problem still challenges human beings today.

The problem, as set out by Epicurus, highlights the difficulties that the problem of evil raises for the religious believer. It questions God's omnipotence, God's goodness and God's omniscience.

Omnipotent

Means infinite or unlimited power. It is a philosophical word often used to describe God.

Omniscient

Means infinite knowledge. Most philosophers today use the word as a quality for God to indicate that God knows everything it is logically possible to know.

WHY THE EXISTENCE OF EVIL CHALLENGES BELIEF IN GOD

For many people the existence of evil in the world, the amount of evil and the suffering evil causes are the greatest challenges to belief in the existence of God. The case against believing in God because of the existence of evil has been well set out by many philosophers, including J.L. Mackie and Anthony Flew.

First, if God is all-powerful why does God not prevent evil?

This challenge to the existence of God is sometimes called the *logical problem*. J.L. Mackie argued it was a logical problem because theists have to show that their beliefs make sense (i.e. clarify the logic of their reasoning). Mackie argues that if God is really omnipotent that must mean God has power over 'causal laws' (*The Miracle of Theism*) – that is, the physical laws of the universe. This raises the challenge: why does God not stop evil events happening if God has the power to stop evil and it costs God no effort to stop evil?

Second, the sheer amount of evil in the world appears to challenge the goodness of creation

As the scientist Richard Dawkins has pointed out, even without human beings, the amount of suffering in the animal kingdom is immense. Does this outweigh the value of good within the world? Religious believers have a problem defending the goodness of the world in the face of the existence of evil and suffering in the world.

Human beings have a capacity to inflict great evil and suffering on one another. Examples include the millions of people killed by the Nazis in the Second World War or the tens of thousands raped and killed in the genocide in Rwanda during the 1990s.

The sheer cruelty of some evil actions seems also to challenge belief in the existence of a good, omnipotent God. Perhaps the most famous challenges are those presented by Dostoevsky in his story *The Brothers Karamazov*. One of the characters, Ivan, puts forward three arguments against God that focus on the problem of evil, some of which were based on incidents recorded in nineteenth-century newspapers in Russia. One of the most poignant of these arguments questioned soldiers throwing babies in the air and killing them with their bayonets – how can free will be worth the price of innocent people suffering and how can anyone believe in the existence of a good, omnipotent God when suffering like this happens? The same point can be made today just by watching the news.

Free will

The ability to make one's own decisions and choose freely between different possible courses of action.

Thought Point

The Brothers Karamazov

If you have the time, read *The Brothers Karamazov* by Dostoevsky. Alternatively, an excellent discussion of the passages of the book which concern the problem of evil may be found in *The Puzzle of Evil* by Peter Vardy.

Mackie argues that the price of having free will is that sometimes humans commit appallingly evil acts. Yet he suggests that if God is really omnipotent, could not God have made human beings so that they always choose freely what is good? (*The Miracle of Theism*). However, theists have replied: what sort of free choice do you have if you are incapable of choosing what is bad? Your answer partly depends on how you define free will.

There is also a huge amount of suffering in nature. Biologists have argued that nature is piteously indifferent to suffering. Nature is not good or evil; all that matters is the passing on of genes from one generation to the next. Any suffering, evil or harm that enables genes to be passed on is not the concern of nature. This does not fit in well with ideas of creation being good and having been made by God, as presented in the creation stories of different religious traditions.

People can argue that a child learns by making mistakes and sometimes mistakes cause suffering, such as learning not to touch hot things because they burn you, but this does not mean we need the whole range of illnesses or wicked acts that occur in the world.

For other people the problem is the fact that evil and suffering seem to be indiscriminate. What this means is that both good and bad people can be affected by it. A very common question to ask is: why do good people suffer while evil ones make a profit? How does this fit in with belief in a good God who is meant to be just?

Thought Point

Is suffering of any benefit?

A rare genetic condition causes children to be born with an inability to feel pain. What are the possible advantages and disadvantages of such a condition?

Thought Point

Nature: good, bad or indifferent

Read the passages below and then answer the questions which follow.

continued opposite

Text 1

And God said, 'Let the earth bring forth living creatures of every kind: cattle and creeping things and wild animals of the earth of every kind.' And it was so. God made the wild animals of the earth of every kind, and the cattle of every kind, and everything that creeps upon the ground of every kind. And God saw that it was good. . . .

So God created humankind in his image, in the image of God he created them; male and female he created them. . . .

God saw everything that he had made, and indeed, it was very good. And there was evening and there was morning, the sixth day. (Genesis 1: 24, 25, 27, 31a)

Text 2

As we shall see, nature is not cruel, only pitilessly indifferent. This is one of the hardest lessons for humans to learn. We cannot admit that things might be neither good nor evil, cruel nor kind, but simply callous – indifferent to all suffering, lacking all purpose. (Richard Dawkins, *River Out of Eden*)

Questions

- Which text presents a more accurate picture of the world?
- Make a list of any evidence that supports the claims of each text.
- Which text appeals more to you?
- Would you teach the ideas presented in these texts to your children (if you had any)?
- In your opinion:

    - Did God make the Earth?
    - Is nature pitilessly indifferent?

NB: It is well worth reading the complete chapters that these two texts come from.

THEODICY

Theodicy is the word used by religious believers for their explanations of how belief in a good, omnipotent God can be maintained in the face of all the evil and suffering present in the world. The word *theodicy* comes from two Greek words: *theos* (meaning 'God') and *dikaios* (meaning 'justice'). Theodicy in philosophical writings has always been taken to mean 'The, or a, vindication of the divine attributes, especially justice and holiness, in respect to the existence of evil; a writing, doctrine, or theory intended to "justify the ways of God to men"' (*OED*).

> Traditional theism holds that God is the creator of heaven and earth, and that all that occurs in the universe takes place under Divine Providence – that is, under God's sovereign guidance . . . **theodicy** – that is, an account of the role evil plays in the world, and a justification for its presence. (*Stanford Encyclopedia of Philosophy* – accessed 11 May 2015)

TYPES OF EVIL

When talking about the problem of evil, philosophers generally discuss two types of evil: natural and moral. It is important that you understand the difference between the two and can apply the terms.

Moral evil

Moral evil is the phrase used by philosophers to refer to evil events or acts that are caused by human beings choosing freely to do the action in question. In philosophical terms you would say that an agent caused the act freely. For example, if you stab someone, that is a moral evil if you choose freely to do it. However, if a lion attacks you and wounds you with its claws, your experience is bad or evil, but the lion's action was not a moral one, because the lion does not think rationally like a human being.

Natural evil

Natural evil refers to events that have bad or evil consequences when experienced by human beings. For example, if a hurricane strikes a city it can cause flooding, devastation, destruction of houses and loss of life. The people in the devastated area experience a natural evil. However, few people today would want to blame an evil spirit for causing the hurricane. Instead, people would understand that the hurricane is just a result of the way in which nature works. If a hurricane struck an area uninhabited by human beings, it would not be a natural evil for human beings and would probably receive little or no news coverage.

Most philosophers today would argue that natural evils are caused by the way the natural world works.

Thought Point

Words

1   Consider the meaning of the following words and then check their definition in a dictionary:

  (a) Good
  (b) Bad
  (c) Evil
  (d) Wicked.

2   What do you normally mean when you describe something as evil? Which of the dictionary definitions does this correspond to?

Damage caused by Hurricane Katrina

Thought Point

Are the terms *natural evil* and *moral evil* easy to apply?

Study the list below and decide which ones are natural evils and which ones are moral evils. Make a bullet point list of the causes of each event referred to.

continued overleaf

1　A hurricane flooding a town leading to hundreds of people drowning.
2　An earthquake destroying a city.
3　A man robbing a bank.
4　A paranoid schizophrenic stabbing a woman.
5　Becoming infected with HIV after receiving a tainted blood transfusion.
6　Killing a person when they step out in front of your car. It was impossible to foresee the accident happening.
7　A person dying of hunger because they had no money and no one gave them food or help.
8　Suffering from hepatitis caught from injecting yourself with heroin using a dirty needle.

Augustine the man (354–430 CE)

As a young man Augustine turned against the Christian faith of his mother and investigated a number of different schools of philosophical thought. However, he ended up becoming a committed Christian and monk, inspired by the preaching of Ambrose of Milan. He wrote a large number of books about Christian doctrine and beliefs, the most famous of which are probably *The City of God* and *Confessions in Thirteen Books*. He was also chosen by the people of Thagaste in north Africa (now part of Libya) to be their bishop.

Evil: a problem to be endured or solved?

There are a number of ways in which the problem of evil, as set out by people like Epicurus, can be solved:

1　Evil is caused by creatures using their free will.
2　Evil is necessary as a means for people to develop some valuable moral qualities, such as compassion.
3　Developing a different understanding of the nature of God.

This chapter explores traditional Christian solutions to the problem of evil, which centre upon (1) and (2) above. If you would like to know about solution (3), have a look at the 'Further reading' section at the end of the chapter.

It is worth noting that theodicies are rational efforts to explain how evil can exist in the world if God exists. In normal life, philosophers put forward these theories as spectators. If you are really suffering from something 'evil', such as cancer or being stabbed, your concern is not solving the problem of evil. Instead, what the suffering person wants and needs is comfort, love, care and compassion.

Most people would say that *the intellectual problem of evil* is very different from the experience of coping with evil and suffering in your own life.

AUGUSTINE'S THEODICY

Augustine's theodicy is greatly influenced by the creation stories found in Genesis 1–3. While thinking about Augustine's theodicy it is worth bearing in mind that he interpreted the Genesis story as a literal account of the origins of the world and also as a mythological story that communicated

THE THEODICY OF AUGUSTINE: KEY IDEAS

1 God:

God the Creator is omnipotent and all-good.

↓

2 Harmonious creation:

Creation is good and in the beginning was harmonious.

↓

3 Hierarchy of beings:

Angels, humans, animals.

↓

4 Privation:

Evil is a privation or lack of goodness in something.

↓

5 The Fall:

Angels and human beings fall through their own free choices and giving in to temptation. Sin enters the world through Adam and Eve.

↓

6 Natural evil:

Disharmony in the world follows the fall of angels leading to natural evil.

↓

7 Free will:

Free will is valuable so God sustains a world within which moral and natural evil occurs.

↓

8 Aesthetic value:

The existence of evil highlights the goodness of creation because of the contrast between good and evil.

values and meaning. While most Christians today would not suggest that the Genesis story is literally true, they still value the ideas Augustine puts forward in his theodicy.

The question to ask is:

Are Augustine's ideas a helpful way to answer the problem of evil?

God the Creator

Augustine had a traditional view of God. According to Augustine, God is all-good, omnipotent and omniscient. This created a problem that Augustine had to solve:

If God is good and he is omnipotent, and he created the world, why is evil in it?

If God created the universe and continues to sustain it in existence for every moment of every day, it means that if people commit acts of evil, God is sustaining and keeping alive those very people while they do those acts.

Privation and evil

Augustine solves the problem of saying God is responsible for evil in the world by defining evil as a *privation*.

What this means is that when we use words such as 'evil' and 'bad' we are saying that something does not meet our expectations of what, by nature, it should be like. Augustine wrote that 'evil is not a substance' (Augustine, *Confessions*).

The philosopher Herbert McCabe ('God, Evil and Divine Responsibility') gave the example of bad grapes and a bad deckchair. We can know what bad grapes are – what they look like and taste like. We can also know what a bad deckchair is like. However, just because we know what bad means in the case of deckchairs and grapes, this does not make badness a thing that exists in the same way as televisions or mobile phones. McCabe argues that badness and evil are about not living up to expectations; something lacks a quality it should have.

Augustine influenced McCabe and it is clear Augustine held the same idea about evil. Augustine rejects the idea that evil is a force or power opposed to God because this would mean that God had a rival and was not omnipotent, which is not part of traditional Christian belief about God.

The idea of evil being a privation also applies to human beings. According to Augustine's view, if you say that a human being is evil, or that

---

Augustine's theodicy

Augustine did not write a book that he called a 'theodicy'. Instead, many of his writings include comments relevant to this topic. So although people refer to the Augustinian theodicy, what they are really referring to is a collection of ideas linked to the writings of Augustine.

God the Creator

Review your earlier work on God the Creator and possible ways to interpret the creation stories. You could refer to the summary of this topic found at the end of Chapter 3.

Privation

Means something is lacking a particular thing that it should have. Augustine gave the example of 'blindness'. He called this a privation, because if you are blind it means that you are unable to see – in other words you lack the attribute of 'sight'. Augustine uses this in his theodicy.

their actions are evil, you are saying that the way they behave does not match expectations about how a human being should behave. For example, if you racially abuse people, rob or torture them, you are not living up to the standards expected of human beings. It is the failure to be what you should be that is wrong.

Thought Point

Evil and privation

Is evil a 'privation' or 'lack' in something? What do you think?

Absence and lack

There is an important difference between absence and lack. Augustine is not concerned with saying that it is bad or evil that human beings cannot breathe like fish under water, because that is not what human beings are like – you should not expect human beings to be able to do this naturally; the ability is just *absent*. However, Augustine's idea of privation does apply when you *lack* something you should have. For example:

1   If you cannot walk – you lack the health you should have. This is a privation in Augustine's thinking.
2   If you are mean – you lack the qualities of generosity and charity. This is a privation in Augustine's thinking.

However, there is an important difference between examples 1 and 2. Example 1 concerns a privation which you are not to blame for. You did not choose to be in this state. Example 2 concerns a privation that you are to blame for, because you choose how you behave.

Thought Point

What does the word 'inhuman' mean?

Describing someone as inhuman, or his or her behaviour as inhuman, comes from the idea of evil being a privation. Consider what the link is.

THE ORIGINS OF EVIL IN AUGUSTINE'S THINKING

In Augustine's thinking, all evil (moral and natural) comes from moral choices. If you choose to do something such as robbing a bank, you lack the quality of respecting others and their property. It is this lack that is wrong and makes the act of robbing the bank wrong. Augustine uses the idea of free will.

Thought Point

Is God to blame for evil?

Augustine made the following comment about evil:

> 'I thought it better to believe that you had created no evil . . . rather than to believe that the nature of evil, as I understood it, came from you'. (Augustine, Confessions)

Discuss:

1   What Augustine believed at first (in bold above)
2   What he believed later (underlined above)
3   Why do you think he changed his mind?

'Evil comes from God' (Augustine)

Where did Augustine's ideas come from?

Augustine's ideas about the origin of evil are influenced by philosophy from later followers of Plato (a school of thought called Middle Platonism) and by ideas drawn from the Bible.

Augustine's claim at first sounds very strange if not plain wrong. Christians, of course, believe that God is good. So how could Augustine say this?

The answer is that Augustine believed that God causes everything that exists. Second, he believed that evil is not a 'thing' but something 'missing' or 'lacking'. So if a person is 'evil', he or she lacks qualities we expect to find in them. As a result Augustine says that 'evil comes from God' because God causes to exist and keeps in existence human beings who have free will and, of course, human beings can become evil through their free choices.

It is important to note that no one can be totally and purely evil according to Augustine because to be evil you have to lack goodness, which means you had goodness to start with. Even the devil has some good in him. Talking about all God had created, Augustine said:

> It was obvious to me that things which are liable to corruption are good. . . . If there were no good in them there would be nothing capable of being corrupted. (Augustine, *Confessions*)

Thought Point

The Genesis stories

Review your work on the Genesis stories from Chapter 3. You can read both creation stories in any Bible in the book of Genesis, chapters 1–3.

The Garden of Eden

God creates the Garden of Eden and the man from dust. In the first Genesis story (Chapter 1) two other points are continually emphasised:

1　Creation is good.
2　Human beings are made in the image and likeness of God.

For Augustine this means that human beings are not just physical creatures but also spiritual. Christians usually interpret this as meaning that human beings are capable of rational thought (unlike animals), and this is a God-like quality.

Second, the Garden of Eden is characterised by a state of harmony. Everything is at peace with everything else. God walks in the Garden in the cool of the day. In addition, there is no suffering. Suffering is a result of disharmony. For example, if you fall over and break your arm it can be painful because you have probably damaged the bones, nerves and muscles of your body – they no longer work in harmony together.

The Fall

Adam and Eve's choice in the story is to eat the fruit of the tree of knowledge of good and evil. Adam and Eve have a choice about whether to know good and evil. In Hebrew the word translated as 'know' does not mean learning a list of facts or vocabulary, it also means to know by experience. You can describe the taste of strawberry yoghurt, what it is and how it is made, but you cannot know the reality of it – what it is like – without tasting it. Eve is tempted by the serpent and uses her free will to choose to do what she is told not to do. Adam is then tempted by Eve. The important feature of the story is that Adam and Eve choose not to be in harmony with God – this is the first sin, often called original sin in Christian thinking. Once disharmony is introduced the original peaceful state of the Garden cannot be restored.

In the story, the fact that Adam and Eve realise they are naked is a sign that they are no longer in harmony with the natural world around them.

Harmony

Refers to objects existing in an ordered way together or living creatures existing in a state of peace and happiness with each other.

The Fall

Refers to the story of Adam and Eve in the Garden of Eden and their disobeying of God. It can be read in Genesis 2: 4 to 3: 1 of the Bible.

Original sin

A reference to the first sin of Adam in the Garden of Eden and its effects, according to traditional Christian beliefs.

Thought Point

Experiment

Buy a packet of sweets and eat one of them. Try to describe the sweets to someone without giving them a sweet. Then give them a sweet. How accurate was your description?

The hierarchy of beings

One interesting idea in Augustine's writings is that he discusses the creation of spiritual beings as well as life on Earth. For Augustine, God creates the full range of types of life – this means physical life such as animals, and purely spiritual life such as angels. He believed that creation was good and perfect in the beginning. That meant that it had to include all types of beings; otherwise creation would lack something and not be good and perfect.

Devils are sometimes described as fallen angels who chose to turn away from God. According to Augustine this brought disharmony into creation and it is the actions of devils that led to natural evil being in the world, because of the disharmony they caused within nature. So, for Augustine, natural evils as well as moral evils are the result of free will.

The consequence of disharmony is suffering. In the story God punishes the man with hard work to survive and the woman with pain in childbirth. These are consequences of the lack of harmony in creation. It is important to note that, for Augustine, God created a good, perfect world – moral choices led to evil in the world.

Perfection

A philosophical term used to indicate the goodness of God. To be perfect means that you lack nothing and could not be better in any way. God is said to be perfect, as God is totally good and could not be more 'good'.

Sharing in Adam's sin

Augustine argued that all human beings were present in Adam's sin. This idea comes from Paul, who wrote that:

> Therefore, just as sin came into the world through one man, and death came through sin, and so death spread to all because all have sinned. (Romans 5: 12)

What Augustine meant is that all human beings are descended from Adam and Eve (remember he interpreted the story literally) and all share in the consequences of Adam and Eve's choice. In Christian theology all people are said to share in Adam's sin because they were *seminally present* in Adam. All future people are born into this disharmonious world.

Augustine and free will

Augustine's theodicy emphasises the fact that human beings and angels choose whether to live in harmony with God or not. This is a free will defence of the problem of evil.

Why create creatures with free will?

Augustine believed that free will is more valuable than having robots who always do God's will. Therefore Augustine would argue that allowing evil to happen is a price worth paying for human freedom. It is very important to understand the consequences of this view:

1   It means that God allows evil things to happen and has made and sustains a world and people who do evil things, such as murder, rape, torture, discriminate and so on.
2   If there was no free will it would also remove all the good choices which people have the chance to make. For example, you could not choose actions that bring joy, happiness and hope, and you could not choose to marry or have children.

It is also worth noting that Augustine argued that when the creation (universe) is viewed as a whole, the contrast between what is good and what is bad highlights the beauty of goodness. This is called the *aesthetic principle* by some philosophers, by which they mean that the contrast between what is good and what lacks goodness is heightened and made clearer in the contrast between goodness and lack of goodness (privation).

CRITICISMS OF AUGUSTINE'S THEODICY

Augustine's ideas dominated Christian thinking for over a thousand years. There is no doubt that Augustine's emphasis on the role of free will in his theodicy is important. However, modern philosophers have put forward a number of criticisms of his theodicy.

1 Plausibility

Many philosophers question whether the theodicy of Augustine is believable in the light of today's understanding of science. First, Augustine interpreted the Genesis story literally and, second, many people think there is no convincing evidence that angels exist. For example, in his book *Evil and the God of Love*, John Hick suggests that Augustine's theodicy is implausible for modern people.

Responses

Alvin Plantinga has suggested that, for Augustine's theodicy to be successful, the existence of angels has to be possible. We do not have to demonstrate the existence of angels.

> **Original sin**
>
> Original sin is defined in many ways by Christian thinkers, but one interpretation is to define it as the inbuilt tendency humans have to do things wrong despite their good intentions. The concept of original sin comes from interpretations of the Genesis story.

Second, philosophers such as Richard Swinburne and Alvin Plantinga have strongly defended the idea that evil arises from humans misusing their free will.

Many Christians today would not interpret the story of creation and the Fall literally, but they would say that its importance lies in what the story tries to tell people about the world, God the Creator and human beings' relationship with God's creation. In other words, the issues the story deals with matter and are still very relevant to people today.

2 Science

Augustine's explanation of the Fall starts from the situation of a perfect world created by God that is then harmed by humans and angels misusing free will. The findings of geologists and other scientists make it quite clear that the Earth developed very slowly over a period of four billion years. Biologists have demonstrated that life has developed through the mechanism of evolution by natural selection. Augustine's belief in a perfect world that is then spoilt by evil cannot be accepted as true in any literal sense.

3 Adam's sin

Augustine states that all people share in the effects of the Fall because they were seminally present in Adam's sin. This is difficult to understand in any literal sense. Biology clearly indicates that every person is a unique individual who inherits half of their DNA from their mother and half from their father. Augustine's ideas rely on an ancient understanding of biology, which said that the life-giving force for a baby came from the man and the flesh from the woman. Furthermore, if human beings were not seminally present in Adam it would appear unjust if God then punishes later human beings for the first human beings' sin.

4 How could the perfect world go wrong?

Over the centuries, philosophers such as Friedrich Schleiermacher (1768–1834) have questioned why a perfect world would go wrong. If angels were created to live in the presence of God, why would they turn away from God?

However, it is worth noting that much literature and history examines why people carry out actions that ruin the good situation they are in, and it is only afterwards, looking back, that people can see that they were better off before.

Thought Point

The perfect house

If you lived in a town where everyone had the same perfect house, would you change your house in any way to make it different from the others?

How does this question relate to Augustine's problem of evil?

5 God's responsibility for natural evils

Even if Augustine's argument that moral evil is caused by misuses of free will is accepted, many Christians are uncomfortable with Augustine's thinking about natural disasters. In particular, Augustine argues, first, for a world in which God is responsible for everything and, second, that suffering is a punishment for the sin of Adam. This does not fit very well with belief in a merciful and kind God. Augustine argued that God was merciful because he sent Jesus to save people, but people today could equally argue: why did God not create a world with less suffering?

THE IRENAEAN THEODICY

The story of the Fall in the Garden of Eden is interpreted literally by Irenaeus. He understands it as a situation in which human beings are led astray by the devil, because while they are in the image and likeness of God they are also far distant from God.

In this sense the state of Adam and Eve in the Garden of Eden is like that of children going astray because they have not yet developed sufficient wisdom to do what is right. While children can be obstinate and difficult it does not mean that their parent abandons the child. Equally, punishment may be appropriate for children as a way to help them to mature. So it is with God.

Irenaeus argues that:

> For, while promising that they [human beings] should be as gods, which was in no way possible for him [Adam] to be, he wrought death in them; wherefore he [the serpent] who had led man captive, was justly captured in turn by God; but man who had been captured, was loosed from the bonds of condemnation. (*Against Heresies*)

Irenaeus then gives an example: he suggests that a conquering army captures a people and the captives are taken away and held for a long time

---

Irenaeus the man (*c.* 130–200 CE)

Irenaeus originated from Smyrna in Asia Minor. He was a Christian preacher and later became the Bishop of Lyon, France. He died in the year 200.

The writings of Irenaeus are important, as he is one of the first Christians to attempt to explain Christian beliefs in an organised way. His greatest work is called *On the Detection and Overthrow of the So-called Gnosis – Against the Heresies*. This book explains Christian beliefs, and also the errors of pagans and other groups claiming to be Christians.

Irenaeus suggested that Adam and Eve in the Garden of Eden are created in the 'image' and 'likeness' of God, meaning that Adam and Eve have free will (making them in the image of God) and are spiritual as well as physical beings (making them in the likeness of God). However, Irenaeus argued that human beings were separate from God because they are mortal. The Garden of Eden for Irenaeus was the historical place where human beings originated. Because human beings had free will they had the ability to grow into relationship with God.

THE IRENAEAN THEODICY: KEY IDEAS

1 God:

God the Creator is omnipotent and all-good

↓

2 Creation is embryonic:

The universe and earth develop over time.

↓

3 Human beings are created in an imperfect state:

Human beings evolve from the 'image' of God into the likeness of God.

↓

4 Soul-making world:

The world is an environment in which people grow and develop
into the likeness of God. Hence, natural evil is present in it.

↓

5 Epistemic distance:

There is an epistemic distance between God and people so
that human beings have the chance to choose freely to grow
into relationship with God.

↓

6 Eschatological aspect:

All will come to be in the likeness of God
eventually, but this will not be in physical life.

↓

7 Free will:

Free will is valuable, so God sustains a world
within which moral and natural evil occur.

as servants and slaves. Some of the captured people end up having children with the captors. Irenaeus suggests that it would be unjust if a rescuer of the captured people only saved the children of the captives and not the parents who were to blame for first being captured. Instead the rescuer saves all those who have been captured, those to blame for the capture and their descendants. In the same way God, according to Irenaeus, saves Adam and Eve, who had first been captured, and their descendants.

It is important to note that in Irenaeus, Adam and Eve go astray but it is not a rebellion in the sense of Augustine's view where Adam and Eve deliberately turn away from God. Irenaeus suggests that God did not specifically curse Adam and Eve in Genesis 3, but cursed the ground and serpent on the ground. Instead Adam and Eve suffer the toil of working the ground and Eve the toil (pain) of giving birth. For Irenaeus punishment had to be given so that Adam and Eve would not 'despise' God, just as children need boundaries that are enforced to develop a sense of morality of their own. Punishment and the consequences of punishment, though hard, are for Irenaeus educative.

For Irenaeus the whole of history is overseen by God and although the world is a hard place in which people experience suffering, for Irenaeus it is necessarily this way as it is a place in which human beings can come to know God. The prophets of the Old Testament point out the right path to God and Jesus' incarnation brings about the presence of God amongst human beings. The incarnation of God in Jesus unites human beings with God once again. Hence, Jesus is the saviour of human beings. Irenaeus further argues that Jesus is the new Adam who obeys God and dies on the cross (the tree) and thus undoes the fault of Adam who took the forbidden fruit from the tree.

However, while Irenaeus' ideas suggest that salvation from God is open to all, he also states very clearly that God judges all and those who reject God and follow the ways of the devil will be punished with him:

> It is therefore one and the same God the Father who has prepared good things with Himself for those who desire His fellowship, and who remain in subjection to Him; and who has the eternal fire for the ringleader of the apostasy, the devil, and those who revolted with him, into which [fire] the Lord has declared those men shall be sent who have been set apart by themselves on His left hand. And this is what has been spoken by the prophet, 'I am a jealous God, making peace, and creating evil things'; thus making peace and friendship with those who repent and turn to Him, and bringing [them to] unity, but preparing for the impenitent, those who shun the light, eternal fire and outer darkness, which are evils indeed to those persons who fall into them. (*Against Heresies*)

The concept of universal salvation is a more modern interpretation of Irenaeus.

Recapitulation

The word 'recapitulation' is often applied to the ideas of Irenaeus concerning the problem of evil.

Recapitulation literally means to 'bring something back to the head or beginning'; it also means to 'summarise or sum something up'. Irenaeus' theodicy is about bringing people back into relationship with God; hence it is called a theory of recapitulation.

Thought Point

Irenaeus' own words

[U]nless God had freely given salvation, we would not now possess it securely. And unless man had been joined to God, he could never have become a partaker of incorruptibility. For it was incumbent upon the Mediator between God and men, by his relationship to both, to bring both to friendship and accord, and present man to God, while he revealed God to man. (Irenaeus, 'The Ante-Nicene Christian Library')

1   What do you think Irenaeus means by the word 'mediator'?
2   Does salvation only come from God? What did Irenaeus think? What do you think?

Thought Point

Criminal tendencies

1   Do people assume that children's attitudes and behaviour reflect those of their parents? Is it right to assume this link and then act on this basis?
2   Does an assumption such as this affect the way people relate to the children of:

- Doctors
- Cleaners
- Lawyers
- Teachers
- Criminals
- Prostitutes?

MODERN IRENAEAN THEODICIES

The early writings of Irenaeus have inspired some modern theodicies that are called 'Irenaean theodicies'. The ideas of the philosopher John Hick are perhaps the most famous example of a modern Irenaean approach to the problem of evil. Many other philosophers have developed Irenaean theodicies, such as Tennant and Schleiermacher. John Hick called Irenaeus the 'patron saint' (Davis, *Encountering Evil*) of this type of theodicy.

The Irenaean theodicy as set out by modern philosophers such as John Hick starts from a belief that God exists. It is an attempt to understand why there is evil in the world.

The key claim of Augustine's theodicy is that the world was perfect and good until evil came into being through people's choices. Augustine's theodicy presents a free will defence. Irenaean theodicies reject these sorts of ideas and the work of modern defenders of the free will defence such as Alvin Plantinga. John Hick argues that Augustinian theodicies are unconvincing to scientifically educated people, as:

1   The idea of Adam, Eve and the Fall is a myth. It is unlikely that it is literally true and hence a fall from grace in the Garden of Eden probably did not happen.
2   The idea that devils (fallen angels) cause natural disasters such as earthquakes is rejected as unbelievable.

JOHN HICK'S IRENAEAN THEODICY

1 The problem to be solved

Hick rejected the mythology of the Garden of Eden story. In his book *Evil and the God of Love* he stated that the role of mythology is to examine some of the great mysteries of human existence, such as evil, using striking imagery that is not easily forgotten. However, the important part of the myth is not the imagery but what the imagery tries to examine: in this case the problem of the existence of evil in God's world.

2 Human beings

Hick followed an idea from Irenaeus about human beings. He suggests that human beings were not created perfect as in Augustine's theodicy. Instead he says human beings develop in two stages:

Stage 1: 'Image'

Hick argues that the idea that humans are created in the image of God is about the evolution of human beings into rational, 'intelligent and religious animals' (Davis, *Encountering Evil*). He emphasised the fact that human beings are one of the forms of life on Earth, not the unique form of life on

Earth. Second, he stated that the evolution of human beings is not from the peaceful Garden of Eden but from a struggle to survive.

Crucially, Hick says that human beings are not perfect. They are spiritually immature. Through their struggle to survive in the world human beings can develop into spiritually mature beings.

Stage 2: 'Likeness'

This word is used to refer to when human beings have achieved 'likeness' with God. By this Hick meant when, in the future, human beings grow into a relationship with God.

3 The Fall

In the Irenaean tradition, the Fall in the Garden of Eden is not nearly as significant as it is for Augustine, because it is a mistake of the immature human being who is only in the 'image' of God. Hick suggests that the only meaning of the term 'Fall' today is to describe how far apart God and human beings are.

Hick argues that human beings were not created in the presence of God. He suggests that if human beings were in God's presence, all their free will would be removed. Effectively, human beings would be overpowered by the presence of God and incapable of any choice. This leads Hick to claim that there is an *epistemic distance* between God and human beings:

> The 'distance' cannot of course be spatial; for God is omnipresent. It must be an epistemic distance, a distance in the cognitive dimension. And the Irenaean hypothesis is that this 'distance' consists, in the case of humans, in their existence within and as part of the world which functions as an autonomous system and from within which God is not overwhelmingly present. (Davis, *Encountering Evil*)

Epistemic distance

The phrase used by John Hick and other philosophers to express the idea that God's existence is not obvious and thus human beings are not overwhelmed by God's presence into believing in God. A measure in the dimension of knowledge. Epistemic distance refers to the degree of difficulty involved in knowing of/about God. Christian apologists argue that God did not want his existence to be so obvious as to force belief upon humans; rather, they ought to '. . . search for me, you will find me; if you seek me with all your heart' (Jeremiah 29:13).

Thought Point

Free choice?

Think about your time in school. Have you ever misbehaved? If you have, would you have behaved in the same way if your mother had been sitting next to you in class?

In some schools teachers ask the parents to come into class with their child if the child misbehaves. Can you think of any disadvantages of this system of discipline?

By this, Hick means that God's presence is not obvious and therefore human beings have a choice whether to believe in God or not.

Peter Vardy has given a modern example to explain this idea. He suggests the idea of a king falling in love with a peasant girl. Rather than forcing her to marry him, the king tries to win the heart of the peasant girl.

Hick argued that if you were perfect, why would you ever sin and make yourself less than perfect? He argued that it would be unlikely that you would do so even if, in theory, you were able to choose to sin and be less than perfect.

Thought Point

Evil actions

Can anything good come from evil actions?

4 Soul-making

Hick argues that we live in a world that is about soul-making. He means that we live in a world in which we can make choices about how to behave and that these choices enable us to develop good habits and virtuous qualities of character – if we choose. For example, virtues such as compassion and charity can only be developed in a world where there is suffering, but developing such qualities makes people more moral. Hick's argument is that virtuous qualities that are developed through effort and choice in life, such as being charitable or conscientious, are much more morally valuable than qualities you are just given or created with.

One example Hick offers is that moral growth can be seen occasionally through the flourishing of ideas and civilisations. Equally, the animal nature of human beings is visible in some of the wicked behaviour of human beings throughout history. One way to illustrate Hick's point could be to contrast the development of the idea of universal human rights with the lack of respect for people's human rights in some countries of the past or present, such as Nazi Germany.

5 Why are there natural disasters?

Hick argues that within an Irenaean theodicy the 'challenging environment' that natural disasters make is also the stimulant for human intellectual and imaginative development. He argues:

In a world devoid both of dangers to be avoided and rewards to be won we may assume that there would have been virtually no moral development of the human intellect and imagination, and hence of either the sciences or the arts, and hence of human civilisation or culture. (Davis, *Encountering Evil*)

Here, Hick is suggesting that the world has to be a real one in which there is danger in order for us to develop from the likeness into the image of God. For the same reason Hick argues that the world functions according to natural laws so that human beings can investigate the world. For the Irenaean theodicy, having a real choice means having a world in which there is the possibility of pain as well as pleasure.

John Hick is well aware of the challenges from people such as Dostoevsky about the sheer amount and depth of evil in the world. He suggests that the only answer may in the end be that in heaven all will be well. This is called an *eschatological answer*. He accepts that from the point of view of the person suffering there is no explanation; all people can do is trust in God. The choice for Hick is either that there is natural evil or that there is no evil, and we do not live in an environment in which we can develop. This explanation is also said to explain the random nature of evil: why it is that good people seem to suffer and evil people thrive. If only evil people suffered, we would not live in an environment in which we could develop.

Eschatological

This is a word used by theologians to refer to what will happen at the end of time or in the last days of the universe. Traditionally it is linked with judgement and afterlife.

6 Eschatological aspect

In the Irenaean theodicy people only become made in the image of God after death. Hick points out that millions of people have already died who were in the likeness not the image of God. This leads him to follow Irenaeus' belief that everyone will eventually be saved and be in the presence of God after death. Hick argues that if God's purpose is to allow humans to develop from the image of God into his likeness, this will be achieved only after death – it is clearly incomplete in life. This leads Hick to support belief in universal salvation – God saving everyone after death; he does not believe in hell.

Purgatory

Purgatory is a state of existence post-death in which people are purified by punishment after death. This is a different state from hell and the nature of punishment is purification, unlike in hell. Belief in Purgatory is most commonly associated with Roman Catholic Christianity, though some other Christians also share this belief.

Thought Point

Daylight robbery

Would you steal what you liked if you knew that in the end you would go to heaven anyway?

Thought Point

If you will be saved – whatever

Would you behave differently if you knew that eventually you would go to paradise with God, whatever you did?

CRITICISMS OF HICK'S THEODICY

Plausibility

Hick rejected the theodicy of Augustine as implausible, but many commentators have questioned the plausibility of his own theodicy, particularly its eschatological aspect. Equally, it is only fair to say that Hick himself is a theist and Christian, and he asks that his argument be viewed as a reasonable interpretation.

Injustice

Traditional Christianity has emphasised the fact that human beings are responsible for their own actions and God will judge them. Many of Jesus' statements echo this thought. Ultimately, justice is seen as a matter of treating people as they deserve. Therefore, many Christians believe that universal salvation is unjust. It is almost like saying you can do wrong in life but ultimately this will not matter.

The existence of suffering

In Hick's theodicy God is explicitly responsible for creating a world in which there are natural disasters, and implicitly responsible for the suffering that arises from them. To other commentators this seems plainly to contrast with the notion of God as loving or good.

Is suffering a price worth paying? Is so much suffering necessary?

Clearly this is a matter of personal opinion. Many would choose to disagree with Hick's idea that it is necessary for the world to be as it is, with all the suffering and evil in it. Even one life lost due to someone else's evil act seems to be one life too many, let alone the millions lost in Nazi Germany (1940s), Vietnam (1960s), Cambodia (1970s), Rwanda (1990s) and so on.

Do the ends justify the means?

Many ethical thinkers do not agree that you may use any means you like to achieve a good end. For example, Immanuel Kant would reject the idea of torturing someone to get information to prevent a terrorist attack because you are harming the person as a means to an end. Dostoevsky's character Ivan Karamazov wanted nothing to do with God's world if it involved appalling suffering being permitted so that good might result.

Many philosophers would question whether it is right to justify the existence of evil so that we live in a world in which we can develop into the likeness of God. Many Christians would reject any idea that a loving God allows or creates situations where evil happens so that people have the chance of living in a world where they can develop into the likeness of God.

The epistemic distance

One could question why God is not more clearly visible, and ask if people would then accept God and not do evil things.

CONCLUSION

There is no doubt of the importance of the Augustinian and Irenaean theodicies as attempts to address the difficult problem presented by the existence of and the amount of evil in the world. Both theodicies emphasise the importance of free will as an explanation of much evil in the world and this certainly appeals to the way in which people think in everyday life.

In addition, there is no doubt that people learn from making mistakes. The idea of a soul-making world also resonates with people's experiences of learning from mistakes and errors.

Both theodicies have been severely criticised. However, whether this means that the problem of evil may be used as an argument against God's existence is another matter. Certainly the logic of the theodicies may be challenged, but is this an argument against God, our definition of God, or really another way of saying that the problem of evil is ultimately a mystery that humans are not in a position to answer?

Swinburne's theodicy

Swinburne argues that some evil is necessary in order for us to achieve higher-order goods. Swinburne accepts that if God is omnipotent he could stop evil, but only if there was no possibility of humans ever choosing to exercise virtues such as courage and selflessness. If there were no famines or disasters, there would be no situations in which humans could exercise charity. He argues that it is better to live in a world where there is evil and suffering than in a 'toy world' where the consequences of human actions do not matter, and if there was not the possibility of human actions producing evil consequences then humans would not need to make moral decisions. God cannot intervene in the world as this would mean no human freedom and no need for responsibility and development. Even death is necessary as it means that humans have to take responsibility for their actions, because if humans were immortal there would always be a second chance and so no risk. Natural evil is necessary to enable death regardless of any suffering caused. Swinburne thought that God created a 'half-finished' universe which gives humans the possibility to choose to make it better. This idea depends on humans having free will.

THE FREE WILL DEFENCE

Both the theodicies of Augustine and Irenaeus rely on human free will. For Augustine human misuse of free will resulted in the introduction of evil into a perfect world and so evil is the responsibility of humans, not of God. For Irenaeus, Hick and Swinburne free will is vital if we are to improve both ourselves and the world in which we live. Both approaches see evil as the result of the human free will, however; without free will there is no possibility of humans having a free loving relationship with God.

Criticisms of the free will defence

Anthony Flew questions the actual meaning of free will. According to Flew freely chosen actions cannot have external causes, they have to be internal to the person in order to be really freely chosen. Flew goes on to say that God could have created a world in which humans could always freely choose to do the right thing – they would be naturally good, but still make free choices according to Flew's definition of a free choice.

In this approach, however, God is manipulating his creation in order to bring about certain results, whereas the free will defence hinges on humans being free to love and worship God as well as being free to reject him.

J.L. Mackie extends the argument further by saying that God could have created a world in which humans were really free but who would never have chosen to do evil. Mackie's argument is a logical one: if it is possible for a person who is free to do the right thing on one occasion, then it is possible for a person to do the right thing on every occasion, so God could have created a world in which everyone is genuinely free, and yet chooses always to do the right thing. Mackie concluded that as God failed to do this he cannot be omnipotent and omnibenevolent.

PROCESS THEODICY

Evil is only a problem if one maintains the traditional God of classical theism. Process theodicy, developed by Alfred North Whitehead (1861–1947) and David Griffin (1943–), states that God is not omnipotent and is not separate from his creation. God is part of creation and can, therefore, influence what happens in the world but cannot determine it. The universe itself is in a constant state of change and process and God can only influence it by his power of persuasion: he tries to influence humans to do his will and to do what is good. Humans are free to ignore this persuasion and God has no control over this, but when evil is committed God suffers along with those involved; God is part of the world and, therefore, affected by it.

God is not powerful enough to stop evil, but process theodicy does not explain why God allowed evil and simply says that evil is an inevitable aspect of natural processes. In spite of the fact that the existence of evil makes it difficult to believe in God, Griffin argues that the universe has produced enough good to outweigh the evil and it is better to have this universe than no universe at all. This encourages believers to fight with God against evil – but is this limited God actually worthy of worship? Is the suffering God any help to someone who is really suffering and faced with the most appalling evil?

Thought Point

The problem of evil – final task

1   How does the following quotation relate to the problem of evil?
2   Is the quotation a satisfactory conclusion to the problem of evil? Give reasons to explain your answer.

continued opposite

> Where were you when I laid the foundation of the earth?
> Tell me, if you have understanding.
> Who determined its measurements – surely you know!
> Or who stretched the line upon it? (Job 38: 4–5)

SUMMARY

1 The problem

Epicurus: Is God willing to prevent evil, but not able to? Then he is not omnipotent. Is God able to prevent evil, but not willing to? Then he is malevolent (evil). Is God able to prevent evil and willing to? Then why is there evil?

2 Why the existence of evil challenges belief in God

If God is all-powerful why does God not prevent evil?
The sheer amount of evil in the world appears to challenge the goodness of creation
Dostoevsky: The Brothers Karamazov
Huge amount of suffering in nature (J.S. Mill, Richard Dawkins)

3 Theodicy

'Theodicy' comes from: theos *(meaning 'God') and* dikaios *(meaning 'justification')*

4 Types of evil

Moral evil
Natural evil

5 Possible solutions

Evil is caused by creatures using their free will
Evil is necessary as a means for people to develop some valuable moral qualities, such as compassion
Developing a different understanding of the nature of God

6 The theodicy of Augustine

Key ideas

God the Creator is omnipotent and all-good
Harmonious creation
Hierarchy of beings: angels, humans, animals
Evil is a privation
Angels and human beings fall through their own free choices
Natural evil: disharmony in the world follows the fall of angels
Free will is valuable so God allows moral and natural evil to occur
Aesthetic value of the existence of evil

Criticisms of Augustine's theodicy

Plausibility
Science
The earth developed very slowly over a period of four billion years
Life has developed through evolution by natural selection
Re Adam's sin: every person is a unique individual who inherits half of
    their DNA from their mother and half from their father

How could the perfect world go wrong?
God's responsibility for natural evils

7 Irenaean theodicy

Key ideas

God the Creator is omnipotent and all-good
The universe and the Earth develop over time
Human beings are created in an imperfect state, evolving from 'image' into
    'likeness' of God
Soul-making world
Epistemic distance
Eschatological aspect
Value of free will

8 Criticisms of Hick's theodicy

Plausibility
Injustice
Is suffering a price worth paying?
Is so much suffering necessary?
Do the ends justify the means?
The epistemic distance
Why is God not more clearly visible?

REVIEW QUESTIONS

Look back over the chapter and check that you can answer the following questions:

1   List the positive and negative features of Augustine's and Irenaeus' theodicies. Do you think either theodicy is adequate? Justify your answer with reasons.
2   Aristotle famously stated that 'we become just by doing just acts, temperate by doing temperate acts, brave by doing brave acts' (Aristotle, *The Nichomachean Ethics*). How could this support the ideas of Christian theodicies?
3   Would you say that 'the existence of evil' is a mystery? If it is a mystery, can 'the existence of evil' be used as an argument against the existence of God?
4   Desmond Tutu wrote in 1977 about South Africa under the apartheid system of discrimination against black people:

    [T]he burning question is not 'Why is there suffering and evil in the universe of a good God?' but the more immediately pressing one of *'Why do we suffer so?' 'Why does suffering seem to single out us blacks to be the victims of a racism gone mad?'* (Appiah-kubi and Torres, *African Theology en Route: Papers from the Pan-African Conference of Third World Theologians*; emphasis added)

    (a) Do you agree with Desmond Tutu about what the key question is (italic above)?
    (b) Do the ideas of the Irenaean and Augustinian theodicies answer Desmond Tutu's question?

Terminology

Do you know your terminology?

Try to explain the following ideas without looking at your books and notes:

(a) Theodicy
(b) The Fall
(c) Epistemic distance
(d) Privation.

Examination Questions Practice

EXAM MISTAKES TO AVOID

1   Make sure that you can clearly explain both the Augustinian and the Irenaean theodicies without confusing them. In addition, when you answer examination questions, you need to show that you understand the theories as well as just describing them.

2   It is important that you are able to compare the Augustinian and Irenaean theodicies as well as criticise them.

Remember: (a) assesses AO1 and (b) AO2. To help you improve your answers look at the AS Levels of Response. See: http://www.ocr.org.uk/qualifications/as-a-level-gce-religious-studies-h172-h572/

SAMPLE AS EXAM-STYLE QUESTIONS

1   (a) **Explain Augustine's theodicy.** (25 marks)

This is a straightforward question to answer, but it is worth learning well as it is the type of question that is frequently set by the examiners.

In your answer you need to explain in a clear manner the key elements of the Augustinian theodicy, such as:

- The link with the Bible story of the creation and the Fall
- The original goodness and harmony of creation as depicted in the Garden of Eden
- The Fall and its consequences
- Suffering as a punishment
- The seminal presence of all human beings in Adam
- The link between free will and natural evil (caused by the fall of angels) and moral evil (caused by the Fall of Adam and Eve)
- Evil as a privation.

(b) **'Reasoned arguments cannot account for the amount of evil in the world.' Discuss.** (10 marks)

There are many ways to approach this question. What you must do is put forward an argument that either supports or disagrees with the statement in the question. Some possible approaches are:

- Theodicies provide a rational defence of belief in God even though evil exists, but they do not offer comfort to a person who is suffering, nor are they intended to.
- Discuss the logical problem with believing in a good, omnipotent, omniscient God in the light of all the evil in the world. For example, you could discuss the particular problem of God being omniscient: would that mean that God always knows what humans will choose to do? If God does

know and is omnipotent, should God not prevent the evil? Consider whether either the Augustinian or Irenaean theodicy can justify the amount of evil in the world.

• Consider whether the sheer amount of evil in the world means that human freedom is too high a price to pay. You could discuss the criticisms from *The Brothers Karamazov* story.

2 (a) Explain how the theodicy of Irenaeus differs from that of Augustine.

(b) How far would you agree that natural evil is not explained by the need for free will?

3 (a) Describe how Augustine and Irenaeus use the concept of human free will in their theodicies.

(b) 'Theodicies are useless for those who experience real suffering.' Discuss.

4 (a) Explain how Irenaeus accounts for the existence of both moral and natural evil.

(b) To what extent is it true that the greatest strength of Irenaeus' explanation of evil is that it points to a loving God?

FURTHER READING

There is a wide range of books available on the problem of evil. A few areas you might follow up are suggested below:

When thinking about the problem of evil in an academic way it is always important to consider the reality of being the victim of great evil and how this relates to any theodicy. You can watch any number of news articles reporting atrocities committed in our world. If you wish to read some books that raise profound questions about humanity's capacity for evil, try either *Night* by E. Wiesel or *The Tenth Circle of Hell* by R. Hukanovic. *Night* is the story of Elie Wiesel in the concentration camps of the Second World War; *The Tenth Circle of Hell* is the story of Rezak Hukanovic's imprisonment during the Bosnian–Serbian conflict of the 1990s.

Richard Swinburne's book *Providence and the Problem of Evil* (1998) is a detailed and thoughtful examination of the problem of evil. It also sets out his own approach to the problem of evil, which provides a good example of the way one modern Christian philosopher has tackled the problem of evil.

D.Z. Phillips' book *The Problem of Evil and the Problem of God* (2012) is an excellent attempt to discuss the problem of evil, showing how it is linked to our idea of God.

If you would like to investigate how other religions have approached the problem of evil you could look at the extract from the great Islamic philosopher Al-Ghazali in E. Stump and Michael J. Murray (eds), *Philosophy of Religion: The Big Questions* (1999). A very interesting short article by S. Brichto about Jewish responses to the problem of evil may be found in the journal *Dialogue* 11 (November 1998).

Peter Vardy and Julie Arliss' book *The Thinker's Guide to Evil* (2003) is an eloquently written examination of the problem of evil and various ways in which people have responded to it. It is a good book to develop your knowledge of this topic for advanced level studies, as it covers many different approaches to the problem of evil.

10 Science and Religion

THE ISSUES

Is it possible to accept the findings of modern science and be religious?
Do the findings of scientists undermine the case for belief in God?

WHAT YOU WILL LEARN ABOUT IN THIS CHAPTER

This chapter explores one of the fundamental questions facing religion in the modern world: how can you be religious and accept a scientific view of the world? The creation stories in the Bible suggest that God is the direct Creator of both the universe and human beings. Animals and plants simply exist for the benefit of human beings.

Yet modern science proposes a very different view of the world. The Big Bang theory suggests that the universe is millions of years old and originated from a fluctuation in space-time, whilst Charles Darwin's theory of evolution explains the origins of all life without any reference to direct or purposeful creation by God. Two questions above all require consideration:

1 Can belief in God be reconciled with scientific discoveries about the formation of the universe?
2 Can belief in God as Creator be maintained if life evolved by natural selection?

THE OCR CHECKLIST

In this chapter you will cover the following aspects of the OCR specification:

Candidates should be able to demonstrate knowledge and understanding of:

- scientific and philosophical views on the creation of the universe; particularly the debate between Creationism and the Big Bang theory;
- Darwinism and various developments of evolutionary theory;
- 'Intelligent Design' and 'Irreducible Complexity';
- Religious responses to challenges posed by scientific views.

Candidates should be able to discuss critically these views and their strengths and weaknesses.

From OCR A Level Religious Studies specification H172.

Complete the table below and the questions which follow it.

Claim	Strongly Agree	Agree	Disagree	Strongly Disagree	No opinion
1. Science concerns facts. Religion concerns opinion					
2. Science provides clear reasons to indicate why religious world views are correct					
3. Science and religion concern completely different fields of human experience					
4. Science and religion work well together					
5. Science and religion answer the same questions in different ways					
6. Science education causes the death of magic and superstition					
7. Science and religion are essential aspects of human existence and experience					
8. Science gives more plausible and reliable arguments than religion					
9. Scientists provide evidence to support their views unlike religious people					
10. Scientists misunderstand religious ideas					

ANALYSIS

1   What assumptions about the nature of science and religion underpin your answers?
2   Which of the claims are 'weakest'?
3   Is there any observable pattern to your choices?
4   Which statements could be supported with empirical evidence?

STARTER

1   Use the internet to research the views of the following scientists regarding religion and creation or the Big Bang theory. Whose case do you find most convincing? Why?

   Richard Dawkins
   Peter Atkins
   John Polkinghorne
   Jocelyn Bell-Burnell
   Arthur Peacock

2   What is the origin of human life? Ask someone to explain their view with reasons.

INTRODUCTION

Before addressing the questions of the origins of the universe and the origins of life it is necessary to explore three key issues in the relationship between scientific ideas and religious beliefs today:

1   The 'how' and 'why' oversimplification;
2   The modern scientific worldview;
3   What is the relationship between science and religion?

For many people who are familiar with modern science the primary issue regarding religious belief and science concerns whether God is the most rational way to explain why the universe exists and why human life exists. In this sense, the issue could be seen as a question: is God the most satisfactory hypothesis to explain the origins of the universe?

   The debates concerning the interaction of science and religion underlie many questions concerning why people hold or reject religious beliefs. In order to understand this debate it is very important to be aware of the following four important issues:

1 Belief in God and modern science

For many people who are familiar with modern science the primary issue regarding religious belief and science concerns whether God is the most rational way to explain why the universe exists and why human life exists. In this sense, the issue could be seen as a question: is God the most satisfactory hypothesis to explain the origins of the universe?

Debates in science and religion are not simply concerned with explaining how the universe began, they also focus upon the matter of explaining why there is any universe here at all. The 'God hypothesis' is one that says that the existence of the universe, i.e. the fact that it is here, can be explained by reference to God.

The God explanation provides an absolute answer to why the universe is here. This is the type of answer that cosmologists like Stephen Hawking are looking for, though of course this explanation goes well beyond the findings of modern science.

For religious believers the question concerning the origins of the universe is particularly important because of the widely held belief in God as the Creator and sustainer of all that exists.

> **Hypothesis**
>
> In scientific thinking a 'hypothesis' is a theory that is put forward to explain the occurrence of some event or object. Hypotheses are then tested against the evidence and the theories are accepted if the evidence supports the theory and the theory is potentially falsifiable. (For more details concerning *falsification* see Chapter 15, 'Religious Language'.)

2 The 'how' and 'why' oversimplification

A view that is often found in books to explain the relationship between science and religion is one that suggests that religion explains 'why' the universe exists or 'why' humans exist, while science explains 'how' things happen as they do. This 'how'/'why' distinction is often repeated but it is an oversimplification. The problem with it is that science quite clearly explains 'why' things happen as well as 'how'. For example, modern accounts of gravity clearly explain why any object with a mass is attracted by other objects that have a mass.

An alternative way to express the 'how' and 'why' principle would be to point to the different types of explanation that occur. At one and the same time, an explanation may:

- identify what something is
- identify the function of an object
- identify the method by which something has been constructed
- identify why the thing was caused to exist
- identify why the thing continues to exist.

> **Stephen Hawking (1942–)**
>
>
>
> Stephen Hawking is a world-renowned theoretical physicist. He is the Lucasian Professor of Mathematics at Cambridge. (This is the same professorial chair that Sir Isaac Newton once held.) He is particularly well known for his work on black holes and his books *A Brief History of Time* and *The Universe in a Nutshell*.

Why modern theories of gravity?

Isaac Newton is, of course, well known for his work on gravity, but it is important to note that within his system of thought God plays the role of sustaining the system. Newton was a deist. Modern accounts of gravity do not rely on holding a deist belief in God.

'God of the gaps' thinking

A view of God that holds God responsible for any aspect of human experience that cannot be otherwise explained. As human knowledge increases, what God is responsible for decreases.

Thought Point

Look at the picture and then complete the table:

Does what the picture shows have a function? If so, what is it?	
How is what the picture shows constructed?	
Why does what the picture shows exist?	
Why does what the picture shows continue to exist?	

3 The modern scientific worldview

When exploring the relationship between science and religion it is very important that you are aware of the origins of the modern view of this. Often, in newspapers, science is depicted as something that gives factual knowledge and is gradually undermining areas that were traditionally considered matters of religious belief. For example, the theory of evolution is often pointed to as evidence that undermines belief in God as Creator. While evolution may do this, it is not clear that it does.

In many Western developed countries there is a prevailing view that science provides facts and religion is based upon views from the past that are mistaken. Typical of this way of thinking are stories often taught to children when young, such as those concerning Christopher Columbus voyaging to prove that the Earth was not flat. In actual fact Columbus' voyage was opposed by the monarchy in Spain on the grounds of its cost and expense, not because of any question concerning whether the Earth was thought to be flat. Indeed, educated people from Graeco-Roman times onwards knew that the world was a sphere. The Ptolemaic view of the universe, with the Earth at the centre of the universe with the sun going around it, always presented the Earth as a sphere.

The myth concerning Columbus proving flat-earth believers wrong originates from books written in the nineteenth century as part of the so-called war between science and religion, such as Andrew Dickson White's book *History of the Warfare of Science with Theology in Christendom* (1896) and Washington Irving's *Life and Voyages of Christopher Columbus* (1828). However, while a number of 'myths' concerning religion and science including the Columbus story circulated, Stephen Jay Gould has observed that flat earth stories are:

> Dramatic to be sure, but entirely fictitious. No period of 'flat earth darkness' ever occurred among scholars (no matter how many uneducated people may have conceptualised our planet in this way, both then and now). Greek knowledge of sphericity never faded, and all medieval religious scholars accepted the earth's roundness as an established fact of cosmology. Ferdinand and Isabella did refer Columbus' plan to a royal commission. . . . They did pose some sharp questions, but no-one questioned the earth's roundness. (*Rocks of Ages*)

A second aspect to the modern worldview is the belief that science provides people with 'facts', unlike religion. This view developed in the nineteenth century, but has been popularised again in the late twentieth century in the work of authors such as Richard Dawkins:

> Faith is the great cop out, the great excuse to evade the need to think and to evaluate evidence. Faith is belief in spite of, perhaps even because of, lack of evidence. (Speech to the Edinburgh International Science Festival, 15 April 1992)

While it is undoubtedly true that science is based on empirical methods, science does not disprove the existence of God. Instead, science such as cosmology helps us to better understand the universe in which we live. Scientific findings may undermine belief that God's role is only to 'fill in the gaps'. For example, if you say that God created life on Earth, because you could not explain it any other way, the theory of evolution will immediately threaten your belief in God the Creator of life. You would have either to modify your belief in God or discard it in the face of the evidence. However, if a religious believer holds the view that God is the Creator of life because God established the scientific laws that enabled life to evolve, then belief in

God is not necessarily undermined by the theory of evolution. Alister McGrath and Joanna Collicutt McGrath state:

> One of the greatest disservices that Dawkins has done to the natural sciences is to portray them as relentlessly and inexorably atheistic. They are nothing of the sort; yet Dawkins' crusading vigour has led to the growth of this alienating perception in many parts of North American conservative Protestantism. (*The Dawkins Delusion?*)

This point cannot be overstated. The assumption that science is correct and religion is incorrect has led to increasing rejection of evolution by many Christians today, particularly in North America. However, the choice is not necessarily between religion and science. Many people can accept theories such as evolution or modern cosmological findings about the origin of the universe as well as being religious; moreover, the fact that people hold these religious views does not mean that they are ignorant.

Thought Point

Science and religion

Consider the following two quotations. What points are they making (and assuming) about the relationship between science and religion? Which view do you find more persuasive? Why?

> I do not see how science and religion could be unified, or even synthesized, under any common scheme of explanation or analysis; but I also do not understand why the two enterprises should experience any conflict. Science tries to document the factual character of the natural world, and to develop theories that co-ordinate and explain these facts. Religion, on the other hand, operates in the equally important, but utterly different, realm of human purposes, meanings and values – subjects that the factual domain of science might illuminate, but can never resolve. Similarly, while scientists must operate with ethical principles, some specific to their practice, the validity of these principles can never be inferred from the actual discoveries of science. (Gould, *Rocks of Ages*)

> I think religion kills. And where it doesn't kill, it stifles. Religion scorns the human intellect by saying that the human brain is simply too puny to understand . . . I don't think that there is any question that science

continued opposite

cannot tackle. And I think that, as it tackles them, it gives people answers that are much more reliable, much more plausible, than the obscure arguments religion provides. I mean, many of the questions religion tries to answer are not real questions. Take one that you've just mentioned, the purpose of the universe. In my view, that's an entirely invented question. (Peter Atkins in Russell Stannard, *Science and Wonders*)

4 Science and religion: friends, enemies or simply different?

The relationship of science and religion is a continuing and ongoing area of debate in the modern world. The table below highlights some common views of the relationship between science and religion. What is worth noting is that there are both atheist and theist scientists, just as some religious people accept the findings of modern science and others do not. Furthermore, the intolerance of religion for science as reflected in some creationists' ideas (see below) is mirrored by the rejection of religion by some scientists. While some scientists argue that religion is undermined by modern science, others do not:

The fact that we wrestle with the problem of pain and suffering shows us that the cold scientific story of a universe of some gainers, as presented to us by Dawkins, is far from sufficient to satisfy our human longing to understand and to make sense of the world in which we live. Questions of meaning and justice cannot be removed from the human agenda. (Polkinghorne, *Belief in God in an Age of Science*)

Table 10.1 Friends, enemies or simply different?

Intelligent Design

The expression *Intelligent Design* has been in use for the last 200 years including by Charles Darwin, but its modern meaning dates back to a ruling by the Supreme Court in America that the teaching of Creationist ideas as science was unconstitutional.

The key features of *Intelligent Design* are that:

- The universe is *irreducibly complex* meaning that objects and organisms in the world are so complex that the complexity of these things cannot be explained by the blind process of evolution.
- The *specified complexity* of organisms and the universe. This refers to the idea that the complexity of the organisms and universe is so great that the only possible explanation of it is that it has been 'specified' by God.
- The physical laws of the universe are just right for life to exist. If the physical laws of the universe were different there would be no life and no stars as we know them to provide energy to sustain life.

All of these features are used as evidence to suggest that the universe is created by God. Often *Intelligent Design* is closely associated with Creationism.

However, the features highlighted by *Intelligent Design* theory have been rejected since the claims of intelligent design cannot be tested and are, in some cases, unfalsifiable. Second, supporters of evolution claim that the complexity of living organisms can be explained by evolutionary theory without need for Creator.

Warfare

The relationship between science and religion in the modern world is often thought to be one of hostility between religious believers and scientists, primarily evolutionary biologists.

Two basic ideas underlie the belief that science opposes religion. First, evolution theory suggests nature is singularly indifferent to human beings. Nature appears to function on its own, and is not directed and displays no purpose. Indeed, from a human perspective, nature can seem cruel.

The second idea derives from the writing of some modern biologists. Richard Dawkins and others have claimed that evolutionary biology has uncovered the secrets of the evolution of life and that religious answers are simply wrong in the light of scientific evidence:

> When you are actually challenged to think of pre-Darwinian answers to the questions 'What is man?', 'Is there a meaning to life?', 'What are we for?', can you, as a matter of fact, think of any that are not now worthless except for their (considerable) historic interest? There is such a thing as being just plain wrong, and that is what, before 1859, all answers to these questions were. (Dawkins, *The Selfish Gene*)

NOMA

NOMA is an idea put forward by Stephen Jay Gould as a way to describe the relationship between science and religion.

NOMA stands for 'Non-overlapping Magisteria'. A Magisteria is an area of authority that someone (historically a teacher) has. Gould's argument is that religion and science can co-exist together because they each concern different areas and fields of human experience. Religion for Gould concerns questions of meaning, purpose and moral values, while science concerns matters of fact and explanations of why things work as they do.

COSMOLOGY

'Cosmology' refers not only to the arguments for God's existence which concern whether God is responsible for the existence of the universe and all that is in it, but also to the field of physics, which is concerned with exploring the origins of the universe.

In particular, cosmology is associated with a theory known as the 'Big Bang theory'. The Big Bang theory is the most widely accepted theory that explains the physical origins and development of the universe. According to the Big Bang theory, the universe is somewhere between 12 and 15 billion years old. All the matter that is within the universe originates from the initial expansion of space from a single point of space-time. The timeline below illustrates some of the most significant dates in the development of the universe from a human perspective.

The key issue for religious believers as well as scientists in the modern world is: how can one explain why the universe exists? It is not a matter of explaining how the universe began, but a matter of explaining why there is any universe here at all.

The Big Bang Timeline

All space-time begins with the Big Bang and all matter and energy in the universe originates from the Big Bang. The timeline below outlines the development of the universe. It is worth noting that the universe continues to expand by inflation even today. Astronomers can detect the expansion of the universe by studying what is known as *Redshift* in the night sky.

Curious?

To find out more investigate the following terms on the internet or in an encyclopaedia:

* The Big Bang theory
* WMAP
* Redshift
* Cosmic Inflation.

0 years ago	Today
10,300 years ago	End of the most recent Ice Age
250,000 years ago	First Homo sapiens
50 million years ago	The Himalayas begin to form
67 million years ago	Dinosaurs become extinct
150 million years ago	First birds
313 million years ago	First reptiles
365 million years ago	First amphibians and trees
1.3 billion years ago	First plants
1.6 billion years ago	First blue-green algae
4 billion years ago	First life on earth
4.45 billion years ago	The earth is completely formed
4.55 billion years ago	Formation of the sun
13.3 billion years ago	The first stars heat
10^{-43}s after	Space and time begin
10^{-35} to 10^{-33}s after	Rapid *Inflation* of the universe
c. 13.7 billion years ago	The Big Bang

IS GOD THE BEST HYPOTHESIS TO EXPLAIN THE EXISTENCE OF THE UNIVERSE?

The key issue for religious believers as well as scientists in the modern world is: how can one explain why the universe exists? It is not a matter of explaining how the universe began, but a matter of explaining why there is any universe here at all. The *God hypothesis* suggests that the existence of the universe, i.e. the fact that it is here, can be best explained by reference to God.

CAN THE ORIGINS OF THE UNIVERSE BE EXPLAINED?

Theories such as the Big Bang theory propose explanations of the development of the universe. Yet an underlying question remains: why did the universe come to exist at all? One needs to consider how the origins of the universe may be explained. There are two obvious approaches: Yes and No.

No

It is impossible that there is an absolute explanation of the origins of the universe. However, this is a rather negative approach, since it starts from the premise that the universe cannot be explained. It would therefore beg the question: can the universe be explained at all? Copleston makes this point in his famous radio debate with Bertrand Russell (see pp. 110ff.).

Yes

There is an absolute explanation for the origin of the universe. Both scientists and theologians may hold this view. This is the position advocated by Copleston in the famous radio debate. There are two forms of it.

First, the idea that the universe is self-explanatory, i.e. if we study the universe we may come to understand all the processes that have caused the universe to exist as it is today. By saying this philosophers mean that the universe is necessary; it is not caused to exist, it just exists; in philosophical terms by necessity. Bertrand Russell held this type of view, when he stated that the universe was a brute fact, hence there is no explanation for its existence. The chemist Peter Atkins also holds this view, believing that humans will eventually find an all-encompassing explanation of the universe, through science.

Second, the belief that the universe itself requires an absolute explanation. Theists believe that the Big Bang theory is not a simple explanation of the universe at all. They argue that for the Big Bang theory to work presumes the existence of various physical laws and laws of quantum mechanics such that the universe had to develop in the way in which it did develop. Therefore, the claim is that the Big Bang theory, far from being simple, is in fact a complex explanation of the universe.

Theists argue that God is a simple, absolute explanation of why the universe exists. This argument rests upon two assumptions; that a 'god' who causes the universe to exist is:

- Consistent with scientific evidence, and
- The most reasonable explanation of why the universe exists.

Why?

The universe itself requires an absolute explanation. Theists believe that the Big Bang theory is not a simple explanation of the universe at all. They argue that for the Big Bang theory to work presumes the existence of various physical laws and laws of quantum mechanics such that the universe had to develop in the way in which it did develop.

Theists argue that God is a simple, absolute explanation of why the universe exists. This argument rests upon two assumptions; that a 'god' who causes the universe to exist is:

(a) consistent with scientific evidence, and
(b) the most reasonable explanation of why the universe exists.

Of course, arguing that God is an absolute explanation of the existence of the universe falls a long way short of saying that this 'god' is indeed the personal God of monotheistic belief. In many ways this problem reflects the issue raised by Thomas Aquinas' Five Ways: Aquinas believed that he had proved the existence of an unmoved mover or uncaused cause which is responsible for the universe. It took him until the end of the set of questions in the *Prima Pars* (first part) of the *Summa Theologiae* to demonstrate that 'god' is indeed the Christian God.

The Cosmological argument

Many of the concepts and criticisms relating to your work on the Cosmological argument relate to the science and religion topic. It is worth looking at your Cosmological argument work again.

God as the simplest explanation of the existence of the universe

Science works on the principle that it looks for explanations for why things are as they are. It uses the principle of Ockham's Razor: *do not multiply entities beyond necessity* – i.e. accept the simplest explanation that resolves a question. In order to believe in God as the Creator of the universe, God has to be the simplest explanation that accounts for the existence of the universe.

What is meant by chance?

In everyday life the word 'chance' is used to mean something which occurs by 'pot luck', for example, meeting a friend unexpectedly in the street or winning the lottery. However, when scientists talk about things happening by chance, they are referring to the fact that the way things happen is not determined. Rather, it is a matter of there being certain probabilities whether a reaction will happen or not, such as the probability of winning the National Lottery when it is stacked 14 million to one against you.

So, to sum up, suggesting that God is the best hypothesis to account for the existence of the universe is acceptable if:

- The hypothesis provides an absolute explanation of the existence of the universe
- It is consistent with scientific evidence
- It is the most reasonable belief there is (Ockham's Razor principle – see p. 211).

Does the universe exist by chance?

If the universe exists as the result of the random development of the Big Bang this could exclude God as the best account of the existence of the universe.

Atheists can argue that the universe is merely a matter of random reactions. It is 'just chance' that the universe is here at all. The claim is that the universe just happened to develop in the way in which it did. It could easily have developed in another way. However, one could argue that the conditions of the universe are finely tuned. If the properties of the universe had been just slightly different then there would be no stars, no planets and no earth as they would not have existed, or if they had existed at all they would not have lasted long. Just slight alterations in gravity, for example, would mean either everything being flung apart or crunched together. Is this fine-tuning just brute fact or a coincidence? Stephen Hawking in his book *The Grand Design* (2010) says that as there is a law such as gravity the universe can create itself from nothing, spontaneously, and so there is no need of God to set the universe in motion.

However, Keith Ward argues that it is more reasonable to suppose that the universe does not exist by chance. Ward argues that blind chance is not a satisfactory explanation of the universe. He suggests that it would have been almost infinitely unlikely that this universe would ever come to exist if it was a matter of blind chance. If this universe is created as a universe in which conscious life can evolve, it is more reasonable to suppose that life should emerge in the universe.

Now, both atheists and theologians interpret the reality around them to try to give reasons for why things are as they are. While atheists suggest that the universe has developed as it has at random, theologians like Keith Ward argue that the random development of the universe is essential for moral freedom to evolve. The idea of an open future requires 'indeterminacy' and does not rule out the existence of God:

> indeterminacy does not contravene the scientific postulate that a reason can be found for why things are as they are (Ward, *God, Chance and Necessity*)

Is it possible to produce a complete understanding of everything? An atheist approach

Scientists such as Richard Dawkins and Peter Atkins argue that there is little or no evidence to support the idea that the existence of God can explain the origins of the universe. Instead it is argued that the universe can be explained by various theories, such as the Big Bang theory or evolution.

The claim is that as our knowledge of the universe expands so we learn more about the workings and development of the universe. The aim is eventually to achieve an absolute explanation of the origins of the universe. This is the task that cosmologists such as Stephen Hawking have set for themselves.

The chemist Peter Atkins has made various criticisms of the idea that God explains satisfactorily the origins of the universe. In particular, he has suggested that it is not necessary to postulate the existence of God to explain the existence of everything. The underlying assumption is that everything can be explained by rational scientific enquiry.

In books such as Daniel Dennett's *Darwin's Dangerous Idea* (1996) and Richard Dawkins' *The Selfish Gene* (1989 [1976]) the assumption concerning the explanatory power of science is applied in fields beyond the actual study of biological evolution via natural selection.

For example, Richard Dawkins proposed the concept of a *meme* that replicates cultural ideas. He states that:

> Just as genes propagate themselves in the gene pool by leaping from body to body via sperm or eggs, so memes propagate themselves by leaping from brain to brain via a process which, in the broad sense, can be called imitation. (*The Selfish Gene*)

Richard Dawkins argues that the idea of God is a *meme*, and like a gene, belief in God by people has continued generation after generation, because the God meme has great psychological appeal which makes its survival generation after generation likely, just as a gene will survive generation after generation in the gene pool if it gives the organism it is in an evolutionary advantage, such as resistance to a disease.

> The survival value of the god *meme* in the *meme* pool results from its great psychological appeal. It provides a superficially plausible answer to deep and troubling questions about existence. (*The Selfish Gene*)

The idea of memes has been developed by authors including Susan Blackmore (*The Meme Machine*, 2000).

Furthermore, atheists such as Richard Dawkins argue that longing for and belief in God can be explained through evolutionary theories and related ideas like *memes*; or alternatively, through human psychology.

Memes

Meme is a word used by Richard Dawkins and Susan Blackmore to refer to a cultural idea or belief that is passed on from person to person and down the generations. *Memes* can function like viruses, in the sense that they can pass on helpful and unhelpful ideas.

Investigate on the internet how *memes* have been applied to religion.

However, Simon Conway Morris has noted that:

one cannot help but notice that the discussion of memes is often pejoratively associated with some notion of 'mind parasites'. But memes are trivial, to be banished by simple mental exercises. In any other context, they are hopelessly, if not hilariously, simplistic. To conjure up memes not only reveals a strange imprecision of thought, but as Anthony O'Hare has remarked, if memes really existed they would ultimately deny the reality of reflective thought. (*Life's Solution*)

Furthermore, the use of scientific theories, such as evolution, as an explanation of aspects of human experience beyond the particular scientific area of study is rejected by Mary Midgley in *The Myths We Live By* (2003). She argues that no one system of human thought fully explains human beings' relationship with and understanding of the world:

Although both rationalists and empiricists tried to claim a monopoly for their own chosen forms of thinking it has become clear, from Kant's time onward, that the tool-bench of thought must allow for a wide variety of methods. (*The Myths We Live By*)

Just as teleological and deontological theories in ethics, and rationalism or empiricism in philosophy, on their own are not complete and satisfactory ways of understanding human thinking, so also it is an error to assume that scientific theories like evolution on its own are a complete explanation of everything. Midgley states that evolution is not a 'universal explanation'; instead, as Darwin himself repeatedly commented in his *Origin of Species*, evolution by natural selection is a biological system – it does not explain other aspects of human experience.

Daniel Dennett's claim in *Darwin's Dangerous Idea* that evolution by natural selection is like a 'universal acid . . . it eats through just about every traditional concept and leaves in its wake a revolutionised world view, with most of the old land-marks still recognisable, but transformed in fundamental ways' is criticised by Midgley because it suggests that evolution theory explains more than just natural selection.

The notion that God is only used to fill in gaps in human knowledge has been another basis for atheists' rejection of belief in God as an explanation of the origin of the universe. In particular, it is claimed that God seems only to be postulated to explain a thing that human beings cannot yet explain scientifically. However, the 'God of the gaps' criticism, has been widely rejected since it is not representative of academic theology.

Related to the 'God of the gaps' argument is the further claim that God is a lazy hypothesis to explain the existence of the universe. Peter Atkins

Perfection

A philosophical term used to indicate the goodness of God. To be perfect means that you lack nothing and could not be better in any way. God is said to be perfect, as God is totally good and could not be more 'good'.

Augustine and free will

Augustine's theodicy emphasises the fact that human beings and angels choose whether to live in harmony with God or not. This is a free will defence of the problem of evil.

Original sin

Original sin is defined in many ways by Christian thinkers, but one interpretation is to define it as the inbuilt tendency humans have to do things wrong despite their good intentions. The concept of original sin comes from interpretations of Genesis 3.

has argued that people believe in God as an absolute explanation of the origin of the universe as a way to hide their ignorance:

> Religion's inwardly directed sentimental glow reflects on issues privately, exchanges information by assurance and assertion, discusses awkward points by warfare, terror, and coercion, and builds up a network of conflicting ideas that conceal ignorance under a cloak of high-flown yet empty prose. ('Awesome Versus Adipose')

The challenge for religious people today is how to explain beliefs such as that God created the world in a scientifically meaningful way, given that scientific explanations of cosmological questions can be investigated empirically in a way that faith claims about events in the past cannot.

A common view in newspapers is that science is gradually replacing any need for religion or any role for religious explanations of the universe. Take, for example, philosopher Julian Baggini's article (*Guardian*, 14 October 2011) 'Religion's truce with science can't hold' subtitled 'Any religious belief seeking to explain the "how"s of the universe is competing with science – and in this sphere science will always win' or scepticism about the work of the Templeton Foundation which funds research into science and religion (see Mitchell Waldrop, 'Religion: Faith in Science'). Many articles attacking religion are also widely available in journals or on the internet, such as Peter Atkins' claim that:

> Science is almost totally incompatible with religion. I say 'almost,' but I do not wish that weasel word to be construed as weakness. The only point of compatibility is that there are well-meaning, honest people on both sides who are genuinely and deeply concerned with discovering the truth about this wonderful world. That having been said, there is no actual compatibility between science and religion ('Awesome Versus Adipose').

However, it is not simply that science is right while religion is misguided or wrong. Both scientists and theologians can be religious and support a modern scientific understanding of cosmological questions such as the origins of the universe, as exemplified in works such as those written by Russell Stannard, Arthur Peacock, Keith Ward and John Polkinghorne. However, amongst Christians there is not one consistent view of cosmology and science; instead there is a range of positions:

- God is the reason that the universe exists and continues to exist (an idea found in writers from Aquinas to Polkinghorne).

GUT

In science the expression 'GUT' is used to refer to a scientific theory that explains the origins and developments of the universe in its entirety. GUT stands for 'Grand Unified Theory'.

Richard Dawkins

Richard Dawkins on . . .

Apparent design in the world

Christian ideas:	Richard Dawkins has stated:
Christians claim that there is evidence of design in the world, which suggests the existence of the designer, i.e. the existence of God	→ 'This appearance of Design is probably the most important reason for the belief, held by the vast majority of people that have ever lived, in some kind of supernatural deity. It took a very great leap of the imagination from Darwin and Wallace to see that, contrary to all intuition, there is another way and, once you have understood it, a far more plausible way, for complex "design" to arise out of primeval simplicity' (*The Blind Watchmaker*)
Paley's watch analogy. Which suggests that there is order and purpose observable in creation.	→ Paley drives his point home with beautiful and reverent descriptions of the dissected machinery of life, beginning with the human eye. . . . Paley's argument is made with passionate sincerity and is informed by the best biological scholarship of the day, but it is wrong, gloriously and utterly wrong. . . . Natural selection the blind, unconscious, automatic process which Darwin discovered, and which we now know is the explanation for the existence and apparently purposeful form of all life, has no purpose in mind. It has no mind and no mind's eye. It does not plan for the future. It has no vision, no foresight, no sight at all. If it can be said to play the role of the watchmaker in nature it is the blind watchmaker. (*The Blind Watchmaker*)
Faith in God	→ [Faith] is the great cop out, the great excuse to evade the need to think and to evaluate evidence. Faith is belief in spite of, perhaps even because of, lack of evidence (speech to the Edinburgh International Science Festival, April 15, 1992)

Task: Critically assess Richard Dawkins' arguments. Are they persuasive?

- Whether to believe in God or reductionist materialism is the biggest question of all, but it is a personal choice (an approach reflected in the work of Keith Ward).

An argument for belief in God: the theist view

While many scientists argue that the Big Bang theories provide a simple explanation of the universe, this claim is also widely disputed on the grounds that the Big Bang theories are complex rather than simple. For example, Big Bang theories are incomplete and depend on the existence of a large number of scientific laws, such as quantum laws. In contrast to the atheist position outlined above, Richard Swinburne argued in his book *The Existence of God* that the argument from design could be reformulated on the basis of the existence of scientific laws which govern the development and workings of the universe. So the problem is explaining how a complex situation came to exist.

Richard Swinburne has put forward what he calls a 'teleological argument'. However, he does not mean a traditional design argument such as Paley's, which can be criticised in the light of modern science. He defines teleological arguments as those which account for the occurrence of general patterns of order in the universe.

In particular, Swinburne points to two types of order in the world:

1 **Spatial order**: e.g. books arranged in alphabetical order in a library, or regular width of car parking spaces, or relations between different members of a family such as father, mother, brother, sister, aunt, uncle
2 **Temporal order**: e.g. regularity of succession, i.e. events follow one after another according to laws of nature, such as Newton's laws. If water boils at 100 degrees Celsius, this is an example of temporal order, since heating the water leads to it boiling at 100 degrees Celsius under standard temperature and pressure, because of the laws of nature.

Thought Point

Richard Swinburne's design arguments

The following two arguments identify key points in, and are drawn from, Richard Swinburne's account of the teleological argument in his book *The Existence of God*.

continued overleaf

Argument 1

- Intricate examples of plants and animals exist in the world around us.
- These plants and animals evolved from inorganic matter by natural processes.
- So the existence of plants and animals depends on the existence of natural laws governing:

    (a) The interaction of inorganic molecules to form organic ones
    (b) Evolution of natural life.

- Therefore, nature produces plants and animals that demonstrate spatial order in the world.
- **Conclusion**: one may infer a creator who establishes the laws of nature so that nature produces variety of life, just as humans build machines which work in a certain way to build other machines.

Argument 2

- The universe exhibits temporal order; meaning that within the universe one can deduce laws that explain why the universe behaves as it does.
- We can attempt to understand the universe because it conforms to some sort of order.

- In science one explains particular phenomena, such as why water turns to ice, by reference to temporal laws which are taken to be universal.
- It is impossible to explain these laws which explain the behaviour of things in the universe, since these very laws themselves are what is used to explain how the universe works.
- The conclusion:

Over centuries long, long ago and over distances distant in millions of light years from ourselves, the same orderliness reigns . . . Yet although a scientific explanation can be provided of . . . e.g. why an electron exerts just the attractive force which it does in terms of more general powers and liabilities possessed by all bodies . . . science cannot explain why all bodies do possess the same very general powers and liabilities. So either the orderliness of nature is where all explanation stops, or we must postulate an agent of power and knowledge who brings about that . . . the most general laws operate . . . the simplest such agent to postulate is one of infinite power, knowledge and freedom, i.e. God.

Do you find Swinburne's arguments persuasive?

John Polkinghorne (*Reason and Reality*, 2011) argues that theology has 'a place within the spectrum of rational enquiry' meaning that theology is not simply vague ideas about God but is a rational activity in which human beings try to understand their experiences of God using rational methods. Polkinghorne argues that 'Creation science' is misguided as it selectively uses science to support its own views. Equally he rejects the approach of scientists who claim that everything can be explained in a reductionist manner as missing out on the richness of human experience.

Polkinghorne argues that first it is a mistake to think that any belief in Creation is concerned with God being the initiator of the universe who starts everything off. Instead he argues that 'The doctrine of creation is concerned, not just with what God did, but with what he is doing; its subject is ontological origin, not temporal beginnings.' The implications following from this are that whatever a theory about the origin of the universe says about whether it has a beginning or not, this does not a have any implication for religious belief; religious belief is concerned with God being the reason that the universe exists and continues existing.

Keith Ward's approach to science and religion debates concerning cosmology points to the problem of relying simply on reductionist materialism to explain all aspects of human experience of the universe. He rejects claims from scientists such as Dawkins and Atkins that everything that exists is ultimately explained by materialism. His argument can be summarised:

- Modern scientific accounts of the origins of the universe are to be accepted and 'render obsolete' religious accounts of creation in historical ancient texts.
- However, what accounts for the Big Bang is not necessarily answerable by science.

It is not clear how cosmological theories of the universe can answer ultimate and existential questions, such as concerning the origins of the Big Bang or what is beyond the universe.

Ward argues that claims about the 'fine-tuning' of the universe such that the physical laws and conditions of the universe are just right to produce life is not evidence for the existence of God since all the 'fine-tuning' arguments ultimately tell people is that the conditions are just right for life to evolve and for us to exist. They do not tell us whether the universe is finely tuned by chance or by the intention of a Creator. Furthermore, Ward accepts that science does not require a Creator figure to progress further in developing a scientific understanding of the universe. Instead modern science reveals the beauty of the universe and the elegant way the universe can be explained in mathematical formulas. Ward argues that science has helped to develop religious understanding of the world and clarify religious thinking. Questions

Anthropic principle
The principle that humans should take into account the constraints that human existence itself imposes on the types of universe that we believe could support human life: the only type of universe we believe capable of supporting human life is the type we occupy.

about the existence of God are ultimately not matters that are answerable by science; instead they form a conceptual framework with which people interpret the world. Ultimately, the individual person has to choose whether to believe in God. Ward suggests that a 'spiritual worldview' may answer ultimate questions about the world concerning issues such as the problem of evil in a way which non-spiritual worldviews cannot. The individual has to decide whether scientific findings about the cosmos suggest that the religious explanations of the universe are persuasive or not:

> The natural sciences are primarily concerned with natural, non-conscious facts. For some, the findings of science point toward a Primordial Consciousness as the source and foundation of all things. For others, science promises to explain the cosmos completely in material terms, without any reference to such a Primordial Consciousness. One of these views is correct. Which one? That remains the biggest question of all. (Ward, *The Big Questions in Science and Religion*)

Thought Point

Explain in your own words what the passage below is saying.

Why do you think that Alister McGrath describes Dawkins' type of approach as 'misleading'?

Does the fact that science cannot prove or disprove God's existence make a Christian cosmology more or less credible?

> Now Dawkins knows perfectly well that 'science has no way to disprove the existence of a supreme being' (Dawkins, R., *The Devil's Chaplain*). This, he argues, cannot be allowed to lead to the conclusion that 'belief (or disbelief) in a supreme being is a matter of pure individual inclination.' But who said anything about 'pure individual inclination'? Where does this idea come from? Dawkins seems to imply that, where the scientific method cannot be properly applied, there is only epistemological anarchy. Without the scientific method, we are reduced to the pure subjectivity of individual opinion. (McGrath, *Dawkins' God*)

CREATIONISM AND EVOLUTION

Since the late nineteenth century Creationists have emphasised the primacy of God above any scientific finding. In particular creationists emphasise the status of the Bible as the Word of God which reveals God as the Creator.

How religious believers should respond to the theory of evolution and other findings of modern science has become a burning issue in the modern world. At the heart of the problem is the question: can you believe in God if you accept the theory of evolution and other modern scientific findings?

In order to understand this issue, two areas need to be considered:

1 The origins of the problem
2 Creationist beliefs and responses to them today.

The origins of the problem with evolution

The origins of the problem with evolution go back to the late nineteenth and early twentieth centuries. As the theory of evolution became more popular, many people began to question the status of the Bible. In particular, people began to question whether the Bible was verbally inspired and revealed truths about God the Creator and the place of human beings in creation. The implication of this questioning was that if the Bible is not verbally inspired then its truth cannot be guaranteed – in which case what is the status of the Bible beyond that of any other book? Furthermore, as the Bible is the basis of the Christian faith, the implication is that the Christian faith and belief in God is not true.

While some Christians did not perceive the theory of evolution to be a challenge to religious belief, others, particularly from Protestant traditions, responded to the theory of evolution with the development of what is now called a 'fundamentalist' approach to Christian belief. During the period 1909 to 1915 a number of works called *Fundamentals of Religion* were published by Protestant conservative evangelical movements in North America. The theory of evolution was rejected precisely because it was thought to challenge the notion of God as Creator, since evolution accounted for the origin of different animals without reference to God. Second, the theory of evolution suggests that human beings are evolved from animals, thus denying that humans are the unique and superior creation of God as stated in Genesis 1–2.

Fundamentalist approaches to scripture claimed to be the heirs of the Reformation reformers who sought the true meaning of scripture behind the interpretation of bishops of the Church. In reality, however, fundamentalism was a new movement as it adopted the empirical approach of science. Fundamentalists attempted to demonstrate the truth of the Bible by using the empirical method of science.

For fundamentalism, science is a tool which can be used to demonstrate the truth of scripture. When science, such as in the theory of evolution, conflicts with religious beliefs in the Bible, the scientific theory is rejected as it does not correspond with the truth claims expressed in scripture.

Darwin's theory of evolution

An account of Darwin's theory of evolution and some the questions and challenges it poses for religious believers can be found in Chapter 7, 'The Teleological Argument'.

Thought Point

The literal meaning of the Bible

Consider the following statements, all based on statements in the Bible:

- God is my rock.
- God is my salvation.
- God became man and dwelt amongst us.
- God is a warrior.

What does each of these phrases mean?

Quite clearly there are various ways in which these statements could be understood as 'literal'. 'Literal' could mean that this is 'literally' what is written down, as in every character in every word is literally as it is. Or, 'literal' could mean that this is 'how it happened' or 'how it is'. This is of course a rather problematic approach if you consider statements like 'God is my rock'.

The problem with claiming that the Bible is the literal Word of God is that the text still needs to be understood, i.e. a question of interpretation remains. In reality, stating that the Bible or any event in the Bible is 'literal' does not resolve the question of what the text communicates. If, for example, you say that Genesis 1 is 'literally' true you could be saying a number of things:

- That the Genesis story happened exactly as described in the Bible;
- That the Genesis story communicates facts that are true in a literal sense, e.g. God is the Creator, these facts cannot be disputed;
- That every word written in Genesis 1 is the literal word of God.

Ultimately, saying the Bible is literally true does not help to resolve questions about the meaning of the biblical passages – if you investigate different Creationist groups you will find that they all believe that the Bible is literal, but what truths they believe the Bible communicates may vary between the different groups.

EVOLUTION

Creationist beliefs

There is no single agreed set of Creationist beliefs since 'Creationism' is a general term to describe the beliefs of a number of conservative, often evangelical, Christian groups. All the groups share a belief that Charles Darwin's theory of evolution should be rejected. At the heart of the rejection of evolution is the widely held belief that evolution challenges the status of humanity as presented in the Bible. The status of the Bible itself is not in question, nor, necessarily, is the question of God being the first cause of the universe (the Victorians had already rejected the cosmology of Genesis in favour of the findings of Galileo and Copernicus). The fundamental problem with evolution is that it places humans on the same level as animals – no longer the distinct pinnacle of creation.

The main different types of Creationism

Young Earth Creationism claims that the book of Genesis is literally true, and God created everything in six days about 100,000 years ago. Scientists disagree with this and say that the earth was formed about 4 billion years ago.

    Old Earth Creationism says that the earth is about 4 billion years old, but God played an active part in the creative process. Humanity, however, was directly created by God.

    Gap Creationism tries to reconcile the age of the earth with the Genesis stories by saying that there were two creations, one before Adam and much later a second one creating Adam and Eve. Most scientists say that the geological evidence shows that this theory is false.

    Day-age Creationism says that the biblical six days were not 24 hours but millions of years. They use Bible references to say that a day for God is like thousands of years, e.g. Psalm 90: 4.

    Progressive Creationism claims that God created different species as shown by the fossil record. The scientific order of creation and the Biblical account are the same, but different forms of organism are separate creations, not the result of evolution from an earlier form.

    Theistic evolution is an approach to evolution which believes that God invented evolution and takes an active part in the process.

    There are a number of key features found in most types of Creationism. First, scripture is the inerrant Word of God and verbally inspired by God, thus it is literally true. Emphasis is placed upon the truth of the biblical text as it is written, rather than on interpretations derived from scripture. Thus,

Verbal inspiration

Verbal inspiration refers to the belief that Holy Scripture is inspired by God. In Christianity, verbal inspiration refers to the divine authorship or revelation of the Bible; in Islam it refers to the divine revelation of the Qur'an.

    The meaning of verbal inspiration is open to interpretation. It could mean that every single word of the holy book is inspired by God or it could mean that the author of the scripture was inspired to write by God.

    The former view is very typical within fundamentalist and conservative Christianity. If every word of, for example, the Bible, is inspired, this means that the Bible is inerrant and, second, that the Bible contains truths that are directly revealed by God.

    The alternative view allows a role for the author, since the author has been inspired to write by God, but the extent to which the author is a writer rather than a typist for a divine dictation varies amongst religious believers.

    (For further information see Chapter 12, 'Revelation and Holy Scripture'.)

Reasons why Creationists reject the theory of evolution

The threat from the theory of evolution led to its rejection by Creationists for a number of reasons that can be summarised as follows:

- The theory of evolution appears to challenge the role of God as Creator of life in Genesis.
- The theory of evolution appears to challenge the status of human beings as a distinct life form at the pinnacle of creation in Genesis.
- The age of the Earth can be calculated by reference to the Bible, either by counting back the number of years to Adam from the stated life spans of the patriarchs in the Old Testament, or by interpreting the Days of Creation (Genesis 1) as symbolic periods of time, such as 10,000 years.
- The geology of the earth can be explained by flood catastrophes, such as Noah's flood in Genesis 6–9.
- Animals on the earth are descended from those that Noah took into the ark to escape the flood.

continued opposite

questions concerning the origin of life are most clearly answered in the book of Genesis with its statements about God as Creator and human beings' place in creation. Features of the world, such as apparently millennia-old rocks can be explained as prematurely aged by God, or the product of past catastrophes such as Noah's flood. Fossils are either the bones of animals that are more recently deceased than archaeology suggests or they are evidence of the flood of Noah (when they were formed).

For fundamentalism, science is a tool which can be used to demonstrate the truth of scripture. When science, such as the theory of evolution, conflicts with religious beliefs in the Bible the scientific theory is rejected as it does not correspond with the truth claims expressed in scripture.

Common features found in most types of Creationism are that:

- Scripture is inerrant;
- Evolution rejected as only being a 'theory';
- Disputed age of Earth;
- Empirical approach;
- Biblical chronology of the Earth.

Thought Point

Theory

What do the following words and phrases mean?

- Theory
- Hypothesis
- It is only a theory
- Law
- Rule.

Second, the theory of evolution is often attacked as being only a 'theory'. This is not a strong argument since it misunderstands the scientific meaning of the word 'theory'. In science, a theory refers to an established explanation of and account of some feature of the physical world that has been established by scientific research, supported by scientific laws. Scientific theories have to be deduced in a logical manner from evidence that has been well supported by research.

Other arguments against evolution as a 'theory' include the claim that there are gaps in the fossil record. However, in itself this is not an argument as there could be other explanations for gaps in the fossil record, such as that the missing fossils are yet to be discovered, or the fact that the conditions and circumstances in which an animal died were not of the specific type for a fossil to be formed – fossils typically form in situations where the dead animal's body is rapidly covered by sediments to prevent exposure to the air and rotting – hence many fossils are found in limestone rocks, which were originally formed under water.

Third, the age of rocks has been challenged. The use of radiometric dating to calculate the age of a rock sample has been attacked as an unreliable method that is open to error, on the grounds that the rate of decay of an element can change. Scientists would counter this by arguing that the circumstances in which the rate at which a radioactive element decays can only change in specified and limited conditions (which are known by scientists) and these circumstances do not affect the accuracy of a radiometric dating.

Fourth, Creationists adopt an empirical approach. Discoveries of scientists of various sorts are used to illustrate the truth of statements within the Bible. One example is the emphasis placed upon archaeological findings concerning flooding, such as the flooding of the Black Sea basin, which is thought to have been caused by the deluge linked to Noah's flood in the Bible. Scientific discoveries point to the fact that in the past sea levels were different (relating to water being trapped as ice during previous ice ages) and catastrophic floods did take place (as evidenced by towns being found at the bottom of what are seas today).

Fifth, many Creationists use the Bible to work out a chronology of the Earth. There are a number of different ways in which this has been done, but the most famous is probably that of James Ussher, who in the eighteenth century used the dates and information in the Bible to work out that creation took place at nightfall preceding 23 October 4004 BCE. Other Creationists interpret biblical events somewhat differently from Ussher's chronology, suggesting that the 'Days' in Genesis 1 represent periods of thousands of years. While there is no doubt that the author of Genesis implies that the list of ancient patriarchs in Genesis goes back to Adam, this is not to say that the number of years of the patriarchs' lives, as given in the Bible, necessarily tells us the date when Adam was made.

Intelligent Design

Finally, some modern Creationists since the 1980s have argued strongly in favour of *Intelligent Design*. When the theory of evolution was first advanced, many Christians rejected it on the grounds that the design that people observed in the world, such as Paley used in his famous design argument,

---

• The theory overlooks the clear signs of design in the universe discovered by modern scientists.

Radiometric dating

Radiometric dating refers to methods of dating the age of physical objects by measuring the amount of radioactive decay of an element within the object being tested. One well-known type of radiometric dating is radiocarbon dating. This refers to the method for calculating the age of physical objects that contain the element carbon. Carbon can exist in a radioactive form (isotope) known as carbon-14, which decays at a known rate to carbon-12. Any new object containing carbon will consist of carbon in its two types (carbon-14 and carbon-12). By measuring the amount of carbon-14 in any object relative to the amount of carbon-12, the object's age can be known.

Radiocarbon dating is effective up to 60,000 years. Other forms of radiometric dating are used for objects like rocks which are older than 60,000 years.

could not be explained by pure blind chance. However, modern Creationists point to the complexity of the world and discoveries such as DNA, or the regularity of the laws of physics, as evidence that the universe is designed by an intelligent Creator.

However, for those religious believers who do not depend on a fundamentalist literalist view of the biblical texts, Darwin did not undermine their beliefs. It could be argued that he took the debate forward and enabled people to further their understanding of God and the universe, rather than simply saying that God is the simple answer to those areas which science does not yet understand.

Darwin's black box

Darwin said:

> If it could be demonstrated that any complex organ existed, which could not possibly have been formed by numerous, successive, slight modifications, my theory would absolutely break down. But I can find no such case. (*On the Origin of Species*)

Simply put, supporters of Intelligent Design such as Michael Behe claim to have found such a case. Behe claims that with the opening of the black box of the cell through the last 40 years of research in molecular and cell biology, there are now numerous examples of complex molecular machines that absolutely break down the theory of natural selection as an all-encompassing explanation of living systems.

Irreducible complexity

In particular, supporters of Intelligent Design point to the irreducible complexity of biological systems, such as the body's blood-clotting mechanism. In addition, various Creationists point to specified complexity within the physical world. *Specified complexity* refers to the complexity of the physical world, such as the messenger RNA (Ribonucleic acid) in nuclei which carries information within the nucleus of a cell. The claim is that the complexity of the biological system must have been specified by an intelligent being.

Something is irreducibly complex if it is composed of several parts and each part is absolutely necessary for the whole structure to function. The implication is that such irreducibly complex structures or machines cannot be built by natural selection because in natural selection each component must be useful to the organism as the molecular machine is built. Behe uses the example of a mousetrap, which has five parts that are absolutely necessary for the mousetrap to work. A mousetrap must contain a solid base to attach the four other parts to, a hammer that clamps down on the mouse, a spring which gives the hammer the necessary power, a holding bar which holds the hammer in position, and a catch to which the holding bar is secured, holding the hammer in coiled tension Take any one of these parts away and the mousetrap can no longer catch mice.

You could probably find all these components lying around in a shed but they are never going to spontaneously self-assemble into a mousetrap. A hammer-like part may accidentally fall from its box into a box of springs, but it's useless until all five parts are assembled so they can function together. In nature these miscellaneous parts would be de-selected unless they produced immediate benefit to the organism.

Behe uses the example of the cilium. Cilia are tiny hair-like structures on the outside of cells that either help move fluid over a stationary cell, such as the cells in your lungs, or serve as a means of propelling a cell through water, as in the single-celled paramecium. A cilium works like oars; however, as it is a hair-like structure, it can bend. There are two parts to the operation of a cilium, the power stroke and the recovery stroke. The power stroke starts with the cilium essentially parallel to the surface of the cell. With the cilium held rigid, it lifts up, anchored at its base in the cell membrane, and pushes liquid backwards until it has moved nearly 180 degrees from its previous position. For the recovery stroke, the cilium bends near the base, and the bend moves down the length of the cilium as it hugs the surface of the cell until it reaches its previous stretched-out position, again having moved 180 degrees back to its original position. How does a microscopic hair-like structure achieve this? Studies have shown that three primary proteins are necessary, though over 200 others are utilised. The protein tubulin forms microtubules which are like long hollow sticks (the oars), the protein nexin acts like a connector between the tubules so that they can bend, and the protein dynein connects two microtubules together and acts like a motor.

The cilium is irreducibly complex as, like the mousetrap, it has all the properties of design and none of natural selection, according to Behe. It would appear, therefore, that natural selection alone cannot account for everything in the natural world.

Those who support Intelligent Design and irreducible complexity often claim to support evolution for the 'big picture' but say that there are things like the cilium which cannot be accounted for by evolution – there needs to be some kind of intelligence. Not all those who support Intelligent Design would claim that this intelligence is God, and, although most supporters are believers, Intelligent Design is not simply another form of Creationism.

However, scientists will continue to search for a better explanation which does not need anything or anyone beyond nature itself to explain it.

Some definitions taken from the American National Academy of Sciences:

Fact

In science, an observation that has been repeatedly confirmed and for all practical purposes is accepted as 'true'. Truth in science, however, is never final, and what is accepted as a fact today may be modified or even discarded tomorrow.

Hypothesis

A tentative statement about the natural world leading to deductions that can be tested. If the deductions are verified, it becomes more probable that the hypothesis is correct. If the deductions are incorrect, the original hypothesis can be abandoned or modified. Hypotheses can be used to build more complex inferences and explanations.

Law

A descriptive generalisation about how some aspect of the natural world behaves under stated circumstances.

Theory

In science, a well-substantiated explanation of some aspect of the

continued opposite

No-one knows whether a natural explanation will be found in the future for something which is claimed to be irreducibly complex and therefore in need of Intelligent Design. For example, consider the claim that the development of blood clotting and immune systems could not be accounted for by evolution: recent research seems to show that they can. Intelligent Design simply focuses on the final stage of evolution. As Dawkins points out in his analogy in *Climbing Mount Improbable*, you can get to the top of a mountain in small steps up a gentle slope rather than by attempting it in one giant leap. Additionally, if only those things with irreducible complexity point to Intelligent Design, what about the rest of creation which is supposedly part of God's plan? How do we explain those features of the natural world which appear to be less than intelligently designed?

Intelligent Design seems to use God to fill the gaps where there is no clear scientific explanation as yet.

Intelligent Design supporters also point to the apparent fine-tuned nature of the universe. Intelligent Design supporters suggest that the fine-tuned way in which the actual physical laws of the universe work together for life to emerge strongly suggests that there must be a designer of the system. A typical example given is the strong force within physics that holds subatomic particles together to form protons and neutrons which make up the nucleus of atoms. The claim is that if the strong force was slightly different, then subatomic particles would not be formed, and if subatomic particles were not formed there would be no atomic particles, and ultimately no life. The implication of this claim is that physical laws like the strong force are so 'fine-tuned' as to suggest that there must be a designer.

Yet it is important to note that, while Creationists have often adopted arguments based on the fine-tuned nature of the universe, not all scientists who research fine-tuning in the universe are Creationists. In addition, the arguments that the universe is fine-tuned for life to emerge may be interpreted to suggest that there must be an intelligent designer behind it, but equally they can be interpreted to suggest that there may not be an intelligent designer. If Stephen Jay Gould is correct in his claim that science and religion are NOMA, then the fact that the universe is fine-tuned may not necessarily have anything to do with religion.

RESPONSES TO THE CREATIONISM AND EVOLUTION CONTROVERSY

The ways in which scientists, theologians and philosophers have responded to questions concerning creation and evolution have varied widely. In essence there are two approaches:

1   A rejection of Creationist claims, such as in the work of Richard Dawkins who says that God the Creator does not exist; and,
2   A rejection of Creationist claims, such as in the work of Keith Ward who argues that God is the sustainer and origin of the created universe.

A number of modern biologists such as Richard Dawkins have attacked both Creationist claims and other religious claims, rejecting all claims that God the Creator exists. This type of approach is sometimes called Neo-Darwinism.

The underlying assumption of Neo-Darwinism is that there is a fundamental opposition between religion and science. Religion and science both have an explanatory role: they explain the origins of life. In the modern world, Neo-Darwinists argue that science should replace religion as it is empirical, unlike religion. Religion, according to this view, is assumed to be unscientific and irrational – a prop from a bygone age which is no longer required. The table on p. 214 highlights this type of view.

For Neo-Darwinists such as Richard Dawkins there is no need to propose a creator; indeed proposing the existence of a Creator God is a mistake. Evolution explains the origin of life.

However, many religious believers reject both the approach of Neo-Darwinists and the claims of Creationists. Keith Ward (*God, Chance and Necessity*) and others have argued that evolution does not have to be interpreted as being in conflict with religion. For Keith Ward the world demonstrates a gradual unfolding design:

> A developing emergent whole, with increasingly complex and beautiful co-adaptedness among organic life forms . . . Competition and struggle exist, as parts of the mechanism by which organic life evolves to new and superior forms. But co-operation and self sacrifice also exist even at quite basic levels of conscious animal life. It is not just a blind will to power which drives evolution forward. It is also a striving to realize the values of beauty, understanding and conscious relationship. (*God, Chance and Necessity*)

God is seen as the sustainer and origin of the created universe; it can be asked whether creation by evolution is any less wondrous than instant direct creation by God.

Thought Point

Evolution and science in conflict?

Read the extracts from scientists and theologians. What does each passage suggest? Which view is most persuasive? Support your answers with reasons.

natural world that can incorporate facts, laws, inferences, and tested hypotheses.
(From: *Science and Creationism: A View from the National Academy of Sciences*, 2nd edn (Free Executive Summary)
http://www.nap.edu/catalog/6024.html)

23 October 4004 BCE

It is worth noting that this date is based on calculations using the Julian calendar. If you use the Gregorian calendar creation took place over one month earlier on the 21 September 4004 BCE.

If you want to know more, investigate the Julian and Gregorian calendars on the internet.

James Ussher (4 January 1581–21 March 1656)

James Ussher was the Anglican Archbishop of Armagh and the head (Primate) of the Anglican Church in Ireland. He is most famous today for his history of the Earth, reaching back to creation, that was based on dates and incidents recorded in the Bible.

continued overleaf

Want to know more?

If you would like to further
investigate claims
concerning whether the
universe is fine-tuned and
whether this suggests that
God exists you could read
either Paul Davies' book
The Mind of God (1993) or
Francis Collins' book *The
Language of God* (2007).
These books offer differing
perspectives on the issue.

Well, let's be clear. God lays it down very clearly in Genesis 1 that he did it in six days. (David Roseveare, a chemist)

I think it's one of the several legs on which belief in God rests. If physics can show that one can account for the creation without invoking a creator of any kind, then that is one of the legs sawn away; it's one more reason why one shouldn't believe in a Creator God. (Peter Atkins, a chemist)

The stories in the Bible are setting out spiritual meanings of very great depth and significance. They're not meant to be literally true. . . . The people who wrote Genesis were not stupid. They knew that for the first few days there wasn't any Sun, so they didn't mean 'day' literally. When people say they believe that literally, they probably haven't quite thought it through. (Keith Ward, a theologian)

(All extracts are taken from Stannard,
Science and Wonders)

The decline of traditional Creationism

In the later part of the twentieth century traditional literalist approaches to the Bible and creation declined in popularity as scientific discoveries in support of evolutionary theory continued. Evidence mounted in favour of the Earth being millions of years old, not simply prematurely aged. Many biologists published books during the 1970s and 1980s which aimed at explaining evolutionary theory in understandable yet scientific terms to lay readers. For example, Richard Dawkins' famous book, *The Selfish Gene* (1976) states in the preface that his first imaginary reader is the 'layman' and that he is working to 'try to popularize subtle and complicated ideas in non-mathematical language, without losing their essence'. Since its first publication, *The Selfish Gene* has sold more than 2 million copies and been translated into over 30 languages.

Second, traditional literalism cannot easily account for specific problems that arise if evolution does not take place over a very long period of time. Philip Kitcher ('Born Again Creationism', 2002) observed that a literalist account of the Genesis creation story found it hard to explain orderly and regular distribution of fossils in the Earth's crust or the difficulty of imagining that animals could cross all the oceans and seas from Mount Ararat where the Ark landed to, for example, New Zealand or Australia. How, for example, would a kangaroo hop all the way to Australia from Noah's Ark? Even more challenging for Creationists is that they:

have to account for the survival of parasites that are specific for our species. During the days on the ark, these would have had to be carried by less than ten people. One can only speculate about the degree of ill-health Noah and his crew must have suffered. (Kitcher, 'Born Again Creationism')

Genetic research has also contributed to the decline in popularity of literalism. For example, the identification of genetic origins of many human diseases and the sharing of disease-causing genes with those in other life-forms has strongly suggested a genetic relationship between human beings and other creatures. The most likely explanation can therefore be argued to be a shared common ancestor. Furthermore, the fact that the genes that cause various diseases have sometimes been identified by studying other living organisms also suggests the idea of the common origin of life. The similarity of many illnesses of human beings and other mammals suggests their common origin. For example, equine motor neurone disease is very similar to amyotrophic lateral sclerosis (a type of human motor neurone disease also known as Lou Gehrig's disease).

The overall result has been that literalist interpretations of the creation story and creation science based on the Bible have lost popularity even amongst Christian fundamentalists.

Modern Intelligent Design arguments against evolution

Since the 1980s, Intelligent Design has emerged as the most popular fundamentalist Christian approach to evolution. Modern Creationists point to the complexity of the world and discoveries such as DNA, or the regularity of the laws of physics, as evidence that the universe is designed by an intelligent creator.

Fundamentalist Christians today who support the idea of God as Creator often believe in Intelligent Design arguments; they are not literalist nor do they derive their approach from the Bible. For a supporter of Intelligent Design the Bible is the authoritative word of God and the Genesis creation stories communicate vital articles of faith:

- God created human beings discretely (independent from evolution);
- Humans are the pinnacle of creation and the rulers over it.

Equally, modern biology's findings concerning, for example, human biology, the genetic structure of the human genome, or the role of DNA in the growth and development of the human body are not disputed. In fact biology and genetics are often studied to degree level and beyond as they reveal the glory of God's creation.

Intelligent Design supporters suggest that the fine-tuned way in which the actual physical laws of the universe work together for life to emerge strongly suggests that there must be a designer of the system. A typical example given is the strong force within physics that holds subatomic particles together to form protons and neutrons which make up the nucleus of atoms. The claim is that if the strong force was slightly different, then subatomic particles would not be formed, and if subatomic particles were not formed there would be no atomic particles, and ultimately no life. The implication of this claim is that physical laws like the strong force are so 'fine-tuned' as to suggest that there must be a designer.

Thought Point

A controversy that has raged since the early twentieth century, as evidenced by the number of legal cases concerning it in the USA, is whether it should be permitted to teach Creationism in state-funded schools. How would you resolve the dilemma?

Challenges to Intelligent Design

Intelligent Design has been widely criticised by both scientists and religious people on the following grounds:

- Fine-tuning of the universe does not necessarily suggest an intelligent designer.
- Intelligent Design is not a scientific theory.
- Intelligent Design is not predictive or testable.
- Scientific evidence challenges the idea of irreducible complexity.
- Chance evolutionary events are possible.
- Observable evidence for evolution.

Other possible explanations of apparent orderliness and design

First, the arguments that the universe is fine-tuned for life to emerge can be interpreted to suggest that there must be an intelligent designer behind it, but equally there may not be an intelligent designer.

Second, from a scientific point of view it is debatable whether Intelligent Design qualifies as a scientific theory. Karl Popper (*Conjectures and Refutations: The Growth of Scientific Knowledge* (1992 [1963])) suggested

All the views expressed in this exercise have been created for the exercise. They are not intended to represent any particular individual's views or opinions and any resemblance is coincidental.

that scientific hypotheses are open to falsification; that is, scientific theories can always be challenged, developed or refuted by new evidence and discoveries. Indeed, scientists delight in developing new hypotheses that replace older ones as better descriptions of the physical universe. For example, Einstein's ideas replaced some of those of Isaac Newton. If Intelligent Design is not open to being challenged or possibly disproved by scientific observations, it is not a scientific theory and therefore is not a challenge to the genuinely scientific theory of evolution.

Furthermore, scientific theories according to Francis Collins (*The Language of God*, 2007) also have a predictive value; meaning that they make predictions about the way the physical universe works, and these predictions are testable. Intelligent Design on the other hand is a 'scientific dead end. Outside of the existence of a time machine, verification of the ID theory seems profoundly unlikely' (Collins, *The Language of God*).

Fourth, Michael Behe's famous example of the flagellum's irreducible complexity is open to challenge as new discoveries have been made. While the entire evolution process of the flagellum is yet to be deduced, research on bacteria has indicated that some parts of the structure that make up the flagellum are also found in bacteria where they are part of the system used by bacteria breaking through healthy cell walls to cause an infection in the cells. In 'The Flagellum Unspun: The Collapse of "Irreducible Complexity"' Kenneth R. Miller argues that biological research shows that parts of the flagellum are also found in bacteria in the protein Type III Secretion System which enables a bacteria to pierce or cross the membrane of a cell and cause an infection in it. This discovery is important as it undermines Michael Behe's claim that the flagellum is an irreducibly complex system; the evidence from Miller's research suggests that the flagellum is not irreducibly complex; various components of the flagellum are found in other parts of nature, indicating that the flagellum could have emerged in small, gradual evolutionary steps.

THE BLOOD-CLOTTING SYSTEM

The blood-clotting system of the human body is given by Michael Behe as another example of irreducible complexity. Compare the two passages below by Michael Behe and Francis Collins and decide which passage you most agree with? Why?

At first glance, clotting seems to be a simple process. A small cut or scrape will bleed for a while and then slow down and stop as the visible blood congeals. However, studies over the past fifty years have shown that the visible simplicity is undergirded by a system of complexity. . . . In all, there are over a score of separate protein parts in the vertebrate clotting system. The concerted action of the

The human blood-clotting cascade, appearing, with its dozen or more proteins, to be a complex system . . . can in fact be understood as the gradual recruitment of more and more elements of the cascade. The system appears to have begun with a very simple mechanism that would work satisfactorily for a low-pressure, low flow hemodynamic system, and to have evolved over a long period of time into the

continued opposite

components results in the formation of a weblike structure at the site of the cut, which traps red blood cells and stops the bleeding. Most of the components of the clotting cascade are involved . . . in the control of timing and placement of the clot. . . . Thus in the clotting cascade, one component acts on another, which acts on a next, and so forth. I argue that the cascade is irreducibly complex, because, if a component is removed, the pathway is either immediately turned on or permanently turned off. (Behe, 'Irreducible Complexity: Obstacle to Darwinian Evolution')

complicated system necessary for humans and other mammals that have a high-pressure cardiovascular system, where leaks must be stopped quickly (Collins, *The Language of God*)

Fifth, while Michael Behe argues that the chance of irreducibly complex systems evolving by chance is very low, it can equally be argued that low chance events can and do still occur. The chance of winning the lottery is very low (approximately 1 in 13 million in the UK National Lottery) and yet people do win it. Furthermore, the fact that an irreducibly complex system exists could simply be because the low chance of it existing has come good. Kitcher ('Born Again Creationism') also suggests that when it comes to evolution we do not know whether the chance of an apparently irreducibly complex system existing is low or high. If one step follows another in a process, it may be that the chance of a particular irreducibly complex system such as a flagellum evolving is high as this is the only way in which evolution could happen and be successful.

Evolution theory's claim that evolution occurred over millions of years also challenges the idea that systems in biology are irreducibly complex. It is possible to point to minor, small changes, happening each generation over time, leading in millennia to huge changes. For example, the complexity of the eye that has impressed people from William Paley to Michael Behe could be explained by small, gradual changes over millions of years. Just from studying biological systems as wide-ranging as light-detecting cells and eyes present in species varying from human beings to worms to golden eagles can suggest the evolution of the eye taking place in gradual steps over millions of years.

David Hume and design in the universe

More information about Hume's arguments can be found in Chapter 7 on the teleological argument.

Finally, the claim for the irreducible complexity of such biological systems as the bacterial flagellum is also open to the same criticisms as those made against William Paley's design argument. In particular, Hume's arguments for other explanations of design rather than God can equally apply to Michael Behe's arguments.

The nature of God as creator could also be questioned if human beings are the direct, irreducibly complex creation of an intelligent agent. How intelligent is the 'intelligent agent' given the fact that many inheritable illnesses exist, such as various types of cancer and Huntington's disease? Furthermore, is the design of the world that of an 'intelligent agent'? For example, what is the purpose of wisdom teeth? Are human beings suited to walking upright? Genetic illnesses and the limitations of the human body in some respects might point to a cruel or unintelligent designer. (This idea is explored further in Chapter 9, 'The Problem of Evil'.)

Why is Intelligent Design so popular amongst religious believers?

Consider the quotation below:

- What is Francis Collins claiming?
- Do you agree with Francis Collins' explanation of the appeal of Intelligent Design?
- What other reasons can you think of to explain the appeal of Intelligent Design?

> The warm embrace of ID by believers, particularly by evangelical Christians, is completely understandable, given the way in which Darwin's theory has been portrayed by some outspoken evolutionists as demanding atheism. But this ship is not headed to the promised land; it is headed instead to the bottom of the ocean. If the believers have attached their last vestiges of hope that God could find a place in human existence through ID theory, and that theory collapses, what happens then to faith? (Collins, *The Language of God*)

CONCLUSION

Ultimately the question concerning whether science and religion are reconcilable remains an open one. The debate rages on, but the decision is yours to make.

REVIEW QUESTIONS

Look back over the chapter and check that you can answer the following questions:

1 Sum up the key differences between the arguments of Richard Dawkins and those of a religious believer in no more than 200 words.
2 Is either modern cosmology or evolution theory a more serious challenge to religious belief? Justify your answer with reasons.
3 Read the quotation below. What do you think Simon Conway Morris is suggesting? Which choice do you support? Why?

> the complexity and beauty of 'Life's Solution' can never cease to astound. None of it presupposes, let alone proves, the existence of God, but all is congruent. For some it will remain as the pointless activity of the Blind Watchmaker, but others may prefer to remove their dark glasses. The choice, of course is yours. (*Life's Solution*)

4 Is it true that belief in modern scientific theories is incompatible with free choice?
5 Why do you think that William Dembski, a key advocate and developer of Intelligent Design theory thinks that Richard Dawkins is a gift to Intelligent Design supporters?

Terminology

Do you know your terminology?

1 Try to explain the following ideas without looking at your books and notes:

- Evolution
- Intelligent Design
- Cosmology
- The Big Bang theory
- Swinburne's design arguments
- Columbus and the flat-earth myth
- NOMA
- The anthropic principle.

Examination Questions Practice

EXAM MISTAKES TO AVOID

Make sure that you understand any scientific knowledge that you refer to in an examination but do not feel the need to explain scientific theories such as evolution or the Big Bang to the examiner. In the Religious Studies examination you will be credited for how well you understand and assess debates concerning these topics.

Second, do not dismiss any view, particularly Creationist or strident atheists' views, as though holders of these views are stupid. There are many reasons why people may hold views that you personally disagree with, but you will lose marks in an examination if you dismiss a view or position out of hand without any balanced consideration.

Remember: (a) assesses AO1 and (b) AO2. To help you improve your answers look at the AS Levels of Response. See: http://www.ocr.org.uk/qualifications/as-a-level-gce-religious-studies-h172-h572/

SAMPLE AS EXAM-STYLE QUESTIONS

1 (a) **Explain how religious people might interpret the theory of evolution.**

This is a common and relatively straightforward essay to complete. In order to gain full marks on a question such as this it is imperative that you demonstrate a breadth of understanding by explaining more than one religious approach. Points to consider include:

- You could explain a Creationist approach to the theory of evolution.
- Explaining reasons why a religious believer might accept the theory of evolution and believe in God the Creator. Reference could be made to different ways in which Genesis 1–2 could be interpreted, including the idea that the Genesis Creation story is a myth.

- Exploring what is meant by Intelligent Design and discussing why these ideas appeal to many religious believers.

(b) **'Science removes any need for belief in a God who created the universe'. Discuss.**

There are a number of valid ways to explore this question. In an examination you would only have time to explore two or three of these ideas:

- You could argue that modern scientific theories to explain the origin of the universe are compatible with religious beliefs. You could suggest that the Big Bang theory only accounts for the universe's existence from the moment of the Big Bang; it does not account for why there is any universe at all. As well as considering the insights of modern scientists you could refer to the Copleston–Russell radio debate (see Chapter 6, 'The Cosmological Argument').

- You could suggest that theories such as the Big Bang theory satisfactorily account for why the universe exists, removing the need for belief in a Creator God. The views of scientists such as Peter Atkins could be used to support this position.
- The implications of the Big Bang theory for belief in a Creator of the universe could be analysed in relation to the problem of 'God of the gaps' religious thinking and the danger of tying religious belief too closely to scientific discovery. Reference could be made to Stephen Jay Gould's concept of NOMA.
- An alternative approach would be to suggest that science might point some people to belief in God as the sustainer of everything. Some of the ideas of Keith Ward or John Polkinghorne could be assessed.

- An evaluation of Richard Swinburne's interpretations of signs of design in the universe such as fundamental laws of physics could be used to suggest that belief in God the Creator is a logical way in which to continue to believe in God and accept modern science.

2 (a) Explain how theories of evolution have posed problems for religious belief.

   (b) How far does religious belief depend on the idea that people were a special creation?

3 (a) Explain why intelligent design is so popular amongst religious believers.

   (b) 'There is absolutely no proof for intelligent design.' Discuss.

4 (a) Explain what is meant by irreducible complexity.

   (b) 'The argument from irreducible complexity is convincing.' Discuss.

FURTHER READING

There is a huge amount of material available concerning both cosmology and evolution. The titles below have been selected to provide a few suggestions of ways to follow up the content of this chapter.

Issues concerning cosmology

There are many books that explore the relationship between science and religion. Francis Collins' *The Language of God* provides a modern exploration of the relationship between science and religion, including evolution, cosmology and Intelligent Design. Alternatively, Keith Ward's book *God, Chance and Necessity* is a detailed account of one way in which a religious believer approaches questions concerning cosmology and evolution.

Issues concerning evolution

If you wish to explore Richard Dawkins' interpretation of evolution a good starting point is his book *River Out of Eden*. Alternatively, the views of Stephen Jay Gould present a different approach to the science and religion debate. His book *Rocks of Ages: Science and Religion in the Fullness of Life* contains an interesting overview of Charles Darwin's evolutionary theory and Darwin's approach to religious belief.

Christian fundamentalism

An excellent resource for exploring fundamentalism is *A Dictionary of Biblical Interpretation* (Coggins and Houlden (eds)) which contains a number of helpful articles on fundamentalism, Creationism and tolerance. A most interesting account of the origins of fundamentalist views in Judaism, Christianity and Islam can be found in Karen Armstrong's book *The Battle for God*.

Journals and the internet

A valuable source of information for this topic is the internet. However, when using the internet be very cautious of biased accounts on many web pages. A large number of web pages are funded by special interest groups that use the internet to suggest a one-sided account of the science and religion debate. It is important that a balanced range of views is considered. Some helpful websites include the following:

http://en.wikipedia.org/wiki/Evolution (an account of the theory of evolution)
http://evolution.berkeley.edu/ (Berkeley University website giving a scientific account of the theory of evolution)
http://www.creationism.org/articles/index.htm (a Creationist website containing a range of articles expressing Creationist views)
http://en.wikipedia.org/wiki/Big_bang (an article about the Big Bang theory)

Many journals regularly carry articles concerning science, evolution and religion. A good starting point for scientific articles written in an accessible manner is *New Scientist*. The Royal Institute of Philosophy's journal *Think* has carried a number of articles discussing issues related to design, science and religion.

THE NATURE OF RELIGIOUS BELIEF

THE ISSUE

How would you explain to an alien what 'religion' is and what religious people believe? Try to list at least five points of information you would tell the alien.

RELIGION AND RELIGIOUS BELIEF

Religious believers have for centuries discussed the meaning and implications of their belief in God and there is no one agreed universal set of religious beliefs.

Part V explores some questions about human existence that puzzle most people at some time in their lives. The chapters examine questions about life after death, miracles, religious language and the holiness or otherwise of some books.

What you will not find in these chapters is much agreement between philosophers and theologians who have written about these topics; instead, a variety of views are presented. Think about which ones you would support and which ones you would reject – in particular, think about how and why you come to these decisions.

11 Life after Death

Life after death

The belief that human life continues in some fashion post mortem.

Resurrection

Refers to the belief that life continues after death through the existence of the person, body and soul, in a new but distinct form of life. Resurrection is a feature of Jewish, Christian and Muslim beliefs.

Soul

Aristotle defined the soul, or psychē (ψυχή), as the 'first actuality' of a naturally organised body, and argued against it having a separate existence from the physical body. In Aristotle's view, the primary activity, or full actualisation, of a living thing is its soul.

THE ISSUE

Is there any such thing as life after death? And if there is, what do we mean by life after death?

WHAT YOU WILL LEARN ABOUT IN THIS CHAPTER

In this chapter you will consider different ideas about life after death, such as resurrection and rebirth, or reincarnation. You will explore what these mean for religious believers and then consider whether these concepts are coherent. You will also consider what is meant by body and soul and consider the relationship between definitions of body and soul and discussions of life after death. Finally, you will consider what is meant by heaven and hell, and the relation of these concepts to life after death.

STARTER

Ask five people to explain what the following phrases mean to them:

- Soul
- Body
- Resurrection
- Reincarnation
- Life after death.

Why does death matter? Read the following quotation and then discuss what you think.

Death, the most dreaded of evils, is . . . of no concern to us, for while we exist death is not present, and when death is present we no longer exist. (Epicurus, *Letters, Principal Doctrines and Vatican Sayings*)

THE OCR CHECKLIST

Candidates should be able to demonstrate knowledge and understanding of:

- distinctions between body and soul, as expressed in the thinking of Plato, Aristotle, John Hick and Richard Dawkins;
- other concepts of the body/soul distinction;
- different views of life after death: resurrection and reincarnation;
- questions surrounding the nature of disembodied existence;
- the relationship between the afterlife and the problem of evil.

Candidates should be able to discuss these areas critically and their strengths and weaknesses.

From OCR A Level Religious Studies specification H572.

Reincarnation or rebirth
The belief that the soul of a person is reincarnated after death. Its status in the next life depends on the conduct of the incarnated soul in its previous existence. Belief in reincarnation or rebirth is associated with Hinduism and other Eastern religions.

INTRODUCTION

Birth and death are the only events common to every human being's life. Birth clearly matters – it is the beginning of human life in a universe full of life and almost limitless possibilities. However, does death matter?

This sounds like a strange question but the reality is that attitudes to death vary enormously. For example, death of a loved one tends to distress people greatly; death of a child is a tragedy – a life compromised. The death of someone in an accident is sad, and death from malnutrition is dreadful. The difference is that the death of people in developing countries from avoidable malnutrition does not distress us in the way that the death of our child or parent can. The reality is that people can see death on the television, in news or drama programmes; this can indeed distress us, but it rarely has the devastating impact of the death of a loved one. Equally, few people living in Western Europe have regularly witnessed the death of people they know, unlike people living in the most deprived parts of the world. In addition, millions of other living creatures die every year as food, pests or for sport.

Thought Point

Question

Why do people's thoughts and feelings about the death of other human beings and living creatures vary so widely?

If you do not believe in an afterlife, death is not something that you personally experience, because your life ends at death. No new memory or experience can be formed of it. While living you may have wanted your life to continue. Once dead, if there is no afterlife, even that wish for continued life is beyond regret and devoid of meaning. The quotation from Epicurus makes this very point, but many people find Epicurus' thought unhelpful. Why?

On the other hand, many people believe death does matter, for three major reasons. First, death is an unknown. It is the end of reality as people experience it every day in their lives. Second, death marks a final parting with people we may have loved and whom the living will continue to miss. Third, for religious people who believe in an afterlife death is the dawn of a new stage of life either with God or, in some beliefs, separated from God in hell.

Thought Point

Does death matter?

Review the quotation from Epicurus at the beginning of the chapter. Do you agree with it? If so, why? Or what do you feel Epicurus should have said?
Discuss your ideas.

CAN I SURVIVE MY DEATH?

For centuries people and philosophers have thought about whether life after death (post mortem) is possible. Belief in life after death is widespread throughout cultures all around the world. The history of belief in life after death can be traced back to the cultures of ancient China, India and the Middle East. The great pyramids of Egypt are a good example of a culture in which the afterlife played a significant part in the belief system of a people.

In more recent centuries, philosophers, theologians and scientists have all examined the question of survival post mortem. In particular, this question has been typically broken down into the following aspects:

- What must survive of me if I am to talk meaningfully of life after death?
- Is belief in life after death coherent?
- Is belief in life after death possible?

All three of these questions are related. The first question points to the great debates that have raged through history concerning the nature of personal identity. This is important because if you talk of personal survival after death, a clear definition of what is meant by 'you' is required. This is the philosophical debate about the mind–body problem and personal identity.

In philosophical history two main approaches have been taken to this problem. One approach, often labelled dualist, argues that human beings consist of a body and soul/centre of identity/spiritual component. In this view survival after death is possible if the soul can survive death. The body is less important in dualist thinking, as it functions as the carrier of the soul.

An alternative view is often called monist. This view suggests that human beings' minds or centres of identity cannot be separated from their bodies. Human beings are a unity of what may be called body and soul. Accordingly the concept of life after death is possible only if humans survive death in some way as a body–soul unity.

The views of dualism and monism lead to the second and third questions above.

Dualism

The view that a human person consists of two distinct elements: the mind/soul and the body. The mind/soul is immaterial whereas the body is physical.

Monism

The belief that human beings are a single unity of body and mind. The mind's existence is dependent on the body.

HOW DO YOU KNOW WHO YOU ARE?

Thought Point

- Who are you?
- How do you know who you are?
- How do other people recognise you as you?
- Are you the same person today as yesterday?
- Will you be the same person tomorrow morning as today?
- Are you:

  - Your mind?
  - Your body?
  - Something else?

NDEs and OBEs

If you would like to investigate accounts of near-death experiences (NDEs) and out-of-body experiences (OBEs) you will find many accounts recorded on internet sites. Richard Swinburne provides an interesting discussion of NDEs and religious experience in *Is There a God?*

Materialism

The view that human beings are physical beings rather than consisting of a physical body and an immaterial soul.

The mind–body problem

There are many books published about this topic. A helpful starting point is Quentin Smith and L. Nathan Oaklander's book *Time, Change and Freedom: Introduction to Metaphysics*. This book is set out in the form of a series of discussions between four philosophers. It is worth reading and discussing.

The questions in the above Thought Point are designed to make you think about how you would define who you are. These issues have puzzled philosophers for centuries. In order to discuss whether life after death is possible, you need to understand two related problems of philosophy – the mind–body problem and the problem of personal identity – so that it is possible to say what needs to survive to be able to talk about me, the individual, surviving after death. There are many ways in which philosophers have approached these problems.

Some philosophers suggest that personal identity is linked to one's body. All of us can recognise our families, and the way we do this is often linked to some form of physical recognition. A person who believes in resurrection could hold this view.

For other philosophers it is the mind that secures personal identity. Supporters of rebirth hold the view that the soul is what gives us identity. According to this view, you are an individual because of the soul you have.

The mind–body problem questions how our mental activities such as thinking relate to the actions of our body. For example, as you read this book you are thinking. When you finish the page you can turn it over and read the next page. The mind–body problem questions the relationship between decisions and thoughts, such as 'I will turn the page' or 'this book is boring', and physical actions such as turning the page.

Some philosophers, such as Plato and Descartes, hold views known as dualist. According to dualism the mind/soul and the body are separate. The mind (or soul) is the centre of identity. The mind/soul and body are somehow joined together, but we also experience them as separate. If you look at your feet you can see your feet and sense your toes, but the experience of seeing your feet and sensing your toes happens in the mind. Descartes famously said, 'I think therefore I am.' Dualists like Descartes and Plato hold that a person consists of mind/soul and body. The strength of this view is that we clearly do experience ourselves as thinking beings distinct from our bodies. For other people this view is credible due to reports concerning people having out-of-body or near-death experiences.

On the other hand, many philosophers are monists. By monism, philosophers mean that the mind and body are not separate and distinct. Rather, the mind is one with the body and inseparable from it. According to this view the mind is the product of the functioning of the brain, and the brain in turn is a physical organ of the body. Typically, monists are materialists – monists argue that the only form of existence is physical, so it is not possible to talk about the existence of a soul separate from the body. Materialists can only support life after death if that life is physical, such as in religious teaching about resurrection. The appeal of this view is that it accords with our knowledge of the world.

PLATO – A DUALIST VIEW

Plato suggests that the soul is distinct from the body. The soul is immortal, whereas the body is mortal. At the end of life the soul is set free from the body. Plato (*Phaedo*) writes that a human person is a soul 'imprisoned' in a body. For Plato the goal of the soul is the World of Forms, which can only be seen indirectly in the physical world.

Plato argues that real knowledge of Forms comes from the soul. He suggests that when we learn, what we are actually doing is recalling to mind the knowledge about the Forms that the soul had before it was incarnated in the body.

Plato's view of the body is rather negative, as the body distracts the soul from seeking knowledge of the World of Forms:

> The body is the source of endless trouble to us by reason of the mere requirement of food; and is liable also to diseases which overtake and impede us in the search after true being: it fills us full of loves, and lusts, and fears, and fancies of all kinds, and endless foolery, and in fact, as men say, takes away all power of thinking. (Plato, *Phaedo*)

Thought Point

Death and philosophy

In *Phaedo*, Plato suggests that philosophy is a preparation for death. Why do you think Plato says this?

Plato suggests that the true philosopher avoids any distractions from the body and concentrates all his or her energy on gaining knowledge of the Forms. His chariot analogy illustrates the divide between the soul's desires and desires of the body. Plato compares the soul to a chariot driver trying to direct the two horses of the chariot; one horse is the mind and the other is the body. Both horses pull in different directions, but the soul tries to direct them to work in harmony.

Plato's description of the soul

In the *Republic* (608d–612a) Plato describes the soul as 'simple' and 'without parts'. This means that the soul cannot be divided up or split into different

---

Soul and Psyche

The word 'soul' comes from the Old English *sáwol*.

The Greek word ψυχή *psychē*, 'life, spirit, consciousness', is derived from a verb meaning 'to cool, to blow', and so refers to the breath.

Greek philosophers such as Socrates, Plato and Aristotle understood the *psyche* to have the logical faculty, the exercise of which was the most divine of human actions. At his trial Socrates said that his teachings were nothing more than an encouragement for his fellow Athenians to excel in matters of the psyche because all bodily goods are dependent on such excellence.

elements. However, when Plato talks about the soul in the body he describes it as 'complex'. By this, Plato means that there are different aspects of the soul. If you think of a diamond, it has different aspects or faces but it is still a single diamond. When Plato talks about the complexity of the soul, it is still 'simple' and 'without parts'. Plato identified three important aspects of the soul when it is incarnate.

Thought Point

Plato's aspects of the soul

1 **Reason**

   (a) Searches for truth
   (b) Rules the soul.

2 **Spirit**
   This includes a number of aspects which can be trained, such as:

   (a) Aggressiveness
   (b) Being honourable
   (c) Emotion.

3 **Desire or mercenary**

   (a) Linked to the idea of seeking pleasures for yourself; Plato identifies many types of desire, such as:

      (i) Desire for what is necessary, like food
      (ii) Desire for what is unnecessary, like luxury items
      (iii) Perverted desires.

   (b) Mercenary, because fulfilment of desires like these requires money.

The evidence for the different aspects of the soul comes from conflict between the aspects of the soul. Anthony Kenny (*A Brief History of Western Philosophy*) gives a helpful example to explain this idea: think of a young child (who has not reached the age of reason) throwing a tantrum. Kenny suggests that this illustrates a lack of harmony in the soul. The child throwing a tantrum shows that spirit and desire are not being directed by reason.

Plato argues that harmony of the soul is a virtue. One way to understand this is to think of what it means to be healthy – health is concerned with all parts of your mind and body working as they should do, together. If you lack health it means some part or other of your mind or body is not functioning as it should, and this affects all parts of you. Lack of harmony in the soul means that not all aspects of the soul work together, and this stops a person obtaining knowledge of the Forms.

According to Plato, injustice comes from disharmony in the soul. This may be understood to relate to the parts of the soul. If the parts of the soul do not work in harmony, then desire, for example, may overpower reason. Many crimes that people commit, such as stealing, are motivated by inappropriate desires and lack of appropriate spirit (attitude) and reasoning.

The implication of this view is that vices such as the habit of stealing things are wrong because they destroy harmony in the soul and prevent one from seeing the truth (the Forms). This is an argument in favour of doing the right thing just because it is good for you to do it, not because it brings you any material benefits such as wealth, popularity, respect and honour.

Thought Point

Disharmony in the soul

Plato suggests that the soul consists of various aspects: spirit, reason and desire. How could the following crimes be explained in terms of disharmony between the aspects of the soul?

- Vandalism
- Perjury (lying in court)
- Fraud
- Drink-driving
- Rape
- Murder.

DOES THE SOUL EXIST?

In *Phaedo* Plato puts forward arguments to show that the soul is immortal and that it exists before incarnation in a body.

The argument from knowledge

Plato argued that learning is a matter of remembering what the soul has previously known in the World of Forms, i.e. it is a matter of recalling

---

Plato talking about desire, the third aspect of the soul

The third [aspect of the soul] has so many manifestations that we couldn't give it a label which applied to it and it alone, so we named it after its most prevalent and powerful aspect: we called it the desirous part, because of the intensity of our desires for food, drink, sex and so on, and we also referred to it as the mercenary part, because desires of this kind invariably need money for their fulfilment. (*Republic*, ed. R. Waterfield)

Virtue in the soul

In ethics a classical argument against doing good, the Ring of Gyges, is from the *Republic*. It is part of Plato's answer to the challenge that people only do good because it brings them some benefit (e.g. not being sent to prison) and is found in his discussion of the importance of harmony in the soul.

knowledge of Forms that you have forgotten. Plato gives the example of 'equals' to explain this point. He suggests that one can see many things that are equal, like stones of equal size. He points out that no one has ever seen the Form of 'equals'. However, that does not stop us using the concept of 'equals' and applying it to many different things. His evidence for this view is that when people come to understand something they recognise it to be true. Ideas in science or mathematics like the laws of physics or fractions are true long before we learn that they are true.

The argument from opposites

Plato argued that the physical world consists of opposites, such as big and small, light and dark, sleeping and waking. He suggested that the opposite of living is death. He argued that if there is such a thing as 'living', which there clearly is, then there must be such a thing as death. For death to be a thing rather than 'nothing', the soul must exist so that one can talk of living and death as opposites. This argument also supports the idea of reincarnation, since if something is dead its opposite is being alive and vice versa, which implies a cycle of death, birth, life, death and so on. Plato himself suggested that souls that were:

> bewitched by it [the body], by its passions and pleasures, that it thinks nothing else real save what is corporeal – what can be touched and seen, drunk and eaten, or used for sexual enjoyment (Plato, *Phaedo*)

would be reincarnated. In *Phaedo* Plato gave the example of tyrants being reincarnated or transmigrated as wolves and drunkards as donkeys, whereas the souls of philosophers who see the Forms enjoy the company of the gods.

Problems with Plato's views on the soul

- Peter Geach rejects Plato's views. He questions what it can mean for the disembodied soul to know the Forms, given that seeing is a process that is linked to the body and experienced through one's senses.
- Is learning really a matter of remembering? For many people learning concerns acquiring new knowledge and is not an act of remembering anything from a previous existence.
- Does the argument from opposites demonstrate the existence of the soul? Many people have questioned whether an argument from opposites can demonstrate the existence of anything, since the assumption that there are pairs of opposites can be challenged.

Peter Geach (1916–2013)

Peter Geach was a British philosopher and Emeritus Professor of Logic at the University of Leeds. Geach said that human beings are essentially rational animals, each one miraculously created. He dismissed Darwinistic attempts to regard reason as inessential to humanity, as 'mere sophistry, laughable, or pitiable.' He argues that there is one reality rooted in God himself, who is the ultimate truthmaker.

- Part of Plato's defence of the existence of the soul relies on the theory of the Forms. As we have seen (pp. 16–18), there are many challenges to the theory of Forms. If Plato's theory of Forms is debatable, this also undermines his theory of the soul as he argues that real knowledge of Forms comes from the soul. He says that instinctively we can know something is beautiful even if we do not know about the Form of beauty. This knowledge comes from the Forms and so he claimed that humans have an immortal soul.

THE SOUL IN ARISTOTLE

Aristotle's interest in the soul arises from his great interest in science, particularly biology. One of his concerns was to explain philosophically what life is. Although we refer to his writing on the soul, this is actually very deceptive, as his concept of 'soul' is nothing like what is commonly meant by the soul today. He saw the soul as having three parts:

- the *logos* (mind, nous, or reason)
- the *thymos* (emotion, spiritedness, or masculine)
- the *eros* (appetitive, desire, or feminine)

However, only the *logos* was immortal.

In Aristotle's writings the soul is a translation of the Greek word *psyche*. The word *psyche* has many different meanings in Ancient Greek which do not correspond to the common idea that the soul is the centre of a person's identity that survives after death.

The soul is the Form and shape of the body. Aristotle argued that the soul is not a substance like matter because matter can be given a Form and be many different things, but what gives matter its shape and function is its Form. So, in just the same way as a marble statue is physically a block of marble but it has the shape and Form of a statue, the soul is the Form of the body. However, the shape and Form of the statue cannot be separated from what the statue is made of. In the same way the soul cannot be separated from the body.

Aristotle gave three examples to illustrate this idea. First, he uses the example of an imprint in wax to suggest that the soul and the body cannot be separated, just as the imprint cannot be separated from the wax. Second, he gives the example of an axe, suggesting that if the axe was living, its body would be the handle and the axe its head, while its Form would be what makes it an axe – for example, the fact that it has the shape of the axe and is suited to chopping. Third, he suggests that if the eye were a body its soul would be the capacity to see.

By suggesting that the soul is the Form of the body, Aristotle means that:

The soul

Aristotle defined the soul, or psychē (ψυχή), as the 'first actuality' of a naturally organised body, and argued against it having a separate existence from the physical body. In Aristotle's view, the primary activity, or full actualisation, of a living thing is its soul.

The body

In Aristotle's thinking the body refers to the matter that a living creature is made of.

Faculty

In Aristotle's writings the word 'faculty' is used to refer to the capacities that are innate to something. For example, the faculty of the eye is sight and of the ear is hearing.

- The soul gives form to the matter which is the body;
- The soul is the principle of life or activity of the body.

Hugh Lawson-Tancred (translator of Aristotle, *De Anima*) gives the example of a car to illustrate this point. In Aristotle's way of thinking the Form of the car is both its shape and its activity – driving.

As the soul is the principle of life of living things Aristotle argued that there are various different faculties of the soul and not all living things have souls with the same faculties. He proposed that there is a hierarchy of faculties of the soul. He suggests that there are three hierarchical levels of natural beings: plants, animals and people. For each he identified three corresponding levels of soul or biological activity: the nutritive activity of growth, sustenance and reproduction which is shared by all life; the self-willed motive activity and sensory faculties, which only people and animals have in common; and finally 'reason', of which only humans are capable.

Plants have the faculty of nutrition. They obviously obtain food and this is what keeps them alive. However, animals not only have this capacity but also other capacities such as perception and desire. Perception concerns seeing the world through different senses, not just sight, while desire refers to appetite, passions, wishing and sensations gained through touch. However, some animals are distinguished from others by their faculty of locomotion – the ability to move. The faculty of intellect distinguishes human beings.

It is important to notice three things:

- Living creations with faculties such as perception and desire also have the lower faculties such as nutrition.
- Aristotle's argument that the human soul is distinguished by intellect was very influential in the Middle Ages. In some Christian writings of this period the distinction between animals and humans is that animals have an irrational soul, i.e. only appetive, while humans have a rational soul.
- The fact that human souls have the faculty of intellect and reason does not mean that they are rational in what they do. Aristotle gave an example to explain the Form of the soul that illustrates this point. A person can learn Greek – this means he actually has this knowledge; however, that does not mean that the person actually uses this knowledge and speaks Greek.

In *De Anima* Aristotle links his ideas about the soul with three of his Four Causes. He states that the soul is 'the cause and principle of the living body', that the soul is the Efficient Cause of the body (it causes movement and life in the body), and it is the Formal and Final Cause of the body (it gives Form to the matter of the body and it causes growth and development in the body).

Does the soul survive after death?

Aristotle's unity of the Form and matter of the body suggests that the soul does not survive after death, as the Form of the body is inseparable from the body. Furthermore, Aristotle's book *De Anima* does not focus on the question of the immortality of a soul. Its concern is to explain plant and animal life. However, confusion has been caused by the fact that Aristotle also suggested that intellectual thought could possibly be separated from the soul and be eternal. Even if thought can survive after death, this is not the same as saying that one's personal identity survives death. Aristotle's writings about the intellectual faculty of the soul are described as 'inconstant' by Anthony Kenny (*A Brief History of Western Philosophy*), by which he means that what Aristotle thought about the soul surviving death is unclear and some of these ideas conflict with other ideas of his.

Thought Point

Aristotle and Christianity

Aristotle's ideas are of great importance to understanding Christian theology. Aristotle's ideas were preserved through the Dark Ages of Europe in Islamic and Jewish culture. During the Middle Ages the works of Aristotle reappeared in Western European culture from the Arabic and Jewish centres of learning in Spain. Thomas Aquinas came across Aristotle's rediscovered works as a student and he spent much of his life incorporating many of Aristotle's ideas into Christian teaching.

- Aquinas presented arguments now known as cosmological arguments that are greatly influenced by Aristotle's ideas.
- The philosophy of Aristotle was used to explain Catholic beliefs about the presence of Jesus in the bread and wine used in the Eucharistic service, the Mass.
- The transcendent prime mover who is pure actuality strongly influenced medieval ideas about the nature of God, as may be seen in Aquinas' *Summa Theologiae*.

However, with regard to the soul, Christianity was influenced by Plato more than by Aristotle. Can you think of the reason why this was the case?

MATERIALISM AND MONISM

Materialists generally argue against any concept of the afterlife, but it is worth noting that a materialist could believe in bodily resurrection. Materialists are often called monists. 'Monist' refers to anyone who believes that there is only one substance – matter – thereby challenging dualism, since it postulates the existence of matter and a non-physical substance (body and soul).

Thought Point

Materialism and bodily resurrection

If you are a materialist you cannot be a dualist or believe in rebirth, but you could believe in bodily resurrection.

Can you explain why?

For materialists, the identity of a person is linked inextricably to the physical body. When the physical body's life ends that person ends. Emotions, feelings and thoughts derive from our brains and are mental processes in the brain. According to materialism, all these characteristics of our experience are explainable by reference to the mental activity of the brain.

Identity theory, for example, claims that all mental activities are centred in the brain. This approach is supported by scientific research which can point to the modification of mood, behaviour and character by drugs. If drugs such as alcohol or antidepressants affect our character, which they clearly do, this suggests that mental activity is not to be linked to an immaterial soul or identity, but to our brain. When our physical life ends, mental activity ceases. The argument is that it is not that a soul has gone to another place but that the life has simply ended.

However, many criticisms of identity theory have been made. Stephen T. Davis ('Philosophy and Life after Death: The Questions and the Options') points to the fact that identity theory has been criticised in relation to how intentionality can be explained. By this, philosophers mean that brain activity consists of nerves functioning in the brain. When you as an individual make a decision, such as whether to listen to music or to open the window, you form an intention. The challenge is that neural activity in the brain has no intentionality. Other philosophical criticisms include the fact that mental events are private or/and do not have a physical location.

Some support for claims that mental activity is fully explainable in terms of neurone activity in the brain has come from recent scientific discoveries. For example, NASA (www.newscientist.com, 22 March 2004) has developed sensors which, when placed on the throat, can detect and recognise words that you say silently to yourself without voicing aloud. Scientists at University College London and the University of California, Los Angeles, carried out research in which people viewed different images ('Thoughts Read via Brain Scans', http://news.bbc.co.uk/1/hi/health/4715327.stm, 7 August 2005). The researchers used a functional magnetic imaging scanner to detect, successfully, when people's attention was focused on different images. In other words, thoughts of the people in the study could be read.

While this research is not 'mind-reading' it strongly suggests that mental activities such as thoughts are in principle detectable as they are caused by physical events in the brain. If this proves to be true it would support philosophers who argue against the dualistic ideas that separate the body and the soul/mind/identity or physical activity in the brain from mental activity and thoughts.

CASE STUDY: RICHARD DAWKINS ON GENES, THE BODY AND CONSCIOUSNESS

Richard Dawkins presents a case in favour of a materialist view of personal identity with no survival post mortem. Dawkins argues that individual human beings cannot survive death. The only sense in which human beings survive death is through the memories of them in other people's minds or through their genes, some of which are passed on to the next generation of offspring. This may be seen in Richard Dawkins' discussion of God's covenant with Abraham:

> He didn't promise Abraham eternal life as an individual (though Abraham was only 99 at the time, a spring chicken by Genesis standards). But he did promise something else.

> *And I will make my covenant between me and thee, and will multiply thee exceedingly . . . and thou shalt be a father of many nations. . . . And I will make thee exceeding fruitful, and I will make nations of thee, and kings shall come out of thee. (Genesis 17)*

> Abraham was left in no doubt that the future lay with his seed, not his individuality. God knew his Darwinism. (Dawkins, *Unweaving the Rainbow*)

Genes do not have any sense of goal or direction. Instead, genes are what DNA is made of. DNA is a protein that makes copies of itself.

Gene

A gene is the term which scientists use for the smallest unit of DNA which can have an effect on the growth of the organism containing the DNA. DNA directs the development of every cell in a living organism. Different genes in isolation or combination have different effects (i.e. they cause different tissues or cells to develop). Similarly, the reason that human beings are different from monkeys, earthworms or yeast is precisely because the DNA in every cell of each of these living organisms is different.

Biologists refer to the effect that a gene has on its environment (i.e. how the organism develops) as its phenotypic effect.

If you want to know more about genes and modern scientific discoveries about the nature of life read Richard Dawkins' book *The Selfish Gene* (1976).

continued overleaf

Dawkins argues that genes are 'potentially immortal' as they are the 'basic unit of natural selection' (*The Selfish Gene*). Our genes have been passed on from previous generations of living organisms.

The role of the body is as '*a survival machine*' for genes. Genes that survive into another generation survive because they make bodies that enable them to be passed on to the next generation:

> A gene can live for a million years, but many new genes do not even make it past their first generation. The few new ones that succeed do so partly because they are lucky, but mainly because they have what it takes, and that means that they are good at making survival machines. (Dawkins, *The Selfish Gene*)

Humans' brains have evolved over a period of three million years and the genes for growth in our brain size were passed on because genes in bodies with bigger brains had a survival advantage. The exact reason why the larger brains of human beings evolved is not fully understood; however, possibilities include the evolution of language actually stimulating further evolution of the brain, because language offers a distinct survival advantage.

Human beings' consciousness has evolved due to the survival advantage it gives. Genes cause each human being to develop a brain as it grows, and the sense of consciousness arises from the brain. This does not mean that genes control and direct our thoughts. Dawkins made the point that you can program a computer to play chess, but when it is actually playing it is not being directed by the programmer; it is playing on its own.

Human consciousness gives the body a greater chance of survival and thus provides a greater chance for the body's genes to be passed on to the next generation. The survival advantage of being conscious is high. Hence, genes which specify the development of a brain and consciousness have an advantage over those that do not. Another way to think about this is the fact that conscious human beings have managed to wipe out some illnesses such as smallpox. The consciousness coded by the genes of human doctors gave them a survival advantage over the genes of consciousless smallpox.

> Whatever the philosophical problems raised by consciousness, for the purpose of this story it can be thought of as the culmination of an evolutionary trend towards the emancipation of survival

Computer analogies and evolution

Dawkins and other scientists have used the development of computers as an analogy to suggest a possible explanation of the development of the human brain and consciousness. You can read more about what Dawkins says in Chapter 12 of *Unweaving the Rainbow* or Chapter 4 of *The Selfish Gene*.

continued opposite

machines as executive decision-takers from their ultimate masters, the genes. Not only are brains in charge of the day-to-day running of survival-machine affairs, they have acquired the ability to predict the future and act accordingly. They even have the power to rebel against the dictates of the genes, for instance in refusing to have as many children as they are able to. (Dawkins, *The Selfish Gene*)

However, it is important to note that this is not the only value of consciousness to us, as thinking human beings. This is one way in which the origins of consciousness can be explained. Consciousness, though, is of value to us in different ways because we have the capacity to understand, enjoy and live life. As Richard Dawkins stated:

What is the use of bringing a baby into the world if the only thing it does with its life is just work to go on living? . . . There must be some added value. At least a part of life should be devoted to living that life, not just working to stop it ending. (*Unweaving the Rainbow*)

JOHN HICK'S REPLICA THEORY – AN ALTERNATIVE MATERIALIST VIEW

John Hick's replica theory ('Resurrection of the Person') presents one way in which the concept of resurrection may be understood. The significance of Hick's theory is that he rejects dualism, while at the same time presenting a defence of belief in bodily resurrection. This contrasts with many philosophers in history who have held monist views and not accepted life after death, or dualist views and accepted life after death.

Hick's starting point is that human beings are a 'psycho-somatic unity'. By this, Hick means that human beings are a unity of physical body and the mind or soul. The two cannot be separated. He does not think that a soul is like Gilbert Ryle's ghost in a machine.

The concept of mind or soul is thus not that of a 'ghost' in the 'machine' but of the more flexible and sophisticated ways in which human beings behave and have it in them to behave. (Hick, 'Resurrection of the Person')

For Hick, the soul is not a separate part of human beings, such as in the work of Plato or other dualists. Hence, Hick's views are not suitably described as dualistic.

Gilbert Ryle's 'Ghost in the Machine'

Gilbert Ryle's book *The Concept of Mind*, first published in 1949, famously challenged philosophical dualism such as that of Descartes. Ryle argued that philosophers often make a category error by assuming that mind and the body can be spoken of as though they are the same kind of thing:

'the dogma of the ghost in the machine'. I hope to prove that it is entirely false, and false not in detail but in principle. It is not merely an assemblage of mistakes. It is one big mistake and a mistake of a special kind. It is namely, a category mistake. It represents the facts of mental life as if they belonged to one logical type or category . . . , when they actually belong to another. (*The Concept of Mind* (2002 [1949])

Ryle noted that a person can talk about mental and physical events, but this does not mean that the mental and physical events are the same type of thing, or that they can be

continued overleaf

compared. In his book Ryle attacked Descartes' dualism and suggested a new approach to understanding the mind–body problem.

Thought Point

Dualism and Hick

Many students in examination answers make the mistake of calling Hick a dualist. Why is this incorrect?

Instead of a dualistic view of the soul surviving death, Hick suggests 'replica theory' to explain what is meant by resurrection. St Paul spoke of the resurrection involving spiritual bodies:

> So it is with the resurrection of the dead. What is sown is perishable, what is raised is imperishable. It is sown in dishonour, it is raised in glory. It is sown in weakness, it is raised in power. It is sown a physical body, it is raised a spiritual body. If there is a physical body, there is also a spiritual body.
>
> What I am saying, brothers and sisters, is this: flesh and blood cannot inherit the kingdom of God, nor does the perishable inherit the imperishable. Listen, I will tell you a mystery! We will not all die, but we will all be changed, in a moment, in the twinkling of an eye, at the last trumpet. For the trumpet will sound, and the dead will be raised imperishable, and we will be changed. For this perishable body must put on imperishability, and this mortal body must put on immortality. (1 Corinthians 15:42–43, 50–53)

and Hick's replica theory is one way to understand Paul.

Hick argues that resurrection is a divine action in which an exact replica of ourselves is created in a different place.

> I wish to suggest that we can think of it as the divine creation in another space of an exact psycho-physical 'replica' of the deceased person. ('Resurrection of the Person')

The replica is in all respects the same as us, but the location of the replica is not on Earth.

Hick argues that resurrection could take place instantaneously at death or after a time lapse determined by God. The replica exists in a 'different space' from us that is observable by God and not by us.

However, the replica of the person is not the same as a copy. Hundreds of copies can be made of an article or picture using a photocopier. Instead,

Hick uses the word 'replica' because each person can only exist in one place and time. Hick rejects the idea of having hundreds or thousands of possible copies of you, because part of being a human person is that we are individuals. What matters is that the replica is the real you; there cannot be another replica floating around in some other place.

In 'Resurrection of the Person', Hick suggested an example to explain replica theory. First, he considered the case of a person disappearing in London and reappearing in New York. He suggested that, for the person who appears in New York to be identifiable, the particular appearance of the person, their character, the arrangement of the matter that makes them must enable a person observing them in New York, who knew them first in London, to recognise who they are. What matters for Hick is the arrangement of matter in the person in New York being such that it constitutes the same person who disappeared in London.

Hick continues by suggesting that you imagine a person who dies in London and is recreated in New York. Hick argues that if a replica of that person exists in New York and a dead body exists in London, it is easier to identify the replica in New York as the person rather than the dead body. He suggests that resurrected persons do not doubt that they are the same person as before. Thus, resurrection is understood by Hick as the creation of a replica by God in a different space.

Philosophers have raised many issues concerning John Hick's replica theory.

Identification of the replica with the original person

Hick argued that the replica and the original person cannot exist at the same time, as persons are individuals. For the replica to be you, it has to be individual. Hick argued that if the replica has the same 'consciousness, memory, emotion and volition' as the original person, it is logical to identify the replica as the same individual as the original person.

However, for some philosophers, what matters is the physical continuity of the person through life, i.e. an individual person consists not just of 'consciousness, memory, emotion and volition' but also of the fact that these are linked to the same physical body throughout life. If the body's life comes to an end then the unity which was that person ends.

Hick insisted that there is continuity because the replica has the 'consciousness, memory, emotion and volition' of the person and there can only ever be one replica of an individual. However, if physical continuity of the body is important when explaining identity, then replica theory is problematic.

Multiple replicas and the nature of the resurrected body

Some philosophers have suggested that there could be multiple replicas. If this were the case then the individuality of a replica would be lost and so none of the copies would be a true replica. Hick rejected this suggestion:

> Our concept of 'the same person' has not developed to cope with such a situation. ('Resurrection of the Person')

Any discussion of life after death is, of course, limited by human beings' inability to talk about what lies beyond our sense experience. Hick acknowledged that discussion of the nature of life as a replica is impossible. Typical questions concern what stage in life the replica is a copy of. If it is a copy at death, are terminal illnesses replicated? Hick suggested that one possibility might be that the healing of illness and disease takes place in the new existence as a replica.

Reductionism

Religious reductionism attempts to explain religion by reducing it to certain non-religious causes. For example: religion can be reduced to humanity's conceptions of right and wrong; religion is mainly a primitive attempt at controlling our environments; religion is a way to explain the existence of a physical world, and religion confers an enhanced survivability for members of a group and so is reinforced by natural selection. Freud wrote that religion was nothing more than an illusion, or a mental illness, and Marx claimed that religion was 'Religion is the sigh of the oppressed creature, the heart of a heartless world, and the soul of soulless conditions. It is the opium of the people'.

In *The Blind Watchmaker*, Dawkins introduced the term 'hierarchical reductionism' for the view that complex systems can be described with a hierarchy of organisations. Each of these is only described in terms of objects one level down in the hierarchy.

Which religion?

You can choose to use any main religious tradition to explain what religious people mean by afterlife, heaven and hell. In this section the example used is Christianity, but you could discuss other traditions, such as Islam.

RELIGIOUS VIEWS ON THE AFTERLIFE

Religious views on the afterlife vary between dualist and monist. Both of these approaches in religious traditions are considered in this section through reference to teachings from Christianity and Hinduism.

CHRISTIANITY AND RESURRECTION

Christians believe that death is not the end of human existence, but it marks an end to physical life and the beginning of a new stage in life. The New Testament refers to the afterlife as a paradise, a state of continued existence with God after death.

Jesus' resurrection is interpreted by Christians as a sign that death is not the end of human existence and that God does not abandon people, even when they are dying.

> But we do not want you to be uninformed, brothers and sisters, about those who have died, so that you may not grieve as others do who have no hope. For since we believe that Jesus died and rose again, even so, through Jesus, God will bring with him those who have died. (1 Thessalonians 4: 13–14)

The story of Jesus in the Gospels concludes with his resurrection. In Christian belief this is the most important and significant event. Jesus not only dies for people, but he also rises from the dead. If you read the accounts of the resurrection a number of points are important: first, Jesus is somehow changed and different; his followers do not at first recognise him and his body is changed. Second, Jesus is not described as being a ghost or vision; he is risen from the dead physically, but his body is transformed and different (see Matthew 28:16, Mark 16:14, John 20:14–16, Luke 24:13–35).

There are many people, Christians and non-Christians, who believe that some sort of non-physical life after death is possible. What is distinctive about Christianity is that it traditionally believes in the resurrection of the body in some way, not just a person's soul or centre of identity. Many philosophers challenge the concept of bodily resurrection, but Peter Geach suggests that resurrection is the only meaningful way in which one can speak of life after death. He states this view on the grounds that a person could not be meaningfully identified with only a spirit existence after death. Instead, he suggests that because people are a unity of body and soul, the only meaningful way to talk about survival after death is to say that souls can be reunited 'to such a body as would reconstitute a man identifiable with the man who died' (Geach, 'What Must Be True of Me if I Survive My Death?').

Since Paul wrote 1 Corinthians 15, Christian belief has been in resurrection and life after death, though it has not always been clearly stated what is meant by resurrection of the body. Christian belief centres on Jesus' resurrection, as illustrated by the following example:

> We firmly believe, and hence we hope that, just as Christ is truly risen from the dead and lives for ever, so after death the righteous will live

for ever with the risen Christ and he will raise them up on the last day. (*The Catechism of the Catholic Church* §989)

While Christianity has argued in favour of the unity of body and soul in an individual person, it has also at times sounded dualistic. From biblical stories Christians believe that at death the soul of a person is separated from her or his body, awaiting the final resurrection and transformation of the person's body to be resurrected like Jesus. At death each person is judged by God in what is called 'The Particular Judgment'. This sounds dualistic, but Christianity also emphasises resurrection of the physical body after death; whether this takes place at the point of death is not always clear because of our notion of time.

The Particular Judgment

Within Christianity the traditional belief has been that every person is judged at the moment of her or his death. This judgment is called 'The Particular Judgment' because each judgment is personal to an individual. The belief is that the good would go to heaven and the bad to hell. However, the word 'judgment' is not a particularly accurate term. The parable of the Last Judgment (Matthew 25: 31–46) tells Christians very clearly that people shape their relationship with God through their own actions. God accepts people as they are.

Thought Point

What do you think?

Look up the following passages. What do you think they are telling people?

From the Bible	*From the Qur'an*
Mark 13: 24–27	Surah 3: 16
Luke 16: 19–31	Surah 3: 25
Luke 20: 9–19	Surah 3: 134–136
Luke 20: 27–40	Surah 3: 185
Luke 23: 39–43	Surah 56: 1–96
Revelation 7: 1–17	

Christian belief in a judgment at death comes from the teaching of Jesus. He stated that:

And the king will answer them, 'Truly I tell you, just as you did it to one of the least of these who are members of my family, you did it to me.' (Matthew 25: 40)

Christians have argued that the way you act in life makes you the character you are and that God judges you according to how you choose to be. The belief is that God in the Jewish Scriptures and Jesus in the New Testament set out principles for people to live by, to remain in relationship with God. Deliberately rejecting these principles is a sign of rejecting relationship with God.

Some people claim that God will forgive them whatever they do, so they can do what they like. However, in the Christian tradition this is a mistaken view, as justice demands that people make up for wrongdoing if they are to be forgiven. God accepts people as they are; forgiveness is on offer if people really repent, but forgiveness also requires people to acknowledge their wrongdoing (contrition), admit their wrongdoing (confession) and make up for their wrongdoing (an act of satisfaction).

HEAVEN AND HELL

Many religious traditions, including Christianity and Islam, believe in a state of existence with God after death, called heaven, and a state of punishment, called hell.

In Christian tradition the experience of afterlife with God is described as a state of existence with God in which people see God face to face; that is, people see or experience God in a new way. In the Roman Catholic tradition this situation of seeing God face to face is called the *Beatific Vision* and the same belief is found in Orthodox Christianity.

This belief originates from the first followers of Jesus who witnessed the events surrounding Jesus' death and resurrection, and it is reflected in the Bible in the writings of Paul and in the Book of Revelation. Paul stated that, in heaven, God is experienced in a different way: 'For now we see in a mirror, dimly, but then we will see face to face' (1 Corinthians 13: 12).

Second, heaven is described in Christian tradition as a state of fulfilment; it is a place in which all human longings and wishes are to be in a right relationship with God: 'Heaven is the ultimate end and fulfilment of the deepest human longings, the state of supreme definitive happiness' (*The Catechism of the Catholic Church* §1024).

Heaven is seen as the ultimate goal or end of human existence to which all human beings are called. It is important to note that in Roman Catholic and Orthodox Christian tradition life after death with God in heaven is something people have to achieve through their actions in life. People have to desire to do what is good (i.e. God's will) and actually do it.

> **Poetry corner**
>
> *Paradise Lost* is an epic poem by John Milton which tells the story of the Fall according to Christian tradition. If you like poetry read *Paradise Lost*, but if you only want to read a short extract, read Book 1 alone.

Gehenna

The image of flames and burning in hell originates from the rubbish dump outside Jerusalem. In the times of the Jewish Scriptures rubbish was burnt in Gehenna and pagan gods were worshipped there. Jews did not live there as it was unclean and associated with pagan worship. Over time a link was made between this place of burning and child sacrifice and the place where unclean people are, bad people, and their cleansing and punishment by fire. The word sometimes translated as 'hell' in Matthew 5: 22 is Gehenna.

Retributive justice

A retributive theory of justice is one in which people who commit wrong acts are punished by law in a way that is proportionate to their wrongdoing. The strength of a retributive theory of justice is that it emphasises that justice involves punishing the wrongdoer, and leaving the good person in peace.

If you want to investigate retributive theories of justice look at the work of Immanuel Kant such as *The Science of Right*.

However, within Christian tradition there is also much emphasis placed upon hell as the fate of people who do wrong in life.

Hell is traditionally characterised by two features: it is a state of separation from God and it is a place of punishment by God. Imagery of fire, pain, suffering and torture is used to describe hell. Many of these images originate from Dante's poetry and later works such as the poems of John Milton. Milton described hell as:

A dungeon horrible on all sides round,
As one great furnace flamed; yet from those flames,
No light, but rather darkness visible
Served only to discover sights of woe
Regions of sorrow, doleful shades

(*Paradise Lost*)

These images convey the idea that hell is a state of suffering after death. In traditional Christian teaching hell is clearly a place of suffering and punishment – a state of suffering because the wicked people in hell lose the chance of a beatific vision with God and they know they have lost it, and a state of punishment because God's justice demands that wrongdoers are punished.

In much Christian teaching hell is interpreted as an aspect of God's justice. People who do wrong deserve to be punished and it is through their wrong actions that people bring punishment on themselves. This is like a retributive theory of justice. In principle, many Christians would argue that a failure by God to punish people would contradict God being just.

The imagery of heaven and hell is often used to teach children the serious consequences of their wrong actions and to highlight the fact that people are judged according to their actions.

However, some people today find these images unhelpful as they believe they do not communicate the idea of a loving and forgiving God. For other people, the eternal nature of the punishment appears unjust – the punishment is punishment alone – it is not educative and does not rehabilitate the person.

The images of hell are a form of negative reinforcement education that may encourage people not to commit an act, but it does not necessarily encourage them to choose what is right for its own sake.

There is a problem related to hell being a place of physical suffering. If it is a place of physical suffering, where is it? Within Christian history there have been many suggestions as to the location of hell, such as under the Earth or on the other side of the moon, but today we know that these places, though inhospitable, are not hell in the traditional sense.

Some writers have focused on the idea that hell is a state of separation from both God and other people that is caused by a person becoming aware of others' 'judgement' on them. In other words, hell may be understood as a state of utter loneliness and separation. Sometimes, through choices in life, people bring this situation on themselves. For example, if you steal from your family and friends and get caught, the effect is that you lose their good will and your relationship with them.

In medieval Christian thought Hell is both a state of separation from God and a state of punishment. As Aquinas stated:

> for mortal sin which is contrary to charity a person is expelled for ever from the fellowship of the saints and condemned to everlasting punishment. (*Summa Theologiae* Supp. 3a, q. 91, a. 1)

Mortal sin is the most serious type of sin within the Catholic tradition and it causes the sinner to be separated from God. For example, murder is a mortal sin. In the thinking of medieval theologians like Aquinas hell is a state of punishment and separation from God which mirrors the separation from the community of people who do wrong on earth. Aquinas argued that hell serves two purposes:

> First, because thereby the Divine justice is safeguarded which is acceptable to God for its own sake . . . Secondly, they are useful, because the elect rejoice therein, when they see God's justice in them, and realize that they have escaped them. (*Summa Theologiae* Supp. 3a, q. 91, a. 1)

The atheist philosopher Sartre's argument is that hell is a state where humans are unable to change who they are and whose existence is determined by other people.

> So that's what hell is; I'd never have believed it . . . .
> Do you remember brimstone, the stake, the gridiron? . . .
> What a joke! No need for the gridiron – Hell is other people.
> (Sartre, 'Huis Clos')

Heaven, hell and the problem of evil

Many Christian theodicies, such as those of Irenaeus, Augustine or Swinburne, place great emphasis on the role of free will as an explanation for the existence of evil. People are morally accountable for their actions precisely because they have free will. However, a traditional challenge to free will defences is: if God is just why does it appear that wrongdoers thrive and good people suffer in this world?

Purgatory

Purgatory is a traditional Christian belief in a place where all people who die in relationship with God, but who are not yet perfect, are purified after death. The imagery again is of a place of suffering; in purgatory the suffering is for the purpose of purifying a person of their wrongdoings in life.

Belief in purgatory derives from the Bible (2 Maccabees 12: 46) but it became a prominent part of Christian teaching in the Middle Ages at the Councils of Florence and Trent. Because purgatory is a place of purification it is different from hell.

> The Church gives the name Purgatory to this final purification of the elect, which is entirely different from the punishment of the damned. (*The Catechism of the Catholic Church* §1031)

Some Christians today find the notion of purgatory problematic since it is very difficult to understand how an individual person who has died can spend time in a physical place being purified, if their life in a physical time-bound existence has come to an end.

For some Christians the justification of this situation comes from the belief that ultimately God holds everyone to account and judges them according to their actions. Hence, God's punishment for some people is to send them to hell because that is what they deserve, and justice demands that they are appropriately punished.

One important aspect of this Christian belief is that God accepts people as they really are. So if people lead a good life and choose to be in good relationship with God and other people, they go to heaven. Equally, if people choose to live a life of wrongdoing, God recognises that they have chosen to live in a state of disharmony and bad relationship with God and other people, so they bring hell on themselves.

Within Roman Catholic and Orthodox Christian traditions no one is predestined to go to hell; God loves everyone, and wishes to forgive everyone and be in good relationship with everyone if that is what they want.

> Do not be astonished, brothers and sisters, that the world hates you. We know that we have passed from death to life because we love one another. Whoever does not love abides in death. All who hate a brother or sister are murderers, and you know that murderers do not have eternal life abiding in them. We know love by this, that he laid down his life for us – and we ought to lay down our lives for one another. How does God's love abide in anyone who has the world's goods and sees a brother or sister in need and yet refuses help? (1 John 3: 13–17)

However, if people choose to lead a life of wrongdoing, effectively turning their back on God, then those people by their actions choose to be separate from God (i.e. in hell). It is not that God wishes for people to go to hell, but people through their actions choose hell as their fate:

> The Lord is not slow about his promise, as some think of slowness, but is patient with you, not wanting any to perish, but all to come to repentance. (2 Peter 3:9)

> God predestines no one to go to hell; for this [to happen], a wilful turning away from God (a mortal sin) is necessary, and persistence in it until the end. (*The Catechism of the Catholic Church* §1037)

The closing phrase 'persistence in it until the end' is important because it indicates another aspect of Christian theology: God's forgiveness. If people turn away from sin, repent and believe in God, they can rebuild their relationship with God. To end up in hell you have to continue in your wrongdoing and never repent what you have done.

If God does not judge people, two challenges to theodicies arise. First, the value of free will is undermined, as free will would become a licence to do what you like without the constraint of possible judgment. However, the weakness of this challenge is the fact that you can be moral without believing in God, and many humanists, for example, have strict moral codes of behaviour without the code of behaviour being dependent on God.

More significantly, Richard Swinburne (*Providence and the Problem of Evil*) argues that free will demands the possibility of people being able to choose to develop an utterly corrupt and bad character. Swinburne argues that a failure to let a person choose to be bad would mean that God does not give us genuine free will about what sort of person we are:

> It is good that God should allow people the choice of forming their characters in such a way as to not be open to future change. For if God refused to allow someone to develop an irreformably bad character, that would be refusing to recognise an ultimate moral choice by an independent moral agent. It would be like a jilted lover pestering the beloved on and on, not recognising her right to say a final no. (Swinburne, *Providence and the Problem of Evil*)

Free will defences rely on the existence of free will and people's ability to choose to be good or bad. In this sense heaven and hell, the states of union and separation from God, have to be real possibilities.

Second, if God has the power to judge people, and the knowledge of what people have done, God's goodness and justice can be challenged if God fails to judge and punish people appropriately. In other words, divine justice is meaningful only if it is carried out. If people through their actions choose to reject God, then justice demands that God must reject them.

Although some modern theologians have argued that God's mercy demands that all people are purified and forgiven by God, Swinburne has noted that this sort of belief in universal salvation is not traditional belief and was almost unheard of before modern times (*Providence and the Problem of Evil*).

In addition, many theodicies rely on the concept of God judging people as the basis of moral responsibility. If this is the case, then it is clearly important that heaven and hell are meaningful concepts.

Predestination and Divine Election

Within Christian tradition much emphasis is placed on the importance of free will, moral responsibility and a rejection of any idea of predestination. However, it is important to note that some Christians believe in Divine Election. While this is not the same as predestination, it has led some people to believe in predestination.

The sixteenth-century Protestant reformer John Calvin is associated with what he called the Doctrine of Divine Election. By the Doctrine of Divine Election Calvin meant that some people are destined for a relationship with God while some are not. This may be seen by the way that some people believe in Jesus and some do not. What is important is that whether someone is saved or goes to hell is not a matter of human choice. Calvin ultimately argued that whether a person is among God's elect is a matter only for God, who is omnipotent and omniscient, and is thus a mystery beyond human comprehension (Calvin, *Institutes of the Christian Religion*).

The doctrine of predestination according to Calvin is concerned with the question of the control God exercises over the world. According to the Westminster Confession of Faith (1646), God 'freely and unchangeably ordained whatsoever comes to pass.' Here 'predestination' applies this to salvation, and to the belief that God appointed the eternal destiny of some to salvation by grace, while leaving the remainder to receive eternal damnation for all their sins, even their original sin. Calvin argued that people are predestined and effectually called in due time to faith by God. This is part of the mystery of human existence. People's actions in life are a possible sign of whether they are among the elect or not.

Among some Protestant groups which are offshoots from Calvinism (e.g. followers of Théodore de Bèze) the doctrine of predestination became an important article of belief separating Catholics and Lutherans from some other Protestants. Some support for belief in predestination may be found in the Bible in the Book of Revelation, which refers to the 144,000 servants of God (Revelation 7: 12) who are to be saved.

Ultimately, belief in Divine Election is a belief that God's justice triumphs; the good are saved while the bad go to hell.

Is it true that you will go to hell if you do not believe in God?

This question has been much debated in Christian history. Many Christians over the centuries have argued that Jesus died to save people who believe in him. Since atheism is a denial of God's existence, such people would be judged and condemned by God. In the past, for example in medieval Europe or Ancient Greece, atheism was punishable by death. This attitude was supported in Christian culture by passages in the Bible which clearly say that if you knowingly reject the Holy Spirit you will go to hell.

However, while this attitude has been a part of mainstream popular Christian culture over the centuries, it is not necessarily reflective of Christian teaching. For example, the Roman Catholic Church states that all people must follow their consciences, as well as seek guidance to inform their consciences. Compulsion or threats cannot be used to make people believe. More specifically, to say *'extra ecclesiam nulla salus'* ('outside the Church there is no salvation') is rejected by most Christian denominations, such as Roman Catholics.

This rejection of the belief that you must believe in God to be saved developed among Catholic missionaries who were scandalised by the way the conquerors of the New World (the Americas) treated the native populations. In particular, theologians from Spain suggested that if the person preaching Christianity was scandalous in his behaviour, it was unreasonable to say that people should believe the preaching. Ultimately, God is seen by Christians as the judge of people who decides whether they go to heaven or hell; Christians cannot decide this.

Much Christian teaching today, such as that of the Roman Catholic Church, clearly states that judgment is a matter for God and second that people can only be expected to believe in Christianity if the witness they have seen is credible. In Roman Catholic theology it is possible to be a good person and go to heaven by following your conscience and Natural Law if you are not a Christian and have had no credible opportunity to become a Christian:

> To the extent that they [Christians] are careless about their [non-Christians] instruction in the faith, or present its teachings falsely, or even fail in their religious, moral, or social life, they must be said to conceal rather than reveal the true nature of God and of religion. (Vatican II, *Gaudium et Spes* (1965))

HINDUISM AND REINCARNATION

Reincarnation is a belief held by many religious traditions, such as Hinduism, which contrasts with Christianity's belief in resurrection. The central idea of reincarnation is the belief that the soul of a body is eternal. It is reborn in new bodies generation after generation. Hence, reincarnation is a dualistic religious theory of life after death.

The status of the body in which the reincarnated soul finds itself depends on the actions of the united body and soul in the previous incarnation. If in the previous life the person was morally good, the soul will be reincarnated in a better body (e.g. that of a wealthy person or even a deity). However, if a person is morally bad, the soul will be reborn in a lower status body, even that of a worm or an insect.

Within Hinduism the physical world is believed to be a dreamlike state. Brahman, who is divine and transcendent, is reality. The physical world is temporary, in the sense that it is not ultimate reality which is Brahman. In every body there is an *atman*, 'soul', which animates the body. The soul is the essence of the person. The soul's place in life reflects the law of karma.

Karma

In Hinduism, the law of cause and effect.

Samsara

The cycle of birth, death and rebirth in Hindu belief. The Jiva is reincarnated as a human or other life form depending on the conduct of its last incarnation.

Samsara is the cycle of life, death and rebirth in which the person's previous actions in life determine the soul's place in the next life. Thus, for example, a person who is wicked in life creates papa (bad) karma – this means that their soul might be reincarnated in a lower position in the hierarchy of life. In Hinduism, all living things have an *atman*. Hence the karma reflecting one's actions in life is generally carried to the next incarnation of the soul. The ultimate goal of the soul is to achieve moksha and end the cycle of rebirths. The jiva/atman is then reunited with Brahman.

Evidence that is often put forward to support belief in reincarnation includes the example of children who appear to remember events they were not present at, or people having a sense of *déjà vu*. The problem with this type of evidence is that it is quite possible to explain it in different ways. For example, young children may hear conversations about an event which took place before they were born and in later life believe that they were present at the event, when in reality they only heard a conversation about it. The problem with any claim that a person remembers a previous life is that the memory could be explained in other ways or just be a hoax.

A philosophical problem is the nature of the connection between the previous life and the person who has inherited the soul. Clearly the nature of reincarnation is that memory or the physical body is not the link, in which case what does it mean to say that there is an immaterial soul that connects the two? Swinburne ('The Future of the Soul') rejects reincarnation on precisely this ground, because if there is no continuity between the brain of the new baby and the old person who died, there is no way of saying that the soul is distinctively the soul of that particular person.

Think of a laptop computer – what makes it your computer as opposed to anyone else's? It is all the software you have installed on it, the work you have completed on it, your fingerprints where you have typed on it. If you wiped the hard drive and transferred it from your computer to a physically identical computer, would the new computer be identifiable with your old computer? Indeed, would it be meaningful to talk of any link with the old computer beyond that it has the same hard drive? This is not really saying very much, since there are millions of examples of every type of hard drive and they are all alike. Furthermore, the hard drive has no physical memory of being your hard drive – the hard drive was wiped, just as experience, memory and learning appear to be lost when separated from the brain. If the reincarnated soul has no direct link with the old body it was in, what are you really saying when you say that karma is carried forward when the *atman* is reincarnated?

Stephen T. Davis ('Philosophy and Life after Death: The Questions and the Options') has also pointed out that the doctrine of karma is claimed to explain the problem of suffering, in that people suffer because of sins in their past lives. However, Davis notes that a question arises about this situation. What is the connection between the person suffering and the past

Atman

A Sanskrit word that means 'inner-self' or 'soul'. Atman is the *true* self of an individual beyond identification with phenomena, the essence of an individual. In order to attain liberation from *samsara*, a human being must acquire self-knowledge, which is to realise that a person's true self (*atman*) is identical with the transcendent self Brahman.

life? If the person suffering now has no memories of a past life and the link is only the immaterial soul, how is it just that the person suffers now for sins committed by a different person in a previous life?

Peter Geach ('What Must Be True of Me if I Survive My Death?') also rejects belief in reincarnation on the grounds that a connection with the person who has died cannot be established. Reincarnation rules out any possibility of memories being the link between the dead and the new person. He gives the example of an old man dying and his soul being reincarnated in a newborn baby. He questions what could be between the two, given that, as a person, the old man was a unity of both body and the experiences and memories gained through life. If the baby is you reincarnated, how is the baby you if the baby lacks your body, memories, experiences, feelings and so on?

Thought Point

Morality

Do you think any ethical theory can justify:

- Pogroms
- Witch-hunts
- Persecuting heretics?

ARGUMENTS AGAINST BELIEF IN LIFE AFTER DEATH

Many philosophers have rejected belief in life after death of any sort. Their arguments focus on three key ideas:

1   Belief in an afterlife is the product of human wishful thinking.
2   There is no evidence to suggest that people do survive death.
3   It makes no sense to talk of a person surviving death, since a person is a physical entity.

Many people fear death because it is something unknown. Some philosophers argue that fear of death being the end leads people to believe in continued existence after death.

In his essay 'Can a Man Witness His Own Funeral?' Anthony Flew argues against belief in an afterlife. In particular, he points out that people are mortal. The minds of human beings are united to a physical body and the body is mortal. As far as anyone can tell mental processes do not survive physical death. Furthermore, Flew suggests that 'people are what you meet', meaning that when we talk about Tony Blair or Martin Luther King Jr or Margaret Thatcher we mean a particular physical person. We do not mean a disembodied soul that is called Martin Luther King Jr's soul. For Flew, talk of life after death was 'self-contradictory' – it made no sense because he believed that mental processes did not survive death.

Bertrand Russell also argued that there was no such thing as life after death. His arguments focused on the claim that wishful thinking on the part of human beings was the cause of belief in life after death. For Russell: 'All that constitutes a person is a series of experiences connected by memory and by certain similarities of the sort we call habit' (Russell, 'Belief in Life after Death Comes from Emotion Not Reason').

Russell argued that a person is the experiences that are connected together in the memory of an individual. He suggests that memories are linked to the brain just as a river is associated with its bed. If the riverbed is destroyed, so is any meaningful sense of the use of the word river to what was there before. In the same way, at death a person's brain ceases to function and their body starts to decay. At this point, the person's memories that make them who they are are also lost because the brain, like the rest of the body, dies and rots.

For Russell, 'fear of death' is 'instinctive' and the result of this fear is that people believe in life after death. However, Russell argues that the universe is indifferent to people and there is no evidence of life after death.

Russell also advocates an argument for rejecting belief in life after death. He suggests that:

> Of men in the concrete, most of us think the vast majority very bad. Civilised states spend more than half their revenue on killing each other's citizens. Consider the long history of activities inspired by moral fervour: persecution of heretics, witch-hunts, pogroms leading up to wholesale extermination by poison gas. ('Belief in Life After Death Comes from Emotion Not Reason')

This leads Russell to question two things: first, whether the ethical beliefs that led to these types of activities are really from God, particularly from an intelligent creator God; second, Russell questions whether people really want those who do conduct events such as witch-hunts or pogroms to live for ever. Russell suggests that the world is better understood without God and an afterlife, because if there is evidence in the world for 'deliberate purpose, the purpose must have been that of a fiend' ('Belief in Life after Death Comes from Emotion Not Reason'). For Russell the idea of a God who would let evil people live for ever was not acceptable and nor did it fit with the general idea of God. Therefore it was preferable to attempt to understand life without belief in God.

Thought Point

Good or bad?

Choose some of the following people. Decide whether what you know of the person's actions supports Russell's arguments. If you do not know who any of these people are, research them in an internet encyclopaedia such as www. wikipedia.org:

- Christopher Columbus
- Adolf Hitler
- Myra Hindley
- Ian Brady
- Alexander Fleming
- Albert Einstein
- Pol Pot
- Chairman Mao
- Arthur 'Bomber' Harris.

SUMMARY

1   Does death matter?

No

If you do not believe in an afterlife, death is not something that you personally experience, because your life ends at death

Yes

Death is an unknown
A final parting with people whom we love
For some religious people it is the dawn of a new stage of life with God, or separated from God in hell

2   The origin of belief in the afterlife

Belief in life after death can be traced back to the cultures of ancient China, Egypt, India and the Middle East

3 How do you know who you are?

Personal identity is linked to one's body, mind or both

Dualism

For example: Plato and Descartes
The mind/soul and the body are separate
The mind (or soul) forms the centre of identity; it is somehow joined with
the body
Support for dualism
We clearly do experience ourselves as thinking beings distinct from our
bodies
Reports concerning people having out-of-body or near-death experiences

Plato
People consist of a body and a soul
The soul is imprisoned in the body
After death, the souls of wrongdoers would be re-imprisoned in a body
Two related arguments to support his belief in an immortal soul:

Argument from opposites
Argument that education is about remembering

Challenges to Plato's view:

Peter Geach questioned what it can mean for the disembodied soul
to see the Forms and whether existence without a body is real
human existence
There is no evidence to suggest that death is a state opposite to
but analogous to life

Monism and materialism

The belief that the mind is one with the body and inseparable from it
'Monist' refers to anyone who believes that there is only one substance
Typically, monists are materialists
For materialists the identity of a person is linked to the physical body
Identity theory claims that all mental activities are centred in the brain
Materialists can only support life after death if that life is physical, such
as in religious teaching about resurrection

Richard Dawkins
The only sense in which human beings survive death is through the
memories of them in other people's minds or through their genes,
some of which are passed on to the next generation of offspring
Human beings' consciousness has evolved because of the survival
advantage it gives

Support for materialism and monism
It accords with our knowledge of the physical world
Some support for claims that mental activity is fully explainable in terms of neurone activity in the brain from recent scientific discoveries

Challenges to this view
Stephen T. Davis pointed to the fact that identity theory has difficulty explaining intentionality

John Hick's replica theory
Rejects dualism, while at the same time presenting a defence of belief in bodily resurrection
Human beings are a 'psycho-somatic unity' (Hick, 'Resurrection of the Person')
Hick's replica theory is one way to understand St Paul
Resurrection is a divine action in which an exact replica of ourselves is created in a different place
Resurrection could take place instantaneously at death or after a time lapse determined by God
The replica exists in a 'different space' from us that is observable by God and not by us
The replica of the person is not the same as a copy
John Hick suggested the example of a person disappearing in London and reappearing in New York
Challenges to replica theory:

  Identification of the replica with the original person
  Multiple replicas
  The nature and state of the resurrected body

4   Religious views on the afterlife

Christianity – resurrection

Resurrection and the New Testament
The New Testament refers to the afterlife as a paradise, a state of continued existence with God after death (1 Thessalonians 4: 13–14)
Seeing God face to face is called the *Beatific Vision* (1 Corinthians 13: 12)
Traditional Christianity has taught the resurrection of the body, not just a person's soul or centre of identity. However, this is not necessarily a physical body
Peter Geach suggests that resurrection is the only meaningful way in which one can speak of life after death

At death the soul of a person is separated from her or his earthly body awaiting the final resurrection and each person is judged by God (the Particular Judgment)

God offers forgiveness if people really repent, but forgiveness also requires contrition, confession and an act of satisfaction

Heaven and hell

Christianity and Islam traditionally believe in a state of existence with God after death (heaven) and a state of separation from God (hell)

Heaven is described in Christian tradition:

As a state of fulfilment of all human longings
As the ultimate goal or end of human existence

Hell is traditionally characterised as:

A state of separation from God
A place of punishment by God
As an aspect of God's justice

Problems with belief in hell:

Images do not communicate the idea of a loving and forgiving God
For some people, the eternal nature of the punishment appears unjust; it is not educative
If hell is a place of physical suffering, where is it?

Purgatory

A traditional Christian belief in a place where all people who die in relationship with God, but who are not yet perfect, are purified after death

Heaven, hell and the problem of evil

For some Christians the justification of the existence of God comes from the belief that ultimately God holds everyone to account and judges them according to their actions
Within Roman Catholic and Orthodox Christian traditions no one is predestined to go to hell
Richard Swinburne: universal salvation is not traditional belief (*Providence and the Problem of Evil*)
Many theodicies rely on the concept of God judging people as the basis of moral responsibility

Predestination and Divine Election:

Some Christians believe in Divine Election
By the doctrine of Divine Election Calvin meant that some people are destined for a relationship with God and some are not; this is an aspect of God's sovereignty

Among some Protestant groups which are offshoots from Calvinism (e.g. followers of Théodore de Bèze) the doctrine of predestination became important

Some support for belief in predestination in the Bible in Revelation (Revelation 7: 12)

Hinduism – reincarnation

The central idea of reincarnation is the belief that the soul of a body is eternal

The soul is reborn in new bodies generation after generation

If in the previous life the person was morally good, the soul will be reincarnated in a better body

All living things have a soul or atman

The karma reflecting one's actions in life is carried to the next incarnation of the soul

The ultimate goal of the soul is to be reunited with Brahman

Evidence that supports reincarnation:

Children who appear to remember events at which they were not present

People having a sense of *déjà vu*

Challenges to reincarnation

Remembering a previous life could be explained in other ways (or could just be a hoax)

Richard Swinburne rejects reincarnation if there is no continuity between the brain of the new baby and the old person who died

Peter Geach rejects belief in reincarnation on the grounds that a link with the person who has died cannot be established

5 Arguments against belief in life after death

There is no convincing evidence to suggest that people do survive death

It makes no sense to talk of a person surviving death, since a person is a physical entity

Flew suggested that 'people are what you meet', meaning that when we talk about a person we mean a particular physical person – not separate physical and spiritual ones

Bertrand Russell

Belief in an afterlife is the product of human wishful thinking

At death the person's memories that make them who they are are also lost because the brain, like the rest of the body, dies and rots

The universe is indifferent to people

Do people really want those who conduct events such as witch-hunts or pogroms to live for ever?

The world is better understood without God and an afterlife

REVIEW QUESTIONS

Look back over the chapter and check that you can answer the following questions:

1   Which are more coherent: arguments in favour of resurrection or rebirth?
2   What is the appeal of materialism?
3   Is replica theory more persuasive than belief in a soul?
4   Which argument against life after death is the strongest in your opinion? Justify your answer.
5   Outline Russell's reasons for rejecting belief in life after death. Is his argument persuasive?

Terminology

Do you know your terminology?

1   Try to explain the following ideas without looking at your books and notes:

   •   Replica theory
   •   Disembodied existence
   •   Resurrection
   •   Reincarnation
   •   Materialism
   •   Divine Election.

Examination Questions Practice

EXAM MISTAKES TO AVOID

It is very important that you are able to explain clearly the different views of writers on life after death and the existence of the soul. If you confuse different ideas you will not achieve high marks. In particular, you need to be able to apply the terms 'monism' and 'dualism' accurately to different philosophers. In addition, make sure that you can clearly explain replica theory.

Examination questions on this topic typically ask you whether life after death/disembodied existence/resurrection etc. are 'possible' or 'coherent'. There is an important difference in meaning between *coherent* and *possible*.

For example, a question asks:

'Embodied existence after death is coherent.' Discuss.

The word *coherent* indicates that you need to discuss in your essay whether the concept of embodied existence after death makes sense. In other words, the question is asking you to consider the strength of arguments that support embodied existence after death.

However, if the question asked:

'Embodied existence after death is possible.' Discuss.

the word *possible* indicates that you need to discuss whether embodied existence after death happens, or can happen. The emphasis of the second question is different from that of the first because the focus of the question is whether embodied life after death happens.

Remember: each question assesses AO1 and AO2. To help you improve your answers look at the A2 Levels of Response. See: http://www.ocr.org. uk/qualifications/as-a-level-gce-religious-studies-h172-h572/.

SAMPLE A2 EXAM-STYLE QUESTION

'Theories of resurrection of the body are logically coherent.' Discuss. (35 marks)

This question requires you to consider whether theories of bodily resurrection make sense logically. There are a number of ways to approach this essay.

One approach would be to present theories of the resurrection of the body, and to assess the strengths and weaknesses of the arguments. For example, John Hick's replica theory could be discussed as a modern understanding of resurrection, and the strengths and weaknesses of the theory could be considered to help form a judgement about the coherence of belief in bodily

resurrection. Materialist criticisms of dualist views could be used to support the claim that resurrection is coherent.

The coherence of religious teaching concerning resurrection of the body could be examined. For example, you could assess accounts of Jesus' resurrection in the New Testament as a way to discuss the coherence of believers' faith in bodily resurrection. An examination of the historical origins of belief in bodily resurrection could be used to argue either in favour of or against the coherence of belief in bodily resurrection.

Part of your answer could consider the problem of personal identity and whether a body is necessary to make any sense of meaningful survival after death. Arguments from materialism as well as philosophers who favour bodily resurrection could be used to defend the necessity of a body to make sense of resurrection. Equally, the coherence of the concept of bodily resurrection could be challenged using materialism, or the arguments of philosophers such as Bertrand Russell.

FURTHER READING

There are many books concerning religious beliefs about the resurrection, such as Bible commentaries. A very interesting examination of questions concerning the historicity of the resurrection of Jesus may be found in William Lane Craig's book *The Son Rises: The Historical Evidence for the Resurrection of Jesus*.

Thomas Aquinas' views on life after death may be explored in his *Summa Contra Gentiles*. Brian Davies has published a useful and clear overview of Aquinas' ideas, including a chapter which examines his understanding of life after death (Davies, *The Thought of Thomas Aquinas*).

If you would like to read a challenge to belief in life after death read 'Do We Survive Death?' in *Why I Am Not a Christian: and Other Essays on Religion* by Bertrand Russell. Russell's essay presents a clear and concise challenge to belief in life after death.

There are many books available that examine both life after death and the mind–body problem. If these areas interest you, a starting point could be Richard Swinburne's *Evolution of a Soul* and the collection of essays concerning life after death entitled *Immortality* (ed. P. Edwards).

12 Revelation and Holy Scripture

Essential terminology

Divine inspiration
Infallible
Non-propositional
revelation
Propositional revelation
Revelation
Verbal inspiration

THE ISSUE

Is the Bible a revelation from God? If it is, do we have to obey it?

WHAT YOU WILL LEARN ABOUT IN THIS CHAPTER

In this chapter you will examine what is meant by 'revelation'. You will then consider what it means to say that the Bible is revealed by God. You will assess the claim that the Bible is divinely inspired and that we have to obey it.

STARTER

Look at the list of books below. Are any of these books particularly special? Should any of these books be described as 'holy'? If so, what would the word 'holy' mean?

- The Bible
- *The Selfish Gene* by Richard Dawkins
- *The Story of Philosophy* by Bryan Magee
- The Qur'an
- *Noddy and the Treasure Trail*
- Joseph Conrad – various works
- *The Third Twin* by Ken Follett
- *The Universe in a Nutshell* by Stephen Hawking

Revelation

Refers to any act in which God is revealed to human beings. The characteristic of revelation is that it reveals knowledge of God/God's nature. In Christianity there are two types of revelation:

1 Propositional revelation
2 Non-propositional revelation.

What is the Bible?

There are two ways to answer this question:

1   The Bible is the divinely inspired and revealed Word of God (more about this later in the chapter).
2   The Bible is a collection of separate books and most scholars would argue that the earliest strands of the Bible date from Solomon around 960 BCE and that the New Testament was complete by the 4th century CE.

THE OCR CHECKLIST

In this chapter you will cover the following aspects of the OCR specification:

Candidates should be able to demonstrate knowledge and understanding of the following in relation to God and religious belief:

*   the concept of revelation through sacred writings.

Candidates should be able to discuss these areas critically and their strengths and weaknesses.

From OCR A Level Religious Studies specification H572.

INTRODUCTION – HOLY SCRIPTURE

People speak of 'holy scripture' revealing God or containing revelations from God, but what does this mean?

In religious tradition, some books, such as the Bible and the Qur'an, are given the title 'holy'. The word 'holy' originally meant 'separate' or 'set apart' and this is why it came to be associated with God. God is holy and set apart from the world. Thus, calling books such as the Bible and the Qur'an 'holy' is suggesting their special status with God. For religious believers, books such as the Bible and the Qur'an are set apart by the fact that they are revelatory – they reveal God to the world.

This chapter will examine what it means within the Christian tradition to describe the Bible as revelatory and what the implications of this are. Your choices in the starter exercise indicate one particular problem – how to decide that a book is holy. Is it because God makes the book holy or because God divinely reveals the book? This is the view of the Qur'an within Islam and the Bible in Christianity.

Thought Point

Revelation exercise

1   What do religious believers mean by the word 'revelation'? Write a list of characteristics of a 'revelation'.
2   Do any of the following events qualify as a 'revelation'?

*   A vision;
*   A miraculous healing;
*   Recovering from having cancer;
*   Having a baby;
*   Feeling God is with you;
*   Admiring the beauty of nature;
*   Having a near-death experience;
*   Winning the lottery;
*   Passing your examinations;
*   Understanding mathematics;
*   Becoming fluent in a foreign language;
*   Reading the Bible;
*   Having an out-of-this-world experience;
*   Going to church;
*   Praying.

A few facts about the Bible

*   The Christian Bible is divided into two parts: The Old Testament and The New Testament.
*   The Old Testament consists of 66 books. Traditionally it was broken into three sections in Judaism: Torah (Law), Nevi'im (Prophets), Ketuv'im (Writings).
*   The New Testament consists of 27 books made up of four Gospels, one historical book, Acts of the Apostles, 21 epistles (by Paul and other writers) and one book of prophecy, Revelation.
*   The following types of writing are found in the Bible: prophecy, history, law, poetry, proverbs, prayer, revelations, allegory and myth.
*   The list of books that make up the New Testament was pretty much agreed in the second century CE, but not finalised until the Council of Elvira in c. 305–306 CE.

HOW IS GOD REVEALED TO THE WORLD?

Religious traditions talk about God being revealed to the world in a variety of ways: through holy books such as the Bible and the Qur'an, or through nature, people, miracles and visions. However, the sense in which the word 'revelation' is used varies between, for example, saying God is revealed in nature and saying God is revealed through the Bible.

The term 'revelation' is used to refer to any act in which God is revealed. God revealing himself to a person is often called an act of 'divine disclosure'. Examples of revelations are events such as the Qur'an being revealed to the Prophet Muhammad ﷺ, God appearing to Saul on the road to Damascus, or God giving the Ten Commandments to the Prophet Moses.

In the Judaeo-Christian tradition a 'revelation' is characterised by the fact that something about God or God's nature is revealed to the person who experiences the revelation. Hence, in the above exercise about what a revelation is, any of the events in which you believed God was revealed could be a revelation. Of course revelation may be used in other senses, for example to mean gaining a new insight into something, but the crucial idea in religious traditions is that revelations reveal God.

For Christians, the Bible, from its origins, is revelatory and a source of authority. What this could mean is the topic of this chapter.

REVELATION IN PHILOSOPHY

In philosophy of religion there are two different ways in which people understand the idea of revelation from God:

1 Propositional revelation
2 Non-propositional revelation.

Both of these views are widely held by religious believers, and many religious believers would hold both these views at the same time. It is common for believers in the Christian tradition to suggest that the Bible is a propositional revelation, but that all other religious experiences are non-propositional revelations of God.

Propositional revelation

Proposition

An indicative statement which contends, maintains, asserts or implies something which is held to be true. This may or may not be factual.

The phrase *propositional revelation* refers to God revealing truths about his nature to people. They are called 'propositions' to indicate that the revelations are statements of facts. The key to propositional revelation is that truths about God are revealed as propositions. Since the revelations communicate facts from God or about God, some religious believers argue that the propositions are true – by this they mean that they are beyond debate or doubt.

Jews and Christians would argue that the Ten Commandments revealed to Moses on Mount Sinai are a revelation from God. For some Jews and Christians the Ten Commandments are not debatable or open to question: they are facts laid down by God. In the same manner a Muslim could state that the Qur'an is a propositional revelation. The distinctive feature of propositional revelation is that it reveals knowledge from God which is without error or need of reinterpretation.

There are many possible types of propositional revelation, such as through holy books like the Bible and Qur'an, vision experiences or religious experiences of God. The role of faith with respect to propositional revelation is to accept the revelation that God has revealed. In Islam this same idea is expressed in the concept of *submission to God*, whence the word *Islam* derives.

Thomas Aquinas (*Summa Theologiae*) suggested that 'faith' concerns knowledge about God who is transcendent. Although this is more certain than opinion, it is not as certain as scientific knowledge.

Aquinas argued that even if faith cannot be demonstrated to be true in the same way as science, it is better than opinions. He believed that faith is based on something factual, which opinion, in his thinking, is not. However, faith is not as certain as science because faith cannot be proved true by reason. Propositional revelations are truths revealed by God but they are not demonstrable using human reason. Propositional revelation refers to God directly revealing truths about his nature to people.

It is important to note that believers in propositional revelation do not reject the use of reason. What they are saying is that God's revelations are not provable by human reason, but they would also say that God can be revealed by using reason in the world. A good example of this is the attempts to prove that God exists using cosmological and teleological arguments. Usually a distinction is made between:

- Revelation and
- Natural theology.

The genuineness of a revelation could be assessed by referring to previous teaching of the magisterium.

Natural theology refers to the process of learning about God from the natural world by using reason. Aquinas is a good example of a person who emphasised the role of propositional revelation and natural theology. In Aquinas' thought, revelations can be accepted as genuine if they accord with Church teaching because the existence of God who makes the revelations may be demonstrated using arguments for God's existence.

The criterion of 'according with Church teaching' is important. One criterion for determining whether a propositional revelation is genuine is to see whether it fits in with Church teaching because this teaching in turn was revealed, ultimately going back to Jesus and the apostles.

Knowledge may be from God as well as about God (e.g. in the historical biblical texts). Karl Barth, for example, considered the Bible in propositional terms (as witness to God's word) but was certainly not a fundamentalist.

> **The magisterium**
>
> Within the Roman Catholic Church the teaching authority of the Church is called 'the magisterium'.

Criticisms of propositional revelation

- Propositional revelation suggests that the receiver of the revelation is passive and just receives the revelation. However, many philosophers have suggested that psychologically the human mind does not passively receive knowledge; rather, the human mind actively receives knowledge.

For example, when you learn something your mind remembers it accurately. If you hear a piece of gossip you have to remember it actively to be able to repeat it. Second, we also make mistakes even when trying to learn things accurately. This could mean that propositional revelations of God may not be recorded accurately, as the human mind makes mistakes.

- How can one know which revelations are true propositions? Despite the suggested criteria of fitting in with accepted Church teaching, this does not guarantee that a revelation is genuine. While the after-effects of a revelation could be pointed out, such as Paul becoming a Christian after the revelation on the road to Damascus (Acts 9: 1–31), this is not an absolute proof of the genuineness of the revelation.
- Different religions claim to have received propositional revelations, yet sometimes the truth claims of different religions conflict. How can these contradictions be resolved? How can you know which truth claim is correct? Or does this mean that all revelations from God are limited by the fact that when they are revealed to human beings the person experiencing the revelation may misunderstand it?
- There is no way directly to verify or prove that propositional revelations happen.

Non-propositional revelation

The phrase *non-propositional revelation* refers to the idea that God does not reveal facts or truths to people directly; instead, the religious believer recognises God acting in human history and human experience. For example, a religious believer may come to see God in a beautiful natural scene; the scene reveals God to the person observing it. William Paley was famously impressed by the structure of the human eye, while Arthur Conan Doyle's character Sherlock Holmes was impressed by the beauty of nature.

The argument which Sherlock Holmes is making is an argument from beauty. For many people their thoughts are raised to the possibility of God through the beauty that is found in the world around them. Nature for many people reveals God to them, but this revelation of God is indirect and a matter of interpretation. Hence, this view of revelation is called non-propositional because the revelation is a human being's recognition of God's acts in and through the world.

According to this view of revelation, a religious book, for example the Bible, is a witness to and record of how the revelation of God has been understood in history by religious believers. God has acted in history, and the perceptions of people who witness these revelatory acts are what are recorded in the Bible. One way to express this could be to say that people learn about God through the signs Jesus worked, such as healing the paralysed man (Mark 2: 1–12), and those who witnessed this act interpreted what they saw. These sorts of non-propositional revelation are indirect experiences of God, which lead a person to understand something about God. In this sense faith is about how a person experiences God through events in daily life – faith is a way of seeing the world. A Muslim or Christian may look at a beautiful landscape and understand something about God as the Creator; an atheist may look at the same landscape and gain no understanding of God.

If the Bible is a non-propositional revelation, the role of the reader and how the reader interprets the Bible will be of crucial importance, because the non-propositional revelation takes place in the life of the believer. In other words, every person will see the world in a different way according to the worldview they hold.

The authority of non-propositional revelation stems from the fact that human beings are free to respond to God's revelation or not, since the revelation is not received passively.

Criticisms of non-propositional revelation

- As non-propositional revelations are the result of human understanding and interpretation of events, they do not reveal direct knowledge of God, nor can they be considered as errorless (infallible). Thus there is no way of resolving theological debates apart from appealing to one's own experience. The advantage of the propositional view is that one can appeal to facts revealed by God as a basis for a theological debate.
- In the non-propositional view of revelation, the content of the revelation is a matter of interpretation. Arthur Conan Doyle wrote about the beauty of nature revealing God, as did William Paley and many other writers, but it is equally possible to wonder at the beauty of nature and yet not experience a non-propositional revelation. Richard Dawkins, the evolutionary biologist and critic of religious belief, is equally moved by the beauty he finds in the world around him. For Dawkins the fact that we evolved through our genes and developed a sense of consciousness which enables us to understand a little of our place in the universe and in the process of evolution is wonderful. Consciousness is a great thing. It does not, however, lead Richard Dawkins to belief in God.

> The spotlight passes but, exhilaratingly, before doing so it gives us time to comprehend something of this place in which we fleetingly find ourselves and the reason that we do so. We are alone among the animals in being able to say before we die: Yes, that is why it was worth coming to life in the first place. (Dawkins, *Unweaving the Rainbow*)

Non-propositional revelation
Refers to the idea that God does not reveal facts or truths to people; instead the religious believer recognises God acting in human history and human experience. For example, a religious believer may come to see God in a beautiful natural scene; the scene reveals truths about God to the person observing it.

Sherlock Holmes and revelation

" WHAT A LOVELY THING A ROSE IS.

He [Sherlock Holmes] walked past the couch to the open window, and held up the drooping stalk of a moss rose, looking down at the dainty blend of crimson

continued overleaf

and green. It was a new phase of his character to me, for I had never before seen him show any keen interest in natural objects.

'There is nothing in which deduction is so necessary as in religion', said he, leaning with his back against the shutters. 'It can be built upon an exact science by the reasoner. Our highest assurance of the goodness of providence seems to rest in the flowers. All other things, our powers, our desires, our food, are really necessary for our existence in the first instance. But this rose is an extra. Its smell, its colour are an embellishment of life, not a condition of it. It is only goodness which gives extras so I say again we have much hope from the flowers.' (Arthur Conan Doyle, *The Adventures of Sherlock Holmes*)

Infallible

Used by religious believers to indicate that a teaching does not contain any error or possibility of error.

Thought Point

Does nature reveal God?

Consider whether you think that God can be non-propositionally revealed through nature. Read the following passage. Do you think that a religious believer wrote it?

> After sleeping through a hundred million centuries we have finally opened our eyes on a sumptuous planet, sparkling with colour, beautiful with life. Within decades we must close our eyes again. Isn't it a noble, enlightened way of spending our brief time in the sun, to work at understanding the universe and how we have come to wake up in it. (See Thought Point box 'The answer', p. 300)

It is not possible to appeal to facts of belief or faith according to the non-propositional view of revelation. Religious faith that is based solely on religious experience of a non-propositional revelation cannot claim absolute certainty about its belief systems in the way a believer in propositional revelation can.

THE REVELATION OF GOD THROUGH SCRIPTURE

What sort of revelation of God is gained from the Bible? The answer depends very much on the particular views of the person you ask. For some people the Bible is a propositional revelation from God that reveals his divine word; for other people the Bible is a non-propositional revelation in which God is revealed through the books of the Bible that record the individual authors' experiences of God. Both of these approaches view the Bible as inspired by God, but the meaning of this phrase varies.

THE BIBLE IS THE DIVINELY INSPIRED WORD OF GOD

A propositional revelation view

Christians who hold that the Bible is a propositional revelation of God acknowledge this by stating that the Bible is the Word of God. According to a propositional approach, the role of the authors of the books of the Bible is limited or non-existent since the Bible is God's revelation. The inspiration for each book of the Bible is divine and this is what causes the author to write his or her book. The authority of the Bible derives from the fact that the Bible is a propositional revelation from God that reveals knowledge about God to people.

Among fundamentalist Christians the term *verbal inspiration* is used to indicate the divine origins or authorship of every word in the Bible which the authors of the biblical books were inspired to write. On this view God effectively dictates the books of the Bible. Consequently, a believer in divine dictation would hold that the Bible is inerrant (without error).

While many Christians believe that the Bible is divinely inspired, not all believe in verbal inspiration. However, all Christians who believe that the Bible is, or contains, propositional revelations from God would point out that the Bible reveals propositions about God and God's wishes for human beings that are true. For example, the Ten Commandments were given to Moses by God and these reveal basic commands for human beings about how they should live.

If the Bible is a propositional revelation from God, you can consult the Bible for guidance about moral dilemmas and problems in life. Answers to these problems may be found in the Bible.

Thought Point

If the Bible and its contents are revealed by God, do you have to obey them?

The claim that the Bible is a propositional revelation from God means that it contains truths from God. Look up the following passages in the Bible and then answer the questions that follow:

- Leviticus 19: 27–28
- Leviticus 20: 9
- Deuteronomy 21: 18–21
- Matthew 5: 27–30
- Mark 10: 21–22

1 What is each passage about?
2 Do you agree with the teaching in each passage? Give reasons to support your answer.

continued overleaf

Verbal inspiration
Refers to the divine origins or authorship of every word in the Bible. According to this view God effectively dictates the books of the Bible by divine inspiration.

Biblical fundamentalism

The term 'fundamentalism' is derived from nineteenth and early twentieth century theologians and biblical scholars who opposed liberal approaches to biblical interpretation which doubted things such as the miracles in the Bible or that the Genesis story was historically true. They were working to return to the fundamentals of Christianity. It is only more recently that fundamentalism came to be understood as 'literalism' in a pejorative way.

Biblical fundamentalists today believe that the Bible is the inspired Word of God and that it is without errors. The Bible is the authoritative Christian book that reveals God's will to people. Many fundamentalists interpret stories such as the Genesis creation stories as historically true documents.

continued overleaf

For some fundamentalists, Genesis happened as recorded in the Bible; for others, the days of the Genesis story symbolise periods of thousands of years. Much of the moral teaching in the Bible is strictly followed by fundamentalists, such as teaching about homosexuality or divorce.

Limitations of this approach

- Fundamentalism does not help you to interpret the Bible. The Bible's authoritative status may be accepted, but unless the reader is also inspired to read the Bible in the way God wants, how is the Bible's message any clearer?

- A fundamentalist only accepts one way of interpreting the Bible, but there is no proof that the fundamentalist's approach is the correct one. All the fundamentalist can do is claim that their view is correct, but this is a subjective view.

3   If the Bible is a propositional revelation from God, what do you think is the revelation contained in these passages?

4   Could a person be a Christian who believes that the Bible is inspired and a propositional revelation from God and yet not follow the teaching contained in these passages?

The question of the author's role is interesting. For a fundamentalist the author's role is limited to that of a passive recorder of God's revelation. However, for other Christians the Bible reveals propositions about God but the revelations have been recorded by human beings in their own language and in different styles or manners. In this sense the reader of the Bible also has to interpret and understand it in order to know the revelation it contains from God. This is different from the fundamentalist approach where the Bible is the dictated Word of God revealed directly to us, but both of these approaches would still claim that the Bible is without errors.

AN EXAMPLE OF THE PROPOSITIONAL REVELATION APPROACH TO THE BIBLE

The Roman Catholic Church is an example of a tradition which believes that the Bible is a propositional revelation from God. The Catholic Church teaches that the Bible is indeed the Word of God: God inspired the authors of the Bible and God is in some sense the author of scripture:

> The divinely revealed realities, which are contained and presented in the text of sacred scripture, have been written down under the inspiration of the Holy Spirit. (*The Catechism of the Catholic Church* §105)

The Roman Catholic Church also emphasises the role of the human authors. God communicates to Christians through the Bible in a human way. Thus the reader has to try to understand the intentions of the authors, who, of course, wrote their books using the language and ideas of their time.

In order to discover the sacred authors' intention, the reader must take into account the conditions of their time and culture. The

continued opposite

literary genres in use at that time, and the modes of feeling, speaking and narrating then current. For the fact is that truth is differently presented and expressed in the various types of historical writing, prophetical and poetical texts, and in other forms of literary expression. (*The Catechism of the Catholic Church* §110)

What is interesting is that the Roman Catholic Church indicates that while the Bible is a propositional revelation of the Word of God, it still needs to be interpreted if its message is to speak to Christians today. It is important to note that Roman Catholics do not interpret the Bible literally.

A non-propositional revelation view: the Bible is a record of human experiences of God

Divine inspiration
Refers to the belief among Christians that God inspired the writers of the books of the Bible. It may also refer to other faiths where texts are seen as being 'inspired' rather than as in Islam where the Qur'an is viewed as divine revelation.

Many Christians agree that the Bible is divinely inspired but they would not accept the idea that it is a propositional revelation from God. Instead they would describe the Bible as a record of human beings' experiences of God (i.e. a collection of accounts and stories about people's experiences of God in history). In this sense the Bible would be a non-propositional revelation of God since it would reveal God to people indirectly.

On this view the Bible is still divinely inspired, but the inspiration of God makes the author write down their experiences and understanding of God and God's action in the world. The author would not be divinely dictated to but would use her or his own skills and understanding to record the revelation of God. Matthew's Gospel is often associated with one of Jesus' apostles. On this view his Gospel would be an account of what was revealed through Jesus' life and work as he understood it.

The non-propositional view of the Bible understands the biblical scriptures as presenting pictures and images of God's revelation; for example, from reading the Gospel we can form an image of what Jesus the man was like. However, Jesus' significance is understood through faith, not through statements in the text of the Gospel. In other words, you read the Bible and then work out what the revelation means to you today.

This non-propositional understanding of revelation in the Bible is often associated with what has been called liberal biblical interpretation. One early figure in this movement was Friedrich Schleiermacher (1768–1834) who believed that religious faith was a matter of experience and feeling in the life of the believer. Thus the religious believer in his or her time has to interpret the revelation from the Bible. Schleiermacher himself concluded that the New Testament revealed that Jesus' mission was not about saving people, but about raising people's awareness of God.

Thought Point

Is the non-propositional revelation of Jesus clear?

- Which picture best represents Jesus as revealed in the Gospels?
- Which picture appeals most to you?
- Discuss your answers.
- Can you identify a problem related to the non-propositional view of the Bible? Think about how you could use these pictures as examples in your answer.

Thought Point

Albert Schweitzer

The famous biblical interpreter Albert Schweitzer (1875–1965) said that if you take a liberal approach to the Bible all you do is read your own meaning into a biblical story. What do you think Schweitzer meant by the following comment?

> Each successive epoch found its own thoughts in Jesus, which was, indeed, the only way in which it could make him live. (Albert Schweitzer quoted in J. Pelikan, *The Illustrated Jesus through the Centuries*)

THE AUTHORITY OF SCRIPTURE

THE ORIGIN OF THE BIBLE

The Christian Bible originated in the early Church. In the first and second centuries CE Christianity was gradually establishing itself as a distinct religion: distinct both from Judaism and from pagan religious groups of the time. The leaders of the Church in the second century CE could no longer appeal directly to the first apostles for advice and guidance. Hence a new source of authority was needed. The solution to this problem, which came to be accepted in the second century CE, was to appeal to two sources of authority:

1   The Rule of Faith
2   The Bible: the Old and New Testaments.

The Rule of Faith referred to the traditions, teachings of leaders and beliefs of Christians that had been passed on in Christian communities from the time of the Apostles.

Bishops of the second century CE drew up lists of Christian writings that it was felt truly reflected and represented Christian beliefs, values and teaching. An important aspect of these books was a claim that they had a direct link with the Apostles or Jesus, if not actual apostolic authorship (e.g. John's Gospel was linked to the apostle John, but now scholars suggest that it came from a 'Johannine community' tracing its traditions to John, and reaching its final form about 90–120 CE; whereas Mark's Gospel was linked to the man who ran off naked from the Garden of Gethsemane when Jesus was arrested, but it is now considered to have been written in Syria by an unknown Christian no earlier than 70 CE). Paul, the writer of many letters in the New Testament, claimed that he had experienced a revelation of the risen Jesus on the road to Damascus. Christianity also adopted the entirety of the Old Testament from Judaism, believing that the Old Testament *proclaimed Christ to come* and the New Testament *proclaimed Christ in fact* (i.e. the story of Jesus' presence on Earth).

From its origins, the Bible is a source of authority for Christians. The question of what it means to claim 'the Bible is a source of authority' is one of the major issues for Christian believers.

THE AUTHORITY OF THE BIBLE

What is the authority of the Bible? For the atheist or agnostic the Bible may be a historically important text; it may help to inform one about the society

---

The Church of England on the authority of the Bible

Holy Scripture containeth all things necessary to salvation: so that whatsoever is not read therein, nor may be proved thereby, is not to be required of any man, that it should be believed as an article of the Faith, or be thought requisite or necessary to salvation. In the name of the Holy Scripture we do understand those canonical Books of the Old and New Testament, of whose authority was never any doubt in the Church. (*The 39 Articles: Article 6*), The Book of Common Prayer

---

Apostolic authority

The link between the books of the Bible and Jesus is very important to Christians, as they believe Jesus gave his authority to the apostles (Mark 16: 12–20) and the apostles were witnesses of Jesus' life and work. Peter was commissioned by Jesus as the leader of the apostles (Matthew 16) and given authority by Jesus on Earth in his name. Bishops are successors to the apostles because down the centuries

continued overleaf

the authority of the apostles has been handed on to the bishops. In the Roman Catholic Church the Pope is the leader of the Church because he is the successor of St Peter, the first Pope.

A canon of books

Canon is the word used by biblical scholars for the list of books officially accepted by the Christian Church as part of the Bible. In the time after Jesus' death there was considerable debate among Christians about which books belonged in the Bible.

Judaism had finalised the canon of the books of the Jewish Scriptures at the (hypothetical) Council of Jamnia (c. 70–90 CE). Believing that the Old Testament 'proclaimed Christ to come', Bishop Irenaeus of Lyon suggested a canon of the New Testament in his book *Adversus Haereses* (c. 175 CE) that is virtually identical to the canon of books of the Bible that was finally accepted at the Council of Elvira in the late fourth century CE, and said the New Testament 'proclaimed Christ in fact' (i.e. the story of Jesus' presence on Earth).

and beliefs of peoples living 2,000 to 3,500 years ago. But this does not mean that the Bible is an authoritative document, however historically important it is.

On the other hand, for Christian believers the Bible is a document that is authoritative. Calling the Bible 'scripture' implies this very point. If the Bible is an authority, it should be listened to, so what does saying the Bible is 'authoritative' mean?

Maurice Wiles ('The Authority of Scripture in a Contemporary Theology') points out that authority may have more than one sense. In a 'hard' sense, authority implies something having the status of a law. On the other hand, saying someone is an 'authority' on racing cars, for example, is a statement about the way a person speaks on a subject; it does not necessarily imply that the speaker is always correct. This is a soft view of authority.

The Bible has traditionally been interpreted as an authority akin to the 'law' rather than to an authoritative and learned speaker on a subject. The idea of the canon in the early Church reflects this notion. Furthermore, if you believe that the Bible is divinely inspired and reveals the Word of God, then clearly the Bible is authoritative and should be followed.

However, 'laws' can at times require clarification and interpretation to meet new issues, even though the laws would have been carefully considered and written by the group that first drew them up to fulfil the needs of the community. Consider, for example, laws regarding the privacy of private citizens' affairs; with the development of the internet and computer record-keeping the law has had to be changed to address this new situation. In this sense a law, though authoritative, may seem to be time-bound to a situation.

Christians disagree about whether the Bible is a law in this sense. If the Bible is believed to be divinely inspired and inerrant, it does not in principle need to be reinterpreted and, unlike human laws, the Bible would be seen as timeless. However, for other people who believe the Bible is divinely inspired there is still a need for interpretation, as indicated earlier in this chapter.

Saying the Bible is authoritative may thus imply that the Bible requires interpretation, and that what it reveals about God is not always straightforward and clear.

What if the Bible is divinely inspired?

This chapter has discussed the different possible ways in which people understand the Bible to be revelatory. If the Bible is divinely inspired a number of consequences and issues arise.

1 Verbal inspiration

If the Bible is verbally inspired, every word comes from God, and the implication is that every word should be respected and followed as it is God's Word. What this might mean though is disputed:

- The Bible instructs that the death penalty be used as a punishment for many offences, and many of the punishments in the Jewish Scriptures appear harsh to modern readers; for example, the instructions in the book of Leviticus to execute any woman who commits adultery or who is not a virgin when she marries.
- The meaning of the Genesis story is much disputed among Christians (see Chapter 3 on 'God the Creator').
- Can the Bible be disobeyed? If the Bible were a verbally inspired revelation from God, then disobeying any instruction in the Bible would be a rejection of God's revealed commands.

2 Divine inspiration

The majority of Christians believe that the Bible is divinely inspired, but this still raises questions about the way in which the Bible is to be read and interpreted:

- Disobeying biblical instructions – as for verbal inspiration the idea of disobeying specific instructions from God is problematic, but also an issue arises about what the specific instructions from God are. If the book is divinely inspired but not verbally inspired, then the revelation of God is within the text. Identifying the exact nature of the revelation could be problematic.
- Many Christians today have difficulty accepting some of the laws about moral behaviour from both the New and Old Testaments. For example, Jesus states that divorce is wrong but many Christian Churches permit divorce and in some circumstances remarriage.
- Some of the passages found within the Bible conflict with many Christians' views today. For example, Paul's statements about women's subservience to their husbands do not fit very happily with modern ideas about male and female equality.

If Christians believe that the Bible is divinely inspired but is expressed in the language and culture of the times in which the Bible books were written, then the problem for any reader of the Bible is to identify the knowledge revealed about God in the biblical books.

SUMMARY

1 Holy Scripture

Holy – 'separate' or 'set apart'

Set apart – the Bible reveals God

2 Revelation

Characteristics

Refers to any act in which God is revealed, such as the giving of the Qur'an or the Ten Commandments
God's nature is revealed to the person who experiences the revelation
God may be revealed through nature, people, miracles and visions

Propositional revelation

Refers to God directly revealing truths about his nature to people
The propositions are true – beyond debate or doubt
Aquinas: revelations can be accepted as genuine if they accord with Church teaching
Criticisms of propositional revelation:
Receiver of the revelation is passive and just receives the revelation
Propositional revelations may not be recorded accurately, as the human mind makes mistakes unless God inspires (controls) the writing
How can one know which revelations are true?
Conflicting truth claims of different religions' revelations
There is no way to prove that propositional revelations happen

Non-propositional revelation

The religious believer recognises God acting in human history and human experience
Human beings are free to respond to God's revelation or not
Criticisms of non-propositional revelation:
They do not reveal direct knowledge of God, nor can they be considered as errorless (inerrant)
No way of resolving theological debates apart from appealing to one's own experience
The beauty of nature may reveal God (Paley) or not (Dawkins)

3 The revelation of God through scripture

Propositional view: the Bible is divinely inspired

The role of the authors of books of the Bible is limited or non-existent
Divine and verbal inspiration of the Bible

You can consult the Bible for guidance about moral dilemmas and problems

Non-propositional view: the Bible is a record of human experiences of God

The Bible is divinely inspired: God makes the authors write down their understanding of God and God's action in the world
No divine dictation
The reader has to work out God's message

4   The authority of scripture

Direct link of the books with the apostles or Jesus

Jesus gave his authority to the apostles
Bishops and Pope are successors to the apostles and Peter

Maurice Wiles: 'hard' and 'soft' senses of authority

Hard: authority like law
Soft: an expert speaker on a subject

Issues raised by divine inspiration

Can the Bible be disobeyed?
Some of the passages found within the Bible conflict with many Christians' views today (e.g. statements about women)

REVIEW QUESTIONS

Look back over the chapter and check that you can answer the following questions:

1   How can Christians demonstrate their belief that the Bible is divinely inspired?
2   Does the Bible have any authority for a person living in the twenty-first century?
3   If the Bible is a propositional revelation from God, should all its laws be obeyed? If not, why not?
4   What is the major weakness of non-propositional revelation in your opinion? Explain your answer.

continued overleaf

Terminology

Do you know your terminology?

1   Try to explain the following ideas without looking at your books and notes:

- Propositional revelation
- Non-propositional revelation
- Holy Scripture
- The canon of the Bible
- The two senses of authority.

 # Examination Questions Practice

EXAM MISTAKES TO AVOID

The OCR specification focuses on the concept of revelation and revelation through scripture. You should ensure that your answer focuses on the revelatory nature of scripture and the questions that this concept raises. Do not spend time in the examination telling biblical stories.

Second, make sure you understand and can explain clearly the different concepts of revelation and relate them to the Bible. Every year examination candidates are awarded low marks on this topic because they do not demonstrate that they have a good understanding of propositional and non-propositional revelation. Often students confuse these views. Make sure that you do not make the same mistake.

Remember: each question assesses AO1 and AO2. To help you improve your answers look at the A2 Levels of Response. See: http://www.ocr.org.uk/qualifications/as-a-level-gce-religious-studies-h172-h572/

SAMPLE A2 EXAM-STYLE QUESTION

1   'God is most clearly revealed to humanity through scripture.' Discuss. (35 marks)

This question presents you with a good opportunity to demonstrate your understanding of scripture and revelation.

Note in the question the phrase 'most clearly' – this phrase indicates that your answer should contain some form of comparison of scripture with another way that God is revealed.

Some approaches that you could consider in relation to this question are:

- Explain one view that shows God being clearly revealed in scripture. One way to do this is to discuss divine inspiration and verbal inspiration of the Bible. This can be related to the view that the Bible is, or contains, propositional revelation from God.
- Assess the idea of propositional revelation in scripture and divine inspiration. Evaluate the strengths and weaknesses of the propositional view of the Bible. Use the weaknesses to suggest that perhaps God is not revealed clearly in scripture. Biblical examples, if explained well, may be used to good effect to support this sort of argument.
- An explained biblical example that illustrates the idea of propositional revelation and another that you can use to illustrate a particular weakness with the propositional view of the Bible are a good way to support an argument.
- Pick one other way in which God is revealed to the world and consider whether that revelation is more or less clear than the revelation of God in scripture. If you have studied religious experience and mysticism, one approach could be to compare the revelation of God through scripture with revelation through a vision or mystical experience. The knowledge revealed about God through scripture could be compared to the noetic quality of a mystical experience.

FURTHER READING

There is a huge range of books available about revelation and biblical interpretation. A few suggestions are given below.

Revelation

If you would like to investigate different ways in which the Bible is understood to be revelatory you could read *The Revelatory Text* (1991) by Sandra M. Schneider. This book contains a wide range of articles. Chapter 4 presents a very interesting case study about a feminist interpretation of John 4.

Thought Point

The answer

The extract in the Thought Point on page 288 is from Richard Dawkins' book *Unweaving the Rainbow*. Richard Dawkins does not believe in God.

The authority of scripture

There are a large number of articles examining the authority of scripture printed in biblical commentaries and dictionaries, such as the *The New Jerome Biblical Commentary* (1989) edited by Raymond E. Brown, Joseph Fitzmyer and Roland E. Murphy. A range of interesting and engaging articles on this topic and related issues may also be found in the collection of essays entitled *Fundamentalism and Tolerance* (1991) edited by A. Linzey and P. Wexler. Try also James Barre, *Fundamentalism* (second edition, 2010).

13 Religious Experience

Essential terminology

Authority
Direct religious
    experiences
Indirect religious
    experiences
Ineffable
Mystical experiences
Noetic
Passive
Transience
Vision

Key scholars

Karl Marx (1818–1883)
William James (1842–1910)
Alister Hardy (1896–1985)
J.L. Mackie (1917–1981)
William Alston (1921–2009)
John Hick (1922–2012)
Richard Swinburne (1934–)

THE ISSUE

Many people throughout the world claim to have had a religious experience of some kind. Are these kinds of experiences evidence that God exists?

WHAT YOU WILL LEARN ABOUT IN THIS CHAPTER

In this chapter you will examine what is meant by a religious experience. In particular, you will focus on studying the work of William James and the conclusions he reached. You will also examine the explanations of religious experiences offered by Freud, and Marxist ideas about religion and religious experience.

This chapter also explores other definitions of religious experiences and different types of religious experiences.

STARTER

Read this account of a person's religious experience and then discuss the questions which follow:

One day, when I was at prayer, the Lord was pleased to reveal to me nothing but His hands, the beauty of which was so great as to be indescribable. This made me very fearful, as does every new experience that I have when the Lord is beginning to grant me some supernatural favour. A few days later I also saw the divine face, which seemed to leave me completely absorbed. I could not understand why the

Lord revealed Himself gradually like this since He was later to grant me the favour of seeing him wholly, until at length I realised that His Majesty was leading me according to my natural weakness. (St Teresa of Ávila)

1 What do you think is the origin of an experience like this?
2 How would you explain why experiences like this happen?

THE OCR CHECKLIST ✓

Candidates should be able to demonstrate knowledge and understanding of the following in relation to God and religious belief:

- arguments from religious experience from William James;
- the aims and main conclusions drawn by William James in *The Varieties of Religious Experience*;
- the following different forms of religious experience: visions, voices, 'numinous' experience, conversion experience, corporate religious experience;
- the concept of revelation through sacred writings.

Candidates should be able to discuss these areas critically and their strengths and weaknesses.

From OCR A Level Religious Studies specification H572.

For many people throughout history the strongest demonstration of the existence of God comes from personal experiences of God. The impact of religious experiences on people has been immense: Paul famously became the greatest missionary of Christianity and Muhammad became the Prophet of Islam. However, the real appeal of any argument from religious experience is the fact that people who are not famous also have religious experiences which can have a dramatic and lasting effect on them. Whether religious experiences can be used to argue for the existence of God is therefore a question of identifying what people mean by religious experiences and, second, what is the origin or cause of the experience.

WHAT DOES THE PHRASE 'RELIGIOUS EXPERIENCE' MEAN?

Thought Point

Religious experience

Try to come up with a definition of 'religious experience' of your own. A good starting point for any investigation is the website of the Alister Hardy Trust, an Oxford-based centre for the investigation of religious experience (http://www.uwtsd.ac.uk/library/alister-hardy-religious-experience-research-centre/).

There are many definitions of religious experience which can in a general way be divided into two groups: *direct* and *indirect experiences*.

Direct religious experiences refer to cases where a person encounters God in a direct way. For example, Paul on the road to Damascus met the risen Jesus who communicated with him (Acts 9).

Rudolph Otto (*The Idea of the Holy*) pointed out that a central element of direct experiences of God was an 'apprehension of the wholly other', which Otto called the 'numinous'. By 'numinous' Otto meant the world that is beyond the physical observable universe in which we live. Hence, Otto refers to direct experiences of God as experiences of the 'wholly other' – meaning completely outside of our possible knowledge and experience. Otto uses the Latin phrase *mysterium tremendum et fascinans* (a terrifying and compelling mystery) to explain something which is so totally 'other' – an experience of awe, dread, wonder and rapture. For Otto religious experiences have something different about them which sets them apart from all other experiences and induces a feeling of human nothingness when faced with such a powerful being, so the numinous experience is felt on an emotional level.

Martin Buber (1878–1965) , however, viewed religious experiences as being like intimate personal relationships that he called I–thou relationships, rather than an I–it which is how one might treat objects or when people are treated as objects. I–thou relationships require both parties to interact. For Buber this is how individuals experience God, whereas Otto's idea of how people experience God seems more of an I–it relationship, as there is no idea of any sort of relationship with God.

Otto noticed that people who have religious experiences described them with words such as awe, wonder, beauty, but the actual nature of the experience was ineffable. Other writers such as William James describe religious experiences in similar ways; James refers to religious experiences involving the individual's experience of the 'divine'.

Direct religious experiences
Refer to events where God reveals her/himself directly to the person having the experience. The religious experience is not chosen or willed by the person; the person experiences or observes God in some way.

Ineffable
Used to refer to experiences which it is beyond human powers and abilities to fully describe and communicate.

Indirect religious experiences
Experiences, thoughts or feelings about God that are prompted by events in daily life, for example observing the stars in the sky and having thoughts about the greatness of God the Creator.

continued overleaf

Writers on religious experience distinguish direct experiences of the numinous or God from experiences in daily life. In particular, direct religious experiences involve an experience of God/the numinous/the divine, and they are ineffable. One reason for this is that many religious experiences are not experiences of an object; instead people describe an awareness, feeling, sensation that is directly in the mind of the person having the experience. Direct religious experiences of God are not just about seeing God as if seeing a statue or a picture; they are events in which people are aware of and know God in an intimate and personal way. It is possible that experiences from daily life are ineffable, but these 'ordinary' experiences do not involve God.

Indirect religious experiences, on the other hand, refer to experiences in which the mind of an individual focuses on God. For example, many people feel inspired by the beauty of nature and this leads them to thoughts, feelings and an appreciation of God as the Creator. Alternatively, acts of prayer or worship are types of religious experience. God is not directly revealed to a person, nor is knowledge of God revealed; instead the person learns something about God through what is observed. In the case of indirect experiences, there is sometimes an object which leads to the thoughts and feelings about God.

Some people have suggested that indirect experiences are not necessarily different from ordinary experiences; they are made significant by the person who has the experience and for whom the experience has religious meaning.

Thought Point

Religious experience and ordinary experience

Think of an event that was very important to you. Try to describe the feelings evoked by this event. Was this experience religious? If so, what made it religious?

Thought Point

Ordinary and ineffable

Can you think of events or incidents in daily life, or in your life, which are ineffable?

TYPES OF RELIGIOUS EXPERIENCES

Richard Swinburne (*The Existence of God*) has suggested that there are five recognisable types of religious experience, which he divides into two groups: public experiences and private experiences.

Public experiences

Ordinary experiences

Experiences where a person interprets a natural event as having religious significance (e.g. the beauty of nature or the natural world).

Extraordinary experiences

Experiences that appear to violate normal understanding of the workings of nature (e.g. Jesus turning water into wine at Cana (John 2: 1–11)).

Private experiences

Describable in ordinary language

Experiences such as dreams (e.g. Joseph's dream in the Bible (Matthew 1: 20–21)).

Non-describable experiences

This refers to direct experiences of God in which God/the wholly other/the divine is revealed to people. These experiences go beyond human powers of description. Look at the example from Teresa of Ávila later in the chapter (pp. 307ff.).

Non-specific experiences

These experiences could include things like looking at the world from a religious perspective.

Swinburne's categorisation of religious experience highlights the wide range of types of experience that may be called 'religious experiences'.

Thought Point

Types of religious experience

In which of Swinburne's categories would you put the following:

- Awe at the beauty and intricacies of God's creation, such as DNA.
- A young girl called Bernadette seeing a vision of Mary, the mother of Jesus.
- John Wesley feeling that his heart had been 'strangely warmed' and his sins 'removed' by Jesus.
- The Qur'an being revealed to Muhammad ﷺ by Allah.
- Moses receiving the Ten Commandments from God.
- Siddhattha Gotama achieving enlightenment.
- The story of Pope St John Paul II's life.

Thought Point

Paul's conversion

Look up the different accounts of Paul's conversion (Acts 9: 4–8, 22: 6–10, 26) and try to explain what happened to him. In particular, think about how the event is described.

Vision

An event in which God, or something about God, is seen or observed. Visions are usually divided into three types: corporeal, intellectual and imaginative.

Vision experiences

A vision experience is one in which God or the divine is 'seen' or 'observed'. In the vision information may be revealed, so dreams are described by theologians as noetic and revelatory.

Thought Point

Vision experiences

Look up the following accounts of religious experiences in the Bible. What can you learn about the characteristics and nature of vision experiences from these stories?

- Exodus 3: 1–15
- Genesis 28: 10–22
- Isaiah 6: 1–13
- Ezekiel 1: 4–28

Vision experiences can happen when a person is awake, or in a dream. For example, Teresa of Ávila talked of seeing Christ at her side, saying that she: 'saw Christ at my side – or, to put it better, I was conscious of Him, for neither with the eyes of the body or of the soul did I see anything' (*Autobiography of St Teresa of Ávila*, trans. and ed. E. Allison Peers).

She went on to say that she could not discern the 'form' of the vision, but she was aware that Jesus was there. This is an example of what is called an intellectual vision. This means that what is seen is an experience rather than something being just observed, such as saying: can you see that woman?

There are other types of vision experiences, such as those of St Bernadette of Lourdes. Bernadette had a number of visions of the Virgin Mary, the mother of Jesus. In one of these visions she was told to dig in the ground at the feet of Mary. When she did this she discovered a mountain spring. Today many people visit Lourdes to pray and bathe in the waters of the stream discovered by Bernadette. Many report being healed in some way after visiting Lourdes and bathing there. This vision is an example of one in which knowledge is communicated (Mary tells Bernadette things). It is called a corporeal vision, because Bernadette sees Mary as a form or image like a physical person.

The third type of vision experience is called *imaginative*. This refers to visions that occur in dreams. For example, in the Bible (Matthew 1: 20–21) Joseph, while engaged to Mary, has a dream telling him not to be afraid of marrying Mary, even though she is pregnant and he is not the father. In this case a message of God is received through a dream. Another example is in Luke 2, where the Magi who visit the infant Jesus are warned in a dream not to go to see King Herod again; Herod was plotting to use information from them to find and kill Jesus.

Voices

In the Christian tradition, religious experiences of God can often be associated with the idea of hearing. Hearing in this case means more than an audible voice, but also the communication of knowledge. The voice is usually linked to God. Often the voice of God is one aspect of a religious experience which could, for example, be a mystical experience.

Mystical experiences
Used in many ways by writers on religious experience. In general, it is used to refer to religious experiences where God is revealed directly and the person having the experience is passive. William James identified four characteristics that are typical of mystical and other religious experiences: *noetic*, *passive*, *transient* and *ineffable*.

Noetic

Refers to something which gives knowledge, such as a revelation from God in which God reveals something.

The voice of God usually communicates a message. For example, in the calling of Samuel, God's voice calls Samuel to be a prophet. In the story of Jesus' baptism, God's voice declares that Jesus is his son.

Three features are noticeable: first, the disembodied voice (the voice that does not come from a person speaking) shows the presence of God. Second, the voice communicates a revelation from God, so the message is noetic – it reveals something of God and God's wishes to people. Third, the voice is authoritative and passes on God's authority. For example, at Jesus' baptism the voice of God says:

> 'You are my Son, the Beloved; with you I am well pleased.'
> (Mark 1: 11b)

Thought Point

The voice of God

Read the accounts of Jesus' baptism (Mark 1: 1–9), Paul's conversion (Acts 9: 4–8, 22: 6–10, 26) and the calling of the prophet Samuel (Samuel 1).

- What is learnt about God from these stories?
- What does the voice reveal to the hearer?

Thought Point

Hearing voices

If a friend tells you that he hears voices which tell him things about the future, how would you react? How would you respond to your friend? Would you be concerned that your friend was mentally ill? Would you think that your friend had received a message from God?

The problem with this type of religious experience is: how do you know that the voice is from God? There are a number of cases of manic schizophrenics who have killed people because they claimed to have heard God's voice and God told them to kill the person.

Teresa of Ávila considered this question and suggested that the criteria to use could be:

- Does the religious experience fit in with Christian Church teaching or is it against it?
- Does the experience leave the person feeling at peace with the world and God, rather than distressed?

Teresa suggested that if the experience did not have these effects it was a sign that the experience was not from God, but from the devil. While Teresa did not know that conditions such as schizophrenia are illnesses and claimed they were from the devil, the distinction she makes is useful. For example, if a schizophrenic tries to kill someone because a voice tells them to, another person could reason that the voice is not God because killing goes against Christian teaching that it is wrong to kill. However, other people have pointed out that the fact that what a voice says fits in with Church teaching in no way proves that the person heard the voice of God rather than a voice in their own mind.

Corporate religious experiences

If an individual claims to have experienced God how can we know that what they experienced is true? However, if more than one person claims to have had the same experience, or many people witness the experience, it becomes more difficult to doubt it.

One such example took place in 1916, in the small village of Fatima in Portugal where a group of three children saw visions of a being that claimed to be an angel of God. Then, on 13 May 1917, the children saw a vision that they thought was the Virgin Mary, who told them to return on the same day each month. The children spread the word and large crowds gathered on the 13th of each month to see the vision of the Virgin Mary. On 13 October Mary only appeared to the children but the crowds reported a miracle – the sun trembled and danced in the sky. This was most likely an eclipse and the crowd's reaction the result of well-documented group hysteria.

Pentecostal worship is also often cited as an example of religious experience, the most famous example being the Toronto Blessing.

Does an event like this actually reveal God? And why would an omnipotent God bother anyway?

Conversion experiences

Conversion experiences always lead to a change in the individual's life. This may be dramatic, for example the conversion of St Paul on the road to

Damascus, or simply a gradual realisation. They have great power for the individual concerned, but would not necessarily convince other people. However, belief in conversion and the necessity for it have always been central to evangelical Christianity and its idea of being a 'born again Christian'. Above all, a conversion experience should result in an individual leading a better life as it did with St Paul, and perhaps this is the only way it can be verified.

William James devoted three chapters of his book *The Varieties of Religious Experience: A Study in Human Nature* to the subject of conversion. He starts by considering 'the divided self and the process of its unification', arguing that in a religious conversion the individual experiences a unification of the self and a sense that their life is complete and meaningful. According to James there are two basic types of conversion: the **volitional** type and the type by self-surrender.

The volitional type is when an individual decides that they want to make spiritual changes in their life and they set about bringing this about. For example, a person may choose to become a Muslim, so they begin to study the Qur'an, they pray five times a day, and then when they are on the Hajj with millions of other Muslims, they have a profound experience, which means that their religious beliefs suddenly all make sense and they feel a deep sense of spiritual connection with God.

The self-surrender type of conversion, is where a person feels that they have done all they can to develop their religious beliefs, but are aware of the sinfulness of their life and the type of life they wish to lead. This leads, according to James, to a crisis in which the individual gives himself to God. James says that conversion is something that just happens almost automatically. James says it is like those moments when you are trying desperately to remember the name of someone and simply cannot however hard you try, and then days later for no apparent reason it just seems to pop into your mind. James argues that there are two ways of understanding this process: either as the work of God, or as the work of the subconscious mind. James does not give a clear answer to this.

WILLIAM JAMES' ARGUMENT FROM RELIGIOUS EXPERIENCE

William James' most famous book, *The Varieties of Religious Experience: A Study in Human Nature*, investigated a large number of accounts of religious experiences. He was interested in exploring the nature of the wide variety of religious experiences people have. This interested James because he assumed that religious experience was the source of religious institutions such as churches. Churches, for James, were secondary to each individual person's religious experiences. James suggested that religious experiences were events which were 'solitary' and in which individuals experienced the divine or God – the religious tradition to which the person belongs (if any) is relatively unimportant.

James noted that religious experiences have great authority for the person who has them and can often have a marked effect in a person's life. He noted that, whether gradual or sudden, conversion experiences are characterised by religious beliefs becoming central to a person's life and this in turn affects their behaviour. A classic example is Paul on the road to Damascus – Paul changes from being a persecutor of Christians to being one of the most important Christian preachers and missionaries. It is because religious experiences can so noticeably change people's behaviour that James suggested that religious experiences were the inspiration and source of religious institutions.

One of James' achievements was to identify some of the characteristics of religious experiences as being as wide-ranging as visions to feelings of God's presence. James noted, for example, that many people's religious experiences are marked by a loss of anxiety, the gaining of new knowledge and a changed understanding of the world. Four characteristics were found to be particularly prominent in mystical religious experiences of God:

1 *Ineffable*
   The direct experience of God goes beyond human powers of description.

2 *Noetic*
   Noetic refers to the fact that mystics receive knowledge of God that is not otherwise available. In this sense religious experiences are direct revelations from God.

3 *Transient*
   Religious experiences are described as transient as they are not permanent; however, the effects of the experience are long-lasting and involve a changed view of the universe and the mystic's place in the universe.

4 *Passive*
   Mystical experiences were found to be passive, meaning that the experiences were not under the control of the mystic. Instead, the religious experience is something that happens to the mystic and is from God. James saw this as evidence against arguments claiming that a religious experience can be explained by saying a person willed it.

James the man (1842–1910)

William James was a philosopher and psychologist. He was a pragmatist. He studied medicine at Harvard University and was initially a lecturer in anatomy. Later he became Professor of Philosophy and then Professor of Psychology. He wrote a large number of books on both psychology and philosophy.

Authority

When applied to religious experience the word 'authority' indicates that the person who has the religious experience has some new insight or knowledge about the world and God's relationship with the world. This gives them authority. Many authors argue that the authority is limited to the individual who has the experience; it is not about authority and power over other people.

Pragmatism

Pragmatism originated in the late nineteenth century. But today it is has a number of meanings.

In philosophy, pragmatism suggests that the meaning of a concept

continued overleaf

or idea is derived from looking at the consequences that come from the original idea or concept.

In order to ascertain the meaning of an intellectual conception one should consider what practical consequences might conceivably result by necessity from the truth of that conception; and the sum of these consequences will constitute the entire meaning of the conception. (Peirce in Hartshorne and Weiss (eds), *Collected Papers of Charles Sanders Peirce*, vol. 5)

Pragmatism was put forward by Charles Peirce and later developed by philosophers such as William James and John Dewey, and Simon Blackburn today.

Transience
Refers to the fact that religious experiences are experiences which are temporary. The experiences do not last forever.

Thought Point

St Teresa of Ávila

St Teresa of Ávila was a mystic from Spain. During her life she received a large number of experiences of God which she later described in her autobiography. Read the extract below and think about the questions which follow it:

> I was at prayer on a festival of the glorious Saint Peter when I saw Christ at my side – or, to put it better, I was conscious of Him, for neither with the eyes of the body nor with those of the soul did I see anything. I thought He was quite close to me, and I saw that it was He Who, as I thought, was speaking to me. Being completely ignorant that visions of this kind could occur, I was at first very much afraid, and did nothing but weep, though, as soon as He addressed a single word to me to reassure me, I became quiet again, as I had been before, and was quite happy and free from fear. All the time Jesus Christ seemed to be beside me, but, as this was not an imaginary vision, I could not discern in what form: what I felt very clearly was that he was all the time at my right hand, and a witness of everything I was doing, and whenever as I became slightly recollected or was not greatly distracted, I could not but be aware of His nearness to me. (*Autobiography of St Teresa of Ávila*, trans. and ed. E. Allison Peers)

1   How could William James' four characteristics of a mystical experience apply to this extract from St Teresa's autobiography?
2   Do you have any other thoughts about:

(a) What happened to Teresa?
(b) The origins of this experience?

When discussing the origins of religious experiences, William James suggested that the only possible sign that religious experiences are from God is a 'good disposition' that is the result of the experience (James, *The Varieties of Religious Experience*) which the sign leaves behind. Consider, for example, the stabbing of George Harrison by Michael Abrams in 2001. Michael Abrams believed that he had heard voices telling him to do this; in reality he was mentally ill and had stopped taking his medication. The voices Abrams heard were not from God, as they encouraged him to harm people.

James stated that mystical experiences have authority and meaning only for the individual who has the experience. He did not deny the reality of the mystical experience and suggested that such experiences were ways in which individuals could gain knowledge of God, not otherwise possible. The mystical experience is not a source of authority for the mystic over other people, although James noted the influence of saints, even though saints did not necessarily seek influence or authority over other people for themselves.

While James did not deny the reality of religious experiences, he examined the parallels and similarities between religious experiences and other types of experiences such as dreams and hallucinations. He suggested that religious experiences could also be linked to our subconscious ideas (James, *The Varieties of Religious Experience*).

James concluded that religious experiences on their own do not demonstrate God's existence, although they can suggest the existence of 'something larger':

> I feel bound to say that religious experience, as we have studied it, cannot be cited as unequivocally supporting the infinitist belief. The only thing that it unequivocally testifies to is that we can experience union with something larger than ourselves and in that union find our greatest peace. (James, *The Varieties of Religious Experience*)

James suggested that religious experiences were 'psychological phenomena'. Experiences could be explained as part of a person's psychological make-up. However, he did not believe that this was an argument against belief in God. For James, saying that religious experiences are psychological phenomena is a statement that a religious experience is natural to a person, just like other psychological experiences such as self-awareness or thinking.

In *The Varieties of Religious Experience* James makes it quite clear that religious experience is central to religious belief. James leaves open the possibility of God's existence.

Passive

Describes the common state of a person who has a religious experience. Often people do not seek out or will religious experiences; instead the experiences happen to them – they are passive.

Thought Point

'The Will to Believe'

William James' essay 'The Will to Believe' (1897) defended the possibility of religious belief. It presents a clear set of reasons why the decision to believe in God is a real, live and important choice for individual people to make. He argued that this issue could not be decided by philosophical arguments. If you have time it is worth reading 'The Will to Believe'.

Responses to James' ideas

*   Some people have suggested that religious experiences are similar to hallucinations caused by drugs such as LSD (lysergic acid diethylamide). However, while this may be true, there is no evidence that every person who has had a religious experience is a user of LSD.
*   James claimed that religious experiences are the primary source of religious belief. However, many psychologists and sociologists claim that religious experiences only happen to people who are already members of a religious tradition. It is, however, also the case that religious experiences do sometimes happen to those who have no connection to any religious tradition.
*   J.L. Mackie argued that if mystical experiences are explainable psychologically (which James stated is possible), then mystical experiences can have no authority even for the person who has the experience. Instead, Mackie suggests that people who believe mystical experiences are authoritative are 'insufficiently critical' (Mackie, *The Miracle of Theism*).

ARE RELIGIOUS EXPERIENCES VERIDICAL?

Every year many, many people claim to have religious experiences, as seen in the research of the Alister Hardy research centre or the work of David Hay. When people say that they have had a direct religious experience they mean that they have experienced God or the divine in some way; they are not saying that it 'seemed like' God but was something else.

The issue for many philosophers is: are religious experiences veridical? By this is meant can we actually demonstrate that the religious experiences of people are what they seem to be, i.e. experiences of God, rather than delusions, products of the mind or of some other source such as LSD?

Richard Swinburne (*The Existence of God*) has suggested two principles that may be used to assess claims about religious experience. First, Swinburne suggests what he calls the 'principle of credulity'. Swinburne argued that, other things being equal, we have good reason to believe what a person tells us is correct. In general, if a person tells us that they can see a cat crossing the road, we believe them, even if we have not seen the event. Even if only one person sees the event, they still count.

> The principle of credulity [states] that we ought to believe that things are as they seem to be . . . unless and until we have evidence that they are mistaken. (Swinburne, *Is There a God?*)

Swinburne suggests three reasons why we could have good grounds to disbelieve evidence. First, he suggests that there may be reasons to believe the person was mistaken, for example if they are hallucinating under the influence of drugs. Second, Swinburne points out that if we have 'strong' reasons (*Is There a God?*) to believe that God does not exist, this would count against believing that an experience was religious. Third, there may be evidence that an event was not caused by God. Swinburne gives the example of two twins in an arcade: you could think you saw John and later discover it was his identical twin brother.

Swinburne also suggests a 'principle of testimony'. He argues that it is reasonable to believe what someone tells you. For example, if your best friend tells you about a religious experience he or she has had, do you have reason to disbelieve them? They might call it a strange experience, but would you automatically doubt what they said? You might want to investigate what they said, but that is not a reason to automatically reject what they claim to have experienced. However, if the friend is a renowned joker and liar, this may be what philosophers call a special consideration – this knowledge about your friend would undermine any instinct to believe what your friend tells you.

However, not everyone does have religious experiences and this may be a reason to say that the experiences are caused by something else. People who are dying of thirst in the desert often have hallucinations of oases, but this does not make the hallucination real. If religious experiences are like this, then they do not reveal God. The fact that not everyone has a religious experience is no reason to reject the possibility of some people having such experiences. Richard Swinburne (*Is There a God?*) suggests that people would not necessarily recognise a telephone for what it is unless they had some knowledge of what telephones are and may be expected to be like. The knowledge would enable them to interpret their experience of the object as a telephone. Consequently, it could be that religious people are those who are more likely to have religious experiences precisely because they have a greater chance of recognising a religious experience for what it is by using their religious beliefs.

The Blessing started at the Toronto Airport Vineyard Church on 20 January 1994.

John Arnott, the pastor, asked Randy Clark from St Louis to address a four-day series of revival meetings. After his first sermon people began to laugh hysterically, leap, dance, cry and roar. The phrase 'Holy Laughter' is used to describe uncontrollable laughter from church congregations. This may include weeping, falling to the floor and animal noises such as barking like dogs or roaring like lions.

The Toronto Blessing spread all over the USA and Canada and has now travelled abroad.

> ### The Toronto Blessing
>
> One of the most famous recent events described as a religious experience is the Toronto Blessing.

Followers say this is the work of the Holy Spirit; others claim that the experiences are engineered through mass hysteria.

The principles of credulity and testimony also draw attention to the importance of people's *prior beliefs* – the beliefs they have before the religious experience occurs. If you have come to the decision that it is possible that there is extraterrestrial life, then reports of aliens or their spacecraft being seen are credible. However, if you believe that there is no evidence that aliens exist, or if they do that they can cross vast distances of space to visit Earth, then there is a very low chance of your believing reports about aliens being sighted. In the same way, if other evidence suggests that God could or does exist, it is not then so surprising to hear reports of people encountering God through religious experiences. Swinburne suggests that, taken with other evidence of God's existence, religious experience makes it likely that God exists. However, the philosopher Anthony Flew argued that collecting together a series of weak arguments does not make a strong argument; he gave the example of ten leaky buckets.

William Alston ('Perceiving God') also considered whether it was logical to talk about a person experiencing God and gaining knowledge from the experience. In particular, he explored the fact that many people had religious experiences and believe that these experiences were '*what they seem to be*'.

Alston argued that in normal life the evidence of something is what you can gather from experience. For example, if you say: 'There's a red car' or 'Can you hear that bird singing?' you are referring to things you have observed using your senses. You are not doubted because many other people have had similar experiences using their senses. Alston suggests that if many people using their minds have had a religious experience, is it right to immediately doubt their observation when we would not doubt it in other situations? This leads him later to argue that if our *sense perceptions* are generally reliable, why should we not believe what our senses tell us if we have a religious experience?

Many people claim that you can explain religious experiences naturalistically: for example, by using sociology or psychology. Alston ('Perceiving God') responded that this was a 'double standard' because religious experiences are also sense perceptions. Second, he pointed out that there is no reason to reject an explanation of something just because the explanation is unusual.

In addition, Alston rejected the argument that religious experiences are unverifiable or uncheckable. He suggested that the way you check anything is by making other sense observations. He suggested that other people's religious experiences are also sense observations.

William Alston's arguments do not show that religious experiences are experiences of God, but they do show that it is not fair to simply reject religious experiences as illogical and irrational.

John Hick (*The New Frontier of Religion and Science*) provided further support for religious experiences by saying that they are a different way of experiencing the world from non-religious experiences. Events which one person might see as having an ordinary natural meaning are experienced as showing the presence and activity of God. The religious person adds an extra layer of meaning to the way they see and experience the world. This could be argued to be a purely subjective interpretation, but all experience involves some level of interpretation. Hick is not arguing for the existence of God; he is arguing that experiencing God in the world is not irrational.

Thought Point

Strange experiences

1   Have you ever had an experience or feeling of some power outside of yourself and your normal way of observing the world?
2   If a trusted friend told you any of the following, how would you respond? What would you think? Explain your answers:

- I experienced God last night;
- I felt God's presence with me last night;
- I saw an alien spacecraft fly past last night;
- I saw a Martian in the field;
- I saw a Yeti on the mountain;
- I learnt that human beings are genetically related to earthworms;
- I was abducted by an alien last night;
- The dream I had three months ago came true yesterday.

Thought Point

Recognising religious experiences

Look up 1 Samuel 3 in the Bible. What can be learnt from this story about possible difficulties in recognising a religious experience?

CHALLENGES TO RELIGIOUS EXPERIENCE ARGUMENTS

PHYSIOLOGICAL CHALLENGES

One argument against religious experiences suggests that they have a physiological cause (i.e. they are the product of physical changes in the body). For example, did Paul have epilepsy? This could possibly explain his experience of bright light. Equally, it is known that damage to the brain can cause hallucinations and delusions, as can brain tumours.

The weakness of this challenge is that there is no evidence that every person who has had a religious experience was suffering from an illness that can cause side effects such as hallucinations, visions and delusions in its victims.

PSYCHOLOGICAL CHALLENGES

Following the work of Sigmund Freud, many commentators have suggested that religious experiences are a product of human psychology. If true, this would explain the common occurrence of religious experiences both throughout history and across cultures.

While William James proposed that religious experiences could in some way relate to the human subconscious, he did not believe this was an argument against God's existence.

Freud

For more information about Freud's ideas as well as the challenges to them and to other psychologists' ideas look at Chapter 17 on the psychology and sociology of religion.

Freud's views

Freud began to link religion with neurosis because he noticed that many patients at Salpêtrière mental hospital who suffered from mental illnesses displayed obsessive behaviour. He observed that the patterns of behaviour that had to be followed were remarkably similar to some religious practices, such as formal prayer and worship.

Freud argued that religion is an *illusion*, by which he meant that it expresses people's desires – what they want to believe. In particular, religion meets people's psychological needs. If this is true, religious experience is an illusion that derives from people's psychological needs. In some ways this would make religious experiences very similar to wishful thinking.

Freud suggested that religion originated from a childlike desire for a God who resembles a father figure. This would suggest that religious experiences are a product of desire for a father figure and are infantile and based on guilt.

The great difficulty with challenges to religious experience based on the subconscious is that scientists today still understand relatively little of the relationship between mind and body, and the conscious and unconscious mind. Freud's and Jung's ideas have been criticised in many ways.

SOCIOLOGICAL CHALLENGES

Many sociologists have suggested that the origins of religion and religious experience are to be found in society. A religious experience thus reflects the society in which you live and have grown up. Hence, it is no surprise that Catholics experience visions of Mary and Hindus of Shiva – this reflects the thought world of the society in which they live.

Karl Marx, in particular, has been associated with sociological challenges to religious claims. Marx was influenced by a philosophical movement known as the young Hegelians, who suggested that religion was a form of 'alienation' from one's true self. By this they meant that religion was about mythological beliefs and an unreal god that distracted people from their own reality in the physical world. Hence, he called religion 'the opium of the people' – religion for Marx was like a drug that stopped people seeing the reality of their situation and the world. Religious experiences in this sense create *alienation* by which Marx meant that you are unable to be yourself and to relate, as you should be able to, to the world.

In particular, Marx saw religion as a form of oppression and control of people in society, which prevented people from being truly human and making their own decisions. In this sense religion was to be overthrown. In particular, the power of the clergy (priests, monks and nuns) was criticised, as Marx saw the Church as a form of social control of behaviour. In particular, Marx's writings about class division and economics highlighted the divisions within societies. The Christian Church as an institution of current society was thus part of the whole system that kept working people oppressed and exploited. Marx argued that the Christian teaching about heaven, hell and punishment after death were like the drug opium: it gave people comfort and helped them cope with their situation. For example, if people are judged after death, Marx suggested it was easier to cope with being treated badly in life, as the people who treated you badly would go to hell. However, Marx argued that people would be better off without religion, just as drug addicts are better off if they quit their habit.

Marx's analysis of people's situation was shaped by the economic realities of the time in which he lived. In the UK at the time the vast majority of people lived in poverty, while a wealthy minority had a very high standard of living and education. Marx argued that the economic system (capitalism) caused this situation, but the Church also sustained the status quo, as it was part of the structure of society and it encouraged people to follow the accepted rules of society.

Hence, for Marx, a religious experience would be the product of the culture in which a person lived. It would not be from God but a product of the desperate situation of a person. The origins of the experience would be traceable to the teachings and beliefs of the Church.

Replies to Marx

- Karl Marx did not accept the fact that for many people religion is more than a comfort like a drug. Religious people would argue that their faith is a relationship with God, and God is a real, existing being, not a product of society.
- In many situations around the world religion has been a force for change in society, not a method of controlling people and oppressing them. Martin Luther King Jr fought for black people's civil rights in the USA and his belief in equality came from his Christian faith.
- While Christianity and other religions have oppressed people, they have also been a great source of strength, hope and comfort. Sociologists since the time of Marx have shown that religious belief and practices become more important to people when they live in difficult situations, such as civil wars.
- When Marx's ideas have been put into practice, such as in Russia under Lenin or China under Chairman Mao, they did not necessarily bring happiness to people, but rather caused much suffering.

LACK OF EVIDENCE

Another philosophical problem with religious experiences is the lack of evidence that they have happened, beyond what a person says. Religious experiences may lead to noticeable changes in a person's lifestyle (think of Paul) but this only shows that the person has changed; it does not give any insight into the nature and origins of religious experience.

CONFLICTING CLAIMS

Within the different religious traditions around the world believers claim to experience God or the divine. However, while there are similarities between the effects of these experiences, there are many differences in the descriptions of them. For example, Hindus see Shiva or Lakshmi, and Christians Jesus or Mary. This may be explained in a number of ways:

- Religious experiences are ineffable; if Hindus and Christians have different religious experiences that are differently described, this may be explained by the prior beliefs of the person. The only language that can be used to attempt to communicate an ineffable experience will be drawn from the person's own culture and upbringing: the language and thought world of Christianity for a Christian, and of Hinduism for a Hindu.
- Religious experiences are a product of human psychology. The fact that a Hindu may see Shiva and a Christian Jesus only reflects the prior beliefs and values of that person.

David Hume's argument that the conflicting claims of miracles in different religious traditions cancel each other out could be applied to religious experience as well if religious experiences are considered to be authoritative for the religious tradition as a whole. However, Christianity has suggested for centuries that the authority of religious experiences is for the experiencer only.

CONCLUSION: DO RELIGIOUS EXPERIENCES DEMONSTRATE THE EXISTENCE OF GOD?

People who have religious experiences are no more likely than others to be deluded, ignorant or to misinterpret the world. Nor is it the case that only ignorant people have religious experiences. The large number of people throughout the world who have reported having religious experiences suggests that God exists.

Many philosophers have argued that, taken with other arguments for God's existence, religious experience suggests that it is likely that God exists:

> The existence, orderliness, and fine-tunedness of the world; the existence of conscious humans within it with providential opportunities for moulding themselves, each other, and the world . . . topped up finally by the apparent experience by millions of his presence, all make it significantly more probable than not that there is a God. (Swinburne, *Is There a God?*)

However, as James has suggested, the authority of a religious experience does not extend beyond the person who experiences it. In this sense, a philosophical demonstration of God's existence based on religious experience is not possible.

Part of the problem is that whether one believes that religious experiences happen depends very much on one's prior beliefs. If you believe in God, it is, as William Alston pointed out, rational to believe that people have religious experiences of God. As Swinburne has argued, the principles of credulity and testimony suggest that an account of a direct religious experience of God should be accepted for what it is, unless there is a good reason to take a different view.

Yet many philosophers and psychologists have suggested that the origins of religious experience could be psychological or sociological. If this is the case, religious experiences can still have great significance and meaning to the person who has the experience, even though they do not support an argument for the existence of God. The beneficial effects to people of religious experiences such as conversion have been documented by many people, including William James. Equally, for many Christians, a psychological explanation in no way excludes God, since God is the Creator and the sustainer of his creation – in this view there is nothing more natural than people experiencing God through natural means that are God's creation.

Ultimately, you need to draw your own conclusions about the many millions of people through history who, irrespective of culture, education, religion, class or wealth, claim to have had religious experiences.

SUMMARY

1 Types of religious experience

Classification

Direct experiences
Rudolph Otto (1923) – the 'numinous'
William James – the individual's experience of the 'divine'

Indirect experiences
Experiences in which the mind of an individual focuses on God

Richard Swinburne

Public experiences
Ordinary experiences
Extraordinary experiences

Private experiences
Describable in ordinary language
Non-describable experiences
Non-specific experiences

Vision experiences

God is 'seen' or 'observed'
Visions/dreams can be noetic and revelatory; types:
Intellectual vision
Corporeal vision
Imaginative vision

Voices

The communication of knowledge from God
Characteristics:
The disembodied voice
The message is noetic
The voice is authoritative

Teresa of Ávila's criteria for assessing the source of a religious experience

Does the religious experience fit in with Christian Church teaching?
Does the experience leave the person feeling at peace with the world and
*   God?*

William James

Characteristics of mystical experience:
Ineffable
Noetic
Transient
Passive

Authority of the experience: only for the individual who has it

Challenges to religious experience arguments

Richard Swinburne:
Principle of credulity
Principle of testimony

Physiological challenges
Psychological challenges
Suggestion that religious experiences are a product of human psychology
Freud

> Religion is an illusion
> Religion expresses people's desires
> Religion originates from a childlike desire for a God who resembles
>   a father figure

Sociological challenges

The origins of religious experience are to be found in society

Karl Marx

> Religion is about mythological beliefs and an unreal god that distracted people from the real world
>
> Religion is 'the opium of the people'
>
> Religious experiences create alienation
>
> A religious experience could be the product of the desperate situation in which a person lived

Replies to Marx

> For many people religion is a relationship with God, and God is real
>
> In many situations around the world religion has been a force for positive change in society
>
> Religious belief and practices become more important to people when they live in difficult situations, such as civil wars
>
> Marx's ideas did not bring happiness to people (e.g. in China under Chairman Mao)

Lack of evidence

REVIEW QUESTIONS

Look back over the chapter and check that you can answer the following questions:

1   Outline William James' understanding of religious experience.
2   Why would a follower of Freud or Marx reject religious experience as evidence of God's existence?
3   If a friend told you they had seen God, how would you react to and assess what they told you?
4   Do you think religious experiences are veridical? Explain your answer with reasons.

Terminology

Do you know your terminology?

1   Try to explain the following ideas without looking at your books and notes:

continued opposite

- Noetic
- Transient
- Ineffable
- Authority
- Passive
- Indirect and direct experiences
- The principle of testimony
- The principle of credulity

Examination Questions Practice

EXAM MISTAKES TO AVOID

First, make sure that you can explain what a religious experience is and philosophers' explanations of the characteristics of a religious experience. Second, think about how to present an argument for God's existence based on religious experience, rather than just telling stories about people's religious experiences.

Remember: each question assesses AO1 and AO2. To help you improve your answers look at the A2 Levels of Response. See: http://www.ocr.org.uk/qualifications/as-a-level-gce-religious-studies-h172-h572/.

SAMPLE A2 EXAM-STYLE QUESTION

1   'Arguments about God from religious experience are never convincing.' Discuss. (35 marks)

There are many ways to answer this question, such as:

- Discuss the challenges to religious experience presented by Karl Marx or Sigmund Freud.
- Consider the fact that some people have rejected James' claim that religious experience is primary. For example, many sociologists point out that the most likely people to have religious experiences are those who are already religious. Refer also to weaknesses of this view.

- You could present physiological challenges to religious experience, as well as the problems related to this idea.
- Many commentators, such as William James, suggest that the authority of an experience is limited to the person who has the experience. If this is the case, religious experience arguments are never valid for anyone except the person who had the experience.
- You could argue in favour of religious experience arguments by referring to the arguments of philosophers such as Alston and Swinburne. You could also note the effect for the better that religious experiences have had on many people.

FURTHER READING

There is a wealth of information about religious experiences available on the Alister Hardy Trust website http://www.uwtsd.ac.uk/library/alister-hardy-religious-experience-research-centre/.

If you want to know more about William James' ideas about religious experience, read extracts from *The Varieties of Religious Experience*, which is available in bookshops or anthologies of philosophers' writings. Michael Palmer has written a very useful overview of 'The Will to Believe' essay in *The Question of God*.

If you would like to read about religious experience in general you could read the sections on revelation in William Raeper and Linda Smith, *A Beginner's Guide to Ideas*.

The argument from religious experience is clearly presented and explored in *The Puzzle of God* by Peter Vardy.

See also David Hay, *Exploring Inner Space: Scientists and Religious Experience*. London, Penguin, 1982.

14 Miracles

THE ISSUES

1   How does God interact with human beings?
2   Do miracles happen?
3   If miracles do happen, are they of any importance to anyone apart from the person who experiences the miracle?
4   Reconciling belief in miracles and God not intervening to help all people.

WHAT YOU WILL LEARN ABOUT IN THIS CHAPTER

In this chapter you will explore what is meant by the word 'miracle'. You will consider the way in which God interacts with the world as understood within the Judaeo-Christian tradition. You will reflect on the idea of God interacting with the world through miracles. By studying some of the miracle stories in the Bible you will think about whether God helping some people and not others might imply that God is biased.

You will examine whether there is any reason for people today to believe in miracles and assess David Hume's writings about miracles. You will also assess whether miracles happen by studying the ideas of Maurice Wiles and examining some modern scientists' thinking about whether miracles happen.

STARTER

1   Write down what is meant by the word 'miracle'. Try to refer to one example you have heard of that people call a miracle.
2   Would you call any of the events in the list below a 'miracle'? If you do call any of these events a miracle, what do you mean by the word miracle?

(a) Having a baby
(b) Something beautiful in the natural world
(c) A man living in a country where AIDS is common gets better after he was diagnosed as being HIV positive
(d) Surviving a life-threatening illness and dangerous surgery
(e) A Catholic man and his daughter report that the statue of the Virgin Mary in their garden is crying real tears
(f) Gaining a job you desperately wanted, ahead of 1,020 other applicants
(g) Winning the National Lottery
(h) A severely disabled woman who had TB and was bed-ridden is washed in the pools of water at a Catholic shrine and gets better
(i) A statue in a Hindu mandir is reported to drink milk
(j) Surviving falling 100m down a cliff while mountaineering
(k) Being rescued from a building that was destroyed by an earthquake seven days after the event
(l) Marrying the boy/girl of your dreams
(m) Having a vision of God
(n) God creating the world.

INTRODUCTION

Stories of miraculous events have been reported for as long as humans have lived in communities. In the Bible, Jesus is pictured as healing people and calming storms, while Moses turns his rod into a snake and summons plagues of locusts. In modern times events that have been called miraculous include statues of Nandi in a Hindu mandir (temples) drinking milk (*Daily Telegraph*, 22 September 1995), people being cured of Aids in Zimbabwe (account from an Oratorian priest based in Oxford), and the Virgin Mary appearing at Lourdes.

THE OCR CHECKLIST

Miracle – a study of how God might interact with humanity, by looking at the concept of miracle

Candidates should be able to demonstrate knowledge and understanding of:

continued opposite

- different definitions of miracle, including an understanding of Hume;
- the biblical concept of miracle and the issues this raises about God's activity in the world;
- the concept of miracle, and criticisms made by Hume and Wiles;
- the implications of the concept of miracle for the problem of evil.

Candidates should be able to discuss whether modern people can be expected to believe in miracles, and whether miracles suggest an arbitrary or partisan God. Candidates should be able to discuss these areas critically and their strengths and weaknesses.

From OCR A Level Religious Studies specification H572.

For religious believers, the occurrence of miracles, such as in the Bible, is an example of God acting within the world and being involved in the world. For example, in Joshua 10: 1–15 God is said to hold back the sun in order to help Joshua's army in battle, while in Exodus 13 God sends a wind to drive back the Red Sea to make dry land; Moses then leads the Hebrews across the seabed to safety. When the pursuing troops of Pharaoh cross the ocean floor, God returns the waters of the Red Sea to the seabed and the soldiers of Pharaoh are destroyed.

The Bible pictures God as being involved and active in the world. Philosophers would say that the biblical image of God shows God to be omnipotent and immanent. Immanent is used in philosophy to mean that God is active and closely involved in the physical universe. For your examination, the crucial issue is to explore the meaning of God being active in the world and its significance for religious believers through studying miracles.

WHAT IS MEANT BY THE WORD 'MIRACLE'?

The starter exercise introduced different examples of what might be called 'miracles'. Underlying these examples are some definitions of miracles that have been used by theologians and philosophers. Many of the debates about whether or not miracles happen centre on what people mean by a 'miracle'. Traditional definitions focus on miracles being:

Immanent

Used to express the idea that God is involved and active in the world. Religious people may often talk of God being experienced through other people or in a miracle. These are examples of occasions when God is immanent.

Transcendent

Used to express the idea that God is separate from and completely distinct and different from the physical world. Transcendence also indicates that God is beyond human comprehension and completely 'other' (different from us).

Miracle

This word has a great variety of possible meanings. Some uses of the word 'miracle' are given below and explained in more detail in the text of the chapter:

- A lucky event
- A coincidence
- A sign pointing to God
- An event that breaks the laws of nature
- An event that reveals God
- A natural event that is given a special meaning by someone
- God's direct intervention in history.

- An event caused by God – this is a view traditionally supported by Christians such as Thomas Aquinas;
- A violation of the laws of nature – a definition of miracles commonly associated with David Hume.

These two definitions usually underlie the way in which people approach the question of God acting in the world, for example as recorded in the Bible.

Thought Point

Your turn

Before you read any further write a very short (one-sentence) answer to the following two questions. Your answer may be the same for both questions. If it is, do not worry:

- How would you explain what is meant by the word 'miracle'?
- If you asked a person living in Jesus' time what they meant by the word 'miracle', what do you think they would say?

TWO PRELIMINARY DEFINITIONS OF MIRACLES

THOMAS AQUINAS' DEFINITION OF A MIRACLE

Thomas Aquinas defined the word 'miracle' as:

> that which has a divine cause, not that whose cause a human person fails to understand. (Thomas Aquinas, *Summa Contra Gentiles*)

Aquinas' definition is important, as it highlights a fundamental point for religious believers: miracles are events caused by God. This is reflected in the meaning of the word 'miracle', which comes from the Latin 'miraculum' – an object of wonder. If we take a story such as

continued opposite

Jesus curing the paralytic (Mark 2: 1–12) it is of no interest to a religious believer whether we understand how Jesus cured the man. The point of the story is that God caused the man to be cured and this is an event to be wondered at. In the story, people cannot stop talking about what Jesus did and how God worked through him.

The second point to note is that Aquinas' idea of miracle comes from Aristotle. Aquinas and Aristotle both believed that everything which exists has a nature. Basically, this nature is a statement about what a thing is able to do. For example, you could say that part of the nature of human beings that makes them different from animals is that they can think about the future and the meaning of life and death. When Aquinas talks about a miracle having a 'divine cause' he means that the event in question is not a normal part of the nature of things.

However, many Christians today would add a further point to what Aquinas says. They would add that miracles are not only caused by God but they also reveal something about God to people. (This is explored in the section on Paul Tillich below.)

DAVID HUME'S DEFINITION OF A MIRACLE

The most famous definition of a miracle in the modern world is probably that of David Hume. Hume defined a miracle as a 'violation of the laws of nature' (*An Enquiry Concerning Human Understanding*).

For Hume, a miracle such as Jesus curing the paralytic is an example of an event which suggests that something happened which broke the laws of nature. It is important to understand what Hume means by the laws of nature, as his ideas are slightly different from those of scientists today. Hume uses the laws of nature to show how the universe works. For example, if you throw this textbook off your desk you know that it will fall to the floor. Why?

David Hume

A famous eighteenth-century philosopher whose writings are still important today in debates about God's nature and existence. In his work David Hume presented a set of philosophical arguments against the existence of miracles.

Miracle

The word 'miracle' originates from the Latin 'miraculum' – an object of wonder. For Hume, a law of nature is something which can be tested scientifically and you only say something is a law of nature if every time you test the law you find the same result. If you want to put this philosophically, Hume would say that laws of nature are proved inductively. What this means is that you collect evidence and reach a conclusion, like a judge listening to the evidence in a court case. Your conclusion is beyond reasonable doubt. Hume is not saying that the laws of nature necessarily have to be this way, but he is saying that the laws of nature are the best description of the way in which the universe works, beyond any reasonable doubt. Secondly, Hume believed that the laws of nature were rigid and fixed – meaning that they are statements which describe how the world works. Once discovered, laws of nature are unchanging.

THE BIBLE AND GOD'S ACTIVITY

The Bible paints a picture of God being closely involved with creation and acting in it, and this is clearly seen in the story of Joshua's defeat of the five kings in Joshua 10. There are a number of important points to note in this story:

Thought Point

Hume and the laws of nature

Look at the example statements below:

- A statue of the Virgin Mary crying in a man's garden;
- A statue of Nandi drinking milk in a Hindu temple;
- An infirm, wheelchair-bound woman going to Lourdes, getting better and starting to walk again;
- A man living in South Africa who was dying of Aids getting better;
- A Templar Knight cutting open an oak tree and finding an image of the Virgin Mary inside;
- A car breaking down and coming to a stop just inches away from hitting some children playing in the road.

Question

Which of these events would Hume say violate the laws of nature? Why?

- The victory over the kings is God's, not Joshua's. Joshua is the player who does the acting but the director and producer with the real power and control is God.
- God is described as throwing the enemy into confusion. This idea of God's presence bringing confusion is found in other parts of the Jewish Scriptures as well (e.g. Exodus 14: 24, 23: 27; Judges 4: 15). It emphasises the involvement of God in the victory.
- In the story, God's divine control is illustrated by referring to God's power over nature. So in Joshua 10 God is described as throwing hailstones or stones from on high. It is important to remember that for the people living in the times of the Jewish Scriptures there is no such thing as 'nature'. Instead the natural world is unpredictable and at times displays amazing powers. For example, today we would explain

lightning in terms of weather patterns and the laws of physics. The Jewish Scriptures come from a pre-scientific world in which the natural world is seen as at times chaotic. God's power and involvement in the world are clear because God's will operates through the events in the world. This is completely different from modern ideas about the world and nature being governed by scientific laws, which first originated in early Greek philosophy and saw the world as displaying some form of order.

- God's omnipotence is pictured through the image of the sun being made to stand still. This is a picture of God being immanent and involved in creation, and it fits in with Job 38 in which God gives orders to the sun. It is an example of God's involvement in the world.
- At the end of the story, Joshua returns to the camp with God; God is the victorious leader, not Joshua – Joshua is the servant who accompanies God.

Necessary

The word used in philosophy to say that something has to be that way and cannot be any different (e.g. if a philosopher was discussing necessary existence he or she would be talking about something which has to exist and could not fail to exist).

Thought Point

Do I need to learn miracle stories for the examination?

The OCR specification says that you should consider how God acts in the world in relation to miracles and the Bible. In order to do this you will need to be familiar with some examples of miracles from the Bible. You need to think about how the Bible writers understood these stories as well as some of the interpretations given to them by people today. You can pick any examples you like, but this chapter will look at the examples suggested by OCR to illustrate some different points drawn from the Bible.

Did people in biblical times believe God acted in the world?

In the time when the Bible was being written down there is no doubt that when people spoke of God helping them to victory they meant that God acted in history and helped them to achieve victory. The miracles and other events are signs of God being immanent in history and of God's omnipotence over creation. The book of Joshua is full of stories in which God fights on behalf of the people and is victorious over the enemies of the people of Israel.

Equally, as mentioned above, the miracles of Jesus were clearly signs pointing to God that revealed God to the people. These signs were realities for the people of the time and, by nature, miracles were (and are) remarkable events that people find significant. The Bible clearly depicts events that for the writers and, presumably, the witnesses of the events were direct examples of God intervening in history and, through his power, causing certain events to happen. This is not saying that God violated the laws of nature to make things happen, though of course the idea of the sun standing still sounds as if natural laws are being violated. The reason it is perhaps incorrect to see the miracles of the Bible as violating natural laws is because the stories, particularly those in the Jewish Scriptures, come from a culture lacking any idea about laws of nature. Instead, miraculous interventions by God were the way in which the people explained the world around them. However, the miracles are still signs pointing to God. Joshua and the Israelites are victorious and this is a sign of God's support.

Thought Point

Anthropomorphic imagery

In the Bible God is described in an anthropomorphic way, i.e. God is described in human terms and with human features. In the Joshua story, God speaks and fights for Joshua and the Israelites; in the Garden of Eden God walks in the afternoon. Perhaps the clearest example is Moses' Song of Victory (Exodus 15: 1–18) dedicated to God following the Israelites' escape from Egypt across the Red Sea. In the Song of Victory God is described as covered in glory, strong, a warrior, throwing chariots into the sea, crushing enemies, and even a blast from his nostrils moves the water.

However, it is important to note that these are examples of the limitations of the language people used when talking about God. Elsewhere in the Bible God is described as not being changeable like human beings (Numbers 23: 19) and being a spirit not flesh (Hosea 11: 9), hinting at the belief in God as transcendent and separate from this world rather than God being immanent and closely involved in the world.

God's action in the world in the New Testament

There are numerous examples in the Jewish Scriptures of God acting in the world, but it is also worth noting that there are specific examples of God acting in the world in the New Testament. Apart from the many stories of healing miracles associated with Jesus, two other stories are significant:

1 Jesus' birth

Jesus' birth is an example of God acting in the world and, for Christians, becoming present in the world (Matthew 1–2; Luke 1–2). Jesus is said by Christians to be God incarnate, meaning God made flesh. For Christians, Jesus' life is an example of God acting in the world.

2 Jesus' death and resurrection

The Gospel stories end with the accounts of God raising Jesus from the dead. For Christians the resurrection is the most important act of God in the Bible because it opens up the possibility of eternal life to all people. This eternal life had been lost by Adam and Eve. The importance of this action may be seen from Paul's statement:

> and if Christ has not been raised, then our proclamation has been in vain and your faith has been in vain. (1 Corinthians 15: 14)

BIAS AND GOD

Bias
Unfairly favouring one person or group above another.

One issue that arises from the stories of miracles in the Bible is the accusation of bias against God. For example, Joshua goes into battle and never loses because God favours him and fights with him. In other stories the lack of God's support leads to suffering: King Saul dies in battle after God has rejected him (1 Samuel 31) and God causes King David's first child by Bathsheba to die as a punishment of the parents for their adultery (2 Samuel 12: 16–23). In the Jewish Scriptures a clear picture of God as the God of Israel emerges. However, the New Testament picture is of God acting through Jesus to enable all people to be saved, not just limiting God's actions to the people of Israel.

If the stories of the miracles in the Jewish Scriptures in particular are taken literally, God favours one people, the Israelites, because God and the people had made an agreement (covenant). The people of Israel have to worship God and God protects the people.

However, in the time of the Jewish Scriptures all people believed that their God fought with them. The enemy in Joshua 10:1 is called Adoni-Tzedek, which means 'my lord is righteousness'. Equally, the name Joshua means 'God saves'. The readers of the Jewish Scriptures would have seen the miraculous victory of God as a sign that God is the true God; hence his actions are victorious.

If you look at the world and interpret it using the ideas of modern science, the only way that the sun standing still can be interpreted as an historical event is to say that it is a miracle which violates the laws of nature.

> **The covenant**
>
> Much more could be said about the concept of covenant, but it is not directly relevant here. For further information about this subject have a look at a Bible commentary, such as the *New Jerome Biblical Commentary*.

Saying this raises new questions about why evil exists if God has the power to intervene directly and stop it.

It is worth noting that one important assumption underlies any discussion of God being biased: that God's actions fit in with human ideas of rationality. In other words, God's actions are understandable in terms of logic and reason.

Furthermore, for many religious believers God's actions and God are a mystery, by which they mean that it is beyond human ability to fully understand the purposes and actions of God. This point is made many times in the Bible by people as varied as Job in the Jewish Scriptures and Paul in the New Testament.

CAN MODERN PEOPLE REALLY BE EXPECTED TO BELIEVE IN MIRACLES?

The Bible presents a clear picture of a world in which God is the Creator and in which God is immanently involved. God is seen as acting in the world and as helping his followers. Does this picture of God's activity make sense to modern people?

There are two aspects to answering this question:

1   The problems raised by God acting in the world, as in Joshua 10
2   Arguments against miracles as in Joshua 10 being real.

PROBLEMS RAISED BY GOD'S ACTION IN THE WORLD

In the Bible God is shown as acting in the world by:

* Healing people;
* Throwing hailstones from heaven;
* Defeating armies;
* Drowning soldiers;
* Answering prayers;
* Creating storms.

The problem that many philosophers raise is: if God has such power and is good, why does God not work miracles to help people or to prevent suffering? Many people point to examples such as the millions of people who died in the concentration camps of the Second World War and ask why, if God has the power, he does not work a miracle to help at least the innocent.

In religious traditions such as Christianity, God is described as being both loving and omnipotent. The problem that many people point to is not just the fact that human beings do evil things to each other. This could be explained by saying that God has given people free will to choose how to behave and this is the price to be paid: sometimes people commit evil actions with their free will.

The more serious problem is that the Bible depicts God as holding back the sun, throwing hailstones, and controlling floods and storms. If God has the power to do this, why does he not prevent natural disasters such as tsunamis in which both innocent and guilty people suffer?

Thought Point

Any problem?

In the Judaeo-Christian tradition God is all good, omnipotent and omniscient. God also acts in the world. Is there any problem raised by the following actions of God in the world? (If you want more information about the incidents, read the stories in the Bible and look up the stories in a biblical commentary.)

- God destroying the cities of Sodom and Gomorrah (Genesis 19: 1–29)
- God causing the great flood (Genesis 6: 5–9; 17)
- God causing Eve to have pain in childbirth (Genesis 2: 4–3; 24)
- God asking Abraham to sacrifice Isaac (Genesis 22: 1–19)
- God helping Joshua to capture Jericho and kill every living person and animal in the city (Joshua 5: 13–6; 27).

The fact that miracles seem to happen so rarely in the modern world raises a question about whether God performs miracles 'arbitrarily' – meaning that there appears to be no purpose or pattern to the occurrence of miracles. In other words, miracles seem to be events that occur by chance, at random. If this were the case, it would suggest that God is not so much an omnipotent, omniscient creator but rather a changeable, unpredictable character. The problem of God being arbitrary is explored by Maurice Wiles in his book *God's Action in the World* (see below).

Responses

There are a number of ways religious people can respond to this challenge:

- Responses to the problem of evil defend the existence of natural disasters in the world on the grounds that this is part of the ordered world we live in, and if God intervenes continually to prevent suffering we will not be able to learn and come to understand our world at all.
- Some religious people would claim that God does act in the world but people often fail to recognise God's actions. For example, following the tsunami which struck South East Asia in December 2004, newspaper headlines were printed asking 'Why did God let this happen?' Negative events are often blamed on God, but for some people the miracle is the fact that many people survived the tsunami in extraordinary circumstances, such as drifting on pieces of rubbish washed out to sea until a passing boat rescued them.
- For some religious people the answer is to say that the picture in the Bible of God acting in the world reflects a pre-scientific understanding of the world in which God is seen to act directly through natural occurrences such as the weather. This fits in with what might be called a mythological view of the world. By myths people often mean stories that communicate the values and beliefs of a community. The famous biblical scholar Rudolph Bultmann suggested that all miracles are myths. What this means is that the stories of miracles communicate the eternal reality of the universe – God created it and continues to work in and through it. People in the Bible expressed this through symbolic myths; today we describe the workings of the world through science, but that does not diminish people's sense of wonder at the world, or an awareness amongst many people today of God as the ultimate explanation for why everything exists and of God acting in creation. You could say that the scientific interpretation of the world is the myth or value system that shapes people's thoughts about the world today.

Arbitrary
A decision that is not based on a reason, or the result of rational decision-making.

ARGUMENTS AGAINST MIRACLES BEING REAL

Another response is to suggest that miracles which violate the laws of nature, such as the sun standing still, do not really happen. The most famous argument against miracles that violate the laws of nature is the one put forward by David Hume in section 10 of his *An Enquiry Concerning Human Understanding*.

DAVID HUME ON MIRACLES

David Hume puts forward two separate but very closely related arguments against miracles.

ARGUMENT 1: LACK OF PROBABILITY

David Hume argues that the probability of miracles actually happening is so low that it is irrational and illogical to believe that miracles do occur.

Hume is an empiricist, meaning that he emphasises experience and observations of the world as the way of learning new things. He argues:

- When investigating any story of a miracle, evidence can be collected, such as from human witnesses.
- Laws of nature appear to be fixed and unvarying. For example, the law of gravity is the same throughout the universe so far as we know.
- Miracles appear to violate the laws of nature.
- Conclusion: it is more likely that the report of a miracle happening is incorrect than that the laws of nature have been violated.

Take as an example the story of Jesus raising Lazarus from the dead (John 11). First, according to the Bible, people witnessed the event. Second, our experience of nature is that people who are dead do not come back to life. It is true that many people have had near-death experiences, but once a person has been in a grave or tomb for a day or two they do not come back to life – they start to rot. So, this leads to a conflict between a law of nature (dead bodies do not come back to life) and the miracle story. Hume's question would be: which is more likely – that the law of nature has been violated or that the eyewitness accounts are for some reason mistaken? Hume's conclusion is that miracles do not happen because there is so much clearly testable evidence in favour of the laws of science. Hume's conclusion is printed in the side box, 'Hume's maxim'.

ARGUMENT 2: HUME'S PRACTICAL ARGUMENT AGAINST MIRACLES

David Hume also put forward some related practical arguments against miracles.

> **Hume's maxim**
>
> No testimony is sufficient to establish a miracle, unless the testimony be of such a kind that its falsehood would be more miraculous than the fact which it endeavours to establish. (*An Enquiry Concerning Human Understanding*)

Lack of convincing testimony from educated people

Hume claimed that miracles were not reported as happening to educated people.

Thought Point

Loaded language

The philosopher Keith Ward stated in an interview (Stannard, *Science and Wonders*):

> I do think miracles happen, but I hate the phrase 'violations of the laws of nature'. It was invented by David Hume, who was a wonderful philosopher, but a notorious atheist. And he invented the phrase to make miracles sound ridiculous.

1 Does the phrase 'violation of the laws of nature' make miracles sound ridiculous? If so, why?
2 What do you think is the point that Keith Ward is suggesting?

Hume commented on the fact that stories tend to circulate and get exaggerated and suggested that this sort of gossiping was part of human nature. Among other examples, Hume mentions gossip about young people, commenting that two young people only had to be seen once together and people would think they were getting married. In the modern world urban myths are an example of this tendency: following the devastation caused to New Orleans by Hurricane Katrina in September 2005, it was reported all around the world that law and order had broken down, and the chief of police announced that two baby girls had been assaulted and raped. However, the New Orleans police investigated the matter and could find no evidence that the event had occurred, and very little evidence of a crime wave having occurred. The reports of looting and a breakdown of law and order were not found to be accurate (*Guardian Weekly*, September 2005).

Miracles only seem to happen among ignorant and barbarous people

Hume argued that if you look at the history of countries, their earliest stories are full of miracles, visions and so on, but as the nation develops and becomes educated these sorts of stories disappear. Later in his essay about miracles Hume discusses some parts of Genesis and Exodus, such as the long lives of people like Adam (he lived for 930 years) or the choice of Israel by God, which he says is arbitrary. Hume concludes that none of these events that violate the laws of nature are probable, as this would imply that the laws of nature are false. He says:

> It appears, that no testimony for any kind of miracle has ever amounted to probability, much less proof. (*An Enquiry Concerning Human Understanding*)

It is certainly the case that newspapers and television programmes during the twentieth century did not report many cases of miracles happening.

Thought Point

Are you truthful?

Discuss the following questions:

1   What do you mean if you say someone is 'an honest or truthful person'?
2   Would you describe yourself as honest and truthful?
3   Have you ever told a lie?
4   Have you told more than one lie?
5   How many lies do you have to have told to be called a 'liar', 'dishonest', or 'untruthful'?
6   How do these questions relate to discussions about miracles?

Contradictory reports of miracles occurring in different religions

Hume wrote that if one religion claimed that a miracle proved their religion true, the value of this statement is cancelled out by the fact that other religions equally claim miracles happen that prove the truth of that religion.

The conclusion Hume reaches is that it is much more likely that stories of miracles, such as those in the Bible, are false than that they really happened.

IS HUME'S ARGUMENT THE FINAL WORD?

The argument against miracles and God's activity through miracles put forward by David Hume has been very influential in philosophical history. However, it is not the final word. In recent years many philosophers,

Hume's probability argument: summary

- There are laws of nature which appear to be unvarying and universal, based on past experience.
- Sometimes there are reports of miracles happening which violate these laws of nature.
- Which is more likely?
- The law of nature is wrong?
- The reports about the miracle event violating the laws of nature are incorrect?
- Conclusion: no report about a miracle can ever prove that miracles happen.

such as Richard Swinburne, have defended the idea of God acting and performing miracles.

Thought Point

Hume's own words

> [T]here is not to be found in all history any miracle attested by a sufficient number of men of such unquestioned good sense, education and learning, as to secure us against all delusion in themselves.
>
> With what greediness are the miraculous accounts of travellers received, their descriptions of sea and land monsters, their relations of wonderful adventures, strange men and uncouth manner? . . . Eloquence, at its highest pitch, leaves little room for reason or reflection.
>
> This is our natural way of thinking, even with regard to the most common and credible event. For instance: there is no kind of report which rises so early, and spreads so quickly, especially in county places and provincial towns, as those concerning marriages; in so much as two young persons of equal condition never see each other twice, but the whole neighbourhood immediately join them together.
>
> It forms a strong presumption against all supernatural and miraculous relations, that they are observed chiefly to abound among ignorant and barbarous nations. (*An Enquiry Concerning Human Understanding*)

How persuasive is Hume's argument in your opinion?

Thought Point

Hume's conclusion

> I desire anyone to lay his hand upon his heart, and after a serious consideration declare whether he thinks the falsehood of such a book [the Bible], supported by such a testimony, would be more extraordinary and miraculous than all the miracles it relates. (*An Enquiry Concerning Human Understanding*)

1   What point is Hume making about the Bible?
2   Do you agree with Hume?

Thought Point

David Hume and miracles

1 How would David Hume analyse the following accounts of remarkable events?
2 Would you agree or disagree with a Hume-like analysis? Why?
3 Would you say that any of these events are miracles?

- Five thousand men, not counting women and children, witnessed Jesus multiplying five loaves and two fishes into enough food to feed every person in the crowd and have twelve baskets of leftovers (Mark 6: 30–44).
- A man went to the Catholic shrine of Lourdes and washed his hands in the waters there. After washing his hands the knuckles in one of his hands, which had been damaged in a car crash, were restored to full health (source: an experience that happened to a member of my extended family).
- A statue of Mary in an Italian man's garden is observed to be crying by thousands of people (*Guardian*, Saturday, 6 May 2000).
- A man dying of Aids is cured (source: a priest of the Oxford Oratory; the man who had the experience is a friend of his).
- Medical research has shown that prayer can have beneficial health effects (*British Medical Journal* website).

Thought Point

A problem for Hume

The philosopher Anthony Flew has written extensively about miracles. Read the passage below and then work out the solutions to the questions:

In the History of Herodotus, we read that some Phoenician sailors at the time of Pharaoh Necho II (about 600 BCE) claimed to have circumnavigated the continent of Africa. They sailed from the Red Sea and arrived at the Mediterranean coast of Egypt nearly three years later. The interesting thing for us is their report that during the voyage the position of the sun shifted from south to north. Herodotus, recording that they said this,

continued overleaf

states that he himself does not believe what they said. He had two good reasons for disbelief: first he knew that Phoenician, and not only Phoenician, sailors are apt to tell tall stories; and, second, he believed he knew that what the sailors reported was impossible. Herodotus therefore had good reason to dismiss this story and did, in fact, dismiss it. (Palmer, *The Question of God*)

1 Use Hume's ideas and decide whether Hume would have agreed with the ancient historian Herodotus if Hume had been a person of that time.
2 Is Herodotus correct?
3 What criticism of Hume's argument about miracles is implied by the passage?

(If you need some ideas to help you, look at the box below the 'Further reading' section.)

HUME'S INDUCTIVE PROBLEM

Hume argues that it is irrational to believe in miracles occurring because they violate the laws of nature. He believes in the laws of nature because empirical observations support the claim that there are laws of nature and that these laws are universal. So, Hume is arguing inductively from observations that the laws of nature are such that they cannot be violated. From this Hume concludes that the evidence concerning how the laws of nature function is such that any account of a miracle occurring is much less likely to be true than an account which explains that the miracle did not occur. Consider the examples in the box below:

Thought Point

Arguing inductively

- Living organisms are observed to need oxygen to survive.
- No living organism has been observed that does not need oxygen to survive.

Conclusion: Living organisms cannot survive without oxygen.

- No empirical evidence of unicorns' existence has been found.
- There are approximately 5 billion people living in the world today.

continued opposite

- It is likely that if there were evidence of unicorns existing, at least one of the 5 billion people in the world would have observed it.
- No-one has produced empirical evidence of unicorns.

Conclusion: It is most improbable that unicorns exist.

- What possible new evidence would undermine each of these arguments?

Hume's inductive argument can be challenged by new empirical evidence. The question thus becomes: which interpretation of an account of a miracle best matches the empirical evidence gained from observation and experience? It is important to note that the fact that something is more probable is not, on its own, proof that something is correct. In detective stories, detectives often solve a case by showing that empirical evidence proves that what is improbable is actually true. In the same way the fact that the probability of a miracle occurring is very low is not enough on its own to prove that it is irrational to believe that miracles do occur.

Hume was writing at a time when the only support for miracle stories came from word-of-mouth reports. Today, claimed miracles are sometimes supported by scientific evidence. At Lourdes, there have been 68 carefully attested claims that miracles have occurred. The evidence has been carefully sifted and documented by unbiased scientists working with the latest available medical equipment. Here the doctors are exactly of the sort that Hume demanded – they have reputations to lose and the evidence is incontrovertible. Hume does not say that miracles are not logically possible, but simply says it is unreasonable to believe in them when others speak about them, but he says nothing about whether an individual who experienced one should doubt the evidence of their experience and look for an alternative explanation.

However, the fact that Hume's inductive argument can be challenged does not necessarily mean that Hume is wrong. Instead the question is raised again of whether, based on our experience and knowledge of the world, the occurrences of miracles are improbable or not.

RICHARD SWINBURNE'S ARGUMENT

Swinburne's defence of miracles, like Hume's argument, considers first what is meant by natural laws. Hume emphasises the fixed and universal nature of natural laws. Swinburne agrees with Hume that natural laws are based on people's experiences of observing the world but he emphasises two points distinct from Hume:

1   Laws of nature are generalisations, i.e. they communicate a general picture of how things work as simply as possible.
2   Swinburne says that all natural laws are 'corrigible' (*The Concept of Miracle*). By this Swinburne means that a law of nature is the best description of how the world works that we currently have, but of course a new discovery may mean that a law of nature has to be modified or changed. Hume does not consider this in his argument, which emphasises the fixed nature or unchangeableness of natural laws.

This leads Swinburne to define a miracle as 'an occurrence of a non-repeatable counter-instance to a law of nature'. By this Swinburne means that a miracle is an event that does not fit in with the laws of nature as we understand them, but equally the event on its own is not enough to prove the law of nature inaccurate. In other words, you could not define a new law from this one instance when an event occurs which does not fit in with the law. This event is also a one-off. Hence it is unrepeatable. Furthermore, it would be rather illogical to say that a law of nature is wrong just because of one incident, or that the occurrence of an incident is automatically to be doubted because it seems to break natural laws.

So, Swinburne concludes that laws of nature are good general descriptions of how the world works but that does not remove the possibility of a miracle – *a counter-instance to a law of nature* – occurring.

But do miracles occur?

Richard Swinburne also considers what evidence would be needed to support a belief that a miracle has occurred, and in doing so challenges some of the practical arguments against miracles put forward by Hume (Swinburne, *The Concept of Miracle*).

Next, Swinburne questions how you define when people are educated. Hume gives no method of recognising when you have a suitable large group of educated men, or women, and what level of education is required. This leads Swinburne to consider what actually counts as 'ignorant and barbarous'. It could mean that people lack a familiarity with science, but this does not really help Hume's argument, as many people today are undoubtedly educated and yet still claim to experience miracles.

Finally, Swinburne questions whether miracles in different religions cancel each other out. He suggests that miracles in any religion are not usually about proving one religious tradition's beliefs correct and another religion's beliefs wrong.

For example, if a miracle was reported to have happened at Lourdes (a Roman Catholic shrine) and another miracle was reported to have happened at Makkah (the most holy place in Islam) this does not necessarily have anything to do with proving one religion right and another wrong. Most miracles that have been reported by religious believers concern incidents where God helps someone, mostly by healing them. Just because miracles are claimed to happen in different religions does not mean that miracles cancel each other out.

Swinburne's evidence for miracles

Swinburne (*The Concept of Miracle*) suggests that Hume is wrong to say that no evidence or witness is reliable enough for us to say that miracles happen. Second, Swinburne suggests that there are ways of collecting evidence that would enable one to decide whether a miracle had or had not happened.

Four kinds of historical evidence are identified by Swinburne:

1　Memories of our experiences.
2　Testimony by other people about their experiences.
3　Physical traces of the event, such as the medical examination of a person who has been healed.
4　Understanding of modern science and what is thought to be physically impossible or most improbable. For example, if someone who had Aids claimed to have been miraculously healed this would go against modern science that understands Aids to be incurable.

Having identified the possible evidence that might be available, Swinburne says that, as in any matter of debate, you have to assess the evidence and deduce a conclusion. Swinburne then suggests some factors that you use in any discussion about interpreting events that happened in the past. He divides the arguments into 'main' and 'subsidiary' parts.

Main argument

Accept as many sources of evidence as possible. The more evidence there is to support the miracle claim, the stronger the probability that the miracle actually happened.

Subsidiary arguments

- Different sources of evidence should be consistent; i.e. the sources of evidence should support each other.
- The value you place on a particular piece of evidence should depend upon the 'empirical reliability' of the evidence, meaning, for example,

that if a witness to a miracle is a known liar you would not take his or her evidence as seriously as the evidence from someone whom you know to be honest and truthful.

- Avoid rejecting without good reason pieces of evidence that may be relevant.

Thought Point

Truthful friends?

How would you react to the following situations?

1　Would you:

   (a)　Send for a doctor;
   (b)　Tell your friend that their joke is rubbish;
   (c)　Believe them;
   (d)　Ask for more details about what happened;
   (e)　Suggest to your friend's parents that their child is going a bit funny in the head;
   (f)　Do something else?
   (g)　Would you believe that your friend had experienced a 'miracle'? If yes, what do you mean by a miracle?

Situation 1

A friend of yours who is a known practical joker comes round to see you. Your friend seems to be a bit shaken up and not himself. You ask what is wrong and your friend says that he cannot believe it but he has just observed a miraculous experience in which he saw a child who had been paralysed since birth get out of a wheelchair and walk. Your friend says that, immediately prior to the incident, the child's mother had been heard to say, 'Please God help my child.'

Situation 2

A friend of yours whom you have known for years as a truthful and honest person comes round to see you. Your friend seems to be a bit shaken up and not himself. You ask what is wrong and your friend says that he cannot believe it but he has just observed a miraculous experience in which he saw a child who had been paralysed since birth get out of a wheelchair and walk. Your friend says that, immediately prior to the incident, the child's mother had been heard to say, 'Please God help my child.'

Swinburne's suggestions are not claiming that miracles do happen, but Swinburne is quite clearly saying that it is possible that they happen and, unlike David Hume, you should not automatically be sceptical and reject a story about a miracle without considering the evidence.

The essence of the claim Swinburne makes is that Hume is mistaken in rejecting all witnesses' statements about miracles. We have to examine seriously what a person claims when they say they have witnessed or experienced a miracle but we should not reject it automatically.

GOD'S ACTIVITY IN THE WORLD AS DESCRIBED IN THE BIBLE: A FINAL WORD

There is much controversy about whether God acts in the world and performs miracles. The picture from the Bible is very clear: God does act in the world.

David Hume put forward a strong argument against believing that violations of the laws of nature take place. However, Richard Swinburne and other philosophers have highlighted some weaknesses in Hume's argument.

Swinburne puts forward a strong argument for suggesting that it is possible that miracles happen and he has also suggested evidence that could be considered to help decide if an event is a miracle.

Thought Point

Lourdes

Lourdes is a Roman Catholic shrine in the south of France. St Bernadette saw a vision of Mary, the Mother of Jesus, there and discovered a stream in some

continued overleaf

Lourdes

A Roman Catholic shrine in the south of France to which thousands of people go on pilgrimage. St Bernadette saw a vision of the Virgin Mary there and discovered a stream in the cave (Grotto) in the mountain. Many people who have bathed in the waters of the Grotto have been healed. Some of these healings have been declared to be miracles by the Roman Catholic Church.

caves in the mountain. People came to visit and pray at the shrine and some people who were very ill claimed to have been cured after bathing in the waters in the cave. Today, thousands of people visit Lourdes every year and many people claim to have been cured there. However, the Roman Catholic Church is very cautious about saying that any of the claimed healings there are miracles. If someone says that they have been healed, an international team of doctors investigates their case and medical history. Not all the doctors are Catholics or Christians. Only if all the doctors agree that the case is a miracle will the Church consider saying publicly that it is a miracle.

Does Swinburne's argument support this sort of approach?

MIRACLES TODAY

1   Write down your own definition of a miracle.
2   Read the story of Jeanne Fretel. Is this a miracle according to your definition? Construct an argument either in favour of or against its being a miracle.

THE JEANNE FRETEL CASE

Jeanne Fretel was born on 7 May 1914. In later life she caught tuberculosis. In October 1948 she joined her diocese's pilgrimage to Lourdes. She was seriously ill with tuberculosis and peritonitis. She was declared incurable by her doctor, who wrote in her notes:

> The patient becomes more and more feeble. She can only take small amounts of liquid; meningitic signs were appearing. The abdomen is very distended and very painful. Pus runs abundantly from the natural outlets . . . accompanied by black blood. Cardiac attacks are very frequent and endanger the patient's life. All hope seems lost.

At Lourdes all her symptoms of illness disappeared. She received communion at the church and then bathed in the pool in the cave underneath the church, called the Grotto, where Roman Catholics believe that the Virgin Mary appeared. When she left the Grotto her symptoms of illness had gone. On her return home her doctor stated that she had been 'completely cured' (D.J. West, *Eleven Lourdes Miracles*).

THE MODERN DEBATE ABOUT THE DEFINITION OF MIRACLE

The definition of a miracle makes a major difference to how a possible miraculous event, such as the Jeanne Fretel story, is interpreted. The general pattern of a discussion may be as follows:

David Hume suggests that miracles are a violation of the laws of nature. Keith Ward (Stannard, *Science and Wonders*) has responded to this claim by suggesting that the phrase *violation of the laws of nature* is unhelpful since it sets up a thought that there is something wrong with believing in miracles. Richard Swinburne in his criticisms of David Hume specifically does not use the phrase *violation of the laws of nature*; instead, he calls miracles 'counter-instances to a law of nature'.

For David Hume laws of nature are rigid and fixed. Therefore, to suggest an event like a miracle, which violates the laws of nature, has occurred immediately sounds problematic. However, if, as Swinburne suggests, laws of nature are expressions of probability, then a counter-instance to these laws does not necessarily involve a violation of the laws of nature.

THE CONTINGENCY DEFINITION OF MIRACLES

An alternative way in which religious people use the word 'miracle' is to refer to a sign pointing to God. This view is often called the contingency definition of miracles and it is this definition which is very popular with modern philosophers of religion.

The crucial point is that miracles are signs from God; that is, miracles are events of great religious significance. For example, in John's Gospel Jesus feeds the five thousand. This is interpreted as a sign by the people that Jesus is from God; after the feeding of the five thousand the people try to crown Jesus king. The event had significance to the people of the time and would have reminded them of Moses feeding the people in the desert when the Israelite slaves were escaping from Egypt (Exodus 16) or Elijah the Prophet's actions (2 Kings 4: 42ff).

In the New Testament, Jesus is pictured as a worker of signs (Greek: *semeion*) and performing works of power (Greek: *dunamis*). The word that is never used is 'miracle', or any translation of it. The early Church used this word but, for the first Christians writing about Jesus, his miracles are signs from God. These signs are remarkable or wonderful, but the crucial point is that the remarkable sign is from God as opposed to anyone else. For example, Jesus curing a person is a sign of God's love for His people, or God rescuing the Hebrew slaves from Egypt is a sign of God acting to save his

> **Did you know?**
>
> In John's Gospel the word 'sign' (Greek: *semeion*) is used 17 times to refer to Jesus' miracles and people believing in his signs.

people. Because these events are religiously significant they are still recalled and celebrated by Christians and Jews today.

In addition, within the Bible, events that people today call miracles are carried out by many biblical characters, such as the witch of Endor, the magicians of Pharaoh and Simon Magus. The point about the miracles of Jesus is that they are of religious significance – meaning that they reveal something about God to people.

For some modern philosophers such as Paul Tillich, miracles are better seen as signs with religious significance. For Paul Tillich, miracles are not about God violating the laws of nature or acting like a magician:

> The supernaturalistic theory of miracles makes God a sorcerer and a cause of 'possession'. It confuses God with demonic structures in the mind and in reality. (Tillich, *Systematic Theology*)

R.F. HOLLAND ON MIRACLES

Along with the idea of miracles being signs pointing to God is the contingency definition of miracles. This definition of miracles points to the fact that the word 'miracle' is applied to a set of coincidental events that are given religious significance and continue to have this significance after the event. The most famous explanation of this idea is probably a story by R.F. Holland – you can read the story yourself in the box below.

A child riding his toy motor car strays on to an unguarded railway crossing near his house and a wheel of his car gets stuck down the side of one of the rails. An express train is due to pass with the signals in its favour and a curve in the track makes it impossible for the driver to stop his train in time to avoid any obstruction he might encounter on the crossing. The mother coming out of the house to look for her child sees him on the crossing and hears the train approaching. She runs forward shouting and waving. The little boy remains seated in his car looking downward, engrossed in the task of pedalling it free. The brakes of the train are applied and it comes to a rest a few feet from the child. The mother thanks God for the miracle; which she never ceases to think of as such, although, as she in due course learns, there was nothing supernatural about the manner in which the brakes of the train came to be applied. The driver had fainted, for a reason which had nothing to do with the presence of the child on the line, and the brakes were applied automatically as his hand ceased to exert

---

continued opposite

pressure on the control lever. He fainted on this particular afternoon because his blood pressure had risen after an exceptionally heavy lunch during which he had quarrelled with a colleague, and the change in blood pressure caused a clot of blood to be dislodged and circulate. He fainted at the time when he did on the afternoon in question because this was the time at which the coagulation in his blood stream reached the brain. (Holland, 'The Miraculous')

QUESTIONS

1   Is this story an example of a miracle? Whatever your answer, what do you mean by a miracle?
2   Work out from this story Holland's definition of a miracle.
3   What do you think is the most important point Holland is making through this story?

The crucial point of this story is that the train stopping just in time is a coincidence according to one view, but it is a matter of religious significance for the mother, and the religious significance of the event for the mother continues long after the event itself. The natural explanation of why the train came to a stop does not affect the religious significance of the event for the mother. What Holland went on to argue is that a coincidence as in the train story can be interpreted as religiously significant and people can argue about this, but the story in no way shows that any intervention by God in the world involves a violation of the laws of nature. Equally, there is no direct way of assessing whether the mother's claim that a miracle happened is true.

It is really important to note for later in the chapter that Holland's view of miracles is not about the laws of nature being violated as David Hume claimed, but equally Holland's view of miracles is not like the biblical picture of God intervening in history.

PAUL TILLICH ON THE CONTINGENCY DEFINITION OF MIRACLES

The theologian and philosopher Paul Tillich has also supported a contingency definition of miracles. According to Tillich, a miracle is a sign event – something that is of religious significance and tells us about God. This idea comes from the miracles in the Bible, which are signs from God. Tillich emphasised the fact that, from the time immediately after Jesus' death, what has been emphasised is the strange or unnatural nature of a miracle, not its role as a sign in Jesus' ministry. There are many stories in the New Testament, apart from the aforementioned feeding of the five thousand. This suggests that the miraculous nature of miracles has been overemphasised, instead of focusing on their role as signs. For example, if you read the story of Jesus healing the paralysed man in Mark 2: 1–12, Jesus specifically heals the man as a sign from God that he has authority to forgive sins. This connects with the belief that illness could be caused by sin, which was commonly held in Jesus' time. So, Jesus healing the man is a sign of his authority over sin.

Emphasising the fact that miracles are 'sign events' leads Tillich to identify some characteristics of miracles:

- Miracles are astonishing but 'without contradicting the rational structure of reality' (Tillich, *Systematic Theology*), by which Tillich meant that miracles are astonishing events but that does not mean that they have to violate the laws of nature.
- Miracles point people to what Tillich called the 'mystery of being' (Tillich, *Systematic Theology*), i.e. God – meaning that they reveal something about God's nature.
- Miracles are 'received as a sign event in an ecstatic experience' (Tillich, *Systematic Theology*), meaning that the miracle event reveals God to people and it is this revelation which causes the ecstatic overwhelming experience for the recipient.

One illustration of these characteristics could be the aforementioned story of Jesus' cure of the paralytic. In the story Jesus forgives the man's sins and then heals him as a sign of this forgiveness (Tillich's revelation of 'the mystery of being'). The paralysed man gets up off his sick bed and goes around praising God (Tillich's ecstatic response which is the result of the miracle).

Thought Point

Read Luke 6: 17–26

Discuss how Tillich and Holland might interpret this story.

HOW ARE CONTINGENCY MIRACLES DIFFERENT FROM OTHER EXPERIENCES IN LIFE?

This question is really important because if contingency miracles are no different from other events in life (e.g. they are a matter of interpretation), then this would suggest that miracles are merely a product of a person's brain, i.e. the way a person's mind thinks and interprets things.

However, this is not what Tillich is saying. The crucial point of Tillich's definition of miracles is that they are revelatory – they reveal something about God and this revelation is from God. This is what is distinctive about miracles and makes them more than just a matter of different interpretations of life experiences. According to Tillich, the person who receives the revelation knows what they have received through faith. This revelation of God can occur through the natural world without violating natural laws because God is the Creator and sustainer of everything.

The problem with the contingency definition of miracles

Many philosophers reject the arguments of Holland and Tillich. The most common argument against this view is that, while they might argue that miracle experiences are revelatory and that the ecstatic response shows this, there is no real way to prove that a person who has experienced a miracle really did experience a miracle rather than its being a product of their thoughts and mind.

Hume, contingency and miracles

The contingency definitions of miracles from Holland and Tillich suggest that miracles are signs revealing God. In this view, no miracle event has to involve a violation of the laws of nature. Hence, the contingency approach avoids many of the criticisms put forward by David Hume. It also reflects some biblical traditions that emphasise the nature of miracles as signs.

However, the contingency view does not well reflect the picture of God causing miracles and healings such as in the stories of the Jewish Scriptures. If stories such as the capture of Jericho are taken literally, God appears to do things that violate the laws of nature. If that is the case, God does act very directly in the world and the action itself is important as well as the sign it gives.

What should we make of the Jeanne Fretel story?

The assessment depends very much on which definition of miracles is in question.

David Hume would undoubtedly point to the fact that an event has occurred which seems to be most improbable. However, although doctors described Jeanne Fretel as having no hope, which would seem to indicate that she would probably die, a natural explanation of her recovery, although unlikely, might be theoretically possible. Hume's practical arguments could be used to suggest that perhaps Jeanne's symptoms had not been properly observed before or after the event, or that the story has grown with being repeated. Ultimately, Hume would probably point to the fact that though recoveries from such serious illnesses are improbable, it does not make them unheard of, and thus to suggest that this is a miracle is misguided.

Richard Swinburne's approach to miracles would suggest that the evidence should be looked at but not prejudged. In particular, Swinburne would think the statements and testimony of doctors, witnesses and Jeanne Fretel particularly important. His approach would indicate that you should make a judgement about what seems most probable, but this does not rule out the possibility that a miracle – a counter-instance to a law of nature – has occurred. Furthermore, Swinburne could point to the fact that many other miracles are reported to have occurred at Lourdes and in some cases there is a lot of documentary and witness evidence concerning the people healed. Taking all this evidence together may suggest that there is good reason not to dismiss the story of Jeanne Fretel.

An assessment of the Jeanne Fretel story following some of R.F. Holland's suggestions could focus on the event as a reality in the life of Jeanne Fretel. Certainly Jeanne believed she had been miraculously healed and this belief continued long after the event. Jeanne also believed that God was revealed to her through this event. Paul Tillich suggested that miracles could be characterised as astonishing, revealing the mystery of God and causing an ecstatic response. Some of these features could be identified in the story of Jeanne Fretel. Jeanne certainly believed that she had been cured and believed God was responsible for this. In addition, there is no doubt from the doctor's own records that the event could be described as surprising or astonishing – that she was so near death and yet was completely cured following a visit to Lourdes. This could match some of Tillich's criteria for miracles.

DO MIRACLES VIOLATE THE LAWS OF NATURE?

David Hume defined miracles as violations of the laws of nature and he would have rejected the account of Jeanne Fretel's healing as evidence of a violation of the laws of nature. Is the definition of a miracle as a 'violation of the laws of nature' satisfactory?

Richard Swinburne has suggested that 'laws of nature' can be understood in a rather different way from that of Hume. He suggests that laws of nature are 'probabilistic' – meaning that the laws of nature are actually describing what will probably happen. Sometimes, of course, most unlikely things do happen. For example, think of a perfect unspoilt beach – mile after mile of golden yellow sand – but somewhere on it I have put one grain of red sand. If I ask you what colour the sand is you would be correct to say it is golden yellow. If I asked you to pick up a grain of sand the likely colour it would be is golden yellow. However, the possibility remains that you could find the grain of red sand. It is a really unlikely possibility, but it could happen.

Thought Point

Jumping and diving

Jumping

If someone jumps from the thirtieth floor of a skyscraper, what do you think will happen to her or him?

Is there any chance of surviving falling this distance without the aid of a parachute or other artificial device?

Diving

For how long can a human being hold their breath under water? For how long can you hold your breath under water?

What do you think the world record time is?

Swinburne explains that the laws of nature are probabilistic by referring to the fact that the quantum laws that govern the whole universe have been clearly shown by scientists to be probabilistic (i.e. quantum laws tell you what is likely to happen, not what will certainly happen).

Thought Point

Richard Swinburne on God's action in the world and quantum theory

Quantum theory indicates that the most fundamental laws of nature, the laws governing the behaviour of very small-scale particles, are probabilistic, i.e. indeterministic; but that, in general, small-scale indeterminacies cancel out on the large scale, leading to virtually deterministic behaviour of the medium-sized objects with which we interact – tables and chairs, trees and persons. . . . But other divine interventions in the world, God moving material bodies over several metres, for example, would require the occurrence of events immensely improbable given natural laws, which we may call 'quasi-violations' of natural laws. (Swinburne, *Providence and the Problem of Evil*)

Read Swinburne's argument carefully and decide whether or not he is saying that miracles violate the laws of nature.

The suggestion that Swinburne and other philosophers have put forward is that:

God's intervention will simply be a matter of inclining things to behave on a certain occasion in this way rather than that, which will be compatible with the probabilistic patterns of behaviour which humans may discover and formulate as 'laws'. (Swinburne, *Providence and the Problem of Evil*)

If this view is correct, God's action in the world may be compatible with nature. Hence, for example, some people have suggested that stories such as Moses leading the Israelites across the Red Sea could be an example of God violating the laws of nature, but equally the sea and weather all combining to cause this great flood could be explained in natural terms. However, the likelihood of such a coincidental set of events happening as to drive the Red Sea back to allow the Israelites a clear path across the sea is unlikely in the extreme.

MAURICE WILES ON GOD'S ACTION IN THE WORLD

The Christian theologian Maurice Wiles rejected the idea of God acting in the world and violating the laws of nature; he would thus reject the idea of explaining the Jeanne Fretel story in terms of God's activity. Wiles suggested that the sole activity of God was to create and sustain the world. God does not intervene in the world in the way that David Hume and other philosophers had in mind.

Maurice Wiles rejects the traditional idea of God causing miracles to happen that appear to violate the laws of nature. In his book *God's Action in the World* Wiles puts forward a set of arguments for not believing that miracles happen:

- If miracles are violations of the laws of nature they have to occur infrequently to avoid the concept of laws of nature becoming meaningless.
- The pattern of the occurrence of miracles appears strange.
- The large number of evil events that are not prevented by God raises questions about God's omnipotence and goodness.

Maurice Wiles argues against a view of God which suggests that God acts in the world and is good, and yet does not prevent the Holocaust of the Second World War and the Nazi concentration camps. In taking an interventionist view of God's action in the world, Wiles sees God's actions as arbitrary and partisan. If God does intervene and undermine the laws of nature, why would he choose to do so for some and not for others?

> If the direct action of God, independent of secondary causation, is an intelligible concept, then it would appear to have been sparingly and strangely used. Miracles must be by definition, relatively infrequent or else the whole idea of the laws of nature . . . would be undermined, and ordered life as we know it would be an impossibility. Yet even so it would seem strange that no miraculous intervention prevented Auschwitz or Hiroshima, while the purposes apparently forwarded by some of the miracles acclaimed in traditional Christian faith seem trivial by comparison. (Wiles, *God's Action in the World*)

For example, many writers have pointed to the problem of God's omnipotence in relation to the vast amount of evil in the world. If God has the ability to intervene directly to prevent evil happening, why does he not do so? In the case of miracles, many people perceive there to be a contradiction between one person being healed, such as Jeanne Fretel, and thousands dying in events such as the 2004 tsunami. Wiles' ideas imply that a view of God who acts in the world and works miracles leads you into all the difficulties for religious believers associated with the problem of evil.

Miracles, then, raise serious questions about God's justice, not only the issue of seemingly trivial actions ascribed to God when serious events are ignored, but also if God is always interfering in human affairs where does that leave the claim that humans are free beings with the gift of free will? According to Wiles, if human freedom is undermined then the free will defence as a response to the problem of evil no longer works. In order to answer this problem, Wiles proposes that everything in the world, whether perceived as good or evil, is 'part of the ongoing activity which contribute to the one divine act of God's creation' (Wiles, *God's Action in the World*). In this way humans act freely but these actions also further the single divine act.

Keith Ward counteracts Wiles' ideas about miracles by saying that Wiles has misunderstood God's special acts in the world. The continuous process of creation does not undermine human freedom and neither do special acts of God such as miracles because God acts with rather than against human freedom, and as God is a God of love he would be expected to act in human history. Wiles, however, disagrees and simply accepts that as God is the Creator he has some responsibility for evil and suffering in the world: 'If evil is something inherent in the creative process, so too must be the overcoming of that evil' (Wiles, *God's Action in the World*).

The idea that God acts in special or particular cases in response to prayers or other needs is also rejected. For Maurice Wiles, God acting in the world in this way leads to questions about miracles showing God to be arbitrary or biased. Wiles considers that such a God would not be worthy of worship: 'An interventionist account is both implausible and full of difficulty for a reasoned Christian faith' (Wiles, *God's Action in the World*). Ward, in reply, argues that the constraints of creation do not always allow God to act. For example, if God always acted to save everyone from suffering we would never develop our moral sense or understand the consequences of our actions – so Ward seems to agree with Wiles that God cannot act without undermining our freedom. However, this does not mean that God has never acted, and in his book *Divine Action* Ward says that it is still possible for God occasionally to perform miracles if they serve his purposes.

Unlike Wiles, Ward does not think miracles cause the moral problem of seeing the actions of God as partisan and arbitrary; instead, he sees miracles as contributing to our knowledge and love of God. Neither does Ward accept that God has responsibility for evil in the world – just as parents are not responsible for the evil acts of their children, why should God be blamed for the evil actions of humanity? The problem with this view is that Ward assumes knowledge of God's purposes. At the same time Wiles also seems sure of the ultimate redemptive outcome of God's single creative act without any direct action in the world.

John Polkinghorne, who is a physicist and a priest, also takes issue with Wiles, saying his view of miracles fails to account for the possibility of answers to prayer. Polkinghorne says that quantum theory suggests our universe has elements of indeterminism and natural laws are not always predictable, so God's actions too may be unexpected – he cites the resurrection as one such act. If God's actions in the world are infrequent, they will not undermine human freedom or science.

An alternative response, which Wiles accepts, is to accept many of the biblical miracles, including the resurrection, as having symbolic significance rather than being seen as historical facts.

Arbitrary

A decision that is not based on a reason, or the result of rational decision-making.

Thought Point

A few questions

Think about the following events. If these events have happened, why do they raise questions about God's ability to act in the world? What questions arise about the nature of God?

- God helping Joshua to destroy Jericho and thousands of people dying in a mudslide and earthquake that occurred in Guatemala in October 2005.
- Jeanne Fretel being healed at Lourdes and over 20,000 people dying in genocidal attacks in Rwanda during the 1990s.

Criticisms of Wiles' views

Christian tradition

Christian tradition clearly depicts God acting in the world in a far more direct way than Wiles suggests. Stories of miracles in the Bible indicate that God acts in the world. If it is believed that God does intervene in the world in a direct way and causes miracles to happen, Wiles' views do not fully reflect the nature of God.

Human rationality

Wiles' argument depends on the fact that human rationality can be applied directly to God. Questions about God's actions being arbitrary and biased only arise if you first suggest that God's actions have to conform to some form of rational order that we understand. For some religious believers, God cannot be limited to what is rationally possible – God is a mystery whose purposes and nature transcend human abilities to interpret and understand them. In the Judaeo-Christian tradition the Book of Job depicts Job challenging God; Job reaches no conclusions but still accepts God – for some believers God's purposes ultimately remain beyond human understanding.

The Christian God

Petitionary prayer

A prayer that makes a particular request of God.

Deist

A person who believes that God started the universe off with one creative act but then effectively left the universe to run without acting in it.

John Polkinghorne argues that Maurice Wiles' view of God's action in the world does not reflect Christian religious experience of God. For example, it is difficult to make sense in a traditional way of the idea of petitionary prayers that make requests of God. Yet many people claim that God answers their prayers.

Second, Polkinghorne points to the fact that many scientists are also Christians but have not rejected the possibility that God does act in the world:

> A minimalist response is to decline to speak on particular divine actions and to confine theological talk to the single great act of holding the universe in being. Not only is such timeless deism inadequate to correspond to the religious experiences of prayer and an intuition of providence but it is also interesting that it has not commended itself to those scientist-theologians who have written on these matters. (Polkinghorne, *Belief in God in an Age of Science*)

Polkinghorne himself suggests that modern science does not exclude the possibility that God acts in the world.

For other modern philosophers of religion, Christian tradition does point to the fact that God can act in the world and leaves the question open about God's ability to act in the world in response to particular needs and situations.

WHY DO MIRACLES MATTER FOR RELIGIOUS BELIEVERS?

Miracles are of great importance for many religious believers, but the reasons that they are important can vary. Broadly speaking, the reasons for miracles being significant may be divided into six groups.

The significance of miracles for religious believers

1 Miracles
support arguments
for God's
existence

6 The miracle of
the resurrection

2 Miracles show
God's providence

5 Miracles show
that prayers are
answered

3 Miracles show
that Jesus is from
God

4 Miracles are
signs of God's
continuing activity
in the world

Of course many people would hold more than one of these views at the same time.

Miracles support arguments for God's existence

For some Christians the occurrence of miracles caused by God in the world is a reason to believe in God. In modern philosophy of religion many philosophers have suggested that while single arguments for God's existence are not, on their own, sufficient to prove that God exists, taken together a range of different arguments for God's existence may be a good reason to believe God exists. This type of view is called a cumulative argument for the existence of God. The philosopher Swinburne suggests:

> The existence of detailed historical evidence for the occurrence of violations of natural laws of a kind which God, if there is a God, would have had reason to bring about, is itself evidence for the existence of God. Though not nearly enough on its own, it makes its contribution; and with other evidence . . . it could be enough to establish the existence of God. (Swinburne, *Is There a God?*)

Cumulative argument
A philosophical argument that is built up with many different arguments and pieces of evidence. A conclusion based on probability is then drawn from all the pieces of evidence. In modern philosophy of religion it is popular to create a cumulative argument for God's existence using the separate different arguments.

Thought Point

Do you agree?

Swinburne suggests that miracles together with other evidence may demonstrate that God exists. What other evidence could he have in mind? Do you agree with him?

Miracles are signs of God's continuing activity in the world

For religious believers, God's continued activity in the world is demonstrated through miracles. If you are a believer in God, the fact that someone is, for example, healed in a miraculous manner demonstrates that God continues to be active in the world.

Miracles show that prayers are answered

Petitionary prayer
The subject 'petitionary prayer' examines questions concerned with whether prayers are answered. For more information about petitionary prayer and miracles have a look at some of the further reading suggested at the end of the chapter.

Many people pray to be healed and go to prayer services of healing. What is striking is that there are a large number of accounts of people being healed in response to their prayers. This is significant for two reasons. First, it shows the nature of God as loving and good (i.e. the miracle is a 'sign-event', in the words of Tillich). Second, the miracle is a sign that God acts in the world. Miracles may be demonstrations of the fact that God responds to prayers in God's own way. In this sense miracles are for the believer a revelation of the nature of God as immanent and active in the world.

The miracle of the resurrection

The vast majority of Christians who have lived in the past 2,000 years would suggest that the resurrection is the important foundational event for Christianity. As Paul said:

> [A]nd if Christ has not been raised, then our proclamation has been in vain and your faith has been in vain. (1 Corinthians 15: 14)

There are a large variety of ways in which the resurrection can be interpreted, but one of those approaches is particularly important here. Many Christians would argue that Jesus' resurrection is miraculous; this could be meant in the sense of a violation of the laws of nature or a 'sign event' that is caused by God and reveals God to people.

The Christian belief in the resurrection and afterlife is a foundational belief of the faith; the resurrection event is a major basis of this belief. For many Christians the particular action of God raising Jesus from the dead is *the sign* of God's activity in the world and love for the world. For example, the Catholic Church has said:

> The Resurrection above all constitutes the confirmation of all in Christ's works and teachings. . . . The truth of 'Jesus' divinity' is confirmed by the Resurrection. (*The Catechism of the Catholic Church* §651–652)

Miracles show that Jesus is from God

For many Christians, miracles are signs that point to God and reveal something about God. In the case of Jesus' miracles these signs or miracles are seen as confirmation that Jesus is from God. Within the New Testament Gospels Jesus' miracles are actually signs and they often follow some other action or saying of Jesus. In particular, Jesus preaches forgiveness of sins, and miracles often accompany this message. In Mark 2: 1–12 Jesus heals a man as a sign of his authority from God to forgive sins, as the Jewish belief was that only God could forgive sins. For many Christians, the signs Jesus works in God's name show that Jesus is the Son of God.

This view is also supported by many of the Christian denominations. The Roman Catholic Church states that:

> The signs worked by Jesus attest that the Father has sent him. They invite belief in him. To those who turn to him in faith, he grants what they ask. So miracles strengthen faith in the one who does his father's work; they bear witness that he is the Son of God. (*The Catechism of the Catholic Church* §548)

God's providence

For many religious believers miracles are examples of God's providence. By 'providence' religious believers mean God's continued action in the world, which sustains it in being and also reveals God to people (e.g. God's providence is revealed through the beauty of nature; the environment provides the food and resources that human beings need). In Christian tradition providence is used in two ways:

The resurrection

How the resurrection can be interpreted is examined in Chapter 11 on life after death.

Providence

A word used in Christian theology to refer to God's goodness and continuing activity in the world for the benefit of creation.

1   *General providence*
This refers to the goodness of creation.

2   *Special providence*
This phrase refers to God acting in the world on particular occasions. An example would be God causing a miracle in response to a person's prayer or need.

CAN PEOPLE BELIEVE IN MIRACLES GIVEN THE FINDINGS OF MODERN SCIENCE?

The answer to this question is crucial, since Christians believe that God acts in the world and many Christians today would also regard the findings of science as important and accurate descriptions of how the world works.

David Hume argued very clearly that scientific discoveries suggested that the chances of a miracle being real were extremely low. However, his arguments, while persuasive, have been criticised by many philosophers, including Swinburne. In particular, Hume so emphasises the fixed nature of natural laws that he leaves little room for them to develop or change as scientific understanding of the world progresses. The theories of special and general relativity of Albert Einstein are the basis of much work in modern physics; however, Einstein's law of general relativity actually replaced Sir Isaac Newton's views on the laws of physics, which Hume would have learnt.

Many modern scientists have debated the reality of miracles as much as theologians and philosophers, and what their debates clearly show is that both sides of the debate can put forward persuasive arguments. Ultimately, the individual person has to decide what is more likely (probable): God causes miracles or miracles are to be explained in other ways by events within the world.

SOME MODERN ARGUMENTS AGAINST MIRACLES

Some scientists present arguments very similar to David Hume's practical arguments. Peter Atkins, a chemist, for example, argues against miracles, suggesting that people seek publicity or are deluded or hallucinate and so on, and that is the reason why they believe in miracles (Stannard, *Science and Wonders*). However, while this may sometimes be the case, this form of argument is open to the points of criticism raised by Richard Swinburne against David Hume: you cannot assume that all people are ill-educated,

Einstein's ideas

If you would like to know more about the history of these ideas and their importance, you could read *In Search of Schrödinger's Cat* by S. Gribbin. This is an excellent and very readable account of some of the great ideas of modern physics.

Modern physics

If you would like to know more about ideas in modern physics, explained in simple terms, have a look at chapters 1 and 2 of *The Universe in a Nutshell* by Stephen Hawking. The illustrations in the book and the text are a superb introduction to some of the big ideas of physics.

and what matters is that the evidence for any miracle claim is tested and assessed.

Richard Dawkins puts forward a different range of points against miracles in conversation with scientist Russell Stannard (Stannard, *Science and Wonders*).

1   People have strange experiences and disturbing experiences, such as 'dreaming of someone for the first time and waking up to discover they are dead' (Stannard, *Science and Wonders*). Other experiences might be great coincidences.
2   Occasionally you would expect people to have coincidental experiences in life to which they attach special significance.
3   Examples of places such as Lourdes could be explained by the placebo effect. People go to Lourdes believing they will be cured and they are then cured.

Richard Dawkins argues very strongly that he would not rule out people being cured by psychological means; however, he would doubt occasions such as people getting up out of a wheelchair and walking again.

It is worth noting that these sorts of arguments against miracles stress a few key points:

*   Miracles are improbable.
*   There are scientific ways of explaining these effects that do not require God as an explanation.

In this sense these arguments are in the same vein as David Hume's practical arguments and his argument against violations of the laws of nature. Of course, the same criticisms raised against Hume's arguments may be applied to many of the points argued by Atkins and Dawkins.

NOT RULING OUT MIRACLES

Few scientists argue in favour of literal belief in a miracle like the incident in Joshua 10, but many scientists do acknowledge the possibility of God acting in the world. However, it is important to understand what this means:

*   Few scientists would talk about God 'violating the laws of nature'.
*   But many would discuss the possibility of God acting in the world through natural laws.

Polkinghorne the man

John Polkinghorne is a physicist and theologian. Having spent many years working as a professional scientist, he became an Anglican priest and studied theology. He has written many books examining the relationship between science and religion, particularly physics and Christian belief.

Quantum mechanics

Refers to the physical understanding of the universe developed in the early twentieth century by the physicists Werner Heisenberg, Paul Dirac and Erwin Schrödinger. Quantum mechanics showed that when it comes to tiny particles (smaller than electrons in atoms) they do not have a definite position and speed.

Instead the tiny particles behave in unpredictable ways. Another way to put this is: some of the basic laws of nature are not fixed laws as Hume thought, but are laws that show that the physical behaviour of particles is a matter of probabilities not certainty.

The scientist and theologian John Polkinghorne argues that God can act in the world, but he explains this in a rather different way from some of the biblical images.

Polkinghorne points out that many scientists who have become theologians, such as Arthur Peacock, do not limit God's role to starting things off. Instead, they see God as active in creation; for example, Arthur Peacock suggests that God acts through events which do not break the laws of nature.

John Polkinghorne also comments on the idea that God only acts through people:

- Intelligent life that can think about what it does has only existed for a few million years; therefore if God acts only through people, it 'implies that God has been an inactive spectator of the universe for most of its history to date, since conscious minds seem not to have been available for interaction with divinity' (Polkinghorne, *Belief in God in an Age of Science*).
- If God works through people, this means that God is working in nature and affecting the physical laws of the world, because Polkinghorne sees human beings as being a unity of body and soul. So, if God acts through you, God is affecting the way the physical processes of the world work by affecting you.

Polkinghorne suggests that:

In unprecedented circumstances, it is entirely conceivable that God will act in totally novel and unexpected ways. (*Belief in God in an Age of Science*)

This leaves open the possibility of God intervening.

It is also worth noting that the laws of nature that govern the universe are not nearly as rigid or set as David Hume assumed. In modern physics quantum mechanics indicates that on the very small scale (e.g. smaller than electrons in atoms) the particles that exist operate in a non-determined way, meaning they do not follow a law of physics that enables you to exactly describe their behaviour. This is not because physics has not found the law; it is because the laws indicate that the behaviour of very small quantum particles is indeterminate (meaning not totally knowable). The significance of this is that the universe is a much more variable environment than Hume imagined. Therefore, some scientists argue that it is an open question whether events happen that do not fit neatly into our understanding of the laws of nature.

The philosopher Richard Swinburne has also suggested that God may occasionally suspend his own laws of nature. Swinburne gives a helpful analogy (*Is There a God?*) to explain this: he compares the laws of nature with parents' rules, pointing out that parents teach rules as laws, but occasionally exceptions are made to the rule in particular circumstances. One illustration could be parents teaching their children the value and importance of the virtue of truth, yet that is not to say that parents are always truthful – the child's surprise party is impossible if the parents always tell the truth.

'GOD'S ACTIONS CAUSE MIRACLES TO HAPPEN' – IS THIS A GOOD THEORY?

It is clear from the debates about the interpretation of miracles that there is no one clear, undisputed view either in favour of or against the occurrence of miracles. The contingency definition of miracles makes miracles a reality in an individual's or group's faith life. Hume and Swinburne disagree about whether there is evidence for miracles or not. Wiles' ideas about God's action in the world certainly fit in with modern science but do not make any sense of traditional Christian claims that God really does act in the world, sometimes in a way that violates the laws of nature.

However, one other way to assess whether God causing miracles is a good explanation of these strange events is to consider whether this is a good theory. Stephen Hawking, the scientist, said that:

> A good theory will describe a large range of phenomena on the basis of a few simple postulates and will make definite predictions that can be tested. If the predictions agree with the observations, the theory survives the test, though it can never be proved correct. (*The Universe in a Nutshell*)

Hawking is suggesting that a good theory is one that is straightforward and uncomplicated, from which you can make predictions about the world that you can test. What you cannot do is prove your theory true, but you can build up more and more evidence that the theory in question is correct.

If we apply this idea to miracles, we could consider the explanation: *God causes miracles*.

This [*God causes miracles*] explains the occasions when miracles are said to have happened.

From the explanation 'God causes miracles' we could predict that more miracles will happen in the future.

Thought Point

For discussion

Is 'God causes miracles' a good explanation for the occurrence of strange events that are labelled as miracles? What do you think?

SUMMARY

1   Definitions

Thomas Aquinas

'That which has a divine cause, not that whose cause a human person fails to understand' (Thomas Aquinas, Summa Contra Gentiles)
Idea of miracle comes from Aristotle
Miracle has a divine cause

David Hume

Violation of the laws of nature

2   God's activity in the Bible

Involved with creation and acts in it (e.g. Joshua 10)

Jewish Scriptures – God is immanent, active and omnipotent

New Testament

e.g. Jesus' birth and Jesus' death and resurrection
The 'Signs' (miracles) of Jesus were real for the first followers of Jesus

3   Problems

Bias and God
If God has such power and is good, why does God not work miracles to help people or to prevent suffering?
Question about whether God performs miracles 'arbitrarily'
Are miracles in the Bible to be taken literally?

& Responses

Free will defence
God does act in the world but people often fail to recognise God's actions

The picture of God acting in the world in the Bible reflects a pre-scientific understanding of the world

4 David Hume: miracles do not happen

Lack of probability
No report about a miracle can ever prove that miracles happen
Practical arguments against miracles
Lack of convincing testimony from educated people
Human beings have a tendency to exaggerate
Miracles only seem to happen among ignorant and barbarous people
Contradictory reports of miracles occurring in different religions

5 Richard Swinburne: miracles possibly do happen

Laws of nature are good general descriptions of how the world works but that does not remove the possibility of a miracle – a counter-instance to a law of nature – occurring

Arguments against Hume

How do you define when people are educated?
What actually counts as 'ignorant and barbarous'?
Miracles in any religion are not usually about proving one religious tradition's beliefs correct and another religion's beliefs wrong

Swinburne's evidence for miracles

Four kinds of historical evidence
Accept as many sources of evidence as possible
The sources of evidence should support each other
The value you place on a particular piece of evidence should depend upon the reliability of the witness
Do not reject without good reason pieces of evidence that may be relevant

6 Do miracles violate the laws of nature?

David Hume defined miracles as violations of the laws
Richard Swinburne has suggested that the laws of nature are 'probabilistic'

7 Maurice Wiles on God's action in the world

The whole universe is the single creative act of God
Rejected the idea of God acting in the world and violating the laws of nature
The pattern of occurrence of miracles appears strange
The large number of evil events that are not prevented by God raises questions about God's omnipotence and goodness

God acting in special or particular cases in response to prayers or other needs is also rejected; it raises questions about God being arbitrary or biased

Criticisms of Wiles' views

Christian tradition depicts God acting in the world in a direct way
Human rationality cannot be applied directly to God
John Polkinghorne argues that Maurice Wiles' views do not reflect Christian religious experience of God
Many scientists are also Christians but have not rejected the possibility that God does act in the world

8   Contingency definition of miracles

Miracles are events of great religious significance

Jesus is pictured as a worker of signs

Paul Tillich

A miracle is a sign event – characteristics
Miracles are astonishing events but they do not violate the laws of nature
Miracles reveal something about God's nature
Miracles cause an overwhelming ecstatic experience for the recipient

R.F. Holland

Set of coincidental events that are of religious significance
The train story example

The problem with the contingency definition of miracles

There is no real way to prove that a person who has experienced a miracle really did experience a miracle

9   Why do miracles matter for religious believers?

Miracles support arguments for God's existence
Miracles are signs of God's continuing presence in the world
Miracles show that prayers are answered
The miracle of the resurrection is a foundational event for the Christian faith
Miracles show Jesus is from God
Miracles reveal God's providence

10   Can people believe in miracles given the findings of modern science?

Modern views against miracles

Peter Atkins: people seek publicity or are deluded or hallucinate

Richard Dawkins
People have strange experiences and disturbing experiences
Places such as Lourdes could be explained by the placebo effect
Miracles are improbable

Not ruling out miracles

The possibility of God acting in the world through natural laws
Many scientists who have become theologians (such as Arthur Peacock)
do not limit God's role to starting things off
The laws of nature that govern the universe are not nearly as rigid or set
as David Hume assumed
Swinburne's parents analogy

REVIEW QUESTIONS

Look back over the chapter and check that you can answer the following questions:

1   A friend asks you what you mean by a 'miracle'. How would you answer?
2   Is life a miracle? What do you think?
3   Why did David Hume reject belief in miracles? Try to present his argument in less than one side of A4 paper.
4   A scientist suggests that miracles never happen. Would you agree with him or her? Would you have any scientific reasons to support your answer?
5   Outline Maurice Wiles' reasons for rejecting traditional views of God acting in the world.
6   Which definition of a miracle most appeals to you? Why?

Terminology

Do you know your terminology?

1   Try to explain the following ideas without looking at your books and notes:

   •   Immanence
   •   Violation of the laws of nature

continued overleaf

- Bias
- Swinburne's four types of evidence
- Hume's arguments against miracles.
- Petitionary prayer
- Quantum theory
- Maurice Wiles' views about miracles.

 Examination Questions Practice

EXAM MISTAKES TO AVOID

Make sure that you remember that miracles are part of the wider topic of God's action in the world which you studied for your AS course. The definitions of miracles from your AS work along with the work you will have done on Hume and Swinburne are an essential part of this topic and preparation for the examinations. In the examination you should be able to demonstrate a good understanding of philosophers' ideas about miracles and God's action in the world.

There are many definitions of miracles by philosophers and theologians. It is important that you can explain the different ideas without confusing them. Practise doing this with a partner.

Remember: each question assesses AO1 and AO2. To help you improve your answers look at the A2 Levels of Response. See: http://www.ocr.org.uk/qualifications/as-a-level-gce-religious-studies-h172-h572/.

SAMPLE A2 EXAM-STYLE QUESTION

1 **Assess Hume's reasons for rejecting miracles.** (35 marks)

The first thing to note about this question is that it will draw on work you have covered at both AS and A2 levels. David Hume is a topic on both.

You will gain 65 per cent of the marks available for this question by clearly explaining Hume's reasons for rejecting miracles. Remember that Hume's discussion focused on the improbability of miracles and the idea of miracles as a 'violation of the laws of nature'. Some examination candidates only write about the practical arguments against miracles and this loses them marks. Points to include could be:

- Lack of probability

  - Hume argued that the laws of nature appear to be unvarying and universal, based on past experience. He claimed that miracles are therefore violations of these laws of nature. Hume concludes that no report about a miracle can ever prove that miracles happen.

- Hume's practical arguments against miracles:

  - Lack of convincing testimony from educated people
  - Human beings have a tendency to exaggerate
  - Miracles only seem to happen among ignorant and barbarous people
  - Contradictory reports of miracles occur in different religions.

Second, this question requires you to **assess** Hume's arguments, so you have a good opportunity to put forward arguments both against and in favour of Hume's ideas. Some points you could discuss in an answer are:

- **Hume's practical arguments**
  To some people Hume's practical arguments are arrogant and make assumptions about people's levels of education that cannot be supported. It is worth remembering that gossip and urban myths are good examples of reasons to agree with David Hume's practical argument that people tend to exaggerate things.
  On the other hand, you could explore Richard Swinburne's reasons for disagreeing with Hume's practical argument, such as: how do you define when people are educated? What actually counts as 'ignorant and barbarous'?

- **Violation of the laws of nature**
  In your essay you should be able to discuss why many people, such as Richard Swinburne, disagree with Hume's rigid definition of the laws of nature.

- **Reasons for believing in miracles**
  You could point to arguments in favour of believing in miracles that challenge the conclusion of Hume's practical arguments. For example, you could assess Swinburne's four kinds of historical evidence for miracles.

- **The definition of a miracle**
  A different approach is to consider whether Hume's definition of a miracle is the correct one. The contingency approach to miracles would provide a good basis to argue that the weakness of Hume's argument is actually the definition of miracles. This point is reflected in Keith Ward's thinking.

- **Hume was right**
  You can, of course, argue the case for Hume being right and it is worth observing that some eminent scientists, such as Peter Atkins and Richard Dawkins, would agree with you.

FURTHER READING

Miracles

Peter Vardy's *The Puzzle of God* (1995) contains an excellent introduction to the problems raised by God's activity in the world and miracles. This book is a good starting point for further reading.

Chapter 7 of Richard Swinburne's book *Is There a God?* contains a thought-provoking defence of belief in miracles in the modern world.

The Question of God by Michael Palmer examines whether miracles are a proof of the existence of God. It provides excellent further reading for this topic and contains a detailed examination of Hume's arguments.

David Hume

If you would like to read part of the original philosophy of David Hume you could take a look at the extract from his *An Enquiry Concerning Human Understanding* in *Philosophy of Religion: The Big Issues*, edited by E. Stump and M.J. Murray (1999).

Petitionary prayer

If you would like to investigate the relationship between miracles and petitionary prayer you could read the helpful chapter on this topic in *The Puzzle of God* by Peter Vardy. There are a large number of articles available about this topic – in particular, the philosopher Eleanor Stump has written widely on this and other subjects. Some of her articles may be found in collections of philosophy of religion articles such as *Philosophy of Religion: The Big Questions* (ed. E. Stump and M.J. Murray).

Science and God's action in the world

There is a range of books available written by scientists. John Polkinghorne has written two books that examine God's action in the world. *Belief in God in an Age of Science* examines the relationship between the two and defends belief in God as well as modern scientific understanding of the origins and development of the universe. *Science and Providence*, as the title suggests, examines what God's providence means. Both books are challenging and stimulating reads that will give you a good insight into the way an eminent physicist who became an Anglican priest approaches religious questions.

15 Religious Language

Essential terminology

Analogy
Equivocal language
Falsification
Myth
Symbols
Univocal language
Verification

THE ISSUE

If God is transcendent and ineffable, how can we talk about God in any meaningful way?

WHAT YOU WILL LEARN ABOUT IN THIS CHAPTER

In this chapter you will examine the ways in which religious people use language to talk about God. You will also explore the challenges to believers' attempts to describe God presented by the logical positivist movement.

STARTER

Who then are you, my God? (Augustine, *Confessions*)

- If a friend asked you 'What do you mean by God?', how would you answer them?
- Do you find any of the following phrases helpful ways to talk about God? Would these phrases help your friend to understand what the word 'God' means?

  - God is like a mother hen.
  - God is a warrior.
  - God is the Lord.
  - God is the ground of being.
  - God is simple.
  - God is ineffable.
  - God is good and not good.
  - God is not a person, nor a body, nor a spirit.

Key scholars

Maimonides (1135–1204)
Thomas Aquinas (1225–1274)
Paul Tillich (1886–1965)
Ludwig Wittgenstein (1889–1951)
Karl Popper (1902–1994)
John Wisdom (1904–1993)
A.J. Ayer (1910–1989)
Norman Malcolm (1911–1990)
Basil Mitchell (1917–2011)
Richard Hare (1919–2002)
John Hick (1922–2012)
Anthony Flew (1923–2010)
R.F. Holland (1923–2013)
Richard Swinburne (1934–)
Brian Davies (1951–)

The starter tasks

The second Starter task referred to a number of ways in which people have described God, and this chapter explores some ways in which language like this can be understood. The images of God as a mother hen, a warrior and the Lord all come from the Bible, while God as the ground of being is a phrase from the work of Paul Tillich. William James, among others, characterised God as ineffable, and Thomas Aquinas wrote in great detail about the meaning of 'God is simple'.

Verification

Refers to the concept of demonstrating the truth or falsity of a statement of fact using empirical evidence. Statements that cannot be assessed, such as 'Martians visit the Earth when no one is watching', are described as 'meaningless'.

INTRODUCTION

There are many ways in which people talk about God and a wide variety of language is used. The problem for any theist is how one talks about God in a meaningful way if God is transcendent and ineffable. For other people, the problem about God-talk is whether it means anything at all. It is these issues which are explored by studying religious language.

VERIFICATIONISM

Verificationism is a philosophical movement which claims that language is only meaningful if it can be verified by a sense-observation or it is a tautology, i.e. a logical truth. A sense-observation refers to the act of gaining a piece of knowledge through your senses, such as touching a piece of fabric, seeing a beautiful sunset or hearing a moving piece of music.

The verification movement was influenced by science, which emphasised the importance of confirming any statement by observation, for example in an experiment. Verificationists aimed to apply the same approach to all use of language when making statements of fact. Moritz, Schlick and other supporters of verification pointed out that the meaningfulness of statements is shown by the method by which you verify the statement.

In other words, if you cannot demonstrate with sense-observations how a statement is true, then the statement is factually meaningless. For a verificationist, language tells us something about the way the world is. Statements that do not tell us something that may be shown to be either true or false by sense-observation are therefore factually meaningless or tautologies. One of the important aims of verificationism was to indicate which areas of philosophical or scientific enquiry are factually meaningless and thus not to be investigated.

For example, if I say 'Water is wet' this statement is meaningful because anyone could put their hand in the water; their sense-observation would confirm whether my statement was true or false. However, a statement such as 'The statue is beautiful' is not confirmable in the same way. One person can look at the statue and say 'True – it is beautiful,' while another person can look at the same statue and say 'No – it is ugly.' It does not matter how many people you ask, the beauty of a statue is not something that can be decided on the basis of observation, nor is it a statement that can be answered with 'true or false' in any certain way.

Verificationists argue that any statement that cannot be proved true or false is 'meaningless', by which they mean that the statement literally has no meaning in a factual sense.

Language that talks about God is meaningless for a verificationist as there is no way to demonstrate the truth or falsity of God-talk by observations and experiments.

The problem with early verificationism's strict scientific approach is that it would mean that many statements people make are meaningless, even when most people think they make perfect sense. Swinburne ('God-talk Is Not Evidently Nonsense') gives the example 'All ravens are (at all times) black.' He points out that while people generally accept ravens are black, there is no way to ever confirm this statement, as however many ravens you look at there is always the possibility of there being one more raven that is not black. Therefore, according to verificationism the statement is meaningless.

A second problem for early verificationists is that no statement can be made about history. If I say that the Battle of Hastings occurred in 1066, there is no way in which to verify this fact by observation. Therefore it is factually meaningless according to verificationism.

AYER AND VERIFICATION

The British philosopher A.J. Ayer (1910–1989) supported verification theory. He suggested that 'The criterion we use to test the genuineness of apparent statements of fact is the criterion of verifiability' (Ayer, *Language, Truth and Logic*). According to Ayer, if a statement is not verifiable it is either meaningless or a tautology.

By 'meaningless' Ayer meant that a statement was not 'factually significant' (*Language, Truth and Logic*). Ayer was not denying that people make other types of statement that are important to them, such as saying that 'God answers my prayers'; it is just that unverifiable statements do not have factual significance:

> The sentence expressing it may be emotionally significant to him; but it is not literally significant. (*Language, Truth and Logic*)

How do you verify a proposition?

Ayer suggested a procedure for deciding whether a statement is verifiable. Ayer called the statement being tested a 'putative proposition' (*Language, Truth and Logic*).

First, Ayer distinguished *practical verifiability* from *verifiability in principle*. *Practical verifiability* referred to statements which could be tested in reality. If someone says that Real Madrid football team wear red shirts this is verifiable in practice – you can observe the team. However, statements such as 'There is life on other planets in the Milky Way Galaxy' are meaningful and verifiable in principle, but in practice we cannot verify these statements as we lack the technology to visit every planet in the Milky Way Galaxy to look for life.

Second, Ayer distinguished *strong* and *weak* verification. Strong verification applied to anything that can be verified conclusively by observation and experience. Weak verification refers to statements that can be shown to be probably true beyond any reasonable doubt by observation and experience.

Ayer (*Language, Truth and Logic*) argued that the sense in which verificationism should be used is the 'weak' sense because the strong sense 'had no possible application' and excluded too many things. He gave the example of general laws that cover an infinite number of cases, such as all human beings are mortal. It is impossible to demonstrate that all human beings are mortal in a strong sense without killing every human being who lives or will live in the future. This is clearly impossible to do, but few people would doubt that all human beings are mortal, as all human observations to date suggest the truth of the statement 'Human beings are mortal.'

Tautology

Tautologies are meaningful according to Ayer. Consequently, in an examination do not say that all unverifiable statements are 'meaningless' according to Ayer.

In logic, a tautology is a statement that something is the case and the statement cannot be confirmed or falsified by any observation. Philosophers like Ayer describe tautologies as 'analytic propositions' (*Language, Truth and Logic*).

For example, 'bachelors are unmarried men'. This is a tautology because the meaning of 'bachelor' is that a man is unmarried.

Which of the following phrases are tautologies?

- Spinsters are unmarried women.
- It is either raining or it isn't.
- UK post boxes are red.
- The prime minister is mortal.

Thought Point

Weak verification

Which of the following statements are verifiable in a *weak* sense? If they are verifiable in a weak sense, how are the statements verifiable?

- Near-death experiences indicate that there is life after death.
- The Yeti walks the Himalayas.
- Unicorns are white.
- God exists.
- Real Madrid is the best football team in Europe.
- Martians live inside the planet Mars.

> **Probable**
>
> Probable is often undefined. The most common way in which it is understood is that something is probable if the likelihood of it occurring on the balance of evidence is greater than 50 per cent. This level of proof is used in civil court trials, such as divorce hearings. In criminal trials, such as for murder cases, the level of proof is higher – the standard is 'beyond reasonable doubt'.

If the principle of verification is applied to religious claims, the claims can appear meaningless because they cannot be supported by observations from sense experience that go beyond reasonable doubt. A good example to consider are the philosophical arguments for God's existence, such as the teleological and cosmological arguments. They have been widely criticised, and one particular failing of these two arguments is an inability to verify the arguments convincingly from sense experience. It may, of course, be argued that there are signs of design in the world but this then becomes a debate about what level of proof satisfies the weak verification criteria. Religious believers would argue that God's existence can be verified, but non-believers would dispute this.

Second, Ayer argued that we can make no meaningful statements about metaphysical ideas (i.e. statements about anything beyond the world of sense experiences) because we can have no knowledge of things beyond experience gained through our senses:

> For we shall maintain that no statement which refers to a 'reality' transcending the limits of all possible sense-experience can possibly have any literal significance; from which it must follow that the labours of those who have striven to describe such a reality have all been devoted to the production of nonsense. (*Language, Truth and Logic*)

Thought Point

Sense experience

Can we know things in any other way except through the five senses of hearing, seeing, feeling, smelling and tasting? What do you think?

If Ayer is correct, religious statements are nonsense if they are referring to God defined in a traditional sense as infinite, impersonal and transcendent, because statements about God do not tell people anything about the world that is verifiable.

Thought Point

Atheism

Ayer also suggested that statements such as 'God does not exist' are meaningless as well. Can you think of the reason why?

Ayer also rejected any argument from religious experience. He accepted that people might claim to have experiences of God, but he argues that a person, such as St Paul, saying they have seen God is recounting a set of emotions that are religious. He suggested that the fact people have religious experiences raised interesting psychological questions, but because religious experiences are not verifiable Ayer rejected them as meaningful statements.

AYER'S SECOND EDITION

When *Language, Truth and Logic* was first published it was widely read and also criticised by a number of philosophers. Ayer responded to many of the criticisms of his theory of verification in the second edition of his book. It is worth noting a number of points he made:

- He rejected the use of 'putative statements'.
- He changed his definition of the principle of verification to: 'A statement is held to be literally meaningful if and only if it is either analytic or empirically verifiable' (*Language, Truth and Logic*).

Ayer changed the definition of verification because he concluded that his distinction between strong and weak verification was not a real distinction, as the strong form of verification could not apply to any statement, and Ayer had come to the conclusion that some statements can be conclusively verified. In particular, he referred to 'basic statements', by which he meant a 'single experience'. He observed that single experiences are what happens and when you have the experience it is a reality. You may not be able to describe it accurately, but the experience itself is verified by its occurrence.

He also rejected his earlier definition of weak verification as 'far too liberal, since it allows meaning to any statement whatsoever' (*Language, Truth and Logic*). To solve the problem with strong and weak verification Ayer suggested two new criteria: directly and indirectly verifiable.

Directly and indirectly verifiable

Ayer suggested that something is:

> directly verifiable if it is either itself an observation-statement, or is such that in conjunction with one or more observation-statements it entails at least one observation-statement which is not deducible from these premises alone. (*Language, Truth and Logic*)

By 'observation-statement' Ayer meant 'a statement which records an actual or possible observation' (*Language, Truth and Logic*). So, for Ayer, direct verification meant a statement that is verifiable by an observation. If you ask the question 'Are post boxes red?', you can verify the answer by observing post boxes.

By 'indirectly verifiable' Ayer meant a statement that is not directly verifiable or analytic and 'in conjunction with certain other premises it entails one or more directly verifiable statements which are not deducible from these other premises alone' (Language, Truth and Logic). One way to understand this is that a statement could be verified if other directly verifiable evidence could support it. For example, scientists predicted and demonstrated the existence of black holes in space. However, black holes in space cannot be directly observed; instead, scientists demonstrated their existence by looking at other evidence which suggested the existence of the thing that we call a black hole.

RESPONSES TO VERIFICATIONISM

There are many criticisms of verificationism, particularly strong verificationism, which is 'generally agreed to be false' (Swinburne, 'God-talk Is Not

Black holes

The reason why you can never see a black hole is that it has such a strong gravitational field that it sucks everything into it, even light. (Light has a mass – a very, very small mass.) As light cannot escape a black hole you cannot see the black hole, because you can only see when light enters your eye; this is a physical impossibility in the case of a black hole.

More about verification and Ayer

If you are interested in verification theory it is well worth reading a copy of Ayer's book *Language, Truth and Logic*. Make sure you read the second edition of the book. Ayer never altered the main text of his book; instead he added extra material to the second edition to respond to criticisms of the first edition. A helpful edition of *Language, Truth and Logic* with an introduction by Ben Rogers is published by Penguin.

Evidently Nonsense'). Whether verificationism makes God-talk meaningless is much debated:

- *Verificationism is unverifiable*
  Many philosophers have pointed out that claiming 'statements are only meaningful if verifiable by sense-observation' is itself unverifiable. You cannot demonstrate this principle by sense-observation.

- *God-talk is eschatologically verifiable*
  John Hick suggested that religion is not meaningless because its truth is verifiable in principle, thus meeting the conditions of verificationism.
  Hick said that the truth of God's existence is verifiable at the end of things (i.e. eschatologically). His story of the Celestial City illustrates this point. Hick imagined two travellers on the journey through life to the Celestial City. The journey is unavoidable. One traveller believes that there is a Celestial City at the end of the journey and views difficulties along the way as learning activities and good events as gifts from the ruler of the Celestial City. The other traveller does not believe there is a Celestial City. This traveller views good events as welcome and bad events as experiences that have to be endured. Whichever one is right at the end of the journey, their views could be verified. Thus Hick argues that religious statements are in principle verifiable.

- *Strong verification*
  Strong verification has been widely criticised for excluding many areas of knowledge. For example, it is not possible to talk meaningfully about history using the strong verification principles as no sense-observation can confirm historical events. Second, as indicated above, Swinburne has argued that strong verification excludes universal statements of any sort. For example, you cannot say water always boils at 100 degrees Celsius at standard temperature and pressure, because there is always the possibility of repeating the test one more time and obtaining a different result. It is worth remembering that A.J. Ayer modified his theory of verification in response to this criticism and stated that 'my "strong" sense of the term "verifiable" had no possible application, and in that case there was no need for me to qualify the other sense of "verifiable" as weak; for on my own showing it was the only sense in which any proposition could conceivably be verified' (*Language, Truth and Logic*).

- *The evidence problem*
  - The problem with weak verification concerns what evidence can count in the verification assessment. While Ayer rejected accounts of religious experience, other researchers have suggested that there

is clear evidence that such experiences happen and that a God causing the experience cannot be ruled out. Are religious experiences therefore a weak form of evidence?
- Richard Swinburne ('God-talk Is Not Evidently Nonsense') pointed out that there are many areas of debate where the problem would be getting people to agree what was admissible evidence to decide the matter. Swinburne refers to debates about the end of the world, the devil or *Poseidon*.

- *Meaningful but unverifiable*
  It is quite possible for a statement to be meaningful without being verifiable. Swinburne ('God-talk Is Not Evidently Nonsense') gives the example of toys in a cupboard. The toys only come out at night when no one observes them. The situation is meaningful even though it is fictitious and unverifiable. Another possible example is Schrödinger's cat. Schrödinger suggested that you imagine a cat in a box with a radioactive source. At any time the radioactive source could emit a radioactive particle that would kill the cat. Is the cat dead or alive? You cannot know. If you open the box to find out, you may trigger the release of the radioactive particle, thus killing the cat. Hence, whether the cat is alive or dead at any point is unverifiable.

FALSIFICATION

Falsification is a different approach to the question of language. Falsification addresses the question: when is a statement scientific as opposed to any other type of statement? One of the most well-known statements of falsification is that of Karl Popper who suggested:

> One can sum up all this by saying that *the criterion of the scientific status of a theory is its falsifiability, or refutability, or testability*. (*Conjectures and Refutations*)

Amongst the examples given by Popper is the comparison of Einstein's theory of gravity with astrology. Popper argued that Einstein's theory of gravity was scientific because it was potentially falsifiable. In other words, its truth or falseness could be tested against empirical observations of the universe. Astrology, on the other hand, was labelled as unscientific because:

> Astrologers were greatly impressed, and misled, by what they believed to be confirming evidence — so much so that they were quite

Falsification
The philosophical theory that an assertion is meaningless if there is no way in which it can be falsified. For example, 'Elves live in the forest but they only come out when no one is looking.'

unimpressed by any unfavourable evidence. Moreover, by making their interpretations and prophesies sufficiently vague they were able to explain away anything that might have been a refutation of the theory had the theory and the prophesies been more precise. In order to escape falsification they destroyed the testability of their theory. It is a typical soothsayer's trick to predict things so vaguely that the predictions can hardly fail: that they become irrefutable. (Popper, *Conjectures and Refutations*)

For Popper falsification was a way to 'demarcate' scientific statements from other kinds of statements. By 'demarcate' Popper meant clearly set apart scientific statements which are supported by some form of empirical evidence from other statements which are unscientific.

Popper himself stated that

It was the problem of drawing a line (as well as this can be done) between the statements, or systems of statements, of the empirical sciences, and all other statements — whether they are of a religious or of a metaphysical character, or simply pseudo-scientific. Years later — it must have been in 1928 or 1929 — I called this first problem of mine the *'problem of demarcation.'* The criterion of falsifiability is a solution to this problem of demarcation, for it says that statements or systems of statements, in order to be ranked as scientific, must be capable of conflicting with possible, or conceivable, observations. (*Conjectures and Refutations*)

Thus if applied to religious belief claims, falsification raises a question about the nature of the claims that religious people make. For example, if a religious person says 'God became incarnate in the person of Jesus' or 'God loves me', the question is whether this statement is 'scientific' or not. If the religious claims are scientific then it must be possible that the religious claims could conflict with sense observations and thus be undermined.

Thought Point

Scientific statements

Consider each of the following statements. Which ones are 'scientific' according to falsification theory? Which statements are not 'scientific'? Explain your answers.

continued opposite

- Unicorns are white.
- Harry Potter is a wizard.
- You exist.
- Water consists of atoms of hydrogen and oxygen.
- Tony Blair is a former prime minister of the United Kingdom of Great Britain and Northern Ireland.
- Chlorine is a halogen.
- Spiders are arachnids.

Falsification theory was famously discussed by Anthony Flew, R.M. Hare and Basil Mitchell in an article entitled 'Theology and Falsification: A Symposium' (Flew and MacIntyre (eds), *New Essays in Philosophical Theology*). Within the article, Flew, Hare and Mitchell present different analyses of falsification and its relationship to religious belief claims, and introduce three parables that are well known today: the explorers in the jungle; the university dons and the partisan.

Antony Flew suggested that believers will allow nothing to falsify their belief claims:

> Now it often seems to people who are not religious as if there was no conceivable event or series of events the occurrence of which would be admitted by sophisticated religious people to be a sufficient reason for conceding 'There wasn't a God after all.' (Flew and MacIntyre (eds), *New Essays in Philosophical Theology*)

Flew presented an analogy to illustrate this. Two explorers in the jungle find a clearing in which weeds and flowers grow. One of them suggests that there is a gardener who looks after the clearing (there are flowers there); the other suggests that there is not. The two explorers set a watch; they even use dogs to hunt for the gardener and put up an electric fence to detect anyone entering. No one is ever detected. One of the explorers says:

> 'But there is a gardener, invisible, intangible, insensible to electric shocks, a gardener who has no scent and makes no sound, a gardener who comes secretly to look after the garden which he loves.' At last the Sceptic despairs, 'But what remains of your original assertion? Just how does what you call an invisible, intangible, eternally elusive gardener differ from an imaginary gardener or even from no gardener at all?'

Flew's argument is that religious believers act in the same way as the believing explorer. Flew gives the example of saying God loves people, even if disaster happens. His argument is that people still go on believing in the loving God. No experience seems to falsify a religious believer's faith. Flew therefore argues that God-talk is meaningless because it is unfalsifiable, in like manner to the *eternally elusive* gardener in his analogy.

Flew suggested that God died a 'death by a thousand qualifications' ('Death by a Thousand Qualifications'). By this phrase, Flew meant that when a religious believer is challenged about the existence of God, or God's nature, their response is to modify the way they talk about God to respond to the challenge. Flew argues that believers end up modifying their statements about God so much when challenged that the statements no longer resemble the original claim about God – in other words, their belief in God dies a 'death by a thousand qualifications'. Study the Thought Point below to understand what Flew meant.

Thought Point

Death by qualification

1   What is the most obvious meaning of these attributes and statements about God?

   * God is all-knowing.
   * God is all-powerful.
   * God answers the prayers of his faithful.
   * God loves us.
   * God's creation is good.

2   What is the most obvious meaning of these statements? How do the following statements challenge the way you define the attributes of God in Question 1?

   * Human beings have free will.
   * God did not prevent Hurricane Katrina from happening.
   * People pray for healing and it does not happen.
   * Many evil people seem to have good lives, while good people suffer.
   * Nature is piteously indifferent to human beings' existence.

Author	Story	Outline of the story	Implication	Possible responses
Anthony Flew	Parable of the two explorers in the Jungle	One of the explorers repeatedly modifies the qualities he attributes to an alleged gardener who looks after the forest clearing. Flew used the parable to suggest that religious believers refuse to let their beliefs be falsified. Instead, when challenged, religious believers qualify their belief, altering it to avoid the criticism. Flew argues that eventually the original belief is lost, 'dying a death of a thousand qualifications'.	If Flew's analogy is an accurate description of religious belief this is a serious challenge to a believer's faith claims as it suggests that: 1 Faith claims are an incorrect and irrational interpretation of the world that goes against the evidence. 2 Religious believers refuse to accept that their beliefs are irrational as they keep qualifying them.	• Religious belief statements are potentially falsifiable. Religious believers do not continually qualify their beliefs. Instead, religious believers clarify and state their beliefs more clearly, e.g. the free will defence is an explanation of belief in God and free will; it cannot be dismissed as a qualification. • Peter Donovan noted that: 'The sense of knowing is never on its own a sufficient sign of knowledge . . . But if the sense of God fails, in the end, to count as knowledge of God, what is to be said about it? Is it of no further philosophical interest and to be discarded, like a pricked balloon, as being simply a great illusion? Nothing that has been said here leads to that conclusion. There is no justification for taking such an all-or-nothing view of religious experience.' (*Interpreting Religious Experience*)

continued overleaf

Author	Story	Outline of the story	Implication	Possible responses
R.M. Hare	Parable of the lunatic who believes the university staff are plotting to kill him	Hare uses the story to show that people have a way in which they see the world. Hare points out that *bliks* may be 'insane ones' or 'sane ones' but he also suggests, following David Hume, that there are no sense-observations available that will help resolve conflicting '*bliks*'. Equally, every person, whether they are atheist, theist, agnostic, verificationist or falsificationist, has a '*blik*' through which they view the world.	Hare's lunatic story does not help traditional religious belief claims. If religious beliefs are *bliks*, this suggests that religious beliefs are an interpretation of the world which could be sane or insane.	• Hare's lunatic story would match anti-realist views of religion as a form of life. • However, religious belief is more than just an approach to life. For many believers it is a belief in reality as it truly is. For traditional religious believers belief statements are not ways of seeing the world, but they are factual claims about how the world is and God's relationship to the world.
Basil Mitchell	The Partisan and the Stranger	Basil Mitchell suggests through the parable that there may be events or things which count against or in favour of a believer's '*blik*'. Second, Mitchell agrees with Flew that theological statements are 'assertions'. Mitchell concludes that religious believers' statements of belief could be: (1) 'Provisional hypotheses'; (2) 'significant articles of faith'; or (3) 'vacuous formulae'. Mitchell concludes that religious statements are not necessarily 'vacuous formulae'.	Mitchell's analogy suggests that religious beliefs are potentially at least statements about how the world is. If this is a correct view of religious belief statements it means that they are meaningful as any claim about how things are in the world is potentially falsifiable.·	• In some ways Mitchell's analogy leads one back to Flew's original issue – if religious statements are assertions about how the world is, they are meaningless, having died a death of a thousand falsifications. • However, a religious believer could equally well reply that religious beliefs are open to falsification and thus are meaningful.

ANTONY FLEW AND JOHN WISDOM

Antony Flew's example of the explorer in the garden was inspired by a similar story by John Wisdom. However, Wisdom uses his story to make a different point from Flew. Study the box below about John Wisdom and consider which story you find more persuasive.

Thought Point

John Wisdom and the gardener

John Wisdom's story about a garden suggested that two people were looking at an overgrown garden. One of the observers notes how uncared-for, overgrown and ill-kept the garden was. Plants and weeds both grow there. The other observer points out signs of order in the garden such as beds of flowers and suggests that there is a gardener. However, no test can show whether a gardener has or has not been at work.

John Wisdom's story was not written as a challenge to God's existence. Instead it suggests that religious language makes statements that are reasonable – the two people observing the garden are both making reasonable statements. However, just as they cannot verify whether a gardener has been at work, the existence or nature of God might be beyond our normal methods of verification; the question is irresolvable. If this is so, then the story may suggest that the existence or nature of God is a matter that is outside the scope of the traditional methods of scientific enquiry.

Think about:

- Whose story is more persuasive: Flew's or Wisdom's?
- Why could John Wisdom's story be used to challenge some conclusions people make using the verification principle but not the falsification principle?

Basil Mitchell, R.M. Hare and falsification

Basil Mitchell, R.M. Hare and Antony Flew famously debated falsification in a series of academic articles (Flew and MacIntyre (eds), *New Essays in Philosophical Theology*).

Hare used the example of a lunatic who believes that his teachers (dons) at university were trying to kill him. This is the way in which the

> **Stories to illustrate religious language**
>
> If you find stories like Wisdom's Garden or Flew's Jungle Explorers helpful ways to think about religious language, look up the articles by R.M. Hare and Basil Mitchell in the 'Further reading' section.

lunatic saw the world and nothing could change his view of the world. Hare coined the word '*blik*' to describe the way in which people see and interpret the world. The important characteristic of the *blik* is that it is not falsifiable and it does not make factual claims about the world that can be tested. No evidence or argument can demonstrate the falseness of a *blik*. If I have a *blik* that invisible Martians always help me when I am ill, this *blik* is untestable, unlike saying that water boils at 100 degrees Celsius.

Thought Point

Hare's lunatic – in Hare's own words

A certain lunatic is convinced that all dons want to murder him. His friends introduce him to all the mildest and most respected dons that they can find, and after each of them has retired, they say, 'You see, he doesn't really want to murder you; he spoke to you in a most cordial manner; surely you are convinced now?' But the lunatic replies, 'Yes, but that was only his diabolical cunning; he's really plotting against me the whole time, like the rest of them; I know it, I tell you.' However many kindly dons are produced, the reaction is still the same. (Flew and MacIntyre (eds), *New Essays in Philosophical Theology*)

- What do you think is the point of Hare's story?
- Think about Hare's example to illustrate the concept of '*blik*' – the lunatic student. Do you think this example is helpful for a religious believer arguing that religious beliefs are meaningful? Think of some reasons to support your answer.

Hare added that there is an important difference between an insane *blik* such as the lunatic student had and a sane *blik*. Although *bliks* are unfalsifiable, he argues that holding the right *blik* matters, which leads him to comment on Flew's jungle analogy:

It is because I mind very much about what goes on in the garden in which I find myself that I am unable to share the explorer's detachment. (Flew and MacIntyre (eds), *New Essays in Philosophical Theology*)

Hare made a number of points about *bliks* and his parable of the lunatic:

- *Bliks* are ways of seeing the world and the difference between different people's *bliks* cannot be solved by observations of what the world is like. For example, if I believe that water sprites makes streams flow downhill and this is my *blik*, and someone else's *blik* is that water flows downhill because of gravity, the difference between the two *bliks* cannot be conclusively solved by observing the world.

- Hare suggested that Flew makes a mistake by treating religious statement as though they are scientific explanations.

In reply, Flew accepted Hare's idea of *bliks* but he added that Christianity does not appear to be a *blik*, as it makes claims about the universe which seem to be what Flew called 'assertions'. 'Assertions' are claims such as 'God created human beings distinct from others species': Christians say they are not just claiming that this is a *blik*. They are saying that God really did this and by implication this claim is testable or falsifiable.

Thought Point

Basil Mitchell's stranger – in his own words

In time of war in an occupied country, a member of the resistance one night meets a stranger who impresses him deeply. They spend that night in conversation. The stranger tells the partisan that he himself is on the side of the resistance – and indeed that he is in command of it, and urges the partisan to have faith in him no matter what happens . . .

. . . sometimes the stranger is seen helping members of the resistance, and the partisan is grateful and says to his friends, 'He is on our side.'

Sometimes he is seen in the uniform of the police handing over patriots to the occupying power. On these occasions his friends murmur against him, but the partisan stills says, 'He is on our side.' He stills believes that, in spite of appearances, the stranger did not deceive him. . . . Sometimes his friends, in exasperation, say, 'Well, what would he have to do for you to admit that you were wrong and that he is not on our side?' But the partisan will not answer. He will not consent to put the stranger to the test. (Flew and MacIntyre (eds), *New Essays in Philosophical Theology*)

- How do you think the story of the partisan and the stranger relates to a believer's faith in God?
- If you were the partisan, would you continue to have faith in the stranger? Explain your answer.
- Is the story helpful?

Mitchell suggested that religious believers do accept evidence that counts against their ideas. He gives the example of the problem of evil and suggests that religious believers do accept that this is a problem, but also that they refuse to doubt their belief because they are committed believers. Mitchell uses the example of a stranger helping the resistance in the war. In his story not all the stranger's behaviour is explainable or understandable, and Mitchell concludes that this resembles God's apparent actions. Mitchell concludes that belief in God can be a 'significant article of faith', although the same evidence might lead other people to reject belief in God. Mitchell argues that believers have to take care that religious beliefs are not just:

> vacuous formulae (expressing, perhaps, a desire for reassurance) to which experience makes no difference and which makes no difference to life. (Flew and MacIntyre (eds), *New Essays in Philosophical Theology*)

In response, Antony Flew agreed with Basil Mitchell's comments about the way theologians address issues such as the problem of evil. However, he argued that, ultimately, if you keep questioning a theologian, explanations have to be qualified:

> I still think that in the end, if relentlessly pursued, he will have to resort to the avoiding action of *qualification*. And there lies that death by a thousand qualifications, which would, I agree, constitute 'a failure in faith as well as in logic'. (Flew and MacIntyre (eds), *New Essays in Philosophical Theology*)

Responses to falsification

• *What can be falsified?*
Swinburne (*The Coherence of Theism*) argues that factual statements can be falsified. However, some existential statements cannot be falsified but this does not stop the statements being meaningful. His toy cupboard story illustrates this point.

Hare has suggested that while the falsification principle could apply to factual statements, it does not apply to existential statements. A Christian's *blik* could include God as Creator and sustainer, and the whole world is seen with this idea in mind. Because *bliks* are a set of values, they are not matters of fact that are falsifiable in the way science is (see Hare's story of the lunatic on p. 392).

- *Verification and falsification*
  Ayer rejected the ideas behind falsification, arguing that statements cannot be conclusively falsified any more than statements can be conclusively verified:

  > Nor can we accept the suggestion that a sentence should be allowed to be factually significant if, and only if, it expresses something which is definitely confutable by experience. (Ayer, *Language, Truth and Logic*)

  He suggested that evidence may strongly suggest that a statement is false, but this does not make it logically impossible that a statement is true. For example, if I claim that unicorns visit my garden when nothing and no one is observing them, evidence strongly suggests, beyond all reasonable doubt, that my claim is false. However, the logical possibility that unicorns visit my garden when unobserved remains. This leads Ayer to argue that weak verification is the appropriate method for assessing which statements are meaningful.

  However, it could be argued that Ayer's claim about Popper's falsification slightly misrepresents Popper's views as falsification is 'the criterion of the scientific status of a theory is its falsifiability, or refutability, or testability' (Popper, *Conjectures and Refutations*). Popper did not say that a theory had to be 'definitely confutable by experience'. Popper himself suggested that

  > Confirming evidence should not count *except when it is the result of a genuine test of the theory*; and this means that it can be presented as a serious but unsuccessful attempt to falsify the theory. (*Conjectures and Refutations*)

CONCLUSION

The principles of verification and falsification both present strong challenges to religious belief. However, they are not the only ways in which to assess religious language, and for many believers the language they use to talk about God is symbolic, mythological or just different from other language. Therefore, believers might claim that the principles of falsification and verification are not relevant challenges to religious language as the nature of religious language is different from that supposed in the verification and falsification debates.

Ayer and falsification

Make sure you do not claim that Ayer was arguing against the work of Flew. Ayer's comments about what became known as the falsification debate were in response to the earlier but also significant work of the philosopher Karl Popper.

Hick and eschatological verification

Beware of using the concept of eschatological verification from John Hick's writings when discussing falsification. Hick pointed out that claims about the afterlife are not open to falsification even if they are eschatologically verifiable.

More details about John Hick's ideas may be found in Chapter 11 on life after death.

Ludwig Wittgenstein (1889–1951)

Ludwig Wittgenstein was one of the most important and influential philosophers of the twentieth century. He was born in Vienna to a wealthy Austrian family. Originally he studied engineering in Berlin and by 1908 he was working on

continued overleaf

The following sections of this chapter explore some of these other ways of understanding religious language.

WITTGENSTEIN AND LANGUAGE GAMES

Wittgenstein suggested that the meaning of words is determined by the Language Game of which the words are part. By this he meant that a word's meaning comes from the circumstance in which it is uttered and the meaning of other words used alongside it. For Wittgenstein words perform a function in a language; they do not just signify an object.

He famously compared the way language works with the game of chess. In chess, rules state how all the pieces can move. However, to talk about how the 'queen' or 'pawns' should move only makes sense in the context of the game of chess. Wittgenstein claimed that the rules of syntax and grammar of a language could function like those of the game of chess. If you use words in a way that does not follow the particular rules of the language them you will be talking 'nonsense'.

For example, to say that the king can move one square in any direction is an instruction that only makes sense in chess, not in any other game. Similarly, to say that the sky is blue makes sense in the English language – it would not make sense in Spanish, since the words 'the', 'is', 'sky' and 'blue' are not part of the Language Game of Spanish. The Language Game has a particular context, and it is in this context that the Language Game makes sense.

By using the phrase 'Language Games' Wittgenstein did not mean that the way words are used and have meaning rigidly follows rules in the way that pieces have to follow rules in a chess game. Instead, he used Language Games as a way of expressing the idea that words only make sense in the context of a background of other words that all belong to the same 'Language Game'. Think of the way words can be used in a very technical way in certain areas of work, which give words a different meaning from ordinary life; one example could be the way 'philosophy' uses words like 'necessary' and 'proposition' in ways that often differ from the everyday usage of these words. For Wittgenstein, language can only be used meaningfully if it is used in the appropriate way in the particular Language Game in question. It is important to note that the Language Game is the reality of our understanding of the world. You cannot escape the Language Games – the Language Games are the reality.

Wittgenstein's Language Games do not refer to language as a whole. Instead he uses the idea of Language Games very loosely to refer to the different way in which language can be used. For example, in the *Philosophical Investigations* he suggests that there can be language games concerned with expressing sensations, storytelling, telling jokes, thanking,

the development of jet engines at Manchester University. He later spent time studying with Bertrand Russell at Cambridge and he developed friendships with G.E. Moore and J.M. Keynes.

Wittgenstein's interest in philosophy really started to develop in 1913 when he lived in an isolated hut in Norway until the start of the First World War. During the war he served in the Austrian Artillery. He was later captured and during his time as a prisoner of war he wrote the notes that would later form his famous book *Tractatus Logico-Philosophicus*.

Having spent some years working as a teacher in Austria, which he did not enjoy, he worked for a time as a monastery gardener.

By 1930 he was again working on philosophy and gave a series of lectures at Cambridge University which became world famous as Wittgenstein developed his philosophy, including the Language Games concept that is important in debates concerning religious language. In 1939 he was appointed as the Professor of Philosophy, succeeding G.E. Moore.

He died in 1951 of cancer.

asking, giving and even cursing. For Wittgenstein, Language Games are a way of expressing the idea that words have meaning only in the context of other words and the context and way in which they are uttered. Speaking is an activity according to Wittgenstein which he called 'a form of life' (Wittgenstein, *Philosophical Investigations*).

Elsewhere, Wittgenstein also says that words function rather like 'tools' by which he means that words can be used in the world and can change it in just the same way that a tool such as a drill could be used in the world and can change the world – it makes holes.

Form of life is a non-technical term which is used in various ways by Wittgenstein. For him, it implied the sociological, historical, linguistic, physiological and behavioural determinants that comprise the matrix within which a language has meaning.

One very important implication of Wittgenstein's work is that language is not private. A Language Game is something that is shared and used by groups of people. Language Games can, of course, develop, evolve, change and drop out of use, but as long as people are using the language, the game exists and, of course, to people using language in that Language Game, the language is meaningful. This is important as it challenges the idea of many philosophers that you can work out how things are by starting from yourself and then deduce how things are. Descartes' famous foundation of knowledge derives from his conclusion that 'I think therefore I am.' Wittgenstein's philosophy implies that no language game is private – it is always shared and therefore Descartes' 'I think therefore I am' statement is actually not private to him alone but is already part of a shared Language Game.

Second, Wittgenstein rejected his earlier empiricist approach to language. This distinguishes him from Logical Positivists such as A.J. Ayer who believed that statements are meaningful only if they are verifiable with reference to a 'sense experience'.

> **Wittgenstein's early philosophy**
>
> Wittgenstein's philosophy went through a number of different stages including earlier theories of language focusing on his Picture Theory and his Theory of Atoms. These ideas were later modified or in some cases rejected. The Language Games theory is only one part of his philosophical work. If you would like to know more about his work see the 'Further reading' section of this chapter.

Thought Point

To which Language Games do the following words belong?

Off-side	Ouch
Check-mate	Touch down
¡Que Suerte!	Hi
Bullseye	Good morning
One hundred and eighty!	A levels

Grammar
The field of linguistics that covers the rules governing the use of language.

Syntax
The study of the principles and rules for constructing sentences.

Language Games and religious language

If the concept of Language Games is applied to religious language it reveals a very different theory of meaning from verification theory. First, religious terminology is a Language Game, and so the language of religious belief, such as 'God', 'omnipotence', and 'perfection', is understandable and meaningful to people who participate in the religious belief Language Game. There is no reason in Wittgenstein's theory to suppose that one particular Language Game is preferable to another. If a religious believer says 'God exists and is a reality in my life' – this has particular meaning and significance to the person who utters it. However, a person who does not share this belief will find difficult, if not impossible, to understand.

The implication of Wittgenstein's Language Games is that you need to be a member of a religious tradition fully to understand the meaning, significance, feeling and aura around a word or expression of belief. For example, 'God loves me' has a particularly deep and significant meaning that may have a distinct resonance for a religious believer while for an atheist 'God loves me' is a statement made by religious people, but the expression lacks the significance that it has for religious people.

The problem with theories like verification when applied to religious belief is that they are a applying a Language Game that is more appropriate for discussing the physical world than believers' statements about God. Thus, according to this way of thinking, verificationism is neither a helpful or meaningful way to understand religious belief.

A real strength of Wittgenstein's theory is that it gives believers a way to express the meaningfulness of religious language at the same time as explaining why talk of God's love or God's existence does not have the same significance or meaning for an atheist.

Thought Point

God does not reveal himself in the world . . . it is not how things are in the world that is mystical, but that it exists. (Wittgenstein, *Tractatus Logico-Philosophicus*)

What do you think this statement means?
Is Language Games theory helpful to religious believers when they discuss religious language?

Challenges to Wittgenstein's Language Games

While Language Games theory may appear to be helpful to understanding religious belief it also removes the link between claims made with language and empirical evidence. In this sense, does Wittgenstein's view lead to religious beliefs being understood in an anti-realist manner? Clearly many believers would claim that some statements they make are true propositions that refer to how things are empirically or metaphysically.

However, it could equally well be argued that religious belief is an activity. It involves sharing a way of life and a language and a manner of speaking about the world and our place in it. In this sense it can be argued that Wittgenstein does capture the essence of what it is to be religious: for many religious believers, religion is not a philosophical enquiry into the nature of belief, but a shared community life, culture, identity and practices, including baptism in Christianity or Salah in Islam, i.e. a form of life.

> ### Anti-realism
>
> In analytic philosophy, the term anti-realism describes any position involving either the denial of an objective reality or the denial that verification-transcendent statements are either true or false.

Thought Point

Read the extract from 'The Groundlessness of Religious Belief' by Norman Malcolm and complete the following questions:

1   Identify Malcolm's argument.
2   Do you agree with Malcolm's argument? Justify your view with reasons.
3   Reflect on the passage below and the various theories of religious language you have studied. Which of the theories of religious language are most persuasive? Why?

In his final notebooks Wittgenstein wrote that it is difficult '*to realize the groundlessness of our believing*' (*On Certainty*). He was thinking of how much mere acceptance, on the basis of no evidence, forms our lives.

The obsessive concern with the proofs [of the existence of God] reveals the assumption that in order for religious belief to be intellectually respectable it ought to have a rational justification. That is the misunderstanding. It is like the idea that we are not justified in relying on memory until memory has been proved reliable. . . .

Present-day academic philosophers are far more prone to challenge the credentials of religion than of science, probably for a number of reasons. One may be the illusion that science can justify its own framework. Another is the fact that science is a vastly greater force in our culture. Still another may be that, by and large, religion is to university people an alien form of life. They do not participate in it and do not understand what it is all about.

THE *VIA NEGATIVA*

The *Via Negativa* suggests that people can only talk about God in negative terms. God is transcendent so you cannot say what God is. However, you can clearly say what God is not: God is not a human being because God is transcendent, so God cannot have a body. Equally, Christians believe that God is good. So, for example, they may not know exactly what they mean when they say God is good, but they know for sure that God is not evil.

The title *Via Negativa* reflects this approach to describing God. It literally means the *negative way* because God can only be described in terms of what God is not. The ideas behind the *Via Negativa* come from the philosophy of Plotinus in the second century CE. Plotinus was at the centre of a movement that renewed interest in the philosophy of Plato. In Plato's philosophy the highest Form is the Form of the Good. In Plotinus' thinking the Form of the Good is linked with God. Because of this link God is seen as being completely separate and beyond this world, just as the Form of the Good is the highest Form of Good, separate from the other Forms of the Good.

The key idea of people who support the *Via Negativa* is that, ultimately, language cannot directly describe God. God is beyond human comprehension, totally ineffable. People who believe in the *Via Negativa* are not saying that you cannot say things about God, such as God is good or God is all-knowing. The problem is that ultimately this language does not tell people about God, because our knowledge of goodness is that of a human being. God's goodness is greater than human concepts. If we talk about God being all-knowing we can debate what this means, but in the end we cannot know for certain what it is to be all-knowing.

Pseudo-Dionysius suggested that if we talk about God being, for example, Good, we then have to say God is not Good, because we do not really know what it means to say that God is Good. Pseudo-Dionysius stated ('The Mystical Theology') that God is 'beyond assertion' and 'beyond denial' – meaning that whatever you say about God ultimately does not tell us about God, and you cannot say absolutely what God is not.

The philosopher Brian Davies (*Philosophy of Religion: A Guide and Anthology*), quoting Pseudo-Dionysius ('The Mystical Theology'), stated that:

> He [God] is beyond assertion since he is 'the perfect and unique cause of all things'. He is beyond denial by virtue of his 'pre-eminently simple and absolute nature, free of every limitation, beyond every limitation'.

Within Christianity the idea of a *Via Negativa* to talk about God has been very influential. Not only does it emphasise the transcendence and otherness of God; the language has also been used by mystics and people who have religious experiences to describe the ineffable nature of their experiences.

Thought Point

Via Negativa and ineffable religious experiences

Read the following extract from the autobiography of St Teresa of Ávila. What difficulty does she have talking about her religious experience on the feast of St Peter? How does the language show the ideas of the *Via Negativa*?

> I went at once to my confessor, to tell him about it. He asked me in what form I had seen Him. I told him that I had not seen Him at all. Then he asked me how I knew it was Christ. I told him that I did not know how, but that I could not help realising that He was beside me, and that I saw and felt this clearly. (*The Autobiography of St Teresa of Ávila*, trans. and ed. E. Allison Peers)

NB: If you want to read more about St Teresa's experience, look at Chapter 13 on 'Religious Experience'.

What is God?

The *Via Negativa*'s argument that you can only describe God in negative ways leaves open the question of what God is. In particular, Flew's story of the explorers in the jungle suggests that if it cannot clearly be stated what is being talked about, how can anyone be sure that there is a 'something' to be talked about, rather than just nothing? If God is not evil, not hurtful, not malicious, not a person, not in time and so on, is God perhaps not anything?

SIGNS AND SYMBOLS

An alternative way to talk about God is to use symbols. In all religious traditions there are symbols that communicate beliefs about God to people. For example, in Christianity the crucifix is a prominent symbol. In the Anglican and Catholic Churches, a bishop carries a stick called a crozier that is curved at the end. The crozier is modelled on a shepherd's crook or staff

Maimonides

Maimonides was a Jewish philosopher of the twelfth century. In his writings he emphasised the use of negative terminology and language to describe God. His book *The Guide for the Perplexed* pointed out that human beings can know that God exists but not know anything about God, because God is not like human beings. For example, God does not feel emotion. Maimonides suggested that this way of talking about God is found in the Jewish Scriptures, where God is described as being 'I am who I am' (Exodus 3): he is beyond any description.

Dionysius who?

Not much is known about the early Church writer called Dionysius. Originally people thought that he was the same Dionysius who was a friend of Paul. Dionysius, a Greek, is a

continued overleaf

person mentioned in the Acts of the Apostles. However, more modern theologians have shown conclusively that the writings linked with the name Dionysius the Areopagite are much later in origin than the time of the apostles. The style they are written in is different from the Greek of the first century CE. Today, Dionysius the Areopagite is often called Pseudo-Dionysius. *Pseudo* is the Greek word for 'false'. After all, the writer is not the same person as the Dionysius of the Acts of the Apostles.

Symbol

Used in religious thought to indicate something which points people to God and also presents something about God to people.

Guernica by Picasso

This famous painting is on display in the Reina Sofia Museum, Madrid. The original is well worth visiting if you are ever in Madrid. Information about the picture and images of it may be found in many art books or on the internet at http://en.wikipedia.org/wiki/Guernica_(painting).

and, for these Christians, symbolises the role of the bishop as a successor of the apostles who is to feed Jesus' flock.

However, it is not just objects which communicate beliefs about God. Various forms of religious action or clothing can be symbolic. In many religious traditions, ritual actions, such as kneeling and standing at certain times when praying in a religious service, indicate worship and submission to God. In Islam the performance of Salah involves following a symbolic pattern of actions while praying, which requires kneeling and standing.

Often the words *sign* and *symbol* are used interchangeably. However, within religious thinking the two are often distinguished. A *sign* is often seen as something which points you in a certain direction or indicates something, just as a road sign does. A *symbol* is something which not only points you in the right direction, but it also communicates a much greater understanding of God than can be put into words. To a Christian the crucifix is symbolic; it not only reminds Christians of Jesus' death on a cross, but it also carries with it the deeper Christian understanding of Jesus' death as a sacrifice or act of redemption.

Paul Tillich was a twentieth-century philosopher and theologian who is famously associated with the use of symbols to describe God. Tillich argued that religious language is symbolic, by which he meant that religious symbols communicate the most significant beliefs and values of human beings. Symbols communicate something which it is often difficult to put into words. In every Roman Catholic church there is a lighted candle near the tabernacle which symbolises the presence of God within the tabernacle. The candle has meaning to Catholics and communicates the idea of the sacred presence of God. The meaning of symbols derives from the culture in which they originate. To a Catholic the lighted tabernacle candle has a sacred and significant meaning. However, this symbol does not resonate with non-Catholics – to a non-Catholic the tabernacle candle is just what it is said to be: a candle. Non-religious symbols function in the same way. The famous painting called *Guernica* by Picasso expresses a view of the Spanish Civil War. To non-Spaniards the painting is an interesting example of painting in the style called *Cubism*. However, to many Spanish people this picture is much more than a painting; it communicates many feelings, values, beliefs and thoughts regarding the Spanish Civil War.

God, in Tillich's thinking, is defined as the *ground of being*. For Tillich, God is the basis of all that exists and also the meaning behind all that exists. For this reason Tillich argues that the *ground of being* must be the ultimate concern of people; material possessions and ideas cannot replace God.

The *ground of being* cannot be comprehended or known in a personal way, but is known through symbols. Symbols include the major theological ideas such as atonement, sacrifice and eternal life. Jesus' life and work thus function as symbols that can reveal the ground of being.

Tillich suggested that, just as the meaning of a symbol originates in a particular society; it can also lose its meaning in a society. He argued that you cannot destroy a symbol; this may be seen clearly in the efforts of dictators to destroy religious and national symbols. These activities have rarely succeeded, and often the support for a symbol has become a sign of resistance. An example of this is the wearing of a crucifix in countries where Christianity is oppressed.

However, as Tillich noted, symbols do lose their meaning, or they can be reinterpreted and come to mean something different. The Hindu symbol of the Swastika was adopted by the Nazi Party in Germany, and in Western European cultures today the Swastika is normally associated with Nazis, not Hindu beliefs.

Tillich gave the example of the Virgin Birth – he suggested that it symbolised the purity of Mary from sin, but for Protestants it had lost its meaning; prayers about Mary were rejected, while on the other hand the Virgin Birth is important to Catholics in a symbolic and/or literal sense.

One difficulty with symbols is that they can be interpreted in different ways by different generations or groups of people. The Adam and Eve story in Genesis 2–3 is an example of a story which is interpreted literally by many people, symbolically by others and as meaningless by some. For some fundamentalist Christians, Adam and Eve's existence is a matter of historical fact; it is not symbolic. For other Christians the story of Adam and Eve is symbolic of the condition of human beings and their state of sin. For others, such as atheists, the Adam and Eve story can be interpreted as being of historical interest, but not of any symbolic value today.

In particular, Tillich suggested that symbols, unlike signs, *participate in* the thing which they point to. So, if the crucifix is symbolic of the significance of Jesus' death, it somehow *participates* in that event. By this Tillich meant that the symbol somehow represents the event and gives access to a deeper level of understanding of the event. Tillich suggested that one way to understand this is to think of music, which can communicate with people on a different level compared to words. Music can be a form of expression; it can capture the mood of the moment as well as communicating feelings and beliefs.

Thought Point

How do you interpret the Bible?

How would you interpret these stories? Are the stories symbolic or literal? What is the significance of these stories for people today?

Music time

Listen to one of the following pieces of music (all readily available online) and try to describe the mood of the piece and what you think the piece communicates:

- *The Ride of the Valkyrie* from the Ring Cycle by Wagner.
- The opening or another part of *The Gadfly Suite* by Shostakovich.
- An extract from *The Dream of Gerontius* by Edward Elgar.
- *In the Hall of the Mountain King* from the *Peer Gynt Suite* by Edvard Grieg.

continued overleaf

- The Wedding at Cana (John 2)
- The Crossing of the Red Sea (Exodus)
- The Great Flood (Genesis 6–9)
- The Cure of the Paralytic (Mark 2: 1–12)
- The Transfiguration of Jesus (Mark 9)
- The Calming of the Storm (Mark 4)

How can a symbol participate in something?

Some philosophers have suggested that it is not entirely clear what participating in a symbol means.

Many Christians do not think that all religious language is symbolic. Instead they would argue that statements such as God is good, just, benevolent or all-powerful have a meaning that is not just symbolic. Furthermore, many religious people take stories from their religious tradition literally. Within the Christian tradition there are many Christians who argue that the creation stories are true in some sense, as well as communicating beliefs in a symbolic way. Additionally, there is no way of knowing whether symbols can ever communicate any truths about the nature of God as this nature cannot be known directly. If statements such as 'God is love' are to be understood symbolically, what does it exactly mean and how can it hope to convey any understanding of what God's love is?

Myth
A story which communicates the values and/or ultimate beliefs of a culture or society.

MYTH

The word 'myth' is used in a variety of ways. For some people 'myth' indicates that a story is fictional and untrue, the type of story that we tell to children. Fables would fit this interpretation of myth. However, the meaning of myth both historically and in religious thinking is much more significant than the idea of a fable or fictional story. For religious people, a myth communicates a particular worldview – the set of values and beliefs a person or group have about the world. This worldview will cover a particular group's response to the ultimate questions about life, death, goodness and evil.

The importance of myths is that they communicate truths – the values of a society. This may be seen in stories such as those of Ancient Greek culture; the stories of people such as Hercules or the behaviour of the gods such as Hera and Zeus tell people about the value system of the Ancient Greek culture from which these stories emerge. Equally, there are myths found in most cultures around the world.

There are many different myths. Commentators such as Peter Vardy (*Religious Language and Virtue Ethics*) have observed that the same ideas and values are communicated in myths from all sorts of different cultures around the world. Creation myths, stories of virgin births and great floods are found in many different cultures.

For Christians today, myths communicate the values of Christianity as well as the response of Christians to some of the ultimate questions in life and to God. Myths such as the Genesis creation stories communicate a deep and real awareness of God as Creator and of human beings' place in creation. Myths are important, as they preserve and hand on the cultural identity of a group in story form. The fact that a myth is a form of story makes it retellable and easier to communicate than, for example, a philosophical theory.

Since myths communicate the identity, experience and values of a community, they are not concerned with the literal truth of the story. There is much debate among some Christians today concerning the literal truth (or not) of the Genesis creation stories. The mythological nature of the story means that the values it communicates are what are really important. Whether a myth is literally true is an interesting question about the historical origins of the myth, but it in some way overlooks the function of myths – to communicate values that preserve identity.

However, there is one way in which the origin of myth does matter. If a myth is just a made-up story like a fable, then it does not communicate any truths about God; it is a fictional story. If, on the other hand, a myth is the expression of values in story form, then myths point, like symbols, beyond themselves to a different reality. In the case of religious myths, the myth may point to and reveal something about God, in like manner to a symbol. The historical truth or not of events recorded in a myth does not stop a myth communicating values to people.

During the nineteenth and early twentieth centuries attempts were made to demythologise myths. The aim of this movement was to remove mythological elements and imagery with the aim of revealing the eternal truths or values communicated by a story, or rather the existential religious experience. Rudolph Bultmann, for example, carried out much work on the New Testament. One aspect of his work was an attempt to remove the supernatural view of the world of the New Testament. This supernatural view of the world referred to the miracles and other occurrences in the text that appear to conflict with modern science.

Ultimately the attempt to demythologise myths came to a halt, because the significance of myths came to be seen as the fact that they communicate values and beliefs in story form. The truths are thus expressed through the story; they are not so clearly separated from the story. However, there is little doubt that the imagery of myths does comes from their culture of origin. There are many myths; for example, the story of Noah and the Flood

> **Myths and Paul Tillich**
>
> If you would like to investigate symbols and myths in relation to Christianity, a good book to look at is *Dynamics of Faith* by Paul Tillich.

(Genesis 6–9) in the Jewish Scriptures, or the account of the Flood in the *Epic of Gilgamesh*. The similarities between such stories are striking. In the case of the Flood story, one possible origin of the story of the Flood is the formation of the Mediterranean Sea. What are now called the Atlas Mountains originally kept the Atlantic Ocean out of the Mediterranean Sea. However, the Atlantic Ocean eventually overcame the barrier presented by the Atlas Mountains and the whole of the Mediterranean Basin was flooded; remains of communities have been found at the bottom of the Mediterranean Sea by archaeologists.

Issues raised by myths

- *What qualifies as a myth?*
  If myths communicate the value system of a community, the myth that is dominant is passed on. A problem arises if there are competing myths that all claim to communicate the truth. There are no agreed criteria for judging which myth communicates truth. Equally, classifying a story as a myth is a statement about the importance of a story. The definition of a story as a myth can therefore be a matter of great debate.

- *How do myths communicate values and truths?*
  Like symbolic language, mythical language causes problems for some believers as it undermines events which many see as historical, such as the birth of Jesus and his resurrection which are understood as revealing Christ to be literally the Son of God. However, just because a myth is not literally true does not mean that it cannot convey an objective truth and point to a higher reality. However, how can we be certain that the myth is communicating the right truth, and wouldn't it be better to make a clear statement of a truth that could be assessed rationally and so proved to be true or false?

  For some people, the fact that truths are communicated in mythological form suggests an evasion from clearly stating values for rational assessment. It is certainly the case that the understanding of the values communicated by myths can change subtly with time. For example, the creation story (Genesis 1) has often been interpreted by Christians as giving humans authority over the Earth to 'dominate' it.

  In more recent years the word 'dominate' has been interpreted as 'stewardship over creation'; this change has partly resulted in growing environmental awareness. If the meaning of a myth does change, can myths communicate 'values' that are eternal truths?

AQUINAS AND ANALOGY

Thomas Aquinas approached religious language in a very different way from the verificationists; he suggested that religious language is meaningful. Second, Aquinas rejected the approach of the *Via Negativa*, partly because it did not say enough about what God is. Aquinas' approach to religious language focuses on the use of analogy.

Aquinas' starting point is to consider the *Via Negativa* as used by Pseudo-Dionysius and Maimonides. Aquinas rejected negative use of language to describe God, since it does not say anything directly about God, and also because, he argues, when believers say 'the living God' (McDermott, *Thomas Aquinas: Selected Philosophical Writings*) they mean more than 'God is not dead.' Aquinas suggested that language means something concrete when applied to God:

> In regard to what they express, these words apply literally to God . . .
> But as regards their manner of expressing it, they don't apply literally
> to God; for their manner of expression is appropriate only to creatures
> (McDermott, *Thomas Aquinas*)

However, he did not suggest that language means the same when applied to God as it does when applied to human beings.

If you say God is Good, does this mean that God is good like a human being? Aquinas' answer was 'no'. Quite clearly God is Good but in a different way from human beings. Goodness in human beings is a label that is used to describe certain types of moral behaviour. God is not Good solely like a human being as, according to Aquinas, God is pure goodness and does not change, and hence using the word 'good' is not about judging God's actions. God does not act as this involves change. Instead, God is just Good. For Aquinas, God's goodness is higher than that of a human being. He suggested that God is Good, but what human beings cannot explain is the way in which God is Good, because human words can only describe the physical world experienced by human beings in a literal way.

Using words in a literal way to describe God is known as *univocal language*. By 'univocal' philosophers mean that a word is applied to two different things but it means the same when applied to both. So, for example, if we said:

- Agamemnon is the name of a Greek warrior.
- The Lord is a warrior.

we are using the word *warrior* to mean exactly the same thing. Aquinas rejects this view precisely because God cannot be a warrior in the same way

Univocal language
Words have the same meaning when applied to different objects or things (e.g. Liz is fat, Mark is fat, the pig is fat).

as a human being, because God is not a human being, nor does God have a body.

Aquinas did not want to reject the use of human terminology to describe God. But he did not believe that *equivocal language* could be used to describe God either. By equivocal language philosophers mean that you use the same word in different ways when applied to different things. For example:

Equivocal language
The use of the same word to mean completely different things when applied to different objects. For example, the word *banger* can mean: (1) a sausage; (2) a firework; (3) an old car in poor condition.

- What a racket[?]

The word *racket* could mean a tennis racket (in American English); equally it could mean that there is lot of noise. These two possible meanings of *racket* are examples of equivocal language. The two ways in which the word *racket* may be used are completely different.

Aquinas rejects equivocal language for describing God precisely because it would prevent a person from making any statements of fact about God. If you said God is Good, it would not mean that God is Good in any way a human being understands, in which case it is utterly meaningless to a human being to say God is Good. Aquinas argued that this contradicted the Christian belief that God can be known from creation and also from what Paul said (Romans 1: 20).

Thought Point

Equivocal language and the Five Ways

Think about how Aquinas' rejection of equivocal language relates to his arguments from cosmology and design.

Aquinas uses analogy to talk about God. An analogy is a comparison between two (or more) things in which the first, simpler thing that is understood is used to help explain the more complex thing that is in some way similar. For example, the human brain could be compared to a computer – the analogy is to compare the human brain to a computer.

Analogies rely on the fact that there is some point of comparison which links the two or more things in the analogy. For Aquinas, analogy may be used to describe God because God is revealed through creation.

Aquinas suggests that when words such as good or just are used to describe God, they are being used analogically. Aquinas uses analogy in two ways, called *analogy of attribution* and *analogy of proportion*.

Analogy of attribution

By *analogy of attribution* Aquinas meant that words such as 'just' may be applied to God and human beings. Aquinas suggested that when we use words such as 'good' or 'just', we are saying that a person has the quality of being good or just. Brian Davies (*An Introduction to the Philosophy of Religion*) gave a very helpful example:

* The bread is good.
* The baker is good.

The word 'good' is used in both cases and has a similar but not the same meaning. Bread can be good – soft, tasty, light. Saying the baker is good does not mean the baker is soft and tasty; instead it is saying that the baker has the qualities necessary to be a good baker.

Aquinas argued that, because God created the world, God is revealed through it. This gives a point of comparison. We can know what it is for a person to be 'good' or 'wise' or 'powerful'. From the ways in which God is revealed we can use words like 'good', 'wise' and 'powerful' to describe God because we can know from the way God is revealed in the world that God is 'Good'. However, what it means for God to be 'Good' is unclear, just as saying the baker is 'good' because he bakes 'good' bread does not make clear what exactly it means for the baker to be 'good', but we deduce from the bread that the baker is indeed good.

Aquinas argued that, because God created the world, God is revealed
The analogy used by Aquinas is:

* The medicine is healthy.
* The urine is healthy.

Aquinas suggests that the medicine being healthy is the cause of the urine being healthy. (In the medieval world one way to check the health of someone was to examine their urine.) 'Healthy' is used in a similar but not quite the same way in both cases. The urine is only healthy because health comes from the medicine. However, Aquinas makes a second point: the medicine is healthy not just because it promotes health, but also because it is in itself healthy.

Hence, if someone says:

* The Pope is good.
* God is good.

'good' is used in a similar sense in both cases, but, furthermore, God being good means that God is the source of goodness, and is good (whatever that means for God). God is the source of goodness because God is the Creator and sustainer of all things; thus goodness in creation comes from God.

Thought Point

Analogy of attribution

Explain what the following statements mean according to the *analogy of attribution*:

- God is just.
- God is loving.

God is good

When Aquinas talks about 'God is good', it is very important to note that he is not talking about moral goodness. Moral goodness refers to a person doing some action which is morally good. In Aquinas' thinking God is not morally good, because God is outside time and he does not change or act. God has the quality of being good, whatever that means for God.

Analogy of proportion

Analogy of proportion refers to the nature of what something is. Aquinas uses the example of 'good' applied to God. If you say that 'this is a good car', you are saying that the car measures up to the idea of what a good car should be like. If you say that someone is a good person, the word 'good' is saying that the person somehow matches certain ideals of what a good person is.

In the case of the statement 'God is good', 'good' is used to indicate that God measures up to what it is for God to be God. God is described by Aquinas as perfectly good, as in Aquinas' thinking God is unchangeable and eternal. So, 'God is good' states that God is whatever it is to be God. It is important to note that Aquinas was not talking about moral goodness. He used the word 'good' to refer to the way in which something lives up to what it should be.

Thought Point

Good, evil and analogy of proportion

Think about what is meant by analogy of proportion. Can you work out what Aquinas meant by 'evil' using analogy of proportion?

continued opposite

Analogy of proportion

Explain what the following sentences mean according to the analogy of proportion:

- God is good.
- The prime minister is good.
- A cockroach is good.

Criticisms of analogy

- *Does analogy tell us anything?*
  Some philosophers have pointed out that while analogy may tell us that God has a certain quality like 'being just', we cannot know what this is for God. If we cannot know what God being just means, does this suggest that 'God being just' is actually meaningless?

- *Literal language*
  Aquinas rejects the literal meaning of words as being applicable to God. Richard Swinburne (*Coherence of Theism*) has suggested that sometimes words could be used univocally to talk about God. For example, if God is good, this could be interpreted to mean that God is good just as human beings can be, but God is good to a greater degree.

MODELS AND QUALIFIERS

The ideas of Ian Ramsey (*Religious Language*) concerning religious language link with analogical language. Ramsey suggested that words and titles applied to God function as 'models', thereby agreeing with Aquinas. By this Ramsey meant that words tell us something about God, but not the whole story, just as models in everyday life help us to understand something. However, models, by nature, tend to be simpler than the original on which they are based. Ramsey acknowledged this point and said that models always need to be qualified – he used the word 'qualifiers'. By 'qualifiers' Ramsey meant that every model has some limits; for example, a model is not necessarily like the original in all respects, or perhaps does not communicate all of the depth or complexity of the original.

An example may help to illustrate this. If we want to understand the workings of the human mind, it could be compared to a computer.

The brain could be likened to the hardware of a computer, whereas memories and ideas implanted in the mind, for example by education and upbringing, could be compared to software. We also know that the human brain processes the light entering our eyes to enable us to see the world. In rare cases where a person has suffered brain damage (the hardware in our analogy), the brain fails to function properly and the person sees in two rather than three dimensions. However, the 'model' of the brain as a computer needs 'qualifiers', such as: the brain is clearly not made of microchip circuits as is a computer, nor can the brain be programmed in the way a computer can be. The fact remains that the analogy can help us to understand something of the functioning of the brain.

Ramsey suggested that eventually a model can help a person to gain real insight and understand more clearly what is being talked about. Ramsey called this a disclosure. If you think about studying something difficult, when you suddenly realise how to solve the problem you see clearly. Quite possibly models have been a way to help you see clearly. In addition, when you have solved something difficult, your reaction is one of fulfilment, satisfaction or even amazement.

Ramsey applied his idea of 'models' and 'qualifiers' to religion to suggest that when we use language to describe God, the language functions as a 'model'. So if we say that the Lord is a warrior, this is a model. However, the 'qualifier' is that the Lord may be a warrior but this is not the same as a human warrior armed with sword and shield. Eventually, Ramsey argues that a person comes to understand by using the model (disclosure) and a new level of understanding is achieved. So the many titles and images of God function as models that can eventually lead us to an understanding of God.

SUMMARY

1   Religious language

Verificationism

Language is only meaningful if it can be verified by sense-observation
If you cannot demonstrate with sense-observations that a statement is true, then the statement is factually meaningless
Language that talks about God is meaningless

A.J. Ayer
Modified verificationism
Distinguished verification in principle and in practice, and strong and weak verification

Ayer later replaced strong and weak verification with *direct* and *indirect* verifiability

Responses to verificationism
Verifying anything – Swinburne's example of black ravens
God-talk is eschatologically verifiable – John Hick
Strong verification has been criticised for excluding many areas of knowledge (e.g. history)
What counts as evidence?
Statements can be meaningful and unverifiable (e.g. Swinburne's toy cupboard)

Falsification

A statement is meaningless if there are no possible falsification criteria
Antony Flew's jungle analogy suggested that God-talk is meaningless
Responses to falsification
Hare's blik, Mitchell's stranger and Swinburne's toy cupboard.

John Wisdom and the gardener

Suggests that religious language makes statements which are reasonable
The existence or nature of God may be beyond our normal methods of verification

Signs and symbols

A sign is often seen as something which indicates something (e.g. a road sign)
A symbol is an object or action which not only indicates something, but also communicates a much greater understanding of the thing than can be put into words

Paul Tillich
Religious language is symbolic
God is defined as the *ground of being*
Jesus' life and work function as a symbol that can reveal the 'ground of being'
A symbol's meaning originates in a particular society; it can also lose its meaning in a society
Symbols, unlike signs, participate in the thing which they point to

Responses
Some philosophers (e.g. John Hick) suggest that it is not entirely clear what participating in a symbol means
Many Christians do not think all religious language is symbolic

Myth

For religious people a myth communicates a particular worldview – the values of a society

Peter Vardy has observed that some ideas and values are communicated in myths from all sorts of different cultures around the world (e.g. creation myths)

Myths (e.g. the Genesis creation story) communicate an awareness of God as Creator and human beings' place in creation

A myth is a form of story which makes it retellable and easier to communicate than a philosophical theory

Myths are not concerned with the literal truth of the story

Myths, like symbols, point beyond themselves to a different reality

Demythologising myths

Rudolph Bultmann attempted to remove or reinterpret in existential terms the supernatural view of the world of the New Testament

Issues raised by myths

What qualifies as a myth?

How do myths communicate values and truths?

The Via Negativa

God can only be spoken of in negative terms

Dionysius: God is good and not good

Issues raised by the Via Negativa

The *Via Negativa*'s argument that you can only describe God in negative ways leaves open the question of what God is

Aquinas and analogy

Aquinas rejected the approach of the Via Negativa, *partly because it did not say enough about what God is*

Aquinas rejected equivocal language for describing God precisely because it would prevent a person from making any statements of fact about God

Aquinas used analogy to describe God

Analogy of attribution

Brian Davies' example: The bread is good; the baker is good

Analogy of proportion

Responses to analogy
Does analogy tell us anything?
Swinburne has suggested that sometimes words could be used univocally to talk about God

Ian Ramsey

Words and titles applied to God function as 'models'
Models always need to be qualified – he used the word 'qualifiers'
A model can help a person to gain real insight and understand more clearly what is being talked about – disclosure
Religious language functions as a 'model' that leads us to an understanding of God

REVIEW QUESTIONS

Look back over the chapter and check that you can answer the following questions:

1   'Statements about aliens are unverifiable and thus meaningless.' How could this argument relate to claims that religious language is meaningless? Do you agree with the statement?
2   Which is a more helpful way to talk about God: symbol or analogy? Explain your answer with examples.
3   Is a symbolic understanding of religious language another way of saying that religious language is unclear and meaningless?
4   Compare the strengths and weaknesses of verification theory and analogy as ways to talk about God.

Terminology

Do you know your terminology?

1   Try to explain the following ideas without looking at your books and notes:

  • Analogy of proportion
  • Analogy of attribution

continued overleaf

- Univocal
- Equivocal
- Symbol
- Myth
- Verification
- Falsification.

 Examination Questions Practice

EXAM MISTAKES TO AVOID

Make sure you stick to the question set. Examination questions tend to focus on one or two of the religious language topics. Do not try to write everything you know about religious language in answer to a question.

Remember: each question assesses AO1 and AO2. To help you improve your answers look at the A2 Levels of Response. See: http://www.ocr.org.uk/qualifications/as-a-level-gce-religious-studies-h172-h572/.

SAMPLE A2 EXAM STYLE QUESTIONS

1 **'Using analogy to express understanding of God is too limiting.' Discuss.** (35 marks)

Analogy can be challenged as it tells us very little about God's nature. Instead, it could be argued that to speak meaningfully of God, language has to be univocal. Some philosophers argue against Aquinas that to be meaningful some language is used univocally to refer to God and human beings; an example could be 'good'. If human beings and God are good, is there a reason to say that the word 'good' means something different when applied to God and human beings?

For some religious believers, qualities of God are directly revealed in history, as, for example, recorded in the Bible or through religious experiences. In this view it is possible that language may be used to talk about God in a univocal way.

The fact that many mystics report religious experiences as ineffable could be used to suggest that analogy reflects the reality of trying to describe God who is beyond human comprehension.

Analogy could be defended as a way to help people talk about the transcendent God that is superior to the *Via Negativa*. Alternatively,

Ramsey's development of 'models' and 'qualifiers' could be used to argue that analogy is not limiting, but gives us a way to talk meaningfully about God who is transcendent.

2   'The verification principle offers no real challenge to religious belief.' Discuss. (35 marks)

There are many possible ways to answer this question. Some alternatives are given below:

- Present the claims of verificationism and why religious beliefs are labelled as 'meaningless'. Falsification theory could be used to develop your answer, but not as the main focus.
- Present some of the challenges to verification, in particular:
    - Consider whether religion could actually meet the conditions of weak verification.

Hick's Celestial City could be used as an explained example to illustrate this point.
    - The logical problem of verifying the verification principle and the fact that Ayer in later life himself criticised the theory.
    - Challenges to verificationism in the work of later philosophers such as Swinburne.
    - Consider the claims that religious language is symbolic, and thus extends beyond religious thinking and beyond the scope of scientific enquiry and verificationism. Tillich's ideas may be used to define this viewpoint.

- Verification approaches could be defended if it is claimed that religious language tells us something factual about God in a univocal sense.

FURTHER READING

Antony Flew's ideas about falsification are clearly explained in his essay 'Theology and Falsification'. A useful extract from this article is printed in Davies (*Philosophy of Religion: A Guide and Anthology*).

A.J. Ayer's book *Language, Truth and Logic* is one of the most famous English philosophy books from the twentieth century. If you want to read an extract, have a look at the Introduction (sometimes printed as the Appendix) and Chapter 1. It is important that you read a copy of the second or later edition, as Ayer modified his ideas in a few significant ways between the first and second editions of the book. As previously mentioned, Ayer added an Introduction/Appendix which highlighted many of the criticisms that had been made of his book as well as responding to them.

Basil Mitchell and R.M. Hare have both written important articles that discuss religious language (see e.g. Flew and MacIntyre (eds), *New Essays in Philosophical Theology*). It is worth reading articles by writers such as Hare, Flew and Mitchell, particularly if you find stories like Flew's jungle helpful ways to think about religious language.

Essential terminology

Eternal
Everlasting
Omnibenevolent
Omnipotent
Omniscient
Simple

16 The Nature of God

Key scholars

Boethius (480–c. 524)
Thomas Aquinas
(1225–1274)
Luis de Molina
(1535–1600)
Nicholas Wolterstorff
(1932–)
Richard Swinburne (1934–)
Brian Davies (1951–)

THE ISSUES

How would you explain to an alien what people mean by 'God'? Is it possible to make logical sense of religious claims that God is eternal, omnipotent and omniscient?

WHAT YOU WILL LEARN ABOUT IN THIS CHAPTER

In this chapter you will examine different ideas about the nature of God. In particular, you will explore whether God is best thought of as existing in time or outside of time. This investigation, in turn, will lead you to consider what is meant by the traditional claims that God is all-powerful (omnipotent) and all-knowing (omniscient), and whether sense can be made of these terms in today's world. Finally, you will reflect on the reasons why these ideas about the nature of God are significant to religious believers.

STARTER

1   What is meant by the word 'God'? Write your answers down individually and then share them with someone else.
2   If an atheist who has never heard anything about religion asked you to explain what the word 'God' means how would you do it?
3   Use the terms 'omnipotent' and 'omniscient' to search for images on a webpage such as www.google.com. What can you learn about the ways in which these words have been interpreted from the images?

THE OCR CHECKLIST

Candidates should be able to demonstrate knowledge and understanding of:

- God as eternal, omniscient, omnipotent and omnibenevolent – and the philosophical problems arising from these concepts;
- the views of Boethius in his discussion of eternity and God's foreknowledge in Book 5 of *The Consolations of Philosophy*;
- the question as to whether or not a good God should reward and punish.

Candidates should be able to discuss these areas critically and their strengths and weaknesses.

From OCR A Level Religious Studies specification H572.

INTRODUCTION: WHAT IS GOD?

This question has perplexed people for thousands of years, and philosophers and theologians have spilt much ink trying to answer it, or, in some cases, explaining why the question is unanswerable.

This chapter explores the way in which philosophers in the Christian tradition have traditionally answered this question. It is very important to distinguish the aims of philosophers from those of religious believers. A religious believer's concern is to use language that communicates the reality of their experience of God and relationship with God. On the other hand, a philosopher's concern is to provide a logically coherent account of what a believer means when they use the word God – philosophers and religious people both talk about God but what they are trying to say about God may differ.

Thought Point

Hymns about God

Study the extract from a traditional Christian hymn. What do you learn about God's nature from it?

continued overleaf

Immortal, invisible God only wise,
In light inaccessible hid from our eyes,
Most blessed, most glorious, the Ancient of Days,
Almighty, victorious, Thy great name we praise.
W. Chalmers Smith (1825–1908)

If you would like to hear the music that accompanies this hymn go to:
http://www.weddingguideuk.com/articles/wordsmusic/hymns/Hymn-
ImmortalInvisibleGodOnlyWise.mid

THE TRADITIONAL DEFINITION OF GOD

The traditional definition of God centres upon five key concepts:

1   Simplicity
2   Eternity
3   Omniscience
4   Omnipotence
5   Omnibenevolence.

This chapter explores the first four terms in this list. Omnibenevolence is considered in relation to the problem of evil in the chapter on that topic.

For the OCR specification you need to be able to explain and assess terms 2–5 on the list. However, it is essential that you understand term 1 in the list if you are to understand many of the other terms, particularly 'eternity'.

GOD'S SIMPLICITY

Christian philosophers use the word 'simple' as a description of God. By 'simple' philosophers are referring to the traditional way in which God was thought of as not being changeable and not having parts or characteristics.

When we talk about people we tend to talk about their characteristics – like eye colour or hairstyle; their mannerisms – a nervous tic; or their character – happy, sad, etc. Describing a person involves describing the different aspects of what makes them them.

When philosophers talk about God being simple they are saying that God does not consist of parts or characteristics. Augustine commented that God is unchangeable and thus cannot lose or gain any characteristics. Aquinas spoke of God being simple as God signifies 'being/existing'. By saying that God is 'simple' philosophers are saying that:

- God is God
  God cannot be broken down or explained in terms of parts. Philosophers like Aquinas say that God's nature (what God is) and God's existence are the same thing, because to talk of God is to talk of a being that exists. Hence in the ontological argument Anselm claims that existence is a predicate of God.

  Thomas Aquinas stated that God is not a kind of thing. Brian Davies (*An Introduction to the Philosophy of Religion*) explains this by suggesting that God is not a thing like 'a human being' but that God is a thing in the same sense as you might talk about 'the human race' as one whole.

- God is unchanging
  God is unchanging because change involves a movement from being one thing to being another. Because God is perfect, God lacks nothing and is not capable of changing into something else and remaining perfect.

  Second, and perhaps more significantly, Christian philosophers have argued that only something unchanging can logically be the cause of the created world that changes. The reason for this claim, as stated by Brian Davies, is:

  > If something changeable accounted for there being a world in which change occurs, it would be part of such a world and could not, therefore, *account* for it. (*Aquinas*)

> **Simple**
>
> What is meant by the word 'simple'? Ask someone and then look up the different meanings of the word 'simple' in a dictionary. Which meaning do you think is important to philosophers?

In other words Davies is claiming that anything that changes is part of the world and not distinct from it, as God is.

- Finally, if God is immaterial as argued by Aquinas and many other philosophers God does not have a body which has characteristics. God simply is God.

Why does the simplicity of God matter?

The simplicity of God matters because it is the implication of any understanding of God's nature that claims that God is not physical.

Thought Point

Odd ones out

Consider what you know about the philosophy of the following thinkers and look up the key ideas of any of these people that you have not heard of. Which ones are the odd ones out regarding God's simplicity? Can you deduce why they are the odd ones out?

Augustine; Anselm; Aquinas; Avicenna; Averroes; Boethius; Hume; Jantzen; Maimonides; Swinburne

Challenge	Response
1. **God changes**	God does not change; instead God is the source of change.
2. **How can a simple God love his people?**	First, God loves us in a non-human way. Second, love concerns what God wills for human beings; it is not a reference to empathy for people
3. **God has no freedom if simplicity is true**	This is a misunderstanding of God's nature. Aquinas argues that God 'wills whatever he does from eternity' (*Summa Theologiae*). E.g. *God is the Creator, so if God is simple, God eternally wills creation.*
4. **God is not described as simple in the Bible**	First, there are many references to God's nature in the Bible some of which are not literal. Second, Malachi 3: 6a suggests that God is unchanging.
5. **The simple God is transcendent and is thus unknowable**	God can be known through revelation. Second, some people claim God can, in a way, be known through the use of analogy of proportion and attribution and the *Via Negativa*.

GOD'S ETERNITY

To some people today it is perhaps curious that so much attention has been paid by philosophers to the concept of God's eternity. The idea of God being eternal is hinted at in a few biblical passages such as:

> For thus says the high and lofty one
> who inhabits eternity, whose name is Holy. (Isaiah 57: 15a)

The idea of God being eternal has also been strongly influenced by classical philosophy (particularly Plato) and his unchanging true reality of the World of Forms, and the later philosophy of Boethius.

However, Nicholas Wolterstorff ('God Is "Everlasting", Not "Eternal"') has suggested that the eternity of God has appealed to people not just because of the influence of classical Greek philosophy but also because the eternal God is different from humans' experience of life in the physical world:

> the feeling, deep seated in much of human culture, that the flowing of events into an irrecoverable and unchangeable past is a matter of deep regret. Our bright actions and shining moments do not long endure.
>
> The gnawing of time bites all. And our evil deeds can never be undone. They are forever to be regretted . . . regrets over the pervasive pattern of what transpires within time have led whole societies to place the divine outside of time – freed from the bondage of temporality. (Wolterstorff, 'God Is "Everlasting", Not "Eternal"')

In today's world people try to stave off aging and the effects of time, but it remains a fact of life that the past flows by and, while it can be regretted, it can no longer be changed. We live in the present moment and our experiences are our reality. In a world before the discovery of antibiotics and modern medical care, where death was a much more prominent feature of life, the notion of the world as a place of change and loss must have been most poignant. In this world the notion of God being other and always existing, as revealed in the Bible, leads to the philosophical understanding of God's nature as eternal and makes believers' conviction that God is eternal more understandable.

In Judaeo-Christian philosophy the concept of God being eternal can have two senses:

- Eternal refers to God existing outside of time.
- Eternal refers to God having no beginning and no end, but time does pass for God.

Anicius Manlius Severinus Boethius (480–c. 524)

Boethius was an early Christian philosopher. He was born into an influential Roman family and eventually became a Roman Consul. In later life he was imprisoned and eventually executed for opposing Emperor Theodoric the Great. Boethius is most famous as a Christian philosopher but he also studied the classical Greek philosophers and was responsible for producing translations of Aristotle's *Organon* (*Logic*) that were used for the next 700 years. In his work he introduced and integrated aspects of Greek philosophy with Christian teaching. He is buried in a tomb in Pavia, Italy.

In this chapter the word *eternal* will be used to refer to God existing outside of time and the word *everlasting* to refer to God always existing but with time passing for God.

THE ETERNAL GOD

Christians since the time of Boethius have thought of God as eternal. Philosophers such as Aquinas and Anselm have suggested that God exists outside of time. Anselm argued that God is eternal because nothing can contain God (*Proslogion* 19). For Thomas Aquinas, time and change are inseparable; since God cannot change, so God cannot be in time.

Six main reasons can be identified to explain why Christians traditionally believe that God is eternal:

* The Bible suggests that God always exists.
* God is not a physical being like us.
* God is the Creator of the universe. Time passing is a feature of the universe. God as the Creator of the universe is therefore outside of time.
* God is the ultimate cause of why things exist and why there is change in the universe. This relates to Thomas Aquinas' first two ways.
* God is perfect and hence is not subject to time because time passing implies imperfection. When time passes you change and lose what you were previously. This argument is found in Anselm's *Proslogion*.
* God exists necessarily (see Aquinas' Third Way to demonstrate the existence of God).

Boethius and Aquinas on God's eternity

The Christian belief that God is *eternal* was strongly influenced by the philosophy of Boethius. Boethius argued that God is changeless (impassable) and does not exist in time. According to Boethius eternity is 'the whole, simultaneous and perfect possession of unending life'. What Boethius is saying is that God's life is not only endless but that it is not like physical life as it does not involve change and as it does not involve experiencing life as a series of events one following another.

Thought Point

Boethius refers to 'the infinity of time' being simultaneously present to God. Boethius stated that:

> Eternity, then, is the whole, simultaneous and perfect possession of boundless life, which becomes clearer by comparison with temporal things. For whatever lives in time proceeds in the present from the past into the future, and there is nothing established in time which can embrace the whole space of its life equally, but tomorrow it does not yet grasp, while yesterday it has already lost. And in this day to day life you live no more than in that moving and transitory moment. Therefore whatever endures the condition of time, although as Aristotle thought concerning the world, it neither began ever to be nor ceases to be and although its life is drawn out with the infinity of time, yet it is not yet such that it may rightly be believed eternal. For it does not simultaneously comprehend and embrace the whole space of its life, though it be infinite, but possess the future not yet, the past no longer. Whatever therefore comprehends and possess at once the whole fullness of boundless life, and is such that neither is anything future lacking from it . . . must necessarily both always be present to itself, possessing itself in the present, and hold as present the infinity of moving time. (*The Consolation of Philosophy*)

1   Identify the key points about God's eternity that are made in this passage.
2   Can you think of any philosophical problems raised by what Boethius states?

As indicated in the Thought Point above, Boethius argued that God's life is limitless and that God possesses the whole of his/her life eternally without end. For God there is no past, present and future. Instead, God exists eternally and all of time is present to God at the same time. God does not see the future as it happens; instead Boethius argues that all time is present to God 'simultaneously'. One way to imagine this is to think of a film you know well. When you watch the film you start at the beginning and the film flows on from beginning to end. However, Boethius argues that if time is like the film God takes in all the film in 'one glance' – all at the same time – the opening title through to the closing credits. The reason that Boethius believes that God is eternal is because God is simple and hence does not learn new things and time does not pass for God:

And God possesses this present instant comprehension of and sight of all things not from the issuing of future events but from his own simplicity. (*The Consolation of Philosophy*)

Thomas Aquinas, quoting Boethius, stated that:

Eternity is simultaneously whole, while time is not, eternity measuring abiding existence and time measuring change . . . the primary intrinsic difference of time from eternity is that eternity exists as a simultaneous whole and time does not. (McDermott, *Thomas Aquinas*)

For Aquinas God exists unendingly without a beginning or conclusion. Hence God must exist outside of time because time consists of parts and the notion of time involves beginnings and ends. For example, all human beings are born, live their lives and die; for Aquinas God is the Creator of the universe and all life, who always exists without end. Time does not pass for God. Aquinas, like Boethius, states that time involves living life 'successively'. By this he means that one event in life follows another, but for God this is not the case. God exists outside of time and the nature of God is to exist.

Some implications of the eternal view of God

- *Implications for religious language*
  God can only be discussed in analogical terms or in terms of a *Via Negativa*, symbols or myths. Thomas Aquinas went as far as to say that any discussion of the nature of God, such as of God's eternity, ultimately indicates something about what God is (using analogical language) and states what God is not (a *Via Negativa*). If God is outside of time, God is transcendent and beyond human understanding.

- *God the Creator*
  As God cannot change God is eternally the Creator, God does not think about creating and then create. Instead it is God's nature to be the Creator. Thomas Aquinas stated that God knows all of creation precisely because God is eternally the Creator and sustains creation in existence. In this sense, all of creation is a work of God.

Table 16.2

Criticism of God's Eternity	Explanation of the Criticism	Response to the Criticism
God knowing all time simultaneously is incoherent	Anthony Kenny famously argued that the notion of all time being simultaneously present to God is incoherent. If all time is simultaneously present to God the meaning of the word 'simultaneous' entails that all of time is happening at the same moment which appears to be incoherent. Kenny stated that: On St. Thomas' view, my typing of this paper is simultaneous with the whole of eternity. Again, on this view, the great fire of Rome is simultaneous with the whole of eternity. Therefore, while I type these very words, Nero fiddles heartlessly on (*The God of the Philosophers*) Richard Swinburne has echoed this criticism stating that he could not 'make much sense' of talk of all events being simultaneously present to God.	Abandon the idea of eternity involving events being simultaneously present to God. Paul Helm has suggested that talk of God being eternal does not involve the *reductio ad absurdum* suggested by Kenny and Swinburne because Helm argues that the eternal God is timeless and acts eternally: God, considered as timeless, cannot have temporal relations with any of his creation. He is timeless in the sense of being time free. This at once provides an answer to the *reductio* brought by philosophers such as Kenny and Swinburne by denying that what any of us is now doing is taking place at the same time as anything God is doing. (Helm, *Eternal God*)
How can God be personal and act in creation?	The Bible implies that God is personal and acts in creation. For example, God responds to the Israelites' prayer for freedom from slavery in Egypt and God intervenes to help Joshua in battle at Ai and at Jericho. These biblical events imply that God is personal and acts in time.	God is not a person. Language that suggests God is acting personally in the Bible reflects the experience of people in past times who described their encounters with God using personal language. Philosophers alternatively would talk about God using language that is analogical or symbolic.

continued overleaf

Criticism of God's Eternity	Explanation of the Criticism	Response to the Criticism
How can God love his people and respond to them?	Love involves a two-way process and ability to respond. If God is eternal how can God love his people and respond to them? In the Bible God responds to people in need out of love. Other philosophers have questioned how an eternal God can respond to people's prayers.	God is loving because God changelessly sustains creation for people. Secondly, God changelessly wills good for people. Regarding God answering prayers: • Aquinas: Prayer is the act of being aware of God's activity in the world, either directly (primary agency) or through others (secondary agency) (*Summa Theologiae* 1a, 19); it is not about making requests. • Maurice Wiles: The universe is part of God's ongoing creative activity; God is always acting – there is no selective response by God, since this would imply God is partial and capricious. • Many people would dispute Wiles' and Aquinas' ideas about petitionary prayers; instead they would claim that God is in time, so God can act and respond.

THE EVERLASTING GOD

One solution to the problems raised by claims that God is eternal has been to suggest that God is everlasting. By 'everlasting' theologians mean that God always exists and will exist without end; however, time passes for God.

Richard Swinburne supports the view that God is everlasting. He argues that the idea of events occurring simultaneously to God cannot be made sense of. Second, he suggests that belief in an everlasting God fits more satisfactorily with God as revealed in the Bible:

> For myself I cannot make much sense of this [all events being simultaneously present to God] suggestion – for many reasons. For example, I cannot see that anything can be meant by saying that God knows (as they happen) the events of AD 1995 unless it means that he exists in 1995 and knows in 1995 what is happening then . . . hence I prefer that understanding of God being eternal as his being everlasting rather than as his being timeless. (Swinburne, *Is There a God?*)

It is important to note that saying God is everlasting is not meant to indicate any lessening of the power of God – it is a statement that God exists without end at all points in time but not that God exists timelessly in the sense of Aquinas and Boethius.

Nicholas Wolterstorff ('God Is "Everlasting", Not "Eternal"') has argued that the only way to understand some of God's actions as indicated in the Bible is to understand them as free actions in response to human beings' behaviour, suggesting that God's actions involve time passing. Second, many discussions of God's knowledge suggest that God's omniscience cannot include knowing a future that does not yet exist. Therefore, God's knowledge increases as the future happens (see 'God's Omniscience' pp. 433–6 for more details).

The picture in the Bible might suggest that God is everlasting rather than eternal. For example, Malachi 3: 6a: 'For I the LORD do not change.' The same idea is reflected in Psalm 102: 27: 'but you are the same, and your years have no end'.

Whether 'have no end' means eternal or everlasting is a matter of debate. Yet, some of the stories in the Bible, such as the story of the ten plagues or God helping Joshua, suggest that God acts in time and it can be argued that God is therefore everlasting.

A further claim is that God can only be understood as Saviour and Redeemer worthy of worship if God is everlasting. As Nicholas Wolterstorff stated:

> He is the Lord of what occurs. And that, along with the specific pattern of what he does, grounds all authentically biblical worship of, and obedience to, God. It is not because he is outside of time – eternal, immutable, impassive – that we worship and obey God. It is because of what he can and does bring about within time that we mortals are to render him praise and obedience. ('God Is "Everlasting", Not "Eternal"')

Ultimately, the Christian belief in God's eternity tells us as much about what God is not as about what God is, and whether God is eternal or everlasting remains open to debate.

GOD'S OMNIPOTENCE

Thought Point

What can God do?

1   Write down your own definition of omnipotence.
2   Answer the following questions about God, justifying your answers with reasons:

continued overleaf

Psalm 68: 32–35

Sing to God, O kingdoms
of the earth;
sing praises to the Lord,
Selah
O rider in the heavens, the
ancient heavens;
listen, he sends out his
voice, his mighty voice.
Ascribe power to God,
whose majesty is over
Israel;
and whose power is in the
skies.
Awesome is God in his
sanctuary,
the God of Israel; he gives
power and
strength to his people.
Blessed be God!

Q. What is learnt about
God in this extract from
Psalm 68?

(a) Can God climb a tree?
(b) Can God make a stone that is too heavy for God to lift?
(c) Can God change the past?
(d) Can God sin?
(e) Can God love?

3 Answer the following questions about you, justifying your answers with reasons:

(a) Can you climb a tree?
(b) Can you make a stone that is too heavy for you to lift?
(c) Can you change the past?
(d) Can you sin?
(e) Can you love?

4 Look at your answers to the questions. What issues or problems are raised by God's omnipotence?

The idea of God being powerful is a key aspect of religious belief. A being worthy of worship is a being who has 'power'. Within the Christian tradition God's power enables all things to be possible (e.g. Luke 1: 37 or Matthew 19: 26). Thomas Aquinas described God as 'active power', communicating this sense of the ability of God to exercise power and to bring about events.

Within biblical tradition omnipotence is also suggested by God's activity in the world and the idea of 'miracles'. Suggestions of God's activity in the world point to the fact that God has power beyond the comprehension and ability of human beings and hence that God is omnipotent.

Within philosophical thinking there have been three main ways in which God's omnipotence has been viewed:

1 Omnipotence concerns God's ability to do anything, including the logically impossible.
2 Omnipotence concerns God's ability to do what is logically possible for a perfect God to do.
3 Omnipotence is a statement of the power of God.

God's ability to do anything including the logically impossible

René Descartes supported the view that God could do anything, including what might seem impossible. For example, following Descartes' definition of omnipotence, God could change the fundamental laws of physics, which as far as we know are unchanging and apply universally.

However, this view has been rejected by many later philosophers since it can be argued that saying God can do the logically impossible does not actually refer to anything, as there is nothing that is 'logically impossible'.

J.L. Mackie ('Omnipotence') stated that the idea of logically impossible actions was 'Only a form of words which fails to describe any state of affairs'.

Omnipotence concerns God's ability to do what is logically impossible for a perfect God to do

According to this view, referring to God as omnipotent is a statement that God's power is different from our powers and abilities, and talk of God's omnipotence is talk of what is logically possible for a being, such as God, to do.

Second, omnipotence in this view is a statement that God has the power to do whatever it is logically possible for God to do. For example, it is logically possible for you to climb Mount Everest; however, the statement that it is logically possible for you to climb Everest does not mean that you have the power to do this. However, in the case of God, saying God is the omnipotent Creator is a statement not only that it is logically possible for God to create but also that God has the power to create.

Aquinas argued that God's power is omnipotent because it is infinite, and the reason that God's power is infinite is that God is not limited. This in turn relies on the idea that God is eternal and therefore not bound by the limitation of physical existence. Aquinas (*Summa Theologiae*) states that 'God's Power can do anything' and 'Whatever involves a contradiction is not held by omnipotence, for it just cannot possibly make sense of being possible . . . For a contradiction in terms cannot be a word, for no mind can conceive it.'

The second quotation from Aquinas is significant because it answers many challenges to God's omnipotence, such as 'Can God climb a tree?' (cf. Wade Savage, 'The Paradox of the Stone'). If God is eternal and not physical then God does not have a body with which to climb and thus the idea that God is not omnipotent because God cannot climb trees is mistaken because the concept of God climbing is illogical.

Aquinas also considered whether God could change past events using his omnipotence and again he rejects this idea as illogical. Consider the following example:

1 The Nazis lost the Second World War.
2 The Nazis won the Second World War.

Perfection of God

In classical Christian philosophy God is described as perfect, meaning first that God lacks nothing from what it is to be truly God. Second, the idea of perfection traditionally relies on the belief that God is eternal and unchanging because change suggests movement from one thing to another, such as less good to more good. If God changes then it implies imperfection and if God is everlasting rather than eternal then God changes and cannot be perfect according to this way of thinking.

The Paradox of the Stone

Can God create a stone so heavy that he cannot lift it? Either God can create such a stone or he cannot. If he cannot he is not omnipotent. If he can there is also something that he cannot do, lift the stone, and therefore he is not omnipotent. A being that is not omnipotent, though, is not God. God, therefore, does not exist.

Aquinas: if God exists then he is a being that can

continued overleaf

lift all stones. A stone that is so heavy that God cannot lift it is therefore an impossible object. God is able to do anything possible, but not anything impossible. So Aquinas can answer the question 'no' without compromising divine omnipotence.

The first statement is true, the second is false. In Aquinas' thinking God could not change the past such that statement 2 is true because this contradicts what we know to be the case; that the Nazis lost the Second World War:

> if you think of it [an event] as a past event and definitively so, then it is not only in itself but also absolutely impossible that it did not take place, for it implies a contradiction. As such it is more impossible than the raising of the dead to life. (Aquinas, *Summa Theologiae*)

Furthermore, it is important to note that God's omnipotence is an aspect of the nature of God and thus, according to this view, God cannot sin because this contradicts the nature of God as good. 'God cannot sin' is more than just saying God does not sin or chooses not to sin; it is a statement that the idea of God sinning goes against God's nature as perfect. Anselm echoed this line of thinking, suggesting that God could not sin as sin involves a lack of control over one's actions. Hence sinning would indicate that God lacks power over his/her activity.

However, omnipotence being defined as the ability of God to do what is logically possible for a perfect God to do has been criticised by philosophers like Peter Geach (*Providence and Evil*). Geach argues that this definition of omnipotence relies on the acceptance of a particular view of God's nature as perfect. This leads Geach to suggest the idea that God's omnipotence is better understood as a statement concerning the power of God. Geach writes:

> I distinguish between almightiness, or power over all things, and omnipotence, or power to do everything. . . . Christians are committed to believing that God is almighty: the source of all power, for whom there is no frustration or failure. But for this, there could be no absolute faith in God's promises. But this very faith requires that there is one feat, in itself logically possible, that God cannot perform, namely promise-breaking. (*Providence and Evil*)

OMNIPOTENCE IS A STATEMENT OF THE POWER OF GOD

Philosophers such Anthony Kenny (*The God of the Philosophers*) have suggested that omnipotence is best understood as a statement of God's power. Kenny states that 'A being is omnipotent if it has every power which it is logically possible to possess.' Kenny's idea is that omnipotence is not only a statement of what is logically possible for God, but also a statement that God has the ability to do whatever is logically possible for God. This is different from human beings who often have the logical capability to do something, but lack the power necessary to achieve the goal.

Table 16.3 Challenges to omnipotence

Challenge	Response
1 Can God change past history?	God cannot change past history as this would involve a contradiction of what we know to be the case. A contradiction is illogical. God cannot do what is illogical unless you adopt Descartes' view of omnipotence.
2 Can God sin?	• God cannot sin as this would stop God being perfect. • God cannot sin, as sin involves change and the eternal God does not change. • Sin involves a lack of power over one's actions (Anselm). An omnipotent being has power of his/her actions, therefore an omnipotent God cannot sin.
3 Omnipotence relies on a pre-existing concept of God's nature as perfect	Omnipotence is an aspect of God's nature and is thus a statement of how God is and is an aspect of God's perfection
4 Can God make a stone that is too heavy for God to lift?	Talk of God omnipotently making a stone that is too heavy for the omnipotent God to lift is incoherent and therefore meaningless. If something is omnipotently made unmovable then that is how the thing is and you do not lack any possible power if you cannot lift the stone as the stone by nature, omnipotently, is unmovable.

GOD'S OMNISCIENCE

Thought Point

Look up each of the following passages in a Bible. What is learnt about God's omniscience from them?

*   A snake in the grass, Adam and Eve (Genesis 3)
*   A bit of boasting about knowledge and power (Job 38: 31–33)
*   A story about lust (2 Samuel 11–12)
*   Knowing people through and through (Psalm 139).

Judaism, Christianity and Islam have always claimed that God is omniscient – all-knowing. The reference to God's omniscience has pointed to the belief that God is aware of all that people do and that God has complete knowledge of the universe; both how it comes to exist and why it exists. God's omniscience also refers to his knowledge of physical creation.

The traditional understanding of omniscience is clearly revealed in the Bible. For example, God is aware of King David secretly arranging for Beersheba's husband Uriah the Hittite to be killed in battle as David desires Beersheba (2 Samuel). God is described as knowing people through and through (Psalm 139: 1–4) and before birth (Jeremiah 1). Omniscience, in this case, signifies complete understanding and full knowledge.

The religious concept of God's omniscience is echoed within philosophers' comments, such as Anselm's claim 'You are supremely perceptive.' (*Proslogion*)

Philosophers and omniscience

Philosophers over the last 2,000 years have written widely about the meaning of omniscience and problems related to it. In general terms the definitions of omniscience can be split up as follows:

- Omniscience – refers to God's unlimited knowledge, including all history, past, present and future. According to this view, God is outside of time and has knowledge of the whole of time from beginning to end. This view fits in with belief that God is eternal.
- Limited omniscience – God's knowledge is limited to what it is logically possible to know or God chooses to limit what he knows to allow humans free will. According to this view God's knowledge changes over time, since God acquires new knowledge as events occur. This view fits in with the belief that God is everlasting.

Thought Point

What do you mean if you know something?

1   Complete the following questions:

(a) 2 + 2 = _____.

(b) Gravity is _____.

continued opposite

(c) Mars is the _____ rock from the sun.

(d) The Earth is _____ years old.

(e) Handel's profession was _____.

2   If you say that you 'know' the answer to these questions:

(a) What exactly do you know?

(b) What is happening in your brain such that you know the answer?

(c) Is the piece of knowledge you have something physical? Does it relate to something physical?

(d) If you did not know that 7 is the square root of 49, would the knowledge that 7 is the square root of 49 still be true?

(e) Having completed the questions, define what is meant by *knowledge*.

How does God know anything?

When discussing God's omniscience it is important to understand exactly what philosophers mean when they talk about God having knowledge. First, if God is eternal, God's knowledge is not the same as human knowledge as God is outside of time and non-physical. Human beings, on the other hand, have knowledge that they gain through their senses.

Second, if God is simple, this means that God does not gain new knowledge in the way humans do through experience and learning. Instead, God just has knowledge. This begs the question, however: if God cannot learn from experience is it meaningful to talk about God having knowledge as we gain knowledge through our experiences gained through our senses and interpreted by our brains?

Thomas Aquinas suggested that God has all knowledge because knowledge is not physical. Aquinas argued that although humans acquire knowledge through their bodies the knowledge itself is not a physical thing. For example, today we know that the square root of 9 is 3. However, 'square roots' are not physical objects. Second, what square roots are does not change even if no one knows what a square root is. Knowledge being non-physical is important because it means that God, who is immaterial, can still have knowledge.

Aquinas suggested that what God knows is 'self-knowledge'. By saying this Aquinas also explains how God can know about creation: God is the Creator and God knows by self-knowledge what he creates, and thus God knows about creation. God's knowledge on this view is not like human knowledge, as it is not gained by using the body's senses.

Why do Christian philosophers claim that God is omniscient?

- God's omniscience is revealed in the Bible;
- God is perfect: if God is perfect then this includes having unlimited knowledge;
- God's actions are intelligent – intelligent action involves all knowledge.

The limits of God's knowledge

In Aquinas' view that knowledge is immaterial and that God's knowledge consists of 'self-knowledge', God has complete knowledge of the creation he sustains.

However, if an everlasting view of God is adopted then God can acquire new knowledge as time passes for God. Thus, as the events of history occur God gains new knowledge. Omniscience on this view is a claim that God can know what it is logically possible to know. So, if the future has not yet happened, there is no future to be known, and God's omniscience is not limited because it is impossible to know what does not exist or has not existed yet. Instead, God is omniscient as God has perfect knowledge of what has occurred and is occurring.

CHALLENGES TO GOD'S OMNISCIENCE

Do human beings have free will if God is omniscient?

The most significant problem regarding belief in God's omniscience has been the question of how one can still accept that human beings have free will if God is omniscient. Consider the following example:

1   At 10.30 I am watching television.
2   At 10.45 I freely choose to turn off the television and go to bed.
3   After turning off the television I go to bed.
4   I am in bed by 11.00.

If God is omniscient, this implies that God knows what I am doing at 10.30 and at 11.00 and at every intervening point between 10.30 and 11.00.

Moreover, if God is eternal then God timelessly knows what I am doing at 10.30 and 11.00. According to Boethius, God takes in all of history in a 'single glance'. This suggests that God knows what I am doing at 10.30, and that God knows the decision I will make even before I have made it at 10.45. If this is correct, it means I do not have a real choice as God already knows what I will do. The clear implication of this is that God has knowledge of future human actions. This creates a problem if free will is defined, in the manner of John Locke, as the ability to do other in a situation. If God has knowledge of our future actions this would undermine claims that human beings have free will as God, being omniscient and perfect, cannot be mistaken. Therefore, whatever God foreknows will happen, has to happen and cannot be any different. As Richard Sorabji puts it, 'If God's infallible knowledge of our doing exists in advance, then we are too late so to act that God will have had a different judgement.' (*Time, Creation and the Continuum*)

The fundamental problem with God having knowledge of future actions of human beings is that it would suggest that future events that we think are contingent on present events and choices actually are not contingent, but necessary. If the future is necessary there is no free choice as the future is already set and follows on from the present.

Religious believers have responded to the challenge of God's omniscience in a number of ways.

First, Boethius argued that God has no foreknowledge as God is eternal. Hence God does not know the future; God just knows everything, including all history, as in a single glance (cf. *The Consolation of Philosophy*). Augustine similarly argues that God simply knows our choices (*De Libero Arbitrio*). For Boethius, God knows everything that is true, but God, being eternal, does not know things at a particular time or in a particular temporal order through history – God simply knows eternally.

However, Anthony Kenny (*The God of the Philosophers*) has famously questioned whether it is meaningful to talk of all events being 'simultaneously present to God' as stated by Boethius, since the nature of 'simultaneity' is that the two or more simultaneous objects occur at the same time in the same way. If all of history is simultaneous to God, this suggests, according to Kenny, that all of history is occurring at the same time: 'The great fire of Rome is simultaneous with the whole of eternity. Therefore, while I type these words, Nero fiddles heartlessly on.' (*The God of the Philosophers*) Boethius could respond to this problem by stating that God knows the 'results' of humans' free actions. So, it is not proper to talk of God having 'foreknowledge' of human actions.

Aquinas built upon the thinking of Boethius and suggested that God takes in all of history as a whole. God's perception of history is like that of someone looking down on history and taking in the broad sweep of all history all at once, as though God, rather than watching a film, takes in every frame of a film from beginning to end all at the same time. In Aquinas' thinking God has a 'bird's-eye' perspective on the whole of history and creation that is *theocentric* (from God's perspective), whereas humans' perspective on history is different because we see events as part of a historical sequence involving past, present and future. Aquinas illustrated this with the analogy of someone walking along the road: 'He who goes along the road does not see those who come after him; whereas he who sees the whole road from a height sees at once all those travelling upon it.' (*Summa Theologiae*) While the walker is making choices, the person looking down from above can see what choices will be made, but this knowledge of the choices that will be made is not causal and thus humans' ability to make free choices is not removed.

Nero and Rome

Investigate why Kenny described Emperor Nero as 'heartless' and what the link is with the great fire of Rome?

Theocentric

Theocentric refers to something being centred on God or from the perspective of God rather than human beings.

The implication of Aquinas' view is that some form of soft determinism is true, since there is a causal link between past events, the present and the future and, from God's perspective, seeing history as a whole, determinism is true even if we experience ourselves as free.

A second solution to the problem of omniscience and human free will is to suggest that God is everlasting rather than eternal. If God is everlasting this suggests that time passes, in some sense, for God. Given that time passes, God learns about the future as it unfolds.

Philosophers have suggested that the past is closed and unchangeable – it cannot be different. The future is open and not necessary, as it has not yet happened. What happens in the future may depend on events that are occurring now, but what exactly will happen in the future remains open. Some philosophers, such as Luis de Molina, have suggested that God's omniscience includes all possibilities for the future. However G.E.M. Anscombe suggested that it is not clear if there is anything to be known about the future: 'There was no such thing as how someone would have spent his life if he had not died as a child.' (*Collected Philosophical Papers*, Vol. 2) Furthermore, the difficulty for Christian believers is that the traditional understanding of God sees God as transcendent, perfect and unchanging (immutable), not everlasting.

Ultimately, the way in which questions surrounding God's omniscience are resolved depends upon whether God is eternal or everlasting. The coherence of any concept of omniscience with regard to God depends upon a person having a theory of knowledge which suggests that knowledge exists immaterially. If a different theory of knowledge is held that suggests that knowledge is not solely immaterial, then it is very difficult to make sense of any claim that God is omniscient unless God is either material or knows things in a way that is utterly different from human beings. However, this second option raises further questions concerning what it means to talk of God's omniscience, if the nature of God 'knowing' things is not analogous in any way to human experience.

Why does it matter if God is omniscient and has knowledge of actions that are in the future from our perspective?

The heart of the problem with omniscience for a religious believer centres on the believer's emphasis on free will. The issue runs as follows:

- People are responsible for their actions and deliberate omissions if they have free will.
- If hard determinism is true, human beings can be held causally responsible for their actions but not morally responsible for their actions.

- The problem is that if human freedom is defended in a libertarian sense, how can religious believers (e.g. Christians) make sense of claims that God is omniscient?

Certainly, in the Bible, God states what will happen and it happens. According to the traditional Christian understanding of God, God cannot be mistaken as this would imply that God is lacking in some way (i.e. he is not perfect).

Thought Point

God's knowledge of future human actions

1 Complete the conclusion to the argument below.
2 Is the argument valid?

The argument

Belief 1: God is omniscient.
Definition: Omniscience concerns knowledge of all that it is logically possible to know.
Belief 2: God is perfect and therefore cannot be mistaken.
Belief 3: God made human beings and gave them free will.
Conclusion: God has/does not have knowledge of future human actions. If God has knowledge of future human actions there is/is not free will.

In ethical theory there are a number of problems relating to the claim that God is omniscient. First, if God's knowledge cannot be mistaken because God is perfect, does God actually know what we will do before we do it, and if God does, do we have a real choice and real moral responsibility for our actions?

Second, many Christian theodicies rely on the free will defence to explain natural and moral evil. If, however, God has foreknowledge of events that are yet to happen from our perspective because he is omniscient and he is omnipotent, the problem concerning God not preventing evil arises once more.

Third, if God sustains everything (God is the Creator), knows what will happen (God is omniscient) and has the power effortlessly to manage what happens (omnipotence), is God responsible for what happens? In which case, are human beings responsible for their actions? Moral philosophy clearly relies on the idea of human beings in some way being morally

---

Distinguishing 'causal determinism' from 'foreknowledge'

A common cause of confusion in Religious Studies examinations is that candidates confuse the meaning of 'determinism' and 'foreknowledge'. In Religious Studies 'foreknowledge' is used to refer to knowledge that an agent has of events that have not yet happened and are in the future from that agent's point of view.

'Causal determinism', on the other hand, is the view that every event that occurs can be explained by reference to the causes that brought it about. 'Causal determinism' suggests that the fact that any event happens is fully explained by understanding the cause or set of causes of the event.

Revise your terminology

Can you explain the meaning of the following words without looking at your notes?

- Foreknowledge
- Omniscience
- Omnipotence
- Libertarian
- Hard determinist
- Soft determinist.

responsible for their actions. This leads into the debate concerning whether God can limit his omniscience, or omnipotently create beings beyond his control – the idea of human beings being beyond God's control does not fit in very well with traditional belief in God the omnipotent Creator. If God is in control, is God responsible for evil happening?

Finally, the question of God's omniscience and free will is significant in relation to religious beliefs about life after death. In many religious traditions God judges people after death, based on their actions in life. The justice of God involves God punishing people if they deserve it. The belief in God's judgment of people therefore relies on the belief that human beings have free will and are morally responsible for their actions. If human beings are not free, this suggests that God's omniscience entails predestination.

Ultimately, the definition of omniscience that you adopt defines whether determinism or free will is accepted. Conversely, your understanding of the nature of God may affect your attitude to the free will and determinism debate.

THE GOOD GOD AND DIVINE REWARDS AND PUNISHMENTS

Many Christians over the centuries have pointed to belief in God's judgment at the end of time. This judgment will separate the just from the unjust. This belief centres on the fact that good and evil are a reality, and people are judged according to which reality their life embodies. In this sense, evil is not the will of God but people will be held to account for how they use their freedom. One question that commonly arises is whether God, who is perfectly good, should punish or reward people.

This is the question that puzzled Boethius: if God is omniscient and foreknows our actions, even though he does not cause them, our actions are necessary and, as such, we could not have done otherwise. As a solution Boethius, as we have seen, appeals to God's eternity. God sees past, present and future simultaneously and they are part of the eternal present for God, so he does not foreknow our actions ahead of time, but sees everything that happens all at once.

Boethius writing in *The Consolation of Philosophy* does not seem to be saying that God exists simultaneously with events and so knows them in the present even if they might be past or future events for us, but simply that God knows them as if they actually are present events. This is explained by introducing the idea of two sorts of necessity which are called 'simple necessity' and 'conditional necessity'. Simple necessity concerns those instances which obey the laws of nature and cannot be otherwise (for example all men are mortal), whereas conditional necessity is explained by the example of a man walking voluntarily: 'If you know someone is walking it is necessary that he is walking.' These two sorts of necessity are vital for Boethius' understanding of God's foreknowledge – every event that happens in the present is both contingent and (conditionally) necessary and this is how Boethius explains God's knowledge – it is like our knowledge, 'But God sees present those future things which happen as the result of free will' so things that happen as a result of free will are in their own nature free, but in relation to God's vision of them they are necessary 'by the condition of God's knowledge'. God is eternal and has no past or future and God does not, therefore, influence actions by seeing them – our actions are necessary because God sees them but they are conditionally necessary as we could have chosen not to do them. As a result, any actions that are the result of our free will can be rewarded or punished by God as he sees them from above.

This view of God as some sort of impartial spectator seeing all our actions as if from a distance is at odds with the Christian view of God who is involved with his creation. Additionally God's omniscience is dependent on human actions which cause problems for his omnipotence. We could, therefore, consider as Ward does, that God cannot know the future because it has not happened yet, and that this lack of knowledge does not limit his omniscience as he still knows everything it is logically possible for God to know, and is still able to reward and punish humans justly.

There are two aspects to the question of divine rewards and punishments: physical rewards and punishments, and rewards and punishments in the afterlife. The primary concern with both is the issue of justice. In this sense, God's goodness demands that people receive their appropriate reward or punishment. On a number of occasions Jesus promises his followers that they will be rewarded appropriately if they suffer on account of his name (Matthew 5: 12). The New Testament states very strongly that God will judge people and hold them to account for their actions in life after death.

Many theologians argue that ultimately, if a person chooses to live their life in a way that is wicked, God's goodness demands two things: (1) that the person has the real freedom to choose to be wicked, and (2) that God's justice demands that people are treated fairly; this would entail that people who are wicked are indeed punished, and people who experience lives full of suffering for which they are not to blame are appropriately compensated. As Richard Swinburne has stated:

> if there are any lives which nevertheless are on balance bad, God would be under an obligation to provide life after death for the individuals concerned in which they could be compensated for the bad states of this life, so that in this life and the next their lives overall would be good . . . Thus God treats us as individuals, each with her own vocation. (*Providence and the Problem of Evil*)

God's omniscience and life after death

This topic is explored in greater depth in Chapter 11, 'Life after Death'.

This issue of God's goodness and punishing and rewarding people is explored in more detail in the chapters on 'The Problem of Evil' (Chapter 9), 'Life after Death' (Chapter 11) and 'Miracles' (Chapter 14).

SUMMARY

REVIEW QUESTIONS

Look back over the chapter and check that you can answer the following questions:

1. Explain concisely the difference between describing God as 'everlasting' as opposed to 'eternal'. Which view is stronger? Justify your answer.
2. Assess whether the concept of God's simplicity is 'coherent'.
3. Read the following passage by Ludwig Wittgenstein. What do you think he is getting at? Is this passage a strong criticism of philosophers' discussions of the nature of God? And, do you sympathise with Wittgenstein? Justify your answers with reasons.

> What is the use of studying philosophy if all that it does for you is to enable you to talk with some plausibility about some abstruse questions of logic, etc. and if it does not improve your thinking about the important questions of everyday life?
> (A letter from Wittgenstein to Norman Malcolm)
> (Malcolm, *Ludwig Wittgenstein*)

   And, what are 'the important questions of everyday life'?
4. Whose views are the most persuasive? Aquinas', Boethius', Swinburne's or Kenny's?
5. Is it true that God's omniscience is incompatible with free choice?

continued opposite

Terminology

Do you know your terminology?

1 Try to explain the following ideas without looking at your books and
   notes:

   - Omniscience
   - Omnipotence
   - Eternal
   - Everlasting
   - Simplicity of God
   - Immutable.

Examination Questions Practice

EXAM MISTAKES TO AVOID

There are two common errors made by students when writing essays
concerning God's eternity, omnipotence and omniscience. First, students
confuse the ideas of different philosophers. It is particularly important not
to confuse the terminology when discussing whether God is eternal or not,
as any confusion will stop you discussing whether God has knowledge or
foreknowledge of human actions in a coherent manner.

Second, in essays it is important that you do not just list criticisms of
ideas linked with omniscience and omnipotence. You must explain to an
examiner what the problem with a particular term is and the implications
of this problem for the way we understand the term in question. For
example, if you were discussing the coherence of omniscience as a concept
you will need to discuss not just criticisms of it but exactly what is meant
by the term, why the term is problematic and the implications of the
criticisms.

Remember: each question assesses AO1 and AO2. To help you improve
your answers look at the A2 Levels of Response. See: http://www.ocr.org.
uk/qualifications/as-a-level-gce-religious-studies-h172-h572/.

SAMPLE A2 EXAM STYLE QUESTIONS

1 **Critically assess the traditional Christian concept of God being eternal.** (35 marks)

Make sure that you clearly explain what is meant by eternity, including the everlasting view of God. There is a lot to fit into this essay. You are quite free to be selective about the criticisms you use – just make sure you include the main ones.

• Explain the traditional notion of eternity:
God is infallible and timeless. Remember to discuss Boethius' claim that *events are simultaneously present to God*; God exists in a *'never passing instant'*. You could also consider Aquinas on God's eternity and 'timelessness'.

• Criticisms of God's eternity: There is a range of different criticisms of God's eternity that could be considered. Some suggestions are given below:

  – *Can God know events which are happening 'now'?* Possible response: God's perception of 'now' is not analogous to ours. Boethius and Aquinas spoke of God taking in everything 'as in a glance'. The downside to this is that it implies some form of soft determinism (Aquinas was happy to accept this).
  – *Incoherency of simultaneously present notion.* Discuss Swinburne's and Kenny's criticisms of the traditional notion of eternity and some responses such as from Paul Helm.
  – *If God is timeless and eternal (as Aquinas states), do we have real freedom?* Discuss the problem of divine knowledge of events that are in the future from a human perspective and some of the responses to it such as from Swinburne. You could also consider Brian Davies' claim that Swinburne's everlasting God would continually be surprised by his creation.
  – *Can an eternal God act in the world?* Swinburne argues that unless God is in a time and subject to change, God can bring nothing about. You could assess this view and responses that suggest that talk of God acting is not analogous to humans acting.
  – *Discuss whether the Bible implies a God in time or outside of time.* The evidence can point both ways (e.g. Malachi 3: 6 *'I the Lord do not change'* – but is God everlasting or eternal)?
  – *Can an eternal God choose to create?* This criticism could be discussed alongside the question of God being the immutable, first cause of everything. Thomas Aquinas' claim that God acts timelessly, in the sense of sustaining the whole universe eternally could be assessed (*Summa Theologiae*, 1a, 19, 3)

FURTHER READING

There is a wealth of material on omnipotence, omniscience and God's eternity available. The titles below have been selected to provide a few suggestions of ways to follow up the content of this chapter.

The attributes of God

A number of introductions to philosophy of religion are widely available that examine the attributes of God. *The Philosophy of Religion: A Critical Introduction* by Clack and Clack gives a helpful overview of the key terminology. If you would like to examine some more modern questions concerning God's nature and the problem of evil, you could consider Jon Sobrino's *Where Is God? Earthquake, Terrorism, Barbarity, and Hope* (2004).

Omniscience, free will and belief in God

Smith and Oaklander's book *Time, Change and Freedom: An Introduction to Metaphysics* (1999) is a detailed examination of philosophical problems concerning belief in God and questions about free will and determinism. It is written as a series of dialogues between four people. Alice and Phil are philosophy degree students, while Sophia and Ivan are philosophy professors.

Each of the characters defends a particular philosophical view. In *Dialogue* 10, pages 130–40 consider whether free will is possible if God exists. As it is written as a dialogue, it is a good idea to read the text in a group. In addition, if any of the terminology in the chapter is unclear, have a look at the glossary at the end of the chapter. If you read this book, bear in mind that many of the other topics in it are related to, but not directly relevant to the Advanced Level Religious Studies course, as the dialogues in the book go well beyond the scope of A level.

The omni qualities

If you would like to read some original philosophical articles and texts concerning the 'omni' qualities of God, many are easily available in the anthology of philosophy of religion articles entitled *Philosophy of Religion: The Big Questions* edited by Stump and Murray (1999).

17 Psychology and Sociology of Religion

This chapter is not part of the specification but provides useful information for students as well as opportunities for stretch and challenge.

THE ISSUES

- Is religious belief explainable as a purely sociological phenomenon?
- Is God a product of the human mind?
- Do psychology and sociology of religion disprove the existence of God?

WHAT YOU WILL LEARN ABOUT IN THIS CHAPTER

This chapter examines sociologists' and psychologists' answers to the question: why are people religious?

In particular, the chapter considers the claim that religious belief is a product of society, and discusses the theories put forward by Durkheim and Weber to explain the existence and influence of religion in society. It also examines how psychologists might explain religious belief, focusing in particular on the ideas of Carl Jung and Sigmund Freud.

STARTER: WHY ARE PEOPLE RELIGIOUS?

Complete the following questionnaire by yourself first of all. Then ask other people one question each. Ask them to explain their views to you. Discuss the results of the survey.

Table 17.1

Questions	Your answer	Another answer
What do you mean by the word 'religious'?		
Are/were you religious?		
Are/were your parent(s) religious?		
Does it benefit people if they are religious?		
Do religions brainwash people?		
Do people believe in God because:		

- it comforts them?
- it helps them cope with difficulty?
- they are in trouble?

Is God a reality?		
Is God a product of human wishes?		
Have religions been a force for good in history?		
Is religion an illusion?		

INTRODUCTION

This chapter examines the relationship between sociology, psychology and religion. Both sociology and psychology explore the origins of religious belief, but they come to very different conclusions. Both of them challenge traditional belief in the existence of God and offer different explanations of the origins, nature and importance of religious belief. The questions in the starter survey of attitudes reflect some of the issues that are raised by the interaction of religion with psychology and sociology.

This chapter examines, first, sociology and religion and, second, psychology and religion.

> **The starter activity**
>
> The questions in the starter activity relate to issues raised by psychological and sociological studies of religion.

SOCIOLOGY OF RELIGION

WHAT IS SOCIOLOGY?

Sociology studies the behaviour of people and society. Sociologists try to understand different patterns of behaviour in society. For example, sociologists investigate the effects and causes of racism, or the possible links between poor education and crime.

Social fact

A type of behaviour or action that is either socially compulsory or unacceptable. For example, blowing your nose in public is unacceptable in some cultures – this is a social fact.

Deviant

A person who chooses not to obey social rules.

For sociologists, society makes you the person you are. Sociologists argue that people's culture, values and beliefs all come from the society in which they grow up. If you had grown up in Saudi Arabia you would most likely be a Muslim and believe that it is wrong for a woman to expose parts of her body, such as a leg or an arm, while for many people in Britain today this is not an issue. Sociologists are interested in the behaviour of groups of people and what leads to change in these groups.

The Thought Point (below) highlights a number of types of behaviour that many people believe to be examples of bad behaviour, especially when committed in public. Sociologists call these types of rules 'social facts'. It is a 'social fact' in many societies that picking your nose in public is unacceptable behaviour. Sociologists are interested in why this behaviour is unacceptable. Some people choose to pick their nose in public anyway – this is an example of behaviour that sociologists call 'deviant'. By 'deviant', sociologists mean a person whose actions break social rules – sociologists are particularly interested in the causes and effects of deviant behaviour, such as crime.

Sociology is also called a 'social science'. This is because sociology is interested in gathering evidence to explain behaviour in society that can be analysed in a scientific way. This is one reason why sociologists are interested in religion: for many people religion comes from belief and is not based on scientifically assessable evidence. Sociologists explore why people sometimes believe extraordinary things, such as stories of alien abductions or miracles.

Thought Point

Anything wrong with . . . ?

- Picking your nose
- Cleaning your ears
- Not shaving
- Exposing any part of your body
- Squeezing a spot
- Kissing.

Does it make a difference if these activities are carried out in public?

SOCIOLOGY AND RELIGION

Sociologists have always been interested in religion for the obvious reason that they are interested in studying the behaviour of people in society and community. Religious people form a community; for example, members of a religion often go together to a place of worship to pray. The sociologist Émile Durkheim commented that 'social interaction is the source of religion' (*The Elementary Forms of Religious Life*).

Second, religion clearly affects people's behaviour. It is part of the cultural environment in which people grow and develop as individuals. Sociologists are interested in the way in which religion shapes people and also in questions concerning deviancy; for example, why some people reject religious belief even though they grow up in a society where religion is important, or the causes and effects of fundamentalist religious behaviour today.

DOES SOCIOLOGY OF RELIGION DISPROVE GOD'S EXISTENCE?

Sociology of religion does not disprove God's existence or claim to do this. However, sociology of religion does challenge the sources of many religious values, activities and beliefs by arguing that they come from society and not from God.

Sociology challenges religious beliefs and religions in a number of ways.

1 Why are people religious?

Most religious people would claim that they are religious because God exists and it is right to respond to God. People who are brought up in a religious tradition such as Christianity or Islam claim that belief in God has been revealed to them.

However, sociologists argue that the time and place of birth are the important factors. Phil Zuckerman gives the example of Costa Rica (*Invitation to the Sociology of Religion*). He asks: why is Costa Rica Catholic? His answer is that it is a result of the conquest of Costa Rica by Europeans and the adoption (often under duress) of the religion of the conquerors: Catholic Christianity.

Many sociologists claim that it is where you are born and the beliefs of your family that influence your religious views. Sociologists would argue that converts are also influenced by others – not just by their families.

> **Brainwashing and sociology**
>
> Sociological research has shown that there is no evidence that religions brainwash people into believing – a claim that is often made against so-called 'cults'.

Thought Point

Many Christians in the USA had slaves in the eighteenth and nineteenth centuries and they did not believe this to be wrong.

1   Was this Christian behaviour?
2   What can you deduce from this example about the influence of society on religious belief?

2 Conversions

Sociologists such as Rodney Starke and Roger Finke (*Acts of Faith*) have suggested that while conversions do happen, they are strongly influenced by society.

This view suggests that religious belief is not really about a faith choice or decision to believe. Instead it is about bringing one's views into line with those of one's neighbours. It is certainly the case that religious beliefs tend to be passed on within families down the generations, as do atheist beliefs.

Response

However, the fact remains that some people do convert to a completely different religious tradition with which they have not had any contact through friends and family. Equally, if the claim about conversion and the passing on of beliefs is true, an interesting question to ask is: why has the level of religious practice continued to be very high in the USA since the Second World War, while it has dropped to much lower levels in the United Kingdom and Spain?

3 Religious experiences

Many religious believers claim to have experienced God in their lives, and religious experience is also the basis of one argument for the existence of God. However, sociologists have suggested that religious experiences are 'socially patterned' (Zuckerman, *Invitation to the Sociology of Religion*), by which they mean that the religious experiences fit in with the religious tradition they come from. For example, a Hindu might experience God as an avatar such as Krishna or Rama, while a Christian may experience God as Jesus or the Holy Spirit. Sociologists suggest that the way in which people talk about experiences that they call religious reflects the tradition they come from.

Response

While this may be true, a religious person could argue that experiences of God are ineffable. Hence, the language you will use to talk about the experience will be drawn from your upbringing. So, of course, if you grew up in a Hindu family, you would use the type of language gained from a Hindu upbringing to describe your experience.

Thought Point

Atheism

If an atheist had an experience that others would call religious, how could they describe it if they had not grown up in any religious tradition?

4 Religion is not separate from the influence of society

Sociologists have shown that religions are greatly influenced by society, and their values often reflect those of the surrounding society in which the religion either originated or exists today. For example, the Anglican Church in Britain changed its teaching in the 1990s and decided to allow women to be ordained as priests. Other examples include the acceptance of abortion by some religious traditions and changing attitudes to marriage and divorce.

These examples and others suggest that while religious traditions sometimes claim their teaching to be divinely revealed, some sociologists would disagree and claim that the teaching of the religious traditions reflects the pervading values of society.

Response

Many religious believers would disagree with the idea that religious beliefs are completely shaped by society. First, many Christians and Muslims would claim that the teaching of their religions is a matter of divine revelation and that society's attitudes are irrelevant. This may be seen in certain teachings of religions which seem to be directly opposed to attitudes found in some societies today. In Western Europe divorce and sex outside marriage are widely accepted, and there is growing tolerance and acceptance of homosexual relationships. However, to many Christians and Muslims all of these activities are immoral as revealed by God, or through Jesus and the prophet Muhammad ﷺ.

Second, it is undoubtedly true that religion has been a real cause of change in society, often for the better. For example, the civil rights campaign in the United States of America was led by church ministers such as Martin Luther King Jr. They campaigned peacefully for equal rights for black people, and their belief in both equal rights and peaceful campaigning came from their religious faith.

SOCIOLOGY OF RELIGION – TWO CASE STUDIES

CASE STUDY 1: ÉMILE DURKHEIM

Durkheim on religion

Durkheim defined religion as:

> A unified system of beliefs and practices relative to sacred things, that is to say, things set apart and forbidden – beliefs and practices which unite into one single moral community called a Church, all those who adhere to them. (*The Elementary Forms of Religious Life*)

As this definition makes clear, Durkheim believed that religion has a unifying role for society – it unites groups of people in a moral community who share a set of beliefs. However, Durkheim does not say that religion relates to a God that exists. For Durkheim, religion is a reality that exists in society – religion cannot be separated from society. He described religion as 'a mode of action', meaning that it was something that united people in society and enabled the people to act together as a society. For example, if you want to build a bridge, you need to work with other people. Durkheim was arguing that religion was in some ways like glue that held society together so that it could achieve results.

Durkheim was not saying that any particular religion was important. Instead, he suggested that societies would go through periods of 'transition' in which the societies' unifying beliefs might

Durkheim the man (1858–1917)

Portrait of Émile Durkheim (b/w photo) by French photographer.
Bibliothèque Nationale, Paris, France/Lauros/Giraudon/The Bridgeman Art Library.
Nationality/copyright status: French/out of copyright

Émile Durkheim was born in Peinl, Lorraine, on 15 April 1858. He is one of the founding figures of sociology. He became the first Professor of the Science of Education and Sociology at the Sorbonne University in Paris in 1913. He also founded the first French sociology journal called *Année Sociologique*. During his life he supported the Republican movement in France and the separation of religion from the state. He died in 1917 at the age of 59.

continued opposite

change or be reinterpreted. The difficult period for society is the period in which the transition takes place. When the Conquistadors from Spain and Portugal invaded Latin and South America in the sixteenth century, they converted the native population, often forcefully, to Christianity. Today most people living in this part of the world are Christian. One of the difficult periods to live in would have been the period of 'transition' or change, when the old religious beliefs were replaced by Christianity.

Thought Point

Society today

Is society today in a period of transition? Can you think of any evidence to suggest that it is?

Durkheim spent much of his adult life investigating the development of religion. To do this he focused on primitive religions as a way to explore the development of religious traditions and beliefs. He focused on the earliest religious tradition he could identify: some Aborigine communities' beliefs. His work was published in his book *The Elementary Forms of Religious Life*.

TOTEMISM

Durkheim (*The Elementary Forms of Religious Life*) suggested that *totemism* was the source of later religious beliefs such as Animism and Naturism, which in turn precede modern religions of today. His investigation of Aboriginal society found that its beliefs were linked with a totemic object, most commonly an animal.

A totem is a sacred thing; that is, a totem is set apart from and different from things in ordinary life. Things in ordinary life are called 'profane'. The totem unites a group and is treated with respect. Durkheim concluded that totems were the emblem of a tribe, the plant or animal that the emblem represents.

Totem
A sacred thing; that is, a totem is set apart from and different from things in ordinary life.

Profane
Something that is not sacred, i.e. the everyday.

continued overleaf

Thought Point

Make a list of things people view as sacred today.

The totem object is treated differently from profane things; for example, a totem should not be killed – this could mean not killing the totem animals or the members of the tribe of the totem animal. The totemic objects are united by 'an anonymous, impersonal force immanent in the world and diffused among its various material objects' (Durkheim, *The Elementary Forms of Religious Life*). Durkheim went on to explain that he meant by this that 'the god of the clan, the totemic principle, can therefore be nothing else than the clan itself, personified and represented to the imagination under the visible form of the animal or plant which serves as totem'. Thus the totem is a symbolic representation of the clan that unites the clan members in belief.

Belief in God comes from belief that the totemic principle is incarnate in each member of the tribe. Durkheim suggested that early people at tribal gatherings thought about the origins of the belief in the totem animal, and this led leaders to conclude that there must have been a founder – a god. People came to believe in immortality because they lived on in the lives of other members of the tribe in whom the totem was also present.

Evil spirits and devils were viewed by Durkheim as the symbolic way in which early people expressed experiences of grief, suffering and mourning.

RELIGION AND EXPERIENCE

Durkheim agreed with William James that religious belief came from real experiences people had. However, Durkheim also went on to say that society is the reality that causes the religious experience. Belief in the totem came from people interacting socially together. William James did not say this.

The crucifix

Look at the picture of the crucifix. What do you think Durkheim would have said about it?

continued opposite

Why is Durkheim's theory a challenge to religious belief?

Durkheim's theory challenges religious belief, as he concluded that the origin of religion is social interaction between people that leads to belief in the totem. If this is the case, there is no divine origin of religion; God does not found religion – instead religious belief is a product of society and people interacting in society that is passed on down the generations. Apart from society, religious belief does not exist.

Criticisms

- Assuming that ancient and modern religions develop in the same way is perhaps not fair to either group, because there is such a marked difference between the totemic beliefs studied by Durkheim and the prominent religious traditions of the world today, such as Hinduism, Judaism, Christianity and Islam.
- Durkheim limited his enquiries to a very small group of Aboriginal tribes of Australia. Modern sociologists have commented on the limited scope of the data he considered, and the fact that these tribes' beliefs are not representative of Aborigines' beliefs.
- Durkheim does not consider the important role of religious leaders (e.g. Jesus in Christianity or the Prophet Muhammad ﷺ in Islam).

Weber the man (1864–1920)

Max Weber was one of the earliest writers on sociology. He was born in Erfurt, Germany. A very able child, by the age of 14 he knew the writings of people such as Homer, Cicero, Kant and Schopenhauer in great detail. When he was 18 he went to Heidelberg University to study law. By 1886 he had passed the equivalent of the 'bar' examinations to become a lawyer. In 1889 he completed his doctorate on legal history. While writing his doctorate he began to study social policy and he became an expert on rural economics and sociology. He became a professor at Freiberg University, and in 1897 a professor at Heidelberg University. However, he became ill, suffering from exhaustion and insomnia. He resigned as a professor in 1903.

continued opposite

CASE STUDY 2: MAX WEBER

Weber's writing on sociology

Although Max Weber was a professor of economics rather than sociology, he wrote a large number of books examining the sociology of religion. He was interested in the effect that religion had on the development of culture and economics in society, particularly in Western Europe. This is reflected in his most famous book, *The Protestant Ethic and the Spirit of Capitalism*. Weber attempted to understand why the cultures of Western Europe had developed in a very different way from those of Asia and China. He concluded that religion was an important factor driving economic development in Western Europe and North America.

Protestant ethics and the spirit of capitalism

Max Weber's most famous book was published in 1904 and is important for two reasons. First, it presents his detailed examination of the relationship between religion and economic development in Western Europe and, second, it is an introduction to many of his later works on the religions of China, India and Ancient Judaism.

Weber argued that Protestant religious beliefs influenced the development of capitalism. He coined the phrase 'Protestant ethic' to describe Protestant attitudes to work and economic activity, and 'the spirit of capitalism' to describe the set of attitudes which value hard work and the acquisition of wealth. Weber noticed that capitalism tended to be characterised by an obsessive pursuit of wealth, greed for profit with little effort. He suggested that capitalism as an economic system had not come from just one thinker or leader; instead it must have a source or sources in society. One of the important sources he identified was Protestant Christianity. Why?

Protestant Christianity and capitalism

First, it is important to be clear about what Weber is not saying: he is not saying that Protestant Christianity aims to promote capitalism

continued opposite

and greed. Instead, what Weber noticed was that some of the tendencies in Protestant beliefs could lead indirectly to an emphasis on economic activity to obtain wealth.

In Protestant theology from the Reformation period, Calvinist reformers highlighted the fact that God saved people by his grace or power. The sign that people had been saved was that they lived a good life, worked hard and followed Christian beliefs. Inevitably, people who worked hard were more likely to become wealthy than those who did not. Thus, indirectly, working hard (a good quality) and the acquisition of wealth became linked. Protestant reformers did not approve of greed or just aiming to make a profit out of your neighbour; but hard work itself was seen as a virtuous activity. Weber argued that this theology encouraged people to become involved in society and to work hard in society. As a side effect this type of theory encouraged what he called 'the spirit of capitalism'. Hence, Weber concluded that the attitudes promoted by some aspects of Protestant Christian thought, albeit unintentionally, were an important factor in the development of capitalism.

Weber went on to argue that the roots of capitalism in Protestant theology promoting good works were gradually forgotten as the capitalist pursuit of wealth became the dominant force in society.

Do Weber's ideas challenge religious belief?

Weber's writings on sociology and economics do not challenge religious belief in the same way as Durkheim's views do. However, it is important to note that if Weber's model of economic development is correct, religion has been a force for change in society but the roots of capitalism in religion decrease in importance and capitalism becomes a force for change in society in its own right. Religion's role diminishes or disappears. If this is correct, Weber's work highlights the decreasing importance of religion as an agent of change in society.

After resigning he published some of his most important writings, including his famous book *The Protestant Ethic and the Spirit of Capitalism*. In 1918 he resumed work as a university professor, first in Vienna and later in Munich. However, he was not popular in Munich due to his left-wing political activities.

He died of pneumonia in 1920.

Capitalism

A form of economic development whose goal is the acquisition of wealth. The word 'capital' refers to the amount of monetary wealth an individual or company possesses.

Weber on religion and capitalism

A glance at the occupational statistics of any country of mixed religious composition brings to light with remarkable frequency a situation which has several times provoked discussion in the Catholic press and literature, and in Catholic congresses in Germany

continued overleaf

namely the fact that business leaders and owners of capital, as well as the higher grades of skilled labour, and even more the higher technically and commercially trained personnel of modern enterprises, are overwhelmingly Protestant. (Weber, *The Protestant Ethic and the Spirit of Capitalism*)

Weber on capitalism

The capitalistic system so needs this devotion to the calling of making money, it is an attitude toward material goods which is so well suited to that system, so intimately bound up with the conditions of survival in the economic struggle for existence, that there can today no longer be any question of a necessary connection of that acquisitive manner of life with any single worldview. In fact, it no longer needs the support of any religious forces, and feels the attempts of religion to influence economic life, in so far as they can still be felt at all, to be as much an unjustified interference as its regulation by the State. (Weber, *The Protestant Ethic and the Spirit of Capitalism*)

PSYCHOLOGY OF RELIGION

WHAT IS PSYCHOLOGY OF RELIGION?

Psychology is the study of the workings of the human mind. While sociology is concerned with the behaviour of human beings in society, psychology is concerned with what goes on in the human mind.

Psychology of religion is concerned with questions such as: Why are individual people religious? What happens in the human mind when a person undergoes a conversion experience? In contrast, sociology of religion explores questions such as: Why have levels of church attendance fallen so much in Britain compared with the USA since the Second World War?

Thought Point

All in the mind?

Why do you think levels of attendance at religious services always increase during wartime?

A key issue that psychology explores is whether religious belief is a product of the human mind. For example: are people religious because it gives them hope or brings them comfort? If these needs are the true origin of religion there is no need to believe that God exists. Instead, God is a product or construction of the human mind.

The two most well-known commentators on psychology and religion are Sigmund Freud and his friend, and later rival, Carl Gustav Jung.

SIGMUND FREUD

The basis of Freud's psychoanalytical work is summed up by Anthony Kenny (*A Brief History of Western Philosophy*) as:

that the greater part of our mental life, whether of feeling, thought or volition, is unconscious; the second is that sexual impulses, broadly defined, are supremely important not only as potential causes of mental illnesses but as the motor of artistic and cultural creation.

In essence Freud argued that religion derives from the unconscious and that sexual impulses are closely related to religion. He argued that religion was:

- An illusion;
- An obsessional neurosis.

The meaning of these two ideas and their relationship to the unconscious part of the mind and sexual impulses are explored below.

Freud's approach to religion may be summarised as follows:

- Science is based on observation of the world; religion is not.
- Psychoanalysis is a science which can help to explain why religious beliefs are appealing.
- Religious belief is caused by the wish for a father figure who saves the believer like a father saving his child.

Religion is an obsessional neurosis

In his book *Obsessive Acts and Religious Practices* (1907) Freud argued that religion is an obsessional neurosis.

By 'neurosis' Freud meant the symptoms of illnesses such as hysteria. Neuroses, according to Freud, are caused by the mind repressing a traumatic experience from conscious thought into the unconscious part of the mind. This repression leads to problems, and sometimes the unconscious repressed experience surfaces again in conscious thought as a neurosis. His evidence for the existence of the unconscious came from so-called Freudian slips, dreams and neuroses. Freud argued that the neuroses were caused by repressed sexuality that is linked to the Oedipus Complex (see below).

Freud began to link religion with neurosis because he noticed that many patients at Salpêtrière mental hospital who suffered from hysteria displayed obsessive behaviour. For example, they followed complicated routines for even simple tasks such as getting up or cleaning their teeth. If the routine was not followed exactly, the patient would became very distressed. He observed that these patterns of behaviour had to be followed and this mirrored some religious practices (e.g. in Christian Eucharistic services there is often a complicated ritual of actions to be followed). One thing that distresses worshippers is the failure of the priest or minister leading the service to follow the ritual exactly.

Essential terminology

Animism
Archetype
Hysteria
Libido – Freud
Libido – Jung
Neurosis
Oedipus Complex

Freud the man (1856–1939)

Sigmund Freud was born in Freiberg, Moravia, although he moved to Vienna in 1860 where he remained until 1938. He fled to London in 1938 to escape the Nazis as his extended family was Jewish, and although Freud was an atheist, culturally he was from a Jewish background.

Freud worked at the Salpêtrière mental hospital in Paris in 1885, and it was from his work there that he was led to the idea of the existence of the unconscious. In 1895 he and Josef Breuer published the important book *Studies in Hysteria* that suggested the use of hypnotism to recall suppressed traumatic experiences from the unconscious part of the mind in order to treat mental illnesses.

Hysteria

The word used by Freud to refer to a range of illnesses that would today be described as mental illnesses, which while they may have physical symptoms (e.g. obsessions) may have no identifiable physical cause.

Neurosis

By 'neurosis' Freud meant the symptoms of mental illness caused by a repressed traumatic experience resurfacing in the conscious mind in a different way.

Oedipus Complex

Refers to Freud's belief that young boys aged around 5 years old are sexually attracted to their mothers and resent their fathers' presence. As the boy develops these feelings are repressed and disappear out of fear that the father will take revenge on the son.

THE OEDIPUS COMPLEX

The Oedipus Complex refers to Freud's belief that young boys are sexually attracted to their mother. Freud argued that the boy became attracted to the mother and resented the father's presence. However, these feelings, according to Freud, gradually diminish out of fear that the father will take revenge and castrate the boy. This is the Oedipus Complex and is normal according to Freud. He suggested that the Oedipus Complex applied to girls in some way, but he never explained this idea fully.

Freud argued that some form of repressed sexual experience caused neuroses. He argued that young boys are used to attention from their mothers, such as being breast-fed. As they grow, they desire that the attention from their mother continues; the father is seen as a rival. However, as the boy gets older these feelings for his mother are repressed into the unconscious. Sometimes a patient develops a neurosis when the unconsciously repressed experience effectively comes into conscious thought again in a different way. One example of neurosis given by Freud is a phobia about animals and insects.

The Wolf Man

One case that Freud wrote about concerned an adult patient of his called Sergei Pankejeff, who had a terror of wolves. He also suffered from serious depression and was obsessively religious. Freud analysed his patient using the Oedipus Complex. Freud identified the cause of the man's problems as having repressed homosexual feelings and the trauma of witnessing his parents having sexual intercourse when he was a young child. Freud concluded that the man's fear of wolves substituted for his fear of his father.

The origins of religion

In his book *Totem and Taboo* (1913) Freud tried to prove that there was a link between neurosis and religion.

Freud linked religion to Animism. In Animism the belief is that the spirits can be controlled by certain rituals and actions. Freud believed that early people who believed in Animism overestimated the mind's ability to control the environment through magic. It is an example of a belief in which the disorderly nature of the world is explained by the actions of spirits. Freud did not believe that spirits were real – Animism for Freud was a way of looking at the world that the mind constructed.

Religion for Freud was like Animism. Religion is a way that the mind interprets the world. God is used as the explanation of why things are as they are in the world. He argued that religious acts of worship, such as praying or the Eucharist, are like magic in Animism – a way of understanding the world and making it explainable. This is why Freud calls religion an obsessional neurosis. It is an example of a case where the mind does not see the world as it really is (using science).

Freud argued that religion derives from the Oedipus relationship between father and son. Freud claimed that:

> The derivation of religious needs from the infant's helplessness and the longing for the father aroused by it seems to me incontrovertible . . . I cannot think of any need in childhood as strong as the need for a father's protection. . . . The origin of the religious attitude can be traced back in clear outlines as far as the feeling of infantile helplessness. There may be something further behind that, but for the present it is wrapped in obscurity. (Palmer, *Freud and Jung on Religion*)

The Oedipus Complex and the primal horde

Freud developed an idea first suggested by Charles Darwin that early human beings lived like great apes in a horde that was ruled over by a dominant male. This male was powerful and had many wives and children. Younger males were driven out of the horde to prevent them from becoming rivals to the dominant male. This type of behaviour has been observed in some mammal species.

However, Freud did not stop there. Instead, he added to Darwin's suggestion the following ideas. He suggested that the young males united together one day to kill the dominant father and become dominant over the horde and gain wives. After the event, the young males felt guilty for what they had done, because although they wanted to replace the father, they had also admired the father in the sense that they wanted his position. Out of guilt the brothers formed a tribe. None of them actually took the place of the father. Instead, they had a totem that like a god united the tribe and ruled over it. The totem replaced the father figure. The totem was most commonly an animal. The members of the horde worshipped the totem and remembered it, and it was forbidden to kill the totem animal. Memories of this event are passed on in the unconscious.

There are two important points to note about the primal horde theory:

1   Freud is suggesting something which could be a historical event.
2   The God father figure originates from this first murder.

Hysteria and repression of sexual instincts

[A]t the bottom of every case of hysteria there are *one or more occurrences of premature sexual experience*, occurrences which belong to the earliest years of childhood. (Palmer, *Freud and Jung on Religion*)

Oedipus

The name Oedipus refers to the character in Greek legend who ends up killing his father and marrying his own mother by accident. Read the story of Oedipus Rex if you would like to know more about it.

Animism

Refers to the belief that spirits give life of some sort to both living creatures and objects. Animism is not a religion but Freud believed Animism led to the development of religion.

Freud on the primal horde

Michael Palmer suggests that belief in God, according to Freud, is an illusion that comes from the:

emotional (and infantile) impulse to return to the past and to become once again the submissive son of the father of the horde. (Palmer, *Freud and Jung on Religion*)

The Oedipus Complex originates from this first crime, as the unconscious mind through the Oedipus Complex is recalling this killing by the primal horde. In the primal horde the brothers both admired and hated their father. In the Oedipus Complex the son both wants to replace his father and fears his father. Freud claimed that some of his child patients exhibiting the Oedipus Complex commonly feared a particular animal instead of fearing their father.

Freud suggested that belief in God arose as a result of the primal horde murder. Over time, out of guilt at what they had done, the brothers remembered the father. Gradually the father figure became like a god and so belief in God commenced.

Freud suggested that Christianity also recalled the memory of the primal horde through the story of Jesus – Jesus is the father figure who is killed and later remembered by his followers and honoured as a god.

Religion is an illusion

Freud argued that religion is an illusion, by which he meant that it expresses people's desires – what they want to believe. Religion meets people's psychological needs. Michael Palmer (*Freud and Jung on Religion*) suggests that Freud has some particular psychological needs of human beings in mind:

* *Coping with threats in the natural world by creating gods who control the natural world*
  Freud suggested that early human beings lived in a world in which the forces of nature were chaotic, beyond comprehension and terrifying. Freud argued that the coping mechanism for these early people was to develop belief in gods who were the controllers of nature.
* *Controlling human instinct, such as aggression and sexual instincts*
  Freud argued that religion helped people to direct and control the libido. Religion does this through its strict laws governing behaviour in society, such as laws concerning sexual intercourse, or the just war theory to limit the scope of war and violence. He believed that religion had had beneficial effects for society.

Freud suggested that the universal longing for a father figure expressed through the Oedipus Complex could be satisfied by religion, where God is the father figure. God can at once be a loving figure and a harsh judge. Freud suggested that God the father is a reflection of people's relationship with their own father. In particular, a person's obedience to their own father is mirrored by the adult obediently following religious rules.

Freud argues that religion has greatly benefited people and society in the past. For example, religion has been a source of laws and customs that have helped societies to develop. However, Freud argues that religion has also not made people happy and has led to people being used. With scientific developments religion should be abandoned because it is a neurosis.

Criticisms of Freud

Freud believed that his arguments would lead to the end of religion once people accepted that religion was a neurosis to be cured. He believed that his psychological theory backed up David Hume's claims that religious beliefs, such as in miracles, were about wish fulfilment. However, Freud's theories are not widely accepted today and have been criticised in many ways.

1 Causes of mental illness

There are many possible causes of obsessional neuroses, not just the Oedipus Complex. This is recognised in modern mental health care; for example, doctors today understand that there are a wide variety of causes of depression and also that bipolar disorder may be related to one's genes (i.e. the tendency to be a manic depressive can be inherited). No one doubts, for example, that sexual abuse can have serious psychological effects on the victims, but it is not true to say that all mental illness is caused by repression of experiences of sexual trauma.

2 Evidence

Freud has been accused of being unreliable. For example, totemism is not a stage of religious development that all communities around the world have gone through. In addition, there is little evidence for sexual aggression among our nearest relatives such as chimpanzees; this would suggest that there is a lack of evidence to support Freud's primal horde theory.

Freud's claims about the scientific nature of his findings as opposed to religion are inaccurate. Many religious people understand science and many scientists have suggested that Freud ignored evidence that did not support his theories.

There is no evidence of an inherited unconscious memory of a crime committed by the primal horde.

3 The Oedipus Complex

There is no agreement about whether the Oedipus Complex actually exists, and if it does, many people suggest that it is not universal. Malinowski has

---

Freud on the origins of belief in God

The notion of a man becoming god or of a god dying strikes us today as shockingly presumptuous; but even in classical antiquity there was nothing revolting in it. The elevation of the father who had once been murdered into a god from whom the clan claimed descent was a far more serious attempt at atonement than had been the ancient covenant with the totem. (Palmer, *Freud and Jung on Religion*)

Libido according to Freud

Libido in Freud's writing refers to the desires of a person and their need to be satisfied. Freud was referring to more than just sexual desire and the wish of adults to have sexual intercourse with a partner. The libido, according to Freud, develops with the person. In adults it is expressed in the desire for children, whereas in babies it is the desire for the mother and to be fed by her. Libido applies as much to children as to adults. Freud himself pointed to the fact that the desires of a person only focus on a person other than a parent after puberty.

suggested that there is no evidence that the Oedipus Complex is universal or inherited. Other scholars have suggested that the Oedipus Complex could be the result of society and upbringing.

4 God as father figure

Freud's image of God as a father figure is limited, in the sense that it is not the only image of God and would be rejected by feminists as a symptom of the male-centred nature of religious thinking. In other words, Freud's father figure God tells us something about his views rather than about God.

In other cultures, there is not a male God figure or necessarily a God figure at all. Anthropologists have discovered some cultures in which the mother is dominant and the father's role in bringing up the child is very limited. All of this somewhat undermines the idea of the Oedipus Complex and primal horde theory being universal.

CARL GUSTAV JUNG

Jung, like Freud, is one of the most famous writers on psychology of religion. However, his views and model of the mind are very different from those of Freud.

According to Jung the mind had three parts:

1 Consciousness
2 Personal unconsciousness
3 Collective unconsciousness.

Jung had a completely different view of the unconscious from Freud. Jung believed that all people inherited a collective unconscious that they share as well as having a personal unconscious. This collective unconscious is not produced from experiences or repressed experiences. Jung believed that the collective unconscious contains images or symbols that resemble trace memories of ancient events that have been handed down to us.

Jung used the word *libido* in a very different way from Freud. For him, libido is *psychic energy* – it is the energy in the mind (psyche) which could be either potential or dynamic. Jung said that this was a conceptual necessity but he acknowledged that it was an unproven hypothesis. For mental health there needed to be a balance in libido between the unconscious and conscious mind. Mental illnesses, according to Jung, are caused by an imbalance in psychic energy. Jung suggested that Freud's theories could not explain the cause of schizophrenia. This was one area of disagreement between them. Instead, Jung suggested that schizophrenia was caused by an imbalance in libidinal energy. For Jung, neuroses were caused by a failure properly to integrate the unconscious and conscious parts of the mind.

Jung observed that many of his patients seemed to be obsessed with images and symbols. He developed a method called *amplification* through which he investigated parallels between the images preoccupying his patients and images and symbolism in religious texts. Jung believed that the link between the symbols of the two groups pointed to the existence of a collective unconscious shared by people.

Archetypes

Jung noted that many symbols and images, such as the association between light and God, were common across the centuries and different cultures. In many ancient cultures the sun had been worshipped, and in Christian culture churches are orientated towards the rising sun; Jesus is called the 'Light of the World'. Jung put forward the hypothesis of archetypes to explain the many cross-cultural symbols that he discovered through research.

Jung used the word *archetype* to refer to symbolic forms that all people share in their unconscious mind. These archetypes are very old and inherited from generation to generation. The archetypes generate images in the conscious mind. Hence, the common symbols used in religion across the generations. However, the meaning of these symbols is undefined in the unconscious mind. Each person interprets the images which come from their unconscious. Jung stated that the 'content' or meaning of each archetype came from the person, but the archetype itself came from the depths of the person's unconscious.

There are many different archetypes in the mind. Jung analysed five in detail: *persona, shadow, anima, animus* and *self*.

For example, he suggested that the *persona* archetype refers to the public image people present to others. The content of this *persona* is dominated by society. Jung gave the example of a 'parson' (priest) who must not only do his job, but also behave as one expects a 'parson' to behave. For Jung this *persona* from society could become a source of problems and neurosis if the individual did not integrate their persona with other parts of their personality.

Jung suggested that *self* was the most important archetype, as it expresses individuality, by which he meant the successful integration of the different parts of the mind. He suggested that the *self* was the goal of life.

God the archetype

Jung suggested that God is an archetype. By this Jung meant that God was a reality from the deepest part of the human collective unconscious. The

Libido – Jung

Jung used the word 'libido' to mean psychic energy – it is the energy in the mind (*psyche*) which could be either potential or dynamic. For mental health there needed to be a balance in libido between the unconscious and conscious mind.

Archetype

Jung used the word *archetype* to refer to symbolic forms that all people share in their collective unconscious. These archetypes are very old and inherited from generation to generation. The archetypes generate images in the conscious mind.

Form of God is unknowable – this is just like any other archetype and also like the Christian belief in the transcendent and ineffable nature of God.

The God archetype is revealed in many different ways and this, according to Jung, explains the existence of different religions around the world. What people know about God comes from the unconscious. This neither disproves nor proves God's existence as a reality, but it limits what we know of God to the collective unconscious. Like Kant, Jung rejected arguments that claimed to prove God's existence as a reality.

For Jung, when people talk about God, they are talking about the symbols and images generated by the God archetype.

Religious experiences are interpreted by Jung as images generated by the God archetype. A person can experience a revelation in the sense that they have no control over the images generated by the God archetype in the unconscious. Religion for Jung is about analysis and discussion of the symbols and images generated by the God archetype. Since religion derives from the God archetype, everyone has the potential, in Jung's thinking, to be religious.

Religion and the God archetype

Jung suggested that a lack of religious feelings or beliefs was psychologically damaging, precisely because it suggested a failure by the person to integrate the unconscious and conscious mind.

'Individuation' was the name Jung gave to the process of integrating the unconscious and conscious parts of the mind to develop the self. Jung suggested that the process of individuation had two stages:

1   The first half of life was characterised by the psyche adapting to society and developing a persona.
2   The second half of life was characterised by a concern with ultimate questions. Individuation and the development of *self* fit into this stage.

Jung suggested that religion was one way to individuation since religion comes from an archetype. Religious images could show the stages of individuation. The example Jung gave was the unity of one God in three persons in the Christian Trinity. Furthermore, because the *self* and God are archetypes, the development of the *self* is a religious activity since the archetypes are beyond comprehension and thus not distinguishable.

Criticisms of Jung

*   Jung's ideas are unverifiable. Jung claims that his ideas are based on psychic facts. However, these cannot be tested and assessed like a

scientific experiment. It cannot be demonstrated that there is a collective unconscious which contains the archetypes.

- The theory of archetypes has been criticised in many ways, such as:

  - For most religious believers God is not an archetype of the mind but a reality with whom people are called to relationship.
  - When religious believers talk about God being transcendent, they mean that God is a reality beyond our time, space and human comprehension, not that God is a reality constructed by the human mind from archetypal images in the human unconscious.
  - For religious believers such as Jews, Christians and Muslims the fact that God has been experienced in history matters. In the case of Christianity, God is believed to have been incarnate in Jesus.
  - Judaism, Christianity and Islam all accept that God can be revealed directly to people and that this does occasionally happen. Jung's theory does not leave room for direct revelation.
  - There is no evidence that the God archetype is the source of similar but distinct images found in different religious traditions. The similarity of images could equally be explained by sociology as a shared historical culture, or indeed as just luck.
  - Many religious traditions do not share common images, mythology or ideas. There are, for example, great differences between the religious thought of the Islamic-Judaeo-Christian tradition and that of Buddhism or Hinduism.

HOW DOES PSYCHOLOGY CHALLENGE RELIGIOUS BELIEF?

In one sense psychology appears to pose no challenge to religious belief. Both Freud and Jung have been widely criticised by theologians, doctors and scholars. In addition, supporters of Jung have widely criticised Freud and vice versa.

However, it is not as easy as that to dismiss the challenge presented by Freud and Jung. First, while Freud's primal horde theory and Oedipus Complex may have been rejected by many people, his challenge that religion is an illusion has been supported by many later writers. There is no doubt that religion does in some way meet people's psychological needs. This can clearly be seen in the increased church attendance during times of war compared with peacetime.

Second, if Jung's suggestion that God is an archetype is correct, God appears to be something drawn from the human mind, which is very different from the Judaeo-Christian tradition's belief in God as a reality who exists, and with whom people are called to be in relationship.

Neither Freud's nor Jung's case has been proven. However, Freud and Jung, though very different, both suggest that the origin of religion is to be found in human psychology. It is this thought alone which questions the origins of religious belief.

SUMMARY

1 Sociology and religion

Sociology challenges religious beliefs:

It suggests that they come from society not from God
Sociologists argue that the time and place of birth are the important
factors governing religious beliefs
Conversions
Are strongly influenced by society
Response
    Some people do convert to a completely different religious tradition
    with which they have not had any contact

Religious experiences
Sociologists suggest that religious experiences fit in with the religious
    tradition they come from (e.g. a Hindu experiences Shiva, a Christian
    experiences Jesus)

Religion is not separate from the influence of society

Responses

Many Christians and Muslims would claim that the teaching of their
    religions is a matter of divine revelation and that religious values are
    different from society's values
That religion has been a real cause of change for the better in society (e.g.
    the civil rights campaign in the United States of America)

Émile Durkheim on religion

Durkheim believed that religion has a unifying role for society
Religion cannot be separated from society
Societies go through periods of 'transition' in which the societies' beliefs
    that unite them might change or be reinterpreted

Totemism

A totem is a sacred thing; things in ordinary life are called 'profane'

Durkheim suggested that totemism was the source of later religious belief such as Animism and Naturism, which in turn precede modern religions of today

Criticisms of Durkheim

Assuming that ancient and modern religions develop in the same way is perhaps not fair to either group

Modern sociologists have commented on the limited scope of the data he considered

Durkheim does not consider the role of religious leaders

Max Weber

Protestant ethics and the spirit of capitalism

Weber argued that Protestant religious beliefs could indirectly lead to emphasis on economic activity to obtain wealth

The roots of capitalism in Protestant theology promoting good works were gradually forgotten as the capitalist pursuit of wealth became the dominant force in society

Do Weber's ideas challenge religious belief?

Weber's work highlights the decreasing importance of religion as an agent of change, and the dominance of the values of economics in society

2 Psychology of religion: are religious beliefs a product of the human mind?

Sigmund Freud

Hysteria and religion – Freud argued that religion is:

An illusion

An obsessional neurosis

Freud's view of religion:

Science is based on observation of the world; religion is not

Psychoanalysis is a science which can help to explain why religious beliefs are appealing

Religious belief is caused by the wish for a father figure who saves the believer as a father saves his child

Religion is an obsessional neurosis:
Caused by repressed sexuality that is linked to the Oedipus Complex
The Oedipus Complex
> Freud's belief that young boys are sexually attracted to their mothers
> Freud argued that some form of repressed sexual experience caused neuroses.
> Freud's case study: The Wolf Man

The Oedipus Complex and the primal horde
> Freud suggested that the primal horde was a historical event
> The God father figure originates from the primal murder

The origins of religion
Freud linked religion to Animism
Religious acts of worship, such as praying or the Eucharist, are like magic in Animism

Religion is an illusion
It expresses people's desires and helps them cope with life
Religion concerns what people want to believe

Criticisms of Freud
There are many possible causes of obsessional neuroses, not just the Oedipus Complex
Evidence:
> Freud has been accused of being unreliable
> There is no evidence of inherited unconscious memory of a crime committed by the primal horde
> There is no agreement about whether the Oedipus Complex actually exists

Freud's image of God as a father figure is limited

Carl Gustav Jung

According to Jung the mind comprised three parts:
Consciousness
Personal unconsciousness
Collective unconsciousness

Libido
The energy in the mind (psyche) which could be either potential or dynamic

Neuroses were caused by a failure to properly integrate unconscious
and conscious parts of the mind

Amplification
Parallels between the images preoccupying Jung's patients and images
and symbolism in religious texts

Archetypes
Refer to symbolic forms that all people share in their unconscious mind
Jung stated that the 'content' of each archetype came from the person,
but the archetype itself came from the person's unconscious
Jung's five archetypes: *persona, shadow, anima, animus* and *self*
God the archetype
God is a reality from the deepest part of the human collective
unconscious
The Form of God is unknowable
When a person talks about God, they are talking about the symbols
generated by the God archetype

Religion
Jung suggested that a lack of religious feelings or beliefs was
psychologically damaging

Individuation
The process of integrating the unconscious and conscious parts of the
mind to develop the self
Two stages:
The first half of life – psyche adapting to society (developing a
persona)
The second half of life – concern with ultimate questions
(individuation of *self*)

Criticisms of Jung
Jung's ideas are unverifiable
The archetypes:
For most religious believers God is not an archetype of the mind
God being transcendent refers to God as a reality beyond our time
and space, not the fact that God is an archetype
For religious believers God being experienced in history matters
Leave no room for direct revelation

REVIEW QUESTIONS

Look back over the chapter and check that you can answer the following questions:

1   Outline in about 250 words either Weber's findings about the role of religion in society or Durkheim's findings about the nature of religion in society.
2   Explain the importance of archetypes in Jung's thinking and why they have been criticised.
3   Would you agree with the following view? Justify your answer with reasons.

> The problem is that almost all the evidence that Freud presents has been discredited in one way or another. (Palmer, *Freud and Jung on Religion*)

Terminology

Do you know your terminology?

1   Try to explain the following ideas without looking at your books and notes:

(a) Social fact
(b) Archetype
(c) Transition period
(d) Illusion
(e) Primal horde theory
(f) Oedipus Complex.

FURTHER READING

There is a lot of information about Freud, Jung, Weber and Durkheim available on the internet and in encyclopaedias. If you want to research any of these great thinkers it is worth looking in libraries or on the internet.

Anthony Kenny's book *A Brief History of Western Philosophy* contains sections on many of the philosophers you study on the OCR course, including an interesting section about Freud.

If you would like to investigate whether religion benefits people, you will find a range of useful articles written by scientists about religion and prayer on the *British Medical Journal* website (http://www.bmj.com/).

Glossary

A posteriori

A Latin phrase meaning 'from what comes after'. Philosophers use it to apply to knowledge which is known through experience.

A priori

A Latin phrase meaning 'from what comes before'. Philosophers use it to apply to knowledge that is gained irrespective of experience, simply by reasoning.

Analogy

The act of comparing one thing with another that shares similar characteristics, to help a person learn about the first thing. For example, if you say a person is 'as cunning as a fox', you are explaining something about how cunning and crafty the person is. Thomas Aquinas divided analogy into two types:

1 **Proportion** – telling us the extent to which a thing corresponds to what it should be
2 **Attribution** – telling us about the qualities of a particular thing.

Analytic

The concept of the subject is contained in the predicate, where the predicate is the part of the sentence which follows after the subject, e.g. triangles have three sides.

Animism

Refers to the belief that spirits give life of some sort to both living creatures and objects. Animism is not a religion but Freud believed Animism led to the development of religion.

Anthropic principle

The principle that humans should take into account the constraints that human existence itself imposes on the types of universe that we believe could support human life: the only type of universe we believe capable of supporting human life is the type we occupy.

Arbitrary
A decision that is not based on a reason, or the result of rational decision-making.

Archetype
An initial model or idea from which later ideas and models of the same thing are all derived.

Archetype – Jung
Jung used the word 'archetype' to refer to symbolic forms that all people share in their collective unconscious. These archetypes are very old and inherited from generation to generation. The archetypes generate images in the conscious mind.

Assumption
A belief or statement which is accepted without being supported by evidence or argument.

Atman
A Sanskrit word that means 'inner-self' or 'soul'. Atman is the *true* self of an individual beyond identification with phenomena, the essence of an individual. In order to attain liberation from *samsara*, a human being must acquire self-knowledge, which is to realise that a person's true self (*atman*) is identical with the transcendent self Brahman.

Authority
When applied to religious experience, the word 'authority' indicates that the person who has the religious experience has some new insight or knowledge about the world and God's relationship with the world. This gives them authority. Many authors argue that authority is limited to the individual who has the experience; it is not about authority and power over other people.

Autonomy
Liberty to follow one's will; personal freedom. Used in philosophy to refer to a person who is able to exercise free will to make decisions. It literally means self-governing. If you are autonomous you are able to use reason to make your own free choices.

Bias
Unfairly favouring one person or group above another.

Big Bang
The essential idea of the Big Bang is that the universe has expanded from a primordial hot and dense initial condition at some finite time in the past and continues to expand.

Body
In Aristotle's thinking 'the body' refers to the matter that a living creature is made of.

Capitalism
A form of economic development whose goal is the acquisition of wealth. The word 'capital' refers to the amount of monetary wealth an individual or company possesses.

Cause
That which produces an effect; that which gives rise to any action, phenomenon, or condition. In philosophy this concept is often linked to the so-called Four Causes of Aristotle.

The Cave
A famous analogy written by Plato which he uses to explain some parts of his theory of Forms.

Contingent
Philosophers use the word contingent to mean that something is not immortal but depends on something else for its existence. For example, human beings are caused to exist by their parents. They do not just exist. So, philosophers would say human beings are contingent beings.

Creatio ex nihilo
This phrase is Latin for '*creation out of nothing*'. It is often used by Christians to communicate the idea that God created the universe out of nothing. God creating the world as described in the Genesis creation stories is often described as being an act of creation '*out of nothing*'.

Creator
A title applied to God. In the Judaeo-Christian tradition it refers to God creating the world as recorded in the Bible, for example in Genesis 1–3, Psalm 8 or Job 38.

Cumulative argument
A philosophical argument that is built up with many different arguments and pieces of evidence. A conclusion based on probability is then drawn from all the pieces of evidence. In modern philosophy of religion it is popular to create a cumulative argument for God's existence using the separate different arguments.

Decalogue
Another term for the Ten Commandments revealed to Moses on Mount Sinai.

Deism
Belief in a God who starts the world off or creates it and then leaves it to run by itself. This view makes God completely separate from, and not involved with, his creation. Also, simply the principle of the universe, but not the one humans have a relationship with.

Deist
A person who believes that God starts the universe off with one creative act but then effectively left the universe to run without acting in it.

Deontological
Philosophical theories which hold that the morality of an act is not totally dependent on its consequences. It is the science of duty; that branch of knowledge which deals with moral obligations; ethics.

Deviant
A person who chooses not to obey social rules.

Direct religious experiences
Refer to events where God reveals her/himself directly to the person having the experience. The religious experience is not chosen or willed by the person; the person experiences or observes God in some way.

Disembodied existence
The idea that a soul can exist separately from its body. Disembodied existence relies on a dualistic view of personhood.

Divine inspiration
Refers to the belief among Christians that God inspired the writers of the books of the Bible. It may also refer to other faiths where texts are seen as being 'inspired' rather than as in Islam where the Qur'an is viewed as divine revelation.

Dualism
The view that a human person consists of two distinct elements: the mind/soul and the body. The mind/soul is immaterial whereas the body is physical.

Effect
The result of a *cause*. For example, the *cause* of a football flying through the air would be the person who kicked it. The *effect* is the result of the action – in this case the ball moving. For more information about *cause* and *effect* see the section on Aristotle.

Ego
Freud's name for the part of the mind which is shaped by and organises 'external influences' such as traumas, bereavements, education and upbringing.

Equivocal language
The use of the same word to mean completely different things when applied to different objects. For example, the word *banger* can mean: (1) a sausage; (2) a firework; (3) an old car in poor condition.

The Fall
Refers to the story of Adam and Eve in the Garden of Eden and their disobeying of God. It may be read in Genesis 2: 4 to 3: 1 of the Bible.

Falsification
The philosophical theory that an assertion is meaningless if there is no way in which it can be falsified. For example, 'Elves live in the forest but they only come out when no one is looking'.

Form
By 'Form' Plato meant the idea of something. For example, if you say 'Look! There's a cat', you have some idea of what a cat is and you can recognise lots of different types of cats. All the different types of cats embody the Form of a cat, some set of characteristics that resemble the idea of what a cat is. The Form of anything is not physical but the eternal idea of what a thing is.

Form of the Good
The highest of all the Forms. Plato said it was also the source of the other Forms.

The Four Causes

The Material Cause – what a thing is made of.

The Efficient Cause – the agent or cause of the thing coming to exist as it is. The existence of a painting or work of art is brought about by the artist who makes it. The artist is the efficient cause.

The Formal Cause – what makes the thing recognisable: its structure, shape and activity.

The Final Cause – The ultimate reason why the thing exists.

Free will
The ability to make one's own decisions and choose freely between different possible courses of action.

Genesis 1–3
The Book of Genesis is the first book of the Christian Bible and Jewish Torah. Chapters 1–2 contain two different accounts of the creation of the world by God, and the Fall is in Chapter 3.

God as judge
A common image of God throughout the Jewish Scriptures and the New Testament. In the parable of the Last Judgment (Matthew 25: 31–46), God is pictured as a king judging people, separating the good from the bad. The good go to heaven, the bad to hell.

God as lawgiver
An image of God commonly used in the Bible, for example when God reveals the Ten Commandments to the Israelites on Mount Sinai.

Grammar
The field of linguistics that covers the rules governing the use of language.

Hume, David
A famous eighteenth-century philosopher whose writings are still important today in debates about God's nature and existence. In his work David Hume presented a set of philosophical arguments against the existence of miracles.

Hysteria
The word used by Freud to refer to a range of illnesses that would today be described as mental illnesses, which while they may have physical symptoms (e.g. obsessions) may have no identifiable physical cause.

Id
Freud's name for the part of the mind in which human instincts such as desire and appetite are based.

Immanent
Used to express the idea that God is involved and active in the world. Religious people may often talk of God being experienced through other people or in a miracle. These are examples of occasions when God is immanent.

Incoherent
A philosophical argument which fails because it is illogical.

Indirect religious experiences
Experiences, thoughts or feelings about God that are prompted by events in daily life, for example observing the stars in the sky and having thoughts about the greatness of God the Creator.

Ineffable
Used to refer to experiences which it is beyond human powers and abilities to fully describe and communicate. In particular, it is used to describe the fact that God is entirely distinct from physical objects and it goes beyond human ability to describe God accurately.

Infallible
Used by religious believers to indicate that a teaching does not contain any error or possibility of error.

Inference
The philosophical word for a conclusion that is reached through a process of reasoning in an argument.

Infinite
Refers to something which has neither a beginning nor an end. Most commonly the idea of infinity is used in mathematics to describe series of numbers that have no beginning or end. For example, the series . . . –3,–2,–1,0,1,2,3 . . . could continue without end.

Intelligent Design
A theory suggesting that the universe shows evidence that it is created by God. Often Intelligent Design is closely linked to Creationism. This is quite different however from Paley's Teleological (Design) Argument.

Irreducible complexity
Meaning that objects and organisms in the world are so complex that the complexity of these things cannot be explained by the blind process of evolution.

Karma
In Hinduism, the law of cause and effect.

Libido – Freud
Refers to the desires of a person and their need to be satisfied. Freud was referring to more than just sexual desire. The libido, according to Freud, develops with the person.

Libido – Jung
Jung used the word 'libido' to mean psychic energy – it is the energy in the mind (*psyche*) which could be either potential or dynamic. For mental health there needed to be a balance in libido between the unconscious and conscious mind.

Life after death
The belief that human life continues in some fashion post mortem.

Lourdes
A Roman Catholic shrine in the south of France to which thousands of people go on pilgrimage. St Bernadette saw a vision of the Virgin Mary there and discovered a stream in the cave (Grotto) in the mountain. Many people who have bathed in the waters of the Grotto have been healed. Some of these healings have been declared to be miracles by the Roman Catholic Church.

Materialism
The view that human beings are physical beings rather than consisting of a physical body and an immaterial soul.

Miracle

This word has a great variety of possible meanings. Some uses of the word 'miracle' are given below:

- A lucky event
- A coincidence
- A sign pointing to God
- An event that breaks the law of nature
- An event that reveals God
- A natural event that is given a special meaning by someone
- God's direct intervention in history.

Monism

The belief that human beings are a single unity of body and mind. The mind's existence is dependent on the body.

Mystical experience

Used in many ways by writers on religious experience. In general, it is used to refer to religious experiences where God is revealed directly and the person having the experience is passive. William James identified four characteristics that are typical of mystical and other religious experiences: noetic, passive, transient and ineffable.

Myth

A story which communicates the values and/or ultimate beliefs of a culture or society.

Natural laws

When discussing the teleological argument, this phrase refers to physical laws of science such as gravity. It must not be confused with the ethical theory called natural (moral) law.

Natural selection

The phrase coined by Charles Darwin to explain his idea that: 'If variations useful to any organic being ever do occur, assuredly individuals thus characterised will have the best chance of being preserved in the struggle for life; and for the strong principle of inheritance, these will tend to produce offspring similarly characterised' (in M. Palmer, *The Question of God*).

Necessary

The word used in philosophy to say that something has to be that way and cannot be any different (e.g. if a philosopher was discussing necessary existence he or she would be talking about something which has to exist and could not fail to exist).

Necessary being

A phrase used in philosophy of religion to refer to something which always exists and cannot fail to exist. Usually it is a phrase that philosophers apply to God.

Anselm stated that God is a 'necessary being' by which he meant God is a being that must exist and it is impossible for God not to exist.

Neurosis

By 'neurosis' Freud meant the symptoms of mental illness caused by a repressed traumatic experience resurfacing in the conscious mind in a different way.

Noetic

Refers to something which gives knowledge, such as a revelation from God in which God reveals something.

Non-propositional revelation

Refers to the idea that God does not reveal facts or truths to people; instead the religious believer recognises God acting in human history and human experience. For example, a religious believer may come to see God in a beautiful natural scene; the scene reveals truths about God to the person observing it.

Oedipus Complex

Refers to Freud's belief that young boys aged around 5 years old are sexually attracted to their mothers and resent their fathers' presence. As the boy develops, these feelings are repressed and disappear out of fear that the father will take revenge on the son.

Omnibenevolence

Used as title for God to say that God is 'good'. Means that God always wills goodness or good things towards people, or all-loving.

Omnipotent

Means infinite or unlimited power. It is a philosophical word often used to describe God.

Omnipresent

All-present. It is used in philosophy as a quality for God to refer to God being present throughout every part of creation.

Omniscient

Means infinite knowledge. Most philosophers today use the word as a quality for God to indicate that God knows everything it is logically possible to know.

Original sin
A reference to the first sin of Adam in the Garden of Eden and its effects, according to traditional Christian beliefs.

Passive
Describes the common state of a person who has a religious experience. Often people do not seek out or will religious experiences; instead the experience happens to them – they are passive.

Perfection
A philosophical term used to indicate the goodness of God. To be perfect means that you lack nothing and could not be better in any way. God is said to be perfect, as God is totally good and could not be more 'good'.

Petitionary prayer
A prayer that makes a particular request of God.

Postulate
Kant uses the word postulate to mean 'assuming as true for the purposes of argument or set forward as a plausible hypothesis'.

Predicate
A quality or property of a subject expressed in a sentence.

Prime mover
The unchanging cause of all that exists. Sometimes this is extended to suggest that the prime mover is God.

Privation
Privation means that something is lacking a particular thing that it should have. Augustine gave the example of 'blindness'. He called this a privation, because if you are blind it means that you are unable to see – in other words, you lack the attribute of 'sight'. Augustine uses this in his theodicy.

Profane
Something that is not sacred, i.e. the everyday.

Propositional revelation
Refers to God directly revealing truths to people.

Providence
A word used in Christian theology to refer to God's goodness and continuing activity in the world for the benefit of creation.

Quantum mechanics
Refers to the physical understanding of the universe developed in the early twentieth century by the physicists Werner Heisenberg, Paul Dirac and Erwin Schrödinger. Quantum mechanics showed that when it comes to tiny particles (smaller than electrons in atoms) they do not have a definite

position and speed. Instead the tiny particles behave in unpredictable ways. Another way to put this is: some of the basic laws of nature are not fixed laws as Hume thought, but are laws which show that the physical behaviour of particles is a matter of probabilities not certainty.

Reductio ad absurdum

'Reduction to absurdity' is a common form of argument which aims to demonstrate that a statement is true by showing that a false, untenable, or absurd result follows from denying it, or to demonstrate that a statement is false by showing that a false, untenable, or absurd result follows from its acceptance.

Reincarnation or rebirth

The belief that the soul of a person is reincarnated after death. Its status in the next life depends on the conduct of the incarnated soul in its previous existence. Belief in reincarnation is associated with Hinduism and other eastern religions.

Resurrection

Refers to the belief that life continues after death through the existence of the person, body and soul, in a new but distinct form of life. Resurrection is a feature of Jewish, Christian and Muslim beliefs.

Revelation

Refers to any act in which God is revealed to human beings. The characteristic of revelation is that it reveals knowledge of God/God's nature. In Christianity there are two types of revelation:

1   Propositional revelation
2   Non-propositional revelation.

Samsara

The cycle of birth, death and rebirth in Hindu belief. The *atman* (*jiva*) is reincarnated as a human or other life form depending on the conduct of its last incarnation.

Social fact

A type of behaviour or action that is either socially compulsory or unacceptable. For example, blowing your nose in public is unacceptable in some cultures – this is a social fact.

Soul

Aristotle defined the soul, or psychē (ψυχή), as the 'first actuality' of a naturally organised body, and argued against it having a separate existence from the physical body. In Aristotle's view, the primary activity, or full actualisation, of a living thing is its soul.

Summum bonum

Literally means the highest good. In Kant's moral thinking the *summum bonum* is the final goal or aim of all moral actions. For Kant the *summum bonum* is the act of both doing your moral duty and willing that doing your duty is rewarded with (or results in) a state of happiness and fulfilment.

Super-ego

The name in Freud's model of the mind for the part of the ego with which humans reason and make decisions. Freud emphasised the way in which parental influence and values mould the super-ego and leave their mark on it.

Symbol

Used in religious thought to indicate something which points people to God and also presents something about God to people.

Syntax

The study of the principles and rules for constructing sentences.

Synthetic

Refers to a proposition or statement the truth or falsity of which has to be verified through experience. Predicates of synthetic propositions are not intrinsic to the subject of the proposition (e.g. the car is green – this may or may not be true).

Teleological

An argument relating to the study of ultimate causes in nature or a study of actions relating them to the ends.

Telos

The Greek word for 'end' or 'result' of a process or course of action.

Theism

Refers to belief in a God who creates the world and continues to sustain it and be involved with it. This is the traditional view of God held by the Jewish, Christian and Islamic traditions.

Theodicy

A philosophical attempt to solve the problem of evil.

Totem

A sacred thing; that is, a totem is set apart from and different from things in ordinary life.

Transcendent

Used to express the idea that God is separate from and completely distinct and different from the physical world. Transcendence also indicates that

God is beyond human comprehension and is completely 'other' (different from us).

Transience
Refers to the fact that religious experiences are experiences which are temporary. The experiences do not last for ever.

Univocal language
Words have the same meaning when applied to different objects or things (e.g. Liz is fat, Mark is fat, the pig is fat).

Verbal inspiration
Refers to the divine origins or authorship of every word in the Bible. According to this view, God effectively dictates the books of the Bible by divine inspiration.

Verification
Refers to the concept of demonstrating the truth or falsity of a statement of fact using empirical evidence. Statements that cannot be assessed, such as 'Martians visit Earth when no one is watching', are described as 'meaningless'.

Vision
An event in which God, or something about God, is seen or observed. Visions are usually divided into three types: corporeal, intellectual and imaginative.

Worldview
A summary of the beliefs and values a person holds about the universe and their place in it. For example, a Christian worldview includes the belief that the universe is a creation of God.

Bibliography

PUBLICATIONS

Ahluwalia, Libby. *Foundation for the Study of Religion*, London, Hodder & Stoughton Educational, 2001.

Al-Ghazali, Abu Hamid. 'Theodicy in Islamic Thought' (1984), in *Philosophy of Religion: The Big Questions*, ed. Stump, E. and Murray, Michael J. Oxford, Blackwell, 1999.

Alexander, David E. *Goodness, God, and Evil* (Bloomsbury Studies in Philosophy of Religion). London, Bloomsbury, 2014.

Allen, R.E. 'Participation and Predication in Plato's Middle Dialogues', in *The Philosophical Review*, Vol. 69, No. 2, pp. 147–64, 1960. Published by Duke University Press on behalf of *The Philosophical Review*.

Alston, William. 'Perceiving God' (1986), in *Philosophy of Religion: The Big Questions*, ed. Stump, E. and Murray, Michael J. Oxford, Blackwell, 1999.

— 'Why Should There Not be Experience of God?' (1998), in *Philosophy of Religion: A Guide and Anthology*, ed. Davies, Brian. Oxford, Oxford University Press, 2000.

Annas, Julia. *An Introduction to Plato's Republic*, Oxford, Oxford University Press, 1981.

Anscombe, G.E.M. '"Whatever Has a Beginning of Existence Must Have a Cause": Hume's Argument Exposed' (1974), in *Philosophy of Religion: A Guide and Anthology*, ed. Davies, Brian. Oxford, Oxford University Press, 2000.

— *Collected Philosophical Papers*, Vol. 2. Oxford, Oxford University Press, 1981.

Anselm. '*Proslogion*', in *Philosophy of Religion: The Big Questions*, ed. Stump, E. and Murray, Michael J. Oxford, Blackwell, 1999.

— 'A Concise Cosmological Argument from the Eleventh Century', in *Philosophy of Religion: A Guide and Anthology*, ed. Davies, Brian. Oxford, Oxford University Press, 2000.

— 'Anselm Argues that God Cannot Be Thought Not to Exist', in *Philosophy of Religion: A Guide and Anthology*, ed. Davies, Brian. Oxford, Oxford University Press, 2000.

— 'Anselm Replies to Gaunilo', in *Philosophy of Religion: A Guide and Anthology*, ed. Davies, Brian. Oxford, Oxford University Press, 2000.

Appiah-Kubi and Torres, Sergio (eds). *African Theology en route: Papers from the Pan-African Conference of Third World Theologians*. Maryknoll, NY, Orbis Books, 1979.

Aquinas, Thomas. *The Summa Theologiae*, ed. Gilby, Thomas. Edinburgh, Eyre & Spottiswoode and McGraw Hill, 1967.

— *Summa Contra Gentiles*, in *Miracles*, ed. Swinburne, Richard. London, Macmillan, 1989.

— *On the Truth (De Veritate)*. Cambridge, MA, Hackett Publishing Inc., 1994.

— 'Summa Contra Gentiles', Anderson, James F. (tr.) in *Philosophy of Religion: The Big Questions*, ed. Stump, E. and Murray, Michael J. Oxford, Blackwell, 1999.

— 'A Thirteenth-century Cosmological Argument', in *Philosophy of Religion: A Guide and Anthology*, ed. Davies, Brian. Oxford, Oxford University Press, 2000.

— 'God and Human Freedom', in *Philosophy of Religion: A Guide and Anthology*, ed. Davies, Brian. Oxford, Oxford University Press, 2000.

— 'Is the World Ruled by Providence?', in *Philosophy of Religion: A Guide and Anthology*, ed. Davies, Brian. Oxford, Oxford University Press, 2000.

— 'One Way of Understanding God-talk', in *Philosophy of Religion: A Guide and Anthology*, ed. Davies, Brian. Oxford, Oxford University Press, 2000.

— 'Why Think of God as Omnipotent?', in *Philosophy of Religion: A Guide and Anthology*, ed. Davies, Brian. Oxford, Oxford University Press, 2000.

— 'A Classic Defence of Divine Simplicity', in *Philosophy of Religion: A Guide and Anthology*, ed. Davies, Brian. Oxford, Oxford University Press, 2000.

— 'Why Ascribe Knowledge to God?', in *Philosophy of Religion: A Guide and Anthology*, ed. Davies, Brian. Oxford, Oxford University Press, 2000.

— 'Why Call God Eternal?', in *Philosophy of Religion: A Guide and Anthology*, ed. Davies, Brian. Oxford, Oxford University Press, 2000.

Aristotle. *De Anima* ('On the Soul'), translation, introduction and notes, Lawson-Tancred, H. London, Penguin, 1986.

— *The Metaphysics*, trans. Lawson-Tancred, H. London, Penguin Classics, 1998.

— *The Nichomachean Ethics*. London, Penguin Classics, 2004.

Armstrong, Karen. *The Battle for God: Fundamentalism in Judaism, Christianity and Islam*. London, Harper Collins, second edition, 2001.

Atkins, Peter. 'Awesome Versus Adipose: Who Really Works Hardest to Banish Ignorance?' *Free Inquiry* magazine, Volume 18, Number 2. Council for Secular Humanism, 1998.

Augustine. 'How Believers Find God-talk Puzzling', in *Philosophy of Religion: A Guide and Anthology*, ed. Davies, Brian. Oxford, Oxford University Press, 2000.

— 'What Is Evil?', in *Philosophy of Religion: A Guide and Anthology*, ed. Davies, Brian. Oxford, Oxford University Press, 2000.

— *Confessions*. London, Penguin Classics, 2002.

— *De Libero Arbitrio (On Free Choice of the Will)* published as *On Grace and Free Will*. Beloved Publishing, 2014.

Ayer, A.J. 'God Talk is Evidently Nonsense' (1946), in *Philosophy of Religion: A Guide and Anthology*, ed. Davies, Brian. Oxford, Oxford University Press, 2000.

— *Language, Truth and Logic*, Dover Publications, 2001 [1936, 1946, 1952].

Barre, James. *Fundamentalism*. London, SCM Press, second edition, 2010.

de Beer, Gavin (ed.) *Charles Darwin and T.H. Huxley: Autobiographies*. Oxford: Oxford University Press, 1983.

Behe, Michael. 'Irreducible Complexity: Obstacle to Darwinian Evolution', in Dembski, William A. and Ruse, Michael (eds). *Debating Design: From Darwin to DNA*. New York, Cambridge University Press, 2004.

Bernardi, Luciano, Sleight, Peter, Bandinelli, Gabriele, Cencetti, Simone, Fattorini, Lamberto, Wdowczyc-Szulc, Johanna and Lagi, Alfonso. 'Effect of Rosary Prayer and Yoga Mantras on Autonomic Cardiovascular Rhythms: Comparative Study', *British Medical Journal (BMJ)*, 323: 1446-9; doi:10.1136/bmj.323.7327.1446, December 2001.

Blackmore, Susan. *The Meme Machine*. Oxford, Oxford University Press, 2000.

Boethius. *The Consolation of Philosophy*. London, Penguin Classics, 1999.

The Book of Common Prayer (1662). Oxford University Press, 1965.

Brown, Raymond E., Fitzmyer, Joseph A. and Murphy, Roland E. *The New Jerome Biblical Commentary*. London, Geoffrey Chapman, 1989.

Burns, Elizabeth and Law, Stephen (eds). *Philosophy for AS and A2*. Oxford, Routledge, 2004.

Calvin, J. *Institutes of the Christian Religion*. Westminster, John Knox Press, 2001.

The Catechism of the Catholic Church. London, Geoffrey Chapman, 1994.

Clack, Beverley and Clack, Brian R. *The Philosophy of Religion: A Critical Introduction*. Cambridge, Polity Press, 2005.

Clark, Michael. *Paradoxes from A to Z*. London, Routledge, third edition, 2012.

Clark, Patrick J. *Questions about God*. Cheltenham, Stanley Thornes, 1999.

Clifford, R.J. 'Genesis', in *The New Jerome Biblical Commentary*, Brown, Raymond E., Fitzmyer, Joseph A. and Murphy, Roland E. London, Geoffrey Chapman, 1989.

Coggins, R.J. and Houlden, J.L. (eds). *A Dictionary of Biblical Interpretation*. London, SCM Press and Trinity International Press, 1990.

Cole, Peter and Lee, John. *Religious Language*. Bromsgrove, Abacus Educational Services, 1994.

Collins, Francis. *The Language of God: A Scientist Presents Evidence for Belief*. London, Pocket Books, second edition, 2007.

Conan Doyle, Arthur. *The Adventures of Sherlock Holmes*. Ware, Wordsworth Editions, 1996 [1992].

Conway Morris, Simon. *Life's Solution: Inevitable Humans in a Lonely Universe*. Cambridge, Cambridge University Press, 2003.

Copleston, F.C. *Aquinas*. Harmondsworth, Penguin Philosophy, 1991.

Cover, J.A. 'Miracles and (Christian) Theism' (1999), in *Philosophy of Religion: The Big Questions*, ed. Stump, E. and Murray, Michael J. Oxford, Blackwell, 1999.

Craig, W.L. *The Son Rises: The Historical Evidence for the Resurrection of Jesus*. Eugene, OR, Wipf and Stock Publishers, 2000.

Crowder, Colin. 'The Design Argument' (1993), in *Dialogue* 1, pp. 3–8.

— 'The Design Argument' (1994), in *Dialogue* 2, pp. 11–19.

Damon, William. 'The Moral Development of Children' (1999), in *Scientific American* 281(2), pp. 56–62.

Darwin, Charles. *On The Origin of Species*. Oxford World's Classics, Oxford University Press, 2008 [1872].

Davies, Brian. *The Thought of Thomas Aquinas*. Oxford, Clarendon Press, 1993.

— *Philosophy of Religion: A Guide and Anthology*. Oxford, Oxford University Press, 2000.

— 'Creationism and All That', in *The Tablet*, 11 May 2002.

— *An Introduction to the Philosophy of Religion*. Oxford, Oxford University Press, 2003 [1993].

— *Aquinas: An Introduction*. London and New York, Continuum, 2003.

Davies, Paul. *The Mind of God: The Scientific Basis for a Rational World*. London, Simon & Schuster, 1993.

Davis, Stephen T. (ed.) *Encountering Evil: Live Options in Theodicy*. Westminster, John Knox Press, 1985 [1981].

— 'Philosophy and Life after Death: The Questions and the Options', in *Philosophy of Religion: A Guide and Anthology*, ed. Davies, Brian. Oxford, Oxford University Press, 2000.

Davis, Stephen T., Kendall, Daniel and O'Collins, Gerald (eds). *The Resurrection*. Oxford, Oxford University Press, 2004.

Dawkins, Richard. *The Selfish Gene*. Oxford, Oxford University Press, 1989 [1976].

— *The Blind Watchmaker*. London, Penguin, 1991 [1986, 1988].

— 'God's Utility Function' (1995), in *Philosophy of Religion: The Big Questions*, ed. Stump, E. and Murray, Michael J. Oxford, Blackwell, 1999.

— *River Out of Eden: A Darwinian View of Life*. London, Phoenix, 1996 [1995].

— *Unweaving the Rainbow*. London, Penguin, 1998.

Day, John. 'Creation Narratives', in *A Dictionary of Biblical Interpretation*, ed. Coggins, R.J. and Houlden, J.L. London, SCM Press and Trinity International Press, 1990.

Deane, S.W. (trans.) *St. Anselm: Basic Writings*. Chicago, IL, Open Court, 1962.

Dennett, Daniel. *Darwin's Dangerous Idea*. London, Penguin, 1996.

Descartes, René. *Philosophical Writings*, trans. Smith, N.K. London, Macmillan, 1952.

— *Anselm's Discovery: A Re-examination of the Ontological Argument*. Hartshorne, IL, Open Court Publishing, 1965.

— *Philosophical Writings*, trans. Smith, N.K. New York, Modern Library Inc., 1973.

— 'Descartes Defends an Ontological Argument', in *Philosophy of Religion: A Guide and Anthology*, ed. Davies, Brian. Oxford, Oxford University Press, 2000.

— *Meditation on First Philosophy*. London, Penguin Classics, 2008.

Dewar, Greg. *AS and A Level Religious Studies: Philosophy and Ethics through Diagrams*. Oxford, Oxford University Press, 2002.

Donovan, Peter. *Interpreting Religious Experience*. London, Sheldon Press, 1979.

— 'Can We Know God by Experience?' (1979), in *Philosophy of Religion: A Guide and Anthology*, ed. Davies, Brian. Oxford, Oxford University Press, 2000.

Dostoevsky, F.M. *The Brothers Karamazov*, trans. McDuff, David. London, Penguin, 2003.

Drane, John. *Introducing the Old Testament*. Oxford, Lion Hudson Plc, 2003.

Draper, Paul. 'Pain and Pleasure: An Evidential Problem for Theists' (1989), in *Philosophy of Religion: The Big Questions*, ed. Stump, E. and Murray, Michael J. Oxford, Blackwell, 1999.

Duns Scotus, John. 'A Fourteenth-century Cosmological Argument', in *Philosophy of Religion: A Guide and Anthology*, ed. Davies, Brian. Oxford, Oxford University Press, 2000.

Durkheim, Émile. *The Elementary Forms of Religious Life* (1912), see Émile Durkheim: *An Introduction to Four Major Works*, Jones, Robert Alun. Beverly Hills, CA, Sage, 1986.

Edwards, Paul (ed.). 'Objections to Cosmological Arguments' (1959), in *Philosophy of Religion: A Guide and Anthology*, ed. Davies, Brian. Oxford, Oxford University Press, 2000.

— (ed.) *Immortality*. New York, Prometheus Books, 1997.

Epicurus. *Letters, Principal Doctrines and Vatican Sayings,* ed. Greer, Russell M. Indianapolis, Bobbs-Merrill, 1964, quoted in Davis, Stephen T. 'Philosophy and Life after Death: The Questions and the Options', in *Philosophy of Religion: A Guide and Anthology*, ed. Davies, Brian. Oxford, Oxford University Press, 2000.

Farr, Bernard. 'The Problem of Evil' (1997), in *Dialogue* 1, pp. 32–40.

Flannery, A. (General editor), (1975) *Vatican II, The Conciliar and Post-Conciliar Documents*. New York, Costello Publishing Inc.

Flew, Antony. 'Death by a Thousand Qualifications' (1953) [1944–5, 1951], in *Philosophy of Religion: A Guide and Anthology*, ed. Davies, Brian. Oxford, Oxford University Press, 2000.

— 'Can a Man Witness His Own Funeral?' *Hilbert Journal* 54:242–50, 1956.

— 'The Presumption of Atheism' (1976), in *Philosophy of Religion: A Guide and Anthology*, ed. Davies, Brian. Oxford, Oxford University Press, 2000.

Flew, Antony and MacIntyre, Alasdair (eds). *New Essays in Philosophical Theology*. London, SCM Press; London and New York, Simon & Schuster, 1972 [1955].

Follett, Ken. *The Third Twin*. London, Basingstoke and Oxford, Pan Books, 1997 [1996].

Freud, Sigmund. *An Outline of Psychoanalysis* (extracts at http://www.mdx.ac.uk/www/study/she13.htm).

— *The Future of an Illusion*. New York, W.W. Norton, 1989.

— *Obsessive Acts and Religious Practices,* Vol. 9: *The Complete Psychological Works of Freud,* ed. Strachey, James. London, Vintage, 2001 [1907].

— *Totem and Taboo*, Vol. 13: *The Complete Psychological Works of Freud*, ed. Strachey, James. London, Vintage, 2001 [1913].

Gaita, Raimond. *Good and Evil: An Absolute Conception*. London, Palgrave Macmillan, 1991.

Gassendi, Pierre, Caterus, Johannes and Descartes, René. 'Descartes replies to critics', in *Philosophy of Religion: A Guide and Anthology*, ed. Davies, Brian. Oxford, Oxford University Press, 2000.

Gaunilo. 'From Reply to Anselm', in *Philosophy of Religion: The Big Questions*, ed. Stump, E. and Murray, Michael J. Oxford, Blackwell, 1999.

'Gaunilo Argues That Anselm Is Wrong', in *Philosophy of Religion: A Guide and Anthology*, ed. Davies, Brian. Oxford, Oxford University Press, 2000.

Geach, Peter. 'What Must Be True of Me if I Survive My Death?' (1969), in *Philosophy of Religion: A Guide and Anthology*, ed. Davies, Brian. Oxford, Oxford University Press, 2000.

— *Providence and Evil*, the Stanton Lectures 1971–2. Cambridge University Press, 1977.

Glover, Jonathan. *Humanity: A Moral History of the Twentieth Century*. London, Pimlico, 2001 [1999].

Gould, Stephen Jay. *Rocks of Ages: Science and Religion in the Fullness of Life*. London, Jonathan Cape, 2001.

Graffy, Adrian. *Alive and Active*. Dublin, Columba Press, 1998.

— *Trustworthy and True: The Gospel Beyond 2000*. Dublin, Columba Press, 2001.

Grayling, A.C. *The Meaning of Things*. London, Phoenix Paperbacks, 2002 [2001].

Gribbin, John. *In Search of Schrödinger's Cat*. London, Black Swan Books, Transworld Publishers, 1991 [1984, 1985].

Hambourger, Robert. 'Can Design Arguments Be Defended Today?' (1979), in *Philosophy of Religion: A Guide and Anthology*, ed. Davies, Brian. Oxford, Oxford University Press, 2000.

Hamilton, Christopher. *Understanding Philosophy for AS Level AQA*. Cheltenham, Nelson Thornes, 2003.

Hartshorne, Charles. *Anselm's Discovery: A Re-examination of the Ontological Proof for God's Existence*. Illinois, Open Court, 1977 [1965].

Hartshorne, Charles and Weiss, Paul (eds). *Collected Papers of Charles Sanders Peirce*, vol. 5. Cambridge, MA, Harvard University Press, vols 1–6 1931–1935.

Hasker, William. 'God, Time and Knowledge', in *Philosophy of Religion: The Big Questions*, ed. Stump, E. and Murray, Michael J. Oxford, Blackwell, 1999.

Hawking, Stephen. *A Brief History of Time*. London, Bantam, 1995.

— *The Universe in a Nutshell*. London, Transworld Publishers, 2001.

Hawking, Stephen and Mlodinow, Leonard. *The Grand Design*. London, Bantam, 2010.

Hay, David. *Exploring Inner Space: Scientists and Religious Experience*. London, Penguin, 1982.

— *Religious Experience Today: Studying the Facts*. Mowbray, Continuum International, 1990.

Helm, Paul. 'A Different Modern Defence of Divine Eternity' (1988), in *Philosophy of Religion: A Guide and Anthology*, ed. Davies, Brian. Oxford, Oxford University Press, 2000.

— *Eternal God: A Study of God without Time*. Oxford University Press, 1988.

Hick, John H. (ed.) *The Existence of God*. New York, Macmillan, 1964.

— 'Resurrection of the Person' (1976), in *Philosophy of Religion: Selected Readings*, ed. Peterson, Michael, Hasker, William, Reichenbach, Bruce and Basinger, David. Oxford, Oxford University Press, 1996.

— 'An Irenaean Theodicy' (1981), in *Philosophy of Religion: The Big Questions*, ed. Stump, E. and Murray, Michael J. Oxford, Blackwell, 1999.

— *Evil and the God of Love*. Basingstoke, Palgrave Macmillan, 1985.

— *The New Frontier of Religion and Science: Religious Experience, Neuroscience, and the Transcendent*. Basingstoke, Palgrave Macmillan, 2006.

Holland, R.F. 'The Miraculous' (1965), in *Miracles*, ed. Swinburne, Richard. London, Macmillan, 1989.

Hornby, A.S. and Wehmeier, S. (eds). *The Oxford Advanced Learners*. Oxford, Oxford University Press, 2002.

Hugh of St Victor. 'De Sacramentis', cited by Aquinas, in Aquinas, Thomas. *Summa Theologiae*, ed. Gilby, Thomas. Edinburgh, Eyre & Spottiswoode and McGraw Hill, 1967.

Hukanovic, Rezak. *The Tenth Circle of Hell*. Foreword: Wiesel, E. New York, Little Brown, 1997.

Hume, David. 'Of Miracles', in *Miracles*, ed. Swinburne, Richard. London, Macmillan, 1989.

— 'Of Miracles', in *Philosophy of Religion: The Big Questions*, ed. Stump, E. and Murray, Michael J. Oxford, Blackwell, 1999.

— 'Dialogues Concerning Natural Religion', in *Philosophy of Religion: The Big Questions*, ed. Stump, E. and Murray, Michael J. Oxford, Blackwell, 1999.

— 'We Cannot Know That the World Is Designed by God', in *Philosophy of Religion: A Guide and Anthology*, ed. Davies, Brian. Oxford, Oxford University Press, 2000.

— 'Why Is a Cause Always Necessary?', in *Philosophy of Religion: A Guide and Anthology*, ed. Davies, Brian. Oxford, Oxford University Press, 2000.

— 'Why We Should Disbelieve in Miracles', in *Philosophy of Religion: A Guide and Anthology*, ed. Davies, Brian. Oxford, Oxford University Press, 2000.

— *An Enquiry Concerning Human Understanding*. Oxford World's Classics edn, Oxford University Press, 2008.

Irenaeus. 'The Ante-Nicene Christian Library', in *A New Eusebius*, Stevenson, J., revised and new edition Frend, W.H.C. London, SPCK, 1992.

— *Adversus Haereses (Against Heresies)* [c. 175 CE] (Alexander Roberts, James Donaldson, A. Cleveland Coxe (eds). Createspace, 2012.

James, William. *The Varieties of Religious Experience: A Study in Human Nature*. London, Penguin Classics, 1983 [1902].

— 'The Will to Believe' (1897). http://educ.jmu.edu//~omearawm/ph101willto believe.html (accessed 4 June 2015).

Jerusalem Bible Popular Edition. London, Darton, Longman & Todd, 1974.

Jones, Robert Alun. *Emile Durkheim: An Introduction to Four Major Works*. Beverly Hills, CA, Sage, 1986.

Kant, Immanuel. 'God as "Postulate" of Sound Moral Thinking' (1956), in *Philosophy of Religion: A Guide and Anthology*, ed. Davies, Brian. Oxford, Oxford University Press, 2000.

— 'A Classic Repudiation of Ontological Arguments' (1965), in *Philosophy of Religion: A Guide and Anthology*, ed. Davies, Brian. Oxford, Oxford University Press, 2000.

— 'The Limits of Design Arguments' (1965), in *Philosophy of Religion: A Guide and Anthology*, ed. Davies, Brian. Oxford, Oxford University Press, 2000.

— *The Moral Law: Groundwork of the Metaphysics of Morals*, trans. Paton, H.J. London, Hutchinson, 1972 [1785].

— *The Science of Right*. New York, NY, www.digireads.com, 2005.

— *Critique of Pure Reason*. London, Penguin Classics, 2007.

Kenny, Anthony. *Wittgenstein*. Harmondsworth, Pelican Books, 1975 [1973].

— *The God of the Philosophers*. Oxford, Oxford University Press, 1979.

— *A Brief History of Western Philosophy*. Oxford, Blackwell, 1998.

Kitcher, Philip. 'Born Again Creationism', in Pennock, R.T. (ed.) *Intelligent Design Creationism and Its Critics: Philosophical, Theological, and Scientific Perspectives*. Cambridge, MA, MIT Press, 2002.

Kretzmann, Norman and Stump, Eleonore. *The Cambridge Companion to Aquinas*. Cambridge, Cambridge University Press, 1994 [1993].

Lane Craig, William. *The Son Rises: The Historical Evidence for the Resurrection of Jesus*. Eugene, OR, Wipf & Stock, 2001.

Leibniz, G.W. 'A Seventeenth-century Cosmological Argument' (1973), in *Philosophy of Religion: A Guide and Anthology*, ed. Davies, Brian. Oxford, Oxford University Press, 2000.

— *Philosophical Texts*. Oxford, Oxford University Press, 1998.

Linzey, Andrew and Wexler, Peter (eds). *Fundamentalism and Tolerance*. London, Bellew Publishing, 1991.

McCabe, Herbert. 'A Modern Cosmological Argument' (1980), in *Philosophy of Religion: A Guide and Anthology*, ed. Davies, Brian. Oxford, Oxford University Press, 2000.

— 'God, Evil, and Divine Responsibility' (1980), in *Philosophy of Religion: A Guide and Anthology*, ed. Davies, Brian. Oxford, Oxford University Press, 2000.

— *God Matters*. London, Geoffrey Chapman, 1987.

McDermott, Timothy. *Thomas Aquinas: Selected Philosophical Writings*. Oxford, Oxford Paperbacks, 1993.

McGrath, Alister E. *Science and Religion: An Introduction*. Oxford, Blackwell, 1999.

— *Dawkins' God: Genes, Memes, and the Meaning of Life*. Oxford, Wiley-Blackwell, 2008.

McGrath, Alister and Collicutt McGrath, Joanna. *The Dawkins Delusion?* London, SPCK, 2007.

McKee, Maggie. 'NASA Develops "Mind-reading" System'. NewScientist.com news service, 22 March 2004.

Mackie, J.L. 'Evil Shows That There Is No God' (1955), in *Philosophy of Religion: A Guide and Anthology*, ed. Davies, Brian. Oxford, Oxford University Press, 2000.

— ' Omnipotence', *Sophia* 1(2:13–25), 1962.

— *The Miracle of Theism: Arguments for and against the Existence of God*. Oxford, Oxford University Press, 1982.

— *Ethics: Inventing Right and Wrong*. London, Penguin, 1990.

McKinnon, Alastair. 'Miracle' (1967), in *Miracles*, ed. Swinburne, Richard. London, Macmillan, 1989.

Magee, Bryan. *The Story of Philosophy*. London, Dorling Kindersley, 1998.

Malcolm, Norman. *Ludwig Wittgenstein: A Memoir* (1958). Oxford, Clarendon Press, 2001.

— 'Anselm's Ontological Argument' (1960), in *Philosophical Review* 69, pp. 42–52.

— 'The Groundlessness of Religious Belief' in *Philosophy of Religion: A Guide and Anthology*, ed. Davies, Brian. Oxford, Oxford University Press, 2000.

Malthus, T. *An Essay on the Principle of Population*. Oxford, Oxford World's Classics, 2008 [1798].

Martin, C.B. 'Why "Knowing God by Experience" Is a Notion Open to Question' (1952), in *Philosophy of Religion: A Guide and Anthology*, ed. Davies, Brian. Oxford, Oxford University Press, 2000.

Midgley, Mary. *The Myths We Live By*. London, Routledge, 2003 (Classics edition 2011).

Mill, J.S. *Nature, the Utility of Religion, and Theism*. Whitefish, MT, Kessinger Publishing, 2004.

Miller, Kenneth R. 'The Flagellum Unspun: The Collapse of "Irreducible Complexity"'. http://www.millerandlevine.com/km/evol/design2/article.html (accessed 4 June 2015).

Milton, John. *Paradise Lost*. London, Penguin Classics, 2000 [1667].

Mitchell Waldrop, M. 'Religion: Faith in Science', *Nature* 470, 323–325, 2011.

Morris, Thomas V. 'A Modern Discussion of Divine Omnipotence' (1991), in *Philosophy of Religion: A Guide and Anthology*, ed. Davies, Brian. Oxford, Oxford University Press, 2000.

— 'A Modern Discussion of Divine Omnipotence' (1991), in *Philosophy of Religion: A Guide and Anthology*, ed. Davies, Brian. Oxford, Oxford University Press, 2000.

— 'Problems with Divine Simplicity' (1991) in *Philosophy of Religion: A Guide and Anthology*, ed. Davies, Brian. Oxford, Oxford University Press, 2000.

Murray, Michael J. 'Coercion and the Hiddenness of God' (1993), in *Philosophy of Religion: The Big Questions*, ed. Stump, E. and Murray, Michael J. Oxford, Blackwell, 1999.

Newman, John Henry. *An Essay in Aid of a Grammar of Assent*, ed. Ker, I. Oxford, Oxford University Press, 1985.

Nielson, Kai. 'Morality Does Not Imply the Existence of God' (1973), in *Philosophy of Religion: A Guide and Anthology*, ed. Davies, Brian. Oxford, Oxford University Press, 2000.

Otto, Rudolph. *The Idea of the Holy*. London, Oxford University Press, 1968 [1923].

Owen, David. 'Hume versus Price on Prior Probabilities' (1987), in *Miracles*, ed. Swinburne, Richard. London, Macmillan, 1989.

Owen, H.P. 'Why Morality Implies the Existence of God' (1965), in *Philosophy of Religion: A Guide and Anthology*, ed. Davies, Brian. Oxford, Oxford University Press, 2000.

Paley, William. 'An Especially Famous Design Argument', in *Philosophy of Religion: A Guide and Anthology*, ed. Davies, Brian. Oxford, Oxford University Press, 2000.

— *Natural Theology*. Oxford, Oxford World's Classics, 2008.

Palmer, Michael. *Freud and Jung on Religion*. London, Routledge, 1999 [1997].

— *Moral Problems in Medicine*. Cambridge, Lutterworth Press, 1999.

— *The Question of God*. London, Routledge, 2002 [2001].

Pelikan, J. *The Illustrated Jesus through the Centuries*. New Haven, CT, Yale University Press, 1997.

Pennock, R.T. (ed.) *Intelligent Design Creationism and Its Critics: Philosophical, Theological, and Scientific Perspectives*. Cambridge, MA, MIT Press, 2002.

Peterson, Michael, Hasker, William, Reichenbach, Bruce and Basinger, David. *Philosophy of Religion Selected Readings*. Oxford, Oxford University Press, 1996.

Phillips, D.Z. *The Problem of Evil and the Problem of God*. London, SCM Press, 2012.

Pike, Nelson. 'Problems for the Notion of Divine Omniscience' (1965), in *Philosophy of Religion: A Guide and Anthology*, ed. Davies, Brian. Oxford, Oxford University Press, 2000.

Plantinga, Alvin. 'A Contemporary Defence of Ontological Arguments' (1975), in *Philosophy of Religion: A Guide and Anthology*, ed. Davies, Brian. Oxford, Oxford University Press, 2000.

— *God, Freedom and Evil*. Grand Rapids, MI, Wm. B. Eerdmans, 1978.

— 'On Ockham's Way Out' (1986), in *Philosophy of Religion: The Big Questions*, ed. Stump, E. and Murray, Michael J. Oxford, Blackwell, 1999.

— 'On Being Evidentially Challenged' (1996), in *Philosophy of Religion: The Big Questions*, ed. Stump, E. and Murray, Michael J. Oxford, Blackwell, 1999.

Plato. 'Life after Death: An Ancient Greek View', in *Philosophy of Religion: A Guide and Anthology*, ed. Davies, Brian. Oxford, Oxford University Press, 2000.

— *Phaedo*. trans. Jowett, Benjamin. The Internet Classics Archive by Stevenson, Daniel C.

— *Republic*. Introduction: Lee, Desmond. London, Penguin, 2003.

— *Republic*. ed. Waterfield, Robin. Oxford, Oxford University Press, 1994 [1993].

— *The Last Days of Socrates*. trans. Tredennik, Hugh. Penguin Classics, Harmondsworth, Penguin, 1972 [1954, 1959, 1969].

Polkinghorne, John. *Science and Providence*. London, SPCK, 1989.

— *Belief in God in an Age of Science*. Yale, Yale University Press, second edition, 2003.

— *Reason and Reality: The Relationship Between Science and Theology*. London, SPCK Publishing, 2011.

Popper, Karl. *Conjectures and Refutations: The Growth of Scientific Knowledge*. London, Routledge, Classics edition 1992 [1963].

Pseudo-Dionysius. 'The Mystical Theology', from *Pseudo-Dionysius: The Complete Works*, Luibheid, C. New Jersey, New York and Mahwah, 1987, in *Philosophy of Religion: A Guide and Anthology*, ed. Davies, Brian. Oxford, Oxford University Press, 2000.

Purtill, Richard L. 'Miracles: What if They Happen?' (1978), in *Miracles*, ed. Swinburne, Richard. London, Macmillan, 1989.

Raeper, William and Smith, Linda. *A Beginner's Guide to Ideas*. Oxford, Lion Publishing, 1991.

Ramsey, Ian T. *Religious Language*. London, SCM Press, 1967.

Ridley, Matt. *The Origins of Virtue*. London, Penguin, 1997 [1996].

— *The Red Queen: Sex and the Evolution of Human Nature*. London, Penguin, 1994 [1993].

Rowe, William. 'The Cosmological Argument' (1978), in *Philosophy of Religion: The Big Questions*, ed. Stump, E. and Murray, Michael J. Oxford, Blackwell, 1999.

— 'The Problem of Evil and Some Varieties of Atheism' (1979), in *Philosophy of Religion: The Big Questions*, ed. Stump, E. and Murray, Michael J. Oxford, Blackwell, 1999.

— 'The Problem of Divine Perfection and Freedom' (1993) in *Philosophy of Religion: The Big Questions*, ed. Stump, E. and Murray, Michael J. Oxford, Blackwell, 1999.

Russell, Bertrand. 'Belief in Life after Death Comes from Emotion Not Reason' (1957), in *Philosophy of Religion: A Guide and Anthology*, ed. Davies, Brian. Oxford, Oxford University Press, 2000.

— *The Problems of Philosophy*. Oxford, Oxford University Press, 1991 [1912].

— *Why I Am Not a Christian: and Other Essays on Religion*. London, Routledge, 2004 [1992].

Ryle, Gilbert. *The Concept of Mind*. Chicago, University of Chicago Press, 2002 [1949].

Saadya, Gaon. 'From the Book of Doctrines and Beliefs' (1960), in *Philosophy of Religion: The Big Questions*, ed. Stump, E. and Murray, Michael J. Oxford, Blackwell, 1999.

Sadowsky, James. 'Can There Be an Endless Regress of Causes?' (1980), in *Philosophy of Religion: A Guide and Anthology*, Davies, Brian. Oxford, Oxford University Press, 2000.

Sartre, Jean-Paul. 'Huis Clos', in *Oxford Dictionary of Quotations* (3rd edn), ed. R.T.B. Oxford, Oxford University Press, 1981 [1979].

Schlesinger, George N. 'From New Perspectives on Old-time Religion' (1988), in *Philosophy of Religion: The Big Questions*, ed. Stump, E. and Murray, Michael J. Oxford, Blackwell, 1999.

Schneider, Sandra M. *The Revelatory Text*. London, HarperCollins, 1991.

Schweitzer, Albert. Quoted in *The Illustrated Jesus through the Centuries*, Pelikan, J. New Haven, CT, Yale University Press, 1997.

— *The Quest of the Historical Jesus*. Foreword: Hillers, Delbert R. Baltimore, MD, Albert Schweitzer Library, Johns Hopkins University Press, 1998.

Scruton, Roger. *A Short History of Modern Philosophy* (2nd edn). London, Routledge, 1999 [1981, 1984, 1996 and 1998].

Smith, Quentin and Oaklander, L. Nathan. *Time, Change and Freedom: Introduction to Metaphysics*. London, Routledge, 1999 [1995].

Smith Churchland, Patricia. 'From Neurophilosophy: Toward a Unified Science of the Mind/Brain' (1986), in *Philosophy of Religion: The Big Questions*, ed. Stump, E. and Murray, Michael J. Oxford, Blackwell, 1999.

Sobrino, J. *Where Is God? Earthquake, Terrorism, Barbarity, and Hope*. London, Orbis Books, 2004.

Sorabji, Richard. *Time, Creation and the Continuum*. London, Bristol Classical Press, 2013.

Spinney, Laura. 'Miracle Worker', in the *Guardian*, 30 September 2004.

Stannard, Russell. *Science and Wonders: Conversations about Science and Belief*. London, Faber and Faber, 1996.

— *The God Experiment*. London, Faber and Faber, 1999.

Starke, Rodney and Finke, Roger. *Acts of Faith: Explaining the Human Side of Religion*. Los Angeles, University of California Press, 2000.

Sterba, P. James (ed.). *Ethics: The Big Questions*. Oxford, Blackwell, 1998.

Stump, E. 'Petitionary Prayer' (1979), in *Philosophy of Religion: The Big Questions*, ed. Stump, E. and Murray, Michael J. Oxford, Blackwell, 1999.

— 'The Problem of Evil' (1985), in *Philosophy of Religion: The Big Questions*, ed. Stump, E. and Murray, Michael J. Oxford, Blackwell, 1999.

Stump, E. and Kretzmann, N. 'Eternity' (1981), in *Philosophy of Religion: The Big Questions*, ed. Stump, E. and Murray, Michael J. Oxford, Blackwell, 1999.

— 'A Modern Defence of Divine Eternity' (1981), in *Philosophy of Religion: A Guide and Anthology*, ed. Davies, Brian. Oxford, Oxford University Press, 2000.

Stump, E. and Murray, Michael J. (eds). *Philosophy of Religion: The Big Questions*. Oxford, Blackwell, 1999.

Swinburne, Richard. 'The Miraculous' (1965), in *Miracles*, ed. Swinburne, Richard. London, Macmillan, 1989.

— 'The Argument from Design' (1968), in *Philosophy of Religion: The Big Questions*, ed. Stump, E. and Murray, Michael J. Oxford, Blackwell, 1999.

— 'God, Regularity and David Hume' (1968), in *Philosophy of Religion: A Guide and Anthology*, ed. Davies, Brian. Oxford, Oxford University Press, 2000.

— 'Historical Evidence' (1970), in *Miracles*, ed. Swinburne, Richard. London, Macmillan, 1989.

— 'Miracles and Laws of Nature' (1970), in *Philosophy of Religion: A Guide and Anthology*, ed. Davies, Brian. Oxford, Oxford University Press, 2000.

— 'Violations of a Law of Nature' (1970), in *Miracles*, ed. Swinburne, Richard. London, Macmillan, 1989.

— *The Concept of Miracle*. Oxford, Oxford University Press, 1974.

— 'Evil Does Not Show That There Is No God' (1977), in *Philosophy of Religion: A Guide and Anthology*, ed. Davies, Brian. Oxford, Oxford University Press, 2000.

— 'The Future of the Soul' (1986), in *Philosophy of Religion: The Big Questions*, ed. Stump, E. and Murray, Michael J. Oxford, Blackwell, 1999.

— (ed.). *Miracles*. London, Macmillan, 1989.

— *The Coherence of Theism*. Oxford, Clarendon Press, 1993.

— *Is There a God?* Oxford, Oxford University Press, 1996.

— *Evolution of a Soul*. Oxford, Clarendon Press, 1997.

— 'God-talk Is Not Evidently Nonsense' (1997), in *Philosophy of Religion: A Guide and Anthology*, ed. Davies, Brian. Oxford, Oxford University Press, 2000.

— *Providence and the Problem of Evil*. Oxford, Oxford University Press, 1998.

— *The Existence of God*. Oxford, Oxford University Press, 2004 [1991, 1979].

Taylor, A. E. *Aristotle*. Mineola, NY, Dover Publications, 2003 [1955].

Taylor, Richard. 'Two Kinds of Explanation' (1966), in *Miracles*, ed. Swinburne, Richard. London, Macmillan, 1989.

St. Teresa of Ávila. 'From *The Autobiography of St Teresa of Ávila*' (1960), trans. and ed. Allison Peers, E. Mineola, NY, Dover Publications, 2010.

The Holy Bible: New Revised Standard Version (Anglicized). Cambridge University Press and Oxford University Press, 1996.

Tillich, Paul. 'Revelation and Miracle' (1951), in *Miracles*, ed. Swinburne, Richard. London, Macmillan, 1989.

— *Systematic Theology*, Vol. 1. Chicago, IL, Chicago University Press, 1973.

— *Dynamics of Faith*. Perennial Classics. New York, Harper Perennial, 2001.

Trethowan, Illtyd. 'Moral Thinking as Awareness of God' (1970), in *Philosophy of Religion: A Guide and Anthology*, ed. Davies, Brian. Oxford, Oxford University Press, 2000.

Tutu, Bishop Desmond. 'The Theology of Liberation in Africa' (1979) [1977], in *Philosophy of Religion: The Big Questions*, ed. Stump, E. and Murray, Michael J. Oxford, Blackwell, 1999.

Van Inwagen, Peter. 'The Magnitude, Duration, and Distribution of Evil: A Theodicy' (1988), in *Philosophy of Religion: The Big Questions*, ed. Stump, E. and Murray, Michael J. Oxford, Blackwell, 1999.

— 'Necessary Being: The Ontological Argument' (1993), in *Philosophy of Religion: The Big Questions*, ed. Stump, E. and Murray, Michael J. Oxford, Blackwell, 1999.

— *Metaphysics*, 7th edition. Boulder, CO, Westview Press, 2014.

Vardy, Peter. *Conscience and the Design Argument* (Notes on Philosophy of Religion and Ethics booklet). London, Heythrop College.

— *Death and Eternal Life*. Unpublished.

— *Religious Language and Virtue Ethics* (Notes on Philosophy of Religion and Ethics booklet). London, Heythrop College.

— *The Puzzle of God*. London, Fount Paperbacks, 1995 [1990].

— *What Is Truth?* Sydney, University of New South Wales Press, 1999.

Vardy, Peter and Arliss, Julie. *The Thinker's Guide to Evil*. Alresford, John Hunt Publishing, 2003.

— *The Thinker's Guide to God*. Alresford, John Hunt Publishing, 2003.

Vardy, Peter and Grosch, P. *The Puzzle of Ethics*. London, Fount, 1999.

Vatican II, *Gaudium et Spes* (1965). http://www.vatican.va/archive/hist_councils/ii_vatican_council/documents/vat-ii_const_19651207_gaudium-et-spes_en.html (accessed 4 June 2015).

Wade Savage, C. 'The Paradox of the Stone' (1967), in *Philosophical Review* 76, pp. 74–9.

— 'The Paradox of the Stone' (1967), in *Philosophy of Religion: The Big Questions*, ed. Stump, E. and Murray, Michael J. Oxford, Blackwell, 1999.

Ward, Keith. *God, Chance and Necessity*. Oxford, Oneworld Publications, 1996.

— *God, Faith and the New Millennium*. Oxford, Oneworld Publications, 1998.

— *Divine Action: Examining God's Role in an Open and Emergent Universe*. West Conshohocken, PA, Templeton Press, 2007.

— *The Big Questions in Science and Religion*, second edition. West Conshohocken, PA, Templeton Foundation Press, 2008.

Webber, Jonathan. 'Cosmological Arguments' (1995), in *Dialogue* 5.

— *Revelation and Religious Experience*. Bromsgrove, Abacus Educational Services, 1995.

Weber, Max. *The Protestant Ethic and the Spirit of Capitalism*. New York, Scribner's Press, 1958.

West, D.J. *Eleven Lourdes Miracles*. London, Duckworth, 1957.

Westermann, C. *Genesis 12–36*. London, SPCK, 1986.

Wiesel, Elie. *Night*. London, Penguin, 1981.

Wiles, Maurice. *God's Action in the World* (Bampton Lectures). London, SCM Press, 1986.

— 'The Authority of Scripture in a Contemporary Theology' (1991), in *Fundamentalism and Tolerance*, ed. Linzey, A. and Wexler, P. London, Bellew Publishing, 1991.

— 'The Authority of Scripture in a Contemporary Theology' (1991), in *Fundamentalism and Tolerance*, ed. Linzey, A. and Wexler, P. London, Bellew Publishing, 1991.

Wisdom, John. *Other Minds*. Oxford, Blackwell, 1952 [1940].

Wittgenstein, Ludwig. *Philosophical Investigations*. Oxford, Wiley-Blackwell, 2009 [1953].

— *Tractatus Logico-Philosophicus*. London, Routledge, 1974 [1921].

Wolterstorff, Nicholas, 'God Is "Everlasting", Not "Eternal"' (1975), in *Philosophy of Religion: A Guide and Anthology*, ed. Davies, Brian. Oxford, Oxford University Press, 2000.

Zimmerman, Dean W. 'Materialism and Survival' (1999), in *Philosophy of Religion: The Big Questions*, ed. Stump, E. and Murray, Michael J. Oxford, Blackwell, 1999.

Zuckerman, Phil. *Invitation to the Sociology of Religion*. London, Routledge, 2003.

JOURNALS

Dialogue (1993) Issue 1

Dialogue (1994) Issue 2

Dialogue (1995) Issue 5

Dialogue (1997) Issue 7

Dialogue (1997) Issue 8

Dialogue (1997) Issue 9

Dialogue (1998) Issue 10

Dialogue (1998) Issue 11

Dialogue (2001) Issue 17

Dialogue (2002) Issue 18

Dialogue (2003) Issue 20

New Blackfriars (1981, vol. 62, no. 727), Herbert McCabe, 'God: III – Evil'

Scientific American (August 1999, vol. 281, no. 2), William Damon, 'The Moral Development of Children'

Think (2003) Issue 5 (London: Royal Institute of Philosophy)

Think (2004) Issue 6 (London: Royal Institute of Philosophy)

Think (2004) Issue 7 (London: Royal Institute of Philosophy)

NEWSPAPERS

Daily Telegraph (22 September 1995)

Guardian (6 May 2000)

Guardian (14 October 2011)

Guardian Weekly (September 2005)

The Tablet (11 May 2002) Brian Davies 'Creationism and All That'

WEBSITES

http://archive.org/stream/outlineofpsychoa027934mbp/outlineofpsychoa027934 mbp_djvu.txt

http://www.bmj.com

http://en.wikipedia.org/wiki/Big_bang

http://en.wikipedia.org/wiki/Evolution

http://en.wikipedia.org/wiki/Guernica_(painting)

http://en.wikipedia.org/wiki/John_Hick

http://en.wikipedia.org/wiki/Max_weber

http://evolution.berkeley.edu

http://news.bbc.co.uk/1/hi/health/4715327.stm

http://plato.stanford.edu/

http://studyspiritualexperiences.weebly.com/

http://subknow.reonline.org.uk/

http://www.creationism.org/articles/index.htm_

http://www.faithnet.org.uk

http://www.harryhiker.com/exercise.htm

http://www.hkbu.edu.hk/~ppp/Kant.html

http://www.importanceofphilosophy.com

http://www.infidels.org/library/historical/charles_darwin/origin_of_species/

http://www.nap.edu/catalog/6024.html

http://www.newadvent.org/

http://www.newadvent.org/summa/

http://www.newscientist.com/article/dn4795-nasa-develops-mindreading-system. html#.VNslz_hwh_t

http://www.nobunaga.demon.co.uk/htm/kant.htm

http://www.pbs.org/wgbh/questionofgod/ownwords/future2.html

http://www.religion-online.org/

http://www.rep.routledge.com/article/DB047

http://www.rsrevision.com/contents/aboutus.htm

http://www.secularhumanism.org/index.php/articles/6968

http://www.srtp.org.uk/

http://www.tere.org/

http://www.thestudentroom.co.uk/showthread.php?t=1114992

http://www.uwtsd.ac.uk/library/alister-hardy-religious-experience-research-centre/.

http://www.weddingguideuk.com/articles/wordsmusic/hymns/HymnImmortal InvisibleGodOnlyWise.mid

Index

Note: references to the Glossary are denoted by 'g'.

Printed in Great Britain
by Amazon

48402776R00303